Past Perspectives

The ten distinguished papers which make up this volume were originally presented at a conference on 'The Greek and Roman Historians', held at the University of Leeds in 1983. Some of the articles are devoted to the detailed investigation of the assumptions, prejudices and methods of work brought to their tasks by writers as separate in time as Herodotus and Ammianus, as opposed in outlook as Thucydides and Dionysius, or as different in practical approach as Xenophon, Plutarch and Tacitus. Other papers, more wide-ranging in scope, examine the validity of the traditions about early Rome, the function of historical writing in Rome of the second and first centuries B.C., and consider the way in which source material contemporary with the death of Julius Caesar can be used as a control to understand and evaluate the growth of later divergent traditions about his assassins. An Epilogue by the editors discusses the main themes which emerge from the collection.

This book will be of value to ancient historians and those interested in ancient historiography.

Past Perspectives

STUDIES IN GREEK AND ROMAN HISTORICAL WRITING

Papers presented at a conference in Leeds, 6–8 April 1983

Edited by I. S. MOXON, J. D. SMART, A. J. WOODMAN

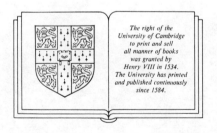

The right of the University of Cambridge to print and sell all manner of books was granted by Henry VIII in 1534. The University has printed and published continuously since 1584.

CAMBRIDGE UNIVERSITY PRESS

CAMBRIDGE

LONDON NEW YORK NEW ROCHELLE

MELBOURNE SYDNEY

Published by the Press Syndicate of the University of Cambridge
The Pitt Building, Trumpington Street, Cambridge CB2 1RP
32 East 57th Street, New York, NY 10022, USA
10 Stamford Road, Oakleigh, Melbourne 3166, Australia

First published 1986

Printed in Great Britain by the
University Press, Cambridge

Library of Congress catalogue card number: 85-5691

British Library Cataloguing in Publication Data

Past perspectives: studies in Greek and Roman historical writing.
Papers presented at a conference in Leeds, 6–8 April 1983.
1. Rome – Historiography 2. Greece – Historiography
I. Moxon, I. S. II. Smart, J. D.
III. Woodman, A. J.
907′.2037 DG205

ISBN 0 521 26625 4

UP

Contents

Contributors

J. COBET. Professor of Ancient History in the University of Essen, and author of *Herodots Exkurse und die Frage der Einheit seines Werkes* (1971).

T. J. CORNELL. Lecturer in Ancient History at University College London. Joint author with J. F. Matthews of *Atlas of the Roman World* (1982), and co-editor of *Classical Quarterly*.

T. J. LUCE. Professor of Latin Language and Literature at Princeton University. Author of *Livy: the composition of his history* (1977) and editor of *Ancient Writers: Greece and Rome* (1982).

I. S. MOXON. Lecturer in Classics at the University of Leeds and editor of the *Proceedings of the Leeds Philosophical and Literary Society* (*Literary and Historical Section*).

C. B. R. PELLING. Fellow and Tutor of University College and Lecturer in Greek and Latin at the University of Oxford. Author of articles on Plutarch, Caesar and Roman history; his commentary on Plutarch's *Antony* is to be published by Cambridge University Press.

ELIZABETH RAWSON. Fellow and Tutor of Corpus Christi College, Oxford. Author of *The Spartan Tradition in European Thought* (1969), *Cicero: a portrait* (1975) and *Intellectual Life in Cicero's Italy* (1985).

CLEMENCE SCHULTZE. Lecturer in Ancient History at The Queen's University of Belfast, at present working on a study of Dionysius of Halicarnassus.

J. D. SMART. Lecturer in Classics at the University of Leeds, at present working on a study of Herodotus.

C. J. TUPLIN. Lecturer in Ancient History at the University of Liverpool. Author of articles on classical Greek history, Roman poetry and medieval hagiography, and of contributions to D. Bowder (ed.), *Who was Who in the Greek World* (1982), R. Talbert (ed.), *Atlas of Classical History* (1984), and A. Watson (ed.), *Justinian's Digest* (forthcoming).

T. E. J. WIEDEMANN. Lecturer in Classics at the University of Bristol. Author of *Greek and Roman Slavery* (1981), contributor to D. Bowder (ed.), *Who was Who in the Greek World* (1982), and currently completing a book, *Adults and Children in the Roman Empire*.

T. P. WISEMAN. Professor of Classics in the University of Exeter. Author of *Catullan Questions* (1969), *New Men in the Roman Senate* (1971), *Cinna the Poet and other Roman Essays* (1974), *Clio's Cosmetics* (1979), *Catullus and his World* (1985), and *Le grotte di Catullo : una villa romana e i suoi proprietari* (forthcoming). With Anne Wiseman he has also produced *The Battle for Gaul* (1980).

A. J. WOODMAN. Professor of Latin in the University of Durham. Editor of Velleius Paterculus' *Caesarian and Augustan Narrative* (1983) and *Tiberian Narrative* (1977), and joint editor with David West of *Quality and Pleasure in Latin Poetry* (1974), *Creative Imitation and Latin Literature* (1979) and *Poetry and Politics in the Age of Augustus* (1984).

Prologue

Greek and Roman historical writing challenges definition. It embraces acknowledged masters such as Thucydides and Tacitus, but also Dionysius of Halicarnassus, who disapproved of the former, and Ammianus Marcellinus, who hoped to imitate the latter. It includes historians as different as Herodotus and Xenophon, and biographers such as Plutarch. Above all, it invites constant speculation as to its very nature: though used by many contemporary historians as if it were a genre no different from their own, it was described by Cicero in terms of rhetoric and by Quintilian in terms of poetics – descriptions which not only appear mutually inconsistent but have little in common with modern historiography.

It was with some of these issues in mind that we proposed to hold a conference on the subject in Leeds on 6–8 April 1983. We invited as speakers a group of scholars who were known to have a personal interest in Greek and Roman historical writing for its own sake, though it must be admitted that the majority are themselves historians by instinct; the one speaker whose interests lay principally in literature, Colin Macleod, died before he was able to deliver his paper, which may now be found as chapter 13 in his *Collected Essays* (1983). Many of the papers were followed by discussion, and some of the points thus raised have been incorporated in the present book in the Epilogue, where we as editors have tried to draw together the main themes of our speakers.

Our conference, which attracted sixty delegates from Great Britain and abroad, received generous financial support from the Leeds Philosophical and Literary Society and from the School of Classics in the University: we happily take this opportunity of expressing our gratitude to these bodies, and also to the Cambridge University Press for making the papers available to a much wider audience than that which heard them delivered.

I.S.M., J.D.S., A.J.W.

September 1984

Herodotus and Thucydides on war

J. COBET

My purpose in this paper is not to present a new analysis of any particular problem, but rather to offer some general reflections on two very well-known texts which by common consent have in one way or another determined the subsequent course of historiography.

I

Herodotus and Thucydides initiate the tradition of historiography as the history of events (*Ereignisgeschichte*), primarily political events and wars. To put it another way: the developing process of politics and war in the Greek world eventually produced in the fifth century B.C. the first historiography in the writings of these two authors. In their texts the continuous thread of the narrative follows the plans and actions of individuals and what results from their interplay. These individual plans and actions are conceived of as essentially discrete and in themselves unqualified to give the course of events a definite direction. Historiography would thus seem originally to depend upon and reflect what may be called the contingency of human action (*Kontingenz*, *Ereignishaftigkeit*).[1] At the same time, there is no doubt in the case of the narratives of Herodotus and Thucydides that their texts as a whole are not simply the record of casual events and individual decisions but follow instead a definite direction. They have been consciously formed with particular emphases in order to reveal a certain meaning underlying the course of events; in other words, their texts, in narrating events, convey at the same time the idea of a directed and purposeful process (*Gerichtetheit*, *Prozesshaftigkeit*).[2] Our historians, in creating their narrative texts, have not simply related what happened, but by the very processes of selection and emphasis they have imparted significance to the chain of events. They have combined separate elements into a unity and, by so doing, they have introduced, whether implicitly or explicitly, a strong element of interpretation. Thus the historical narrative, like other narrative forms, relates and attempts at the same time to explain. Since war constitutes the main element in the narratives of Herodotus and

[1] Meier (1978) 69–97.

[2] Meier (1978).

Thucydides, it is to be expected that their understanding of the course of events, i.e. of history, will be revealed specifically in their presentation of war, the main phenomenon to offer itself for explanation in the course of the historical narrative.

This would appear to be an obvious and uncomplicated starting-point for an examination of the works of Herodotus and Thucydides. But contrast the remarks of Yvon Garlan in his important book on war in Greek and Roman antiquity:

Mais toutes ces 'explications' se situent en réalité à un faible niveau d'élaboration théorique! trop variées, ou trop simples, ou trop générales, ou trop vagues, elles semblent flotter à la surface des faits, parce qu'elles ne rendent jamais compte, directement et globalement, du phénomène guerrier, pris à la fois dans sa spécificité, dans son universalité et dans sa diversité. Faute d'avoir su procéder à une analyse qui dépassât l'observation des circonstances génératrices des conflits particuliers, ou la condamnation de la perversité naturelle du coeur humaine, les Anciens se trouvèrent dans l'incapacité de traiter la guerre comme un sujet en soi.[3]

The ancients were, it would seem, incapable of generalizing in any depth about war. Garlan is here in fact adopting and elaborating a point earlier made by Momigliano (1958):[4]

It was not by chance that Herodotus made war the centre of historical writing, and that his successors accepted his decision. War was the centre of Greek life. Yet the amount of attention that Greek political thinkers gave to causes of war is negligible in comparison to the attention they paid to constitutional changes.[5]

A little further on Momigliano adds: 'They were interested in the causes of *wars*, not in causes of *war* as such.'[6] If Momigliano is right, we are confronted with a paradox: though war is a, or the, main topic in the narratives of Greek historical writers, men like Herodotus and Thucydides do not concern themselves at all with speculation about the nature of war and one need not look in their works for explanations of the phenomenon of war.

I am myself sceptical about the correctness of such a sweeping statement. My own presuppositions are otherwise, as will be clear from my earlier remarks: it seems very likely that, even though there is little explicit discussion of the nature of war, closer examination of the texts of both Herodotus and Thucydides will reveal that both

[3] Garlan (1972) 4.

[4] Momigliano (1958) = (1960a) 13–27. This paper was first given as a lecture at the Second International Congress of Classical Studies in Copenhagen in 1954.

[5] Momigliano (1958) = (1960a) 21.

[6] Momigliano (1958) = (1960a) 22.

authors, in presenting their narratives, were very conscious of war as a phenomenon. To state, as Momigliano does, that 'wars remained the centre of historiography, because you could not escape wars'[7] seems to me to underrate the conscious decision of ancient historians, in particular Herodotus and Thucydides, to devote their narratives of events to subject-matter which consisted mainly of wars. Therefore we may expect to find, at least implicitly, in the works of Herodotus and Thucydides some evidence of reflection on their part about the nature of war. It is my purpose in this paper to attempt to detect and identify such conceptualization of war as I believe to be embedded in the narratives of our writers. I hope this attempt will produce results which will help us to understand what motivated these first historians to write about wars. At the outset I confess that I approach the question myself from the modern standpoint of growing sensitivity about war. Herodotus and Thucydides too may have had experiences in their own lifetimes which inclined them, in deciding to write narratives of events, to select war as the principal topic. What, in short, were their particular experiences in the fifth century and how far do these help in explaining their decision to equate the narrative of events, i.e. the writing of history, with accounts of wars?

II

My first step in investigating the degree of emphasis given to consideration of the nature of war and the significance ascribed to it is to consider the introductory passages which Herodotus and Thucydides have prefixed to their narratives. I observe first that both authors introduce war as their main theme at an early stage of their works, each by means of a specific statement integrated with their introductory sentences. Let us examine their respective specific statements to see if our authors are thinking only of their particular conflicts or also about the nature of war in general.

If one compares the introductory sentences, one sees that Herodotus is less direct than Thucydides in identifying his subject as the history of a particular war. Against the background of generally τὰ γενόμενα ἐξ ἀνθρώπων and more specifically ἔργα μεγάλα τε καὶ θωμαστά, τὰ μὲν Ἕλλησι, τὰ δὲ βαρβάροισι ἀποδεχθέντα he finally introduces the theme of war as the question δι' ἣν αἰτίην ἐπολέμησαν ἀλλήλοισι. These three formulations of Herodotus' intended subject, each more precise than the last, are somewhat loosely connected. This loose connexion of three different levels of subject is not contextually explained, but it would seem to correspond to the way in which

[7] Momigliano (1958) = (1960a) 22.

Herodotus makes the very different parts of his work fit together.[8] This is not the place to discuss the problem of composition. For my present purpose it will be enough to reaffirm that it is the comprehensive theme of the Persian War which undoubtedly gives the whole text its coherence. This means that the last of the three parts of the introductory sentence (δι' ἣν αἰτίην ἐπολέμησαν ἀλλήλοισι) constitutes the transition to the main theme of the *Histories*. The investigation of the αἰτίη of this particular war is meant to demonstrate its comprehensive historical significance. Herodotus does not explicitly state why he chose the Persian War as the central subject of his account of the past, but it is not difficult to infer from the wording of his first sentence, and from all that follows, the obvious reason that it was *the* 'Great Event'[9] in recent times which involved most of mankind. Note his further observation in what serves as a second introduction at the beginning of the Xerxes *logos*: there never was a larger army in known history, neither that of Darius against the Scythians, nor that against Troy (7.20). Great and memorable deeds in the highest degree are to be expected in the context of the Persian War. This further implies that Herodotus in his account of this war has in mind war as a general human phenomenon and as constituting history in its most intense form. All this is much more explicit in Thucydides. He chooses to write about the Peloponnesian War because it is the most remarkable war of all, compared even with the Trojan War (1.10) and now also with the Persian War (1.23), affecting almost all of mankind as a historical force of the highest degree (1.1, κίνησις μεγίστη). Here too, therefore, history appears in its most intense form. I therefore conclude that both authors are concerned to describe not just a particular war but an event of the most general significance, conceiving war to be, as it were, the most pregnant manifestation of history.

Herodotus, in proceeding with his discussion of the Persian War, offers a rationalization of a series of legends as a first answer to the αἰτίη question (1.1–5). Though he evidently does not regard this brief version of reciprocal conflict between Greek and barbarian as a substantial contribution to explanation of the αἰτίη of the particular war in question, we shall surely not be wrong if we conclude that this discussion represents in principle for Herodotus an acceptable approach to discourse about causation in war. That is to say, if one asks for the αἰτίη of a war, one accepts as part at least of the answer – and an important part – the identification of an individual

[8] For a detailed recent interpretation see Hommel (1981) 277–87.

[9] Drews (1973) *passim*. For the epic tradition see below n. 12.

or a group as bearing responsibility. Thucydides, on the other hand, develops his discussion of the scale and significance of war a stage further by tracing, in the particular case of the Peloponnesian War as compared with earlier ones, a correlation between its magnitude and the level of resources invested in it and by deriving from this correlation a criterion for the degree of evolution of human affairs and a measure of the pace of historical change and development. Thucydides' view of causation is that it is a secondary consideration, dependent on the primary question of scale and to be answered less in personal, more in impersonal and material terms.

Next let us consider in more detail the elaboration by Herodotus and Thucydides within their respective introductory passages of the two differing approaches to the nature of war just identified. Herodotus, in his primary concern with αἰτίη, combines four independent legends into two pairs of reciprocal abductions: Io and Europa; Medea and Helen. He is here concerned to apportion responsibility (αἰτίη). The initiative in the first pair belonged to the barbarians, but the Greeks got their own back by taking Europa. The second pair followed the same pattern, except that this time the Greeks began it by carrying off Medea, while Helen's rape evened the score from the point of view of the barbarians. When this happened, however, the Greeks, in the opinion of some observers, overreacted grossly by mounting their enormous expedition against Troy which eventually destroyed the city; it was this disproportionate retaliation which truly began the chain of reciprocal acts of enmity between Greeks and barbarians. Though Herodotus does not accept the condemnatory judgement about the Greeks, he does acknowledge, as suggested above, this mode of discussion of causation in terms of responsibility and he does subscribe to its moral basis. Associated with the concept of responsibility are the divergent realities of violence and suffering (the city of Troy having been destroyed) experienced by one party, and of empire (Πριάμου δύναμις, 1.4.3), glory (ἔργα μεγάλα), success, fortune and happiness (εὐδαιμονίη, 1.5.4) achieved by the other. Again Herodotus is not explicit about these, but there is an implied evaluation of the nature of war in terms of them. And I suggest that Herodotus has a still more fundamental general point about the nature of war in the back of his mind: in addition to the points about responsibility and consequent suffering contrasted with achievement, a rudimentary typology of war is detectable, I believe, in Herodotus' introductory discussion. The extent of responsibility and of suffering/achievement depends upon and is proportionate to the type of military engagement: this may be (1) simple robbery (in the present case, abduction of women); (2)

destruction of a city (e.g. Troy); (3) defeat, subjection, removal of autonomy and reduction to tributary status in relation to the conqueror. This last is what Croesus does to the Ionians and is Herodotus' own view of the true beginning of hostilities between Greeks and barbarians. Here at the end of his introductory argument (1.5) he reaches level 3 and so the type of conflict to which the Persian War is to be attached.

Thucydides in his so-called *Archaeology* (1.2–19) extends the idea of development inherent in Herodotus' rudimentary typology into a strict teleology with Athens and her empire as the logical end of a development of long duration in Greek history. The motive force for historical change in Thucydides' view consists of multiple impulses proceeding in the same direction beyond the conditions of simple subsistence through the accumulation of surplus and revenues and their transformation into means of power such as ships, walled cities, colonies and money reserves. Simple robbery (1), destruction of cities (2), and creation of empire (3) in this order are types of warfare accompanying this evolution. Power and wealth serve the whole mechanism as both means and ends in a self-generating process. Motion at this high level of abstraction explains change in history and attributes to war its key position. As an appendix to Thucydides' introduction we find the facts of glory (ἔργα μεγάλα) and suffering (παθήματα) attached to the notion of war (1.23.1–2), although they stand outside the main argument. At the level of individual events Thucydides finally turns to the question of causes, evidently regarding this as a function of the more abstract level at which he has introduced war as a general phenomenon.

I conclude this section with a summary. Herodotus and Thucydides in their respective introductions present their general and specific arguments for their selection of war as the subject of their historical narratives. Both see war as the focus of historical change. Thucydides does so in a much more explicit way and on a more abstract level than Herodotus, although clearly their respective viewpoints are not far removed from each other. Both see as a central aspect violence, which means suffering to one side and power, wealth and success to the other side, but neither author explicitly develops this in his argument. Evidence for conceptualization is rather to be found in both authors in their respective discussions of causes and in their attribution to war of a special place in the generality of human affairs.

III

I propose next to examine the main body of the texts of Herodotus and Thucydides in order to discover how far the ideas above identified as present in their introductory sections are developed in their works as a whole. My concern will be to investigate the presence of similar conceptual structures under three separate headings. Allowance will be made for differences of degree in conceptualization between each author and under each heading.

(1) *The function of war*

In both our authors war is assessed as ambiguous, as an evil (κακόν) man tries to avoid and at the same time as a regular opportunity to gain fortune (εὐτυχία). The negative assessment seems to represent the popular view of war[10] and is assumed in a number of general statements placed by both authors in the mouths of their main characters: 'Nobody is so stupid as to choose war instead of peace; in peace sons bury their fathers, but in war fathers bury their sons' (Croesus on the pyre, Hdt. 1.87.4); 'All men agree that peace is the best', whereas 'making war is something troublesome as everybody knows by experience' (Hermocrates of Syracuse, Thuc. 4.62.2, 59.2); 'For those who have the choice it is stupid to make war' (Pericles, Thuc. 2.61.1). Herodotus repeats this negative assessment as his own view: 'Civil war is worse than war to the same degree as war is worse than peace' (8.3.1).[11] Thucydides is more cautious and although Melesippus is made to say at the very beginning of the Peloponnesian War that this is the beginning of μεγάλα κακά (2.12.3), I presume that Thucydides himself identifies rather with figures like Archidamus: 'War is not desirable and should be avoided in so far as it is in general not subject to calculation – or else it must be very well prepared' (1.80–85), or Pericles: 'The choice of war is stupid for those who live in good and secure conditions' (τἆλλα εὐτυχοῦσι, 2.61).

Despite these negative assessments the narrative's main concern in both authors is nevertheless precisely with war as effecting in their view the most conspicuous change of human fortune and so as the main source of historical change. Such concern represented a deliberate historiographical choice, and, in thus taking up epic traditions,[12] in reshaping the archaic preference for certain kinds of

[10] In contrast to aristocratic values: Hdt. 1.37.2 (the son of Croesus), 'The most beautiful and noble thing used to be to gain glory by going to war and to the hunt.'

[11] Cf. Herodotus' general statements about the κακά for all Greeks, 6.98 and 5.97.

[12] In Homer also, however, the epithets of war are always negative, e.g. *Il.* 2.833, πόλεμος φθισήνωρ (cf. LSJ s.v. πόλεμος). Note also *Il.* 3.111–12, 'The Achaeans and Trojans

glory and in reacting to general interests and realities of its own time, the first historiography defined history. Herodotus' ἔργα μεγάλα τε καὶ θωμαστά appear in Thucydides' introduction as the general preference accorded to great wars as the paramount object of admiration in a society's consciousness of its present and memory of its past (...παυσαμένων δὲ τὰ ἀρχαῖα μᾶλλον θαυμαζόντων... 1.21.2).

In both historians the choice of subject derives from such a positive assessment of war. It was this which determined their preference for active subjects who by their own actions increase, or lose, their own good fortune. They are much less interested, as we shall see, in the objects of their subjects' action, except in so far as these objects become themselves active subjects through successful resistance, like the Scythians or Greeks against the Persians,[13] or the Peloponnesians against the Athenians. There are, however, important differences between Herodotus and Thucydides. Whereas Herodotus' preference for the active agent of war as his subject unfolds against a broader background of human striving for fortune and a broader catalogue of human activities, Thucydides rigorously concentrates on the evolution of human society towards the full development of those constituents of power which enable a state to threaten or wage war. The Peloponnesian War stands at the end of this linear process, like Aristotle's *polis*, as a *telos* of human evolution. It is his choice of precisely this war as subject of the detail of his narrative (*Ereignishaftigkeit*) which imparts to that narrative its direction (*Prozesshaftigkeit*). Neither in Thucydides nor in Herodotus does war stand at the centre of their narratives by accident: its complex centrality is rather the consequence of conscious and deliberate design.

(2) *The causes of war*

This problem has been studied often and well.[14] All I wish to do now is to bring together from past studies those agreed observations which may help to answer the question of how much conceptualization of war there is in Herodotus and Thucydides at the level of causation.

Herodotus provides many instances of simple description of aggression without mention of causes, which are obviously taken as self-evident. These fall mainly within types (1) and (2) of his rudimentary typology (see above pp. 5–6). In the case of the expansionist acts of aggression by the Lydian kings Gyges, Ardys,

were delighted, hoping for the end of the woeful [ὀϊζυρός] war'. For the importance of the epic tradition for the establishment of the historiographic tradition cf. Strasburger (1966) 62–69 and Strasburger (1972).

[13] Cf. Cobet (1971) 111–17 ('primitive Gegner').

[14] To cite but a recent book: Hunter (1982) esp. c. 5 (with bibliography).

Sadyattes and Alyattes, it is left to the reader to understand their cause to be the simple desire for wealth and power. In many well-known instances, however, Herodotus takes considerable pains to give full treatment of the question of causes. Let us take his first example, the war of Croesus against Cyrus, which is also the climax of Herodotus' first carefully arranged example of change of fortune. If we bring together all the relevant passages, Herodotus gives the following causes for Croesus' warfare:

(i) divine necessity. Croesus had to be drawn into an adventure leading to failure in order to fulfil the divine promise of revenge on Gyges for killing Candaules (1.13, 87, 91)

(ii) (a) the tradition of Lydian expansionism (1.27)
(b) Croesus' own desire to conquer more land (1.73)
(c) his inability to accept natural limits like the Halys (1.28)
(d) his extreme self-confidence in his own luck (1.29–33) and his own interpretation of prophecies about his plans (1.46–56, 71, 73, 91)
(e) his underestimation of his enemy despite prudent warning (1.71)

(iii) revenge for the overthrow of his brother-in-law Astyages by Cyrus (1.73)

(iv) his hope of destroying the Persian empire before it became too powerful (1.46, 71).

All these causes reappear in several other prominent examples, sometimes in a more expanded form. Further motifs are occasionally added. We find for example the motif of the instigator(s), urging the protagonist to war, in Atossa and the Pisistratids with Darius (3.134, 6.94), or Mardonius, the Aleuadae and again the Pisistratids with Xerxes (7.5–6). And the motif of world empire as the ultimate consequence of expansionism appears in Xerxes' justification of war against the Greeks (7.11). It is not possible to combine all these causes into a completely coherent explanation of the respective wars, and it also seems to me impossible to order them in a satisfactory hierarchy, even with the help of categories like 'beginning' (ἀρχή, 5.82, 97), 'pretext' (πρόσχημα τοῦ λόγου, 4.167, 6.133; πρόφασις, 6.133), 'blame' (αἰτίη, 1.26) and 'real reason' (ἐπέμπετο δὲ ἡ στρατιή, ὡς ἐμοὶ δοκέειν, ἐπὶ Λιβύων καταστροφῇ, 4.167), although these are categories used by Herodotus himself. We have to accept the coexistence in Herodotus of extra-human and human causes on different, but partly interconnected, levels. In the end it amounts to the well-known pattern in Herodotus of imperial expansionism, exemplified, along with several smaller instances, in the great figures of Croesus, Cyrus, Cambyses, Darius and Xerxes.[15] In this way Books 1–6 in Herodotus have the same function for the Persian War as Book 1 in Thucydides for the Peloponnesian War. Herodotus offers his pattern, I am sure, as a well considered and generally valid explanation of human history. It represents his attempt to explore the rational element inherent in expansionist policy and at the same time to expose its irrational, although intelligible, roots. The individual guilt of the particular expansionists and the general fate of empire combine to produce a certain concept of evolution and historical change with the necessary downfall of empire as its main constituent.

Although several elements of causation are the same in Herodotus and Thucydides,[16] Thucydides' pattern of causation as a whole is completely different from that of Herodotus. That a pattern exists is, however, generally recognized. Thucydides presents no simple *Ereignisgeschichte*. Certain general threads are clearly apparent in the texture of his narrative and he presents the Peloponnesian War as a paradigmatic historical process, unfortunately incomplete (since he stops in 411 B.C.).[17] In his analysis the Peloponnesian War appears as the inevitable consequence of a certain mechanism of power, the springs of which are embedded in the *Archaeology*. This mechanism operates, as we have seen, through a combination of impulses towards economic progress, which is not an end in itself, but a means of gaining security and power. War is the most important instrument in this process and the highest expression of the general force inherent in this evolution. The most developed stage is reached with the Athenian empire and war is its necessary concomitant. The psychological acceptance of this inevitability by Thucydides' subjects is already shown transformed into action at the beginning of Thucydides' narrative in the Κερκυραϊκά and Ποτειδεατικά (1.24–66). It appears, too, most clearly in Spartan fear of further Athenian expansion (1.23). There is thus in this respect no significant difference between what we used to call the war's 'precipitating causes' (*Anlässe*) and its 'real cause' (*Ursache*). The whole mechanism, the elements of which are elaborated in such famous passages as the first assembly in Sparta (1.66–88), the Mytilenaean Debate (3.36–50), or the Melian Dialogue (5.84–114), is explained in brief by the Athenians in the first assembly in Sparta (1.75–76): We were compelled in the beginning by the very nature of things. *Fear* of being subdued by the Persians made us build up our *power*. This created glory [τιμή], success and advantage

[15] Cf. 'Die fünf Geschehenskreise' in Cobet (1971) 165–71.

[16] As is shown, for example, by a comparison between Xerxes' decision to send the Greek expedition (Hdt. 7.5–18) and the Athenian decision to send the Sicilian expedition (Thuc. 6.6–26); cf. Smart (1977b) 252 n. 20.

[17] See below n. 27.

[ὠφελία]. At the same time we were consequently *feared* and hated, and this in turn created a need for *security*. This means keeping all those around us in *fear*. As such *fear* might fail to be effective, our own *fear* requires *war*.

(3) *The effects of war*

For both our authors war represents historical change in its most spectacular and intense form. The essence of this change is violence, which in the form of war achieves its most complex manifestation and involves affected groups, states and societies in many different ways. Not all of these different ways are, of course, mentioned, let alone elaborated, in our two authors. Thucydides, in expressing the greatness of the Peloponnesian War, is concerned in the first place with the number of cities and nations involved, and in particular with the amount of resources engaged. His main concern is to treat this war as a contest for power, success and fortune, and he investigates its effects from this point of view. Herodotus' approach, as we shall see, is very similar. Both authors would seem to be more concerned with the positive, than with the negative, effects of war.

We have, however, already noted a number of passages in both authors which might suggest the opposite conclusion (see above p. 7). Most significantly at the end of his introduction Thucydides changes his otherwise positive perspective and concludes with a summary of παθήματα never before seen in Greece in such a short space of time (1.23): 'Never were so many cities captured and depopulated [...] never were there so many refugees and there was never so much killing.' In addition nature contributed earthquakes, solar eclipses, drought, famine and plague. We find a corresponding passage in Herodotus, although it is more general and placed in the middle of his narrative, at the point when Datis and Artaphernes in 490 B.C. were approaching Eretria and Marathon: 'There was an earthquake at Delos, obviously indicating to mankind the coming evils [κακά]; there were more κακά in Greece during the three generations of Darius, Xerxes and Artaxerxes than in twenty generations before' (6.98). Herodotus intends by this remark to include both phases of the Persian War as well as at least the beginning of the Peloponnesian War. A little earlier, concerning the Athenian and Eretrian participation in the Ionian revolt in 499 B.C., Herodotus states: 'These ships were the beginning of κακά for the Greeks and the barbarians' (5.97.3). Similarly, to return to Thucydides, at the very beginning of the hostilities between Sparta and Athens we have seen how Melesippus is made to say: 'This day will be the beginning of great evils [μεγάλων κακῶν] for the Greeks' (2.12.3).

These remarks are well placed and meant to influence the reader's perception of the general nature of war. War is success and fortune on one side, but on the other side it is death, loss of home, and misery. This is a general consequence of war for all involved, as well as in particular for those who have the misfortune to lose. Thucydides at the end of his account of the Sicilian expedition describes it as follows: ἔργον τῶν κατὰ τὸν πόλεμον τόνδε μέγιστον [...] καὶ τοῖς κρατήσασι λαμπρότατον καὶ τοῖς διαφθαρεῖσι δυστυχέστατον. The Athenians were completely defeated; massively κακοπαθήσαντες, they lost everything; only a few of them returned home (7.87.5–6). There would seem here to be manifest expression of the negative effects of war. But how far in fact are Herodotus and Thucydides concerned to go into detail in their accounts of their respective wars concerning war's negative side of misfortune, suffering and personal pain?

A few passages revealing general concern for the calamities of war occur at points where the number of people killed seems extremely high. For example, Herodotus comments on the defeat by the Messapians of Tarentum: φόνος Ἑλληνικὸς μέγιστος οὗτος δὴ ἐγένετο πάντων τῶν ἡμεῖς ἴδμεν (7.170.3). One might add Thucydides' remarks on Tanagra (φόνος πολύς, 1.108.1), Ambracia (πάθος μέγιστον, 3.113.6), or the Sicilian disaster (πλεῖστος φόνος, expressed as an understatement: 'not less than any other in this war', 7.85.4). In both authors we also find some passages showing a feeling for especially severe effects of war and fighting which go beyond what might be called the routine level of suffering in war and which therefore give occasion for some sympathy with the victims. This is the case with some exceptional atrocities and unusually heavy losses. Herodotus describes how the Persians came upon a group of men taking supplies to the Greeks near Plataea and killed men and animals alike 'without mercy' (ἀφειδέως ἐφόνευον, 9.39.2). In Thucydides there are the cases of Aegitium, of Mycalessus and again, of course, of the Athenians at Syracuse. At Aegitium many Athenians were killed by the Aetolians in pitiful ways because of especially difficult conditions; they were all 'in the prime of life and the best men the city lost in this war' (3.98). Mycalessus in Boeotia was sacked by Thracians and many inhabitants were killed in many ways; neither old nor young were spared (φειδόμενοι); the slaughtered included children and women, even animals, and a whole class of pupils (7.29.4–5). 'Mycalessus suffered a calamity proportionately no less lamentable than anything else in this war' (7.30.3). The last stages of Athenian experience in Sicily are associated with expressions of pity rarely found elsewhere in Thucydides: he reports οἰμωγή and στόνος during their last battle (7.71.6); and at the point when they commence their withdrawal, he both describes the scene in general (τῇ τε ὄψει ἑκάστῳ ἀλγεινὰ καὶ τῇ γνώμῃ αἰσθέσθαι, 7.75.2) and goes on to detail the unburied dead, who bring grief and fear to their relatives, and the abandoned wounded and sick, who reduce their comrades to tears and helplessness (7.75.3–4); finally he describes the lamentable situation in the quarries of Syracuse (7.87). At Athens the reaction is grief, fear and consternation; each suffered private loss and the whole city lost its youth (8.1). Finally there is one other group of passages which reveal some sympathy on the part of the writer. Herodotus in a few of his many examples of destruction and killing calls those affected by it ἀναίτιοι, i.e. undeserving of their fate. Not that he believes that in all other cases where cities were sacked and people killed these were in some sense guilty, but normal wars seem to have their rules which define cases of unjust involvement. The city of Pteria was destroyed by Croesus although, as seems to be implied, it had no part in the conflict between the Lydians and the Persians (1.76). The Medes became slaves of the Persians ἀναίτιοι, obviously because as such they were not involved in the conflict between Cyrus, Harpagus and Astyages (1.129). Xerxes proposes to subdue all Greeks, αἴτιοι as well as ἀναίτιοι (7.8γ.3), with the latter belonging in the category of those whom, according to Mardonius, the Persians have already subdued although they had done them no wrong (ἀδικήσαντα οὐδέν, 7.9.2). Thucydides' more intellectual approach is shown in the case of the Chians. Although he does not use a term such as ἀναίτιος, he makes it clear that he much deplores the fact that the well-maintained *chōra* of Chios, after surviving twenty years of the Peloponnesian War, was finally in 412 B.C. devastated by the Athenians. His sympathy is clearly with the prudent policy of the islanders, who calculated so well for so long and in their final false estimation of the Athenian situation were no different from all other Greeks at that moment (8.24).[18]

However, these examples of more detailed and sympathetic reports of misfortune seem in fact to constitute the exception rather than the rule. What is normally found with some frequency is the simple and rather stereotyped report of the routine effects of war. Figures of those killed in a battle occur more often in Thucydides than in Herodotus, but in general in their description of the effects of ancient warfare I find no difference between the two authors in the various types of which they take regular note: plunder and pillage,[19] destruction of

[18] See below n. 28.

[19] E.g. Hdt. 1.6.3, 1.88, 1.105–6, 5.81.3, 6.5.3, 6.17; Thuc. 6.7.1, 6.95.1, 8.3.1, 8.28.3.

crops and fields,[20] or destruction of houses and temples, that is, of whole cities,[21] dispersal of the inhabitants,[22] their slaughter, at least of the males (regarded as an act of some barbarity),[23] their enslavement, at least of the women and children (the single most-mentioned effect of war),[24] or even transference of complete populations elsewhere,[25] and final resettlement of the conquered land by the conquerors.[26] All these regular and negative consequences of war are usually mentioned with no particular regard for the conquered; they may be understood just as well by the reader as an expression of the conqueror's success.

So far no significant difference is apparent between Herodotus and Thucydides, with the exception of the few examples of misfortune which they respectively present as unjust. Herodotus here reflects the view of popular morality and public opinion, whereas Thucydides reveals his own personal and rational perspective, which did not lightly admit negative effects in a policy, such as that of the Chians, which generally followed lines regarded as prudent. There are two further passages in Thucydides which reflect negative effects of war in a way not to be found in Herodotus. In the famous passage at 2.65 Thucydides describes in detail the individual suffering and pain of the Athenian citizens after two years of war which had seen the destruction of the Attic countryside and the great plague. The result of this suffering was a general desire for peace. Here Thucydides is not interested in the negative effects of war as such, but is concerned to make clear the great efforts which Pericles had to make in order to achieve the continuation of his policy for final success in the Peloponnesian War; his success as a statesman was in great part due to his ability to make the Athenian citizens endure all these hardships. The passage's focus is thus not wartime suffering, but political leadership in response to such suffering. A still more general interest of the author is to be found in Thucydides' concluding chapter on the *stasis* at Corcyra and its intrinsic connection with the Peloponnesian War (3.82). Here the meaning of war's description as βίαιος διδάσκαλος is that under the pressure of war its own necessities and violence replace the ease of normal, everyday life (ὑφελὼν τὴν εὐπορίαν τοῦ καθ' ἡμέραν). War produces circumstances which push human nature

[20] E.g. Hdt. 1.17, 1.76.1, 3.58.3, 8.50, 8.121.1; Thuc. 1.30.2, 1.114.1, 2.23.1, 2.25–26, 2.31, 2.47.2, 2.55, 2.56, 2.57.2, 2.79.2, 2.85.6, 3.1.1, 3.26.3, 4.2.1.

[21] E.g. Hdt. 1.76.2, 1.103.2, 4.123.1, 5.101, 6.19, 6.32, 6.96, 8.32–33; Thuc. 2.56.6, 3.68.

[22] E.g. Hdt. 1.76.2, 1.150; Thuc. 1.114.3, 2.27, 2.68.6.

[23] E.g. Hdt. 1.167, 3.140.5, 3.147, 6.19.3, 8.127; Thuc. 1.30.1, 1.50.1, 2.5.7, 3.36.2, 3.68, 4.130, 5.32.1, 5.116.4, 7.29.

[24] E.g. Hdt. 1.76.2, 1.155–56, 3.59.3, 3.140.5, 6.19.3, 6.96, 7.181.3; Thuc. 1.29.5, 1.55.1, 1.98.1, 2.68.7, 3.36.2, 3.68.2, 5.3.4, 5.32.1, 5.116.4.

[25] E.g. Hdt. 2.107.1, 4.204, 5.15.3, 6.20, 6.119.

[26] E.g. Hdt. 5.77.2, 6.20, 8.127; Thuc. 1.98.2, 1.114.3, 2.27, 2.68.6, 3.68, 5.32.1, 5.116.4.

beyond civilized limits and normal social conventions, thus exposing to the analytical interests of Thucydides what he regards as the true, but in the circumstances of war almost unbearable, realities of human behaviour. At this point there is clearly indicated a theoretical concern on the part of Thucydides with war in general.

With this last exception the historical narratives of Herodotus and Thucydides are not much concerned with exploration of the negative effects of war in daily life. Their central interest is in what positive gains their subjects as the agents, rather than the victims, of war intend thereby to achieve. One thinks of Minos κατεστραμμένου γῆν πολλὴν καὶ εὐτυχέοντος τῷ πολέμῳ (Hdt. 1.171.3), or Bias advising the Ionians to settle the island of Sardinia and to rule over the natives in order to gain fortune (εὐδαιμονέειν Ἑλλήνων μάλιστα, Hdt. 1.170). On this level the effects of war, according to Herodotus' rudimentary typology, are as follows: (1) booty, (2) gaining land and destroying rival cities and settlements, and (3) gaining power and fortune through revenues and empire (εὐτυχία, δύναμις and ἀρχή). The last type is the most 'progressive'. It creates for an agent of war the most fortune and the most possibilities for action and is the type most explored in Herodotus' and Thucydides' narratives. What the Cimmerians did to the Ionian cities was simple robbery (ἐξ ἐπιδρομῆς ἁρπαγή, Hdt. 1.6.3), whereas Croesus created an empire and secured regular φόρος from wherever possible (1.6.2, 1.27.1), while at the same time making agreements with neighbours too strong to be subdued (φίλος, 1.6.2; ξεινίη, 1.27.5). In Thucydides the Athenians founded their empire similarly by fixing a financial φόρος or a certain number of ships to be contributed to warfare under their leadership (1.96) and the subsequent 'Fifty Years' is precisely τῆς ἀρχῆς ἀπόδειξις (1.97.2). The subjects of their respective narratives are, for Herodotus, Croesus and the Persians, or rather the Persian kings, and, for Thucydides, the Athenians and their political leaders. The main concern within the narrative is their preparation of the means of war and their actual warfare.

One last point about the effects of war as a subject in our two texts. There is, as we have seen, no elaborated concern with personal grief and pain as the daily experience of war; it is mentioned, but mostly taken for granted, as an experience familiar to everybody and not worth description except for extreme examples. What we do find considerably elaborated is the change from fortune to misfortune (εὐτυχία – δυστυχία) from the viewpoint of the subjects whom each author chose as the centre of his respective narrative. This change in fortune is thus intrinsic to the general conceptualization of the theme of war. If the efforts of the narrative's subjects are defined within the theme of war and empire, then exploration of the failure of these efforts is an integral part of the same theme. It occurs repeatedly in Herodotus as the well-known κύκλος τῶν ἀνθρωπηίων πρηγμάτων (1.207). Polycrates is the best example of this pattern (3.39, 3.122), but it provides the basic structure for the Croesus *logos*, and indeed for all the *logoi* of the Persian kings. These are essentially explorations of the human and extra-human, i.e. divine, causes for the regular change from great good fortune to misfortune. Herodotus' preference for kings and tyrants as the subjects of his narrative and for a causation which includes τὸ θεῖον serves to define the personalized and divinely conditioned fate of his subjects as the determining factor in the course of war. The weeping Croesus, recalling Solon and his own fate and advising Cyrus and Cambyses (1.86, 2.14), is a symbol of this. Thucydides is more sophisticated in explaining the change of fortune. He excludes extra-human causes and takes as his subjects cities, not individual rulers. Nevertheless, he also attaches to the change a tragic element in so far as incalculability is part of his general concept of war. The Athenians, for example, speak of τοῦ δὲ πολέμου τὸ παράλογον and the longer the war, the more room there is for pure chance (τύχη, 1.78) to decide its outcome. Thucydides himself in the above-mentioned passage on the Chians, whose *chōra* was devastated by the Athenians, conveys his feeling that something happened which was unjust but obviously normal in war. Although the Chians displayed εὐδαιμονία *and* σωφροσύνη for such a long time, they finally failed: ἐν τοῖς ἀνθρωπείοις τοῦ βίου παραλόγοις ἐσφάλησαν (8.24.5). The Sicilian expedition is shaped by Thucydides as the tragic climax of his whole narrative and his report of the reaction at Athens to its failure (8.1), in strong contrast to the situation at the start of the expedition (6.30–32), is a comment on the incalculability of a long war (1.78). Instead of increasing their fortune, they suffered extreme misfortune (δυστυχέστατον, 7.87.5).

This change from fortune to misfortune appears consistently in the form of the failure of imperial expansion. The reasons for this failure are different according to the respective patterns of Herodotus and Thucydides. With Herodotus empire develops within itself forces which bring about its fall, but it is not a completely abstract historical process, since within this general development there is room for *personal guilt*. Thucydides, on the other hand, seems to think in terms of general progress and the failure of empire is rather a matter of *mistakes* committed by incapable political leaders.[27] It is they who are

[27] Thucydides 'lived to see the final result twenty-seven years later. His intelligence and his strong concentration on the events as they happen have shown him that neither Pericles' ideals for Athens nor Nicias' personal virtue were equal to the demands made

responsible for the realization of the opportunities the circumstances offer; their ability to realize those opportunities depends on their insight into the general mechanism of power and human nature as well as into the circumstances of a given situation; unfortunately these circumstances are not always calculable, as the Chians discovered, whose σωφροσύνη did not suffice to keep their εὐδαιμονία (8.24).[28] Nevertheless Thucydides' conceptualization of war seems to contain the view that war, albeit atrocious, has to be accepted as an unavoidable element of social progress; it has, however, to be carefully planned. Herodotus seems to me rather to suggest the idea that war should not happen at all.

IV

I have tried so far to substantiate my belief that Herodotus and Thucydides, in presenting their narratives of their specific conflicts, show evidence of reflection on the general nature of war and its historical significance. The discussion has revealed both similarities and differences in their conceptions of war's significance, its causes and its effects. How can we account for these similarities and differences?

There is a current controversy about the date of publication of Herodotus' work.[29] If one adopts the traditional dating, represented for example by Jacoby,[30] that it was published by 425 B.C., then Herodotus' presentation and handling of the Persian War will reflect his experience of the period before and just after the beginning of the Peloponnesian War. That is to say he will have shared with Thucydides the experience of the approach and outbreak of the Peloponnesian War, but he will not have seen, as did Thucydides, the failure of the Athenian expedition to Sicily in 413 and Athens' final defeat in 404. However, other views about the date of publication of the *Histories* have been adopted recently: either after the end of the Archidamian War[31] or after 404 B.C.[32] The first of these views has some limited

by the war itself. The real coldness of Thucydides' unfinished work is that it falls silent without telling us whether he finally found anything to take their place' (Pouncey (1980) 150).

[28] Proctor (1980) starts his analysis of the whole of Thucydides from 8.24 (pp. 1–7); Pouncey (1980) 184 n. 3 takes the same passage as a hint of Thucydides' final judgement on the whole of the Peloponnesian War.

[29] Jacoby (1913b) 229–32, Fornara (1971a) 25–34, Cobet (1977) 2–27, Smart (1977b) 251–52, Evans (1979a) 145–49, Flory (1980) 23–26, Fornara (1981) 149–56.

[30] Jacoby (1913b) 229–32.

[31] Fornara (1971a) 25–34 and Fornara (1981) 149–56.

[32] Smart (1977b) 251–52. Malitz (1982) 265–67 has shown that consideration of general probabilities confirms the *communis opinio* that Thucydides gave his *History* its final, present form in full knowledge of Herodotus' published work. This should constitute a serious argument against Smart's late date.

significance for the interpretation of details within the work and the reason for their inclusion, but Herodotus' experience of the war remains as different as before from that of Thucydides.[33] If, however, the second view is correct, then the experience of the two historians will have been common throughout and we shall be confronted with differently articulated reactions to the same, common experience. The differences between the two historians will in this case have to be explained without recourse to the traditional supposition of an interval of time between them.

Herodotus expressed in his account of the Persian War the view that such war, indeed war in general, lies within the reach of human responsibility and in that sense both could and should be avoided. Thucydides' conceptualization of war, on the other hand, conveys its necessary inevitability as the general course of history. However, many elements of function, causation and effects of war are similar in both authors. These similarities are to be explained against the background of their common political experience, common up to 425 B.C. in any case. The differences between their respective conceptions may be explained in terms of differences in personality, in personal experience, or in closeness to Athens and her political leaders. Nevertheless, since my own preference is to retain Jacoby's date for the publication of the *Histories*,[34] I ask myself whether the distance between Thucydides' own stern view and the view of Herodotus is not to be explained by the experiences of 413 B.C. and 404 B.C.: he, unlike Herodotus, 'lived through the whole of it' (Thuc. 5.26).

[33] Fornara (1971b) cc. 3–5. For further references see Cobet (1977) 26–27.
[34] As I will try to reaffirm in a short article to appear elsewhere.

Thucydides and Hellanicus

J. D. SMART

H.-P. Stahl in his influential work, *Thukydides. Die Stellung des Menschen im geschichtlichen Prozess*,[1] includes a careful examination of the content and chronological location of Thucydides' account of the Theban attack on Plataea at 2.2–6. He maintains that its content was intended to show within the particular detail of a particular event the disjunction of reality from prior plan through the operation of what he later calls 'men's incapability of self-comprehension within the conditions of their own objective reality';[2] and that its ambiguous[3] chronological location between the prior plan and the posterior reality of the total war was intended to give it a general programmatic function within the *History* as a whole. Here Stahl seems to me to have misinterpreted both Thucydides' motive in choosing the Theban attack on Plataea as the *archē* of the war and his intention in describing the attack as he does. I believe that chronological location and particular content are indeed related, as Stahl insists, but that what Thucydides wants thereby to impress upon his readers is not an intensely pessimistic view of the insufficiency of *gnōmē* within the human condition,[4] but more positive instruction in the sophistic priority of *phusis* over *nomos*.

At the present end of Book 1 and the beginning of Book 2 (1.145–2.2.1) Thucydides moves from the war's *prophasis* to its *archē*, clearly defined by six chronological indicators (2.2.1) as the Theban attack on Plataea. He finds it necessary to justify his choice of the attack to begin the war: it constituted a clear breach of the Thirty Years Peace (2.2.1, with 2.7.1, λελυμένων λαμπρῶς τῶν σπονδῶν) so that thereafter (2.1, ἐνθένδε ἤδη) the Athenians and Peloponnesians, along with their respective allies, moved into a state of continuous war and employed heralds in their communications with one another (2.1), whereas beforehand the Peace, although being undermined (1.146, σπονδῶν γὰρ ξύγχυσις τὰ γιγνόμενα ἦν), had continued in

[1] Stahl (1966).

[2] Stahl (1966) 171. My translation.

[3] Stahl (1966) 72: 'Die Plataia-Erzählung gehört weder zum Krieg noch zu seiner Vorgeschichte – und hat doch mit beiden gemeinsame Züge.'

[4] For contemporary views of Thucydides' purpose in composing his *History* and their division into the optimistic and the pessimistic see Parry (1969) 107–8.

force and there had been no employment of heralds (1.146, ἀκηρύκτως).[5] Other possible beginnings are rejected by Thucydides elsewhere in his narrative:

(1) At 1.53 after the battle of Sybota in 433 the Corinthians approach the Athenians without a κηρύκειον and the Athenians are made very explicitly to deny that they are beginning war.

(2) At 1.66 after the battle of Potidaea in 432 Thucydides most emphatically denies that the war had thus begun: ἰδίᾳ γὰρ ταῦτα οἱ Κορίνθιοι ἔπραξαν. There has been some misunderstanding of ἰδίᾳ here. Gomme[6] believed that Thucydides thereby wished to indicate that Corinthian military support for Potidaea's revolt did not represent a public act of the Corinthian state but rather an unofficial venture organized by private individuals at Corinth. Earlier, however, at 1.60, Thucydides had described the dispatch of troops to Potidaea as an act of 'the Corinthians' with Aristeus as *stratēgos*. He must, then, as De Ste Croix[7] has insisted, mean by ἰδίᾳ at 1.66,

[5] Rawlings (1981) 19–36 refers ἐνθένδε ἤδη at 2.1 backward to the return of the Spartan ambassadors at 1.145 (καὶ οἱ μὲν ἀπεχώρησαν ἐπ' οἴκου καὶ οὐκέτι ὕστερον ἐπρεσβεύοντο) rather than forward to the Theban attack on Plataea at 2.2.1. He thereby attempts an explanation of 5.20.1, αὐτόδεκα ἐτῶν διελθόντων καὶ ἡμερῶν ὀλίγων παρενεγκουσῶν, understood as 'ten years plus a few days', as the interval not between the Peace of Nicias and the attack on Plataea at 2.2.1, but rather between the Peace of Nicias and the diplomatic *archē* of the war at 1.145. As he rightly insists (cf. Andrewes *HCT* 4.18–21), 'ten years plus a few days' is an impossible description for Thucydides to have used for an interval between the Peace of Nicias carefully placed at the end of winter (5.20.1, τελευτῶντος τοῦ χειμῶνος ἅμα ἦρι) and the attack on Plataea similarly carefully placed at the beginning of spring (2.2.1, ἅμα ἦρι ἀρχομένῳ): an interval thus defined as *less*, rather than more, than ten seasonal years cannot be described as ten (seasonal) years *plus* a few days; see further Meritt (1979) 109–10. Even so, the formal and detailed statement at 2.2.1, introduced by γάρ, leaves no doubt that ἐνθένδε ἤδη refers forward to the Theban attack on Plataea. The only possible solution to the problem is to follow Stahl against Steup (cf. Classen–Steup (1912) 5.53) in taking ἡμερῶν ὀλίγων παρενεγκουσῶν to mean 'with [sc. only] a few days *subtracted*', i.e. 'ten years *minus* a few days' (cf. Dio 43.26.1 with LSJ s.v. παρά III 5b). Gomme's reference to τοῦ κώδωνος παρενεχθέντος at 4.135.1 (*HCT* 3.683) is not pertinent and, if Thucydides could more simply have written παρελθουσῶν at 5.20.1 and προσθεμένας at 5.26.3, as the scholiast suggests, then one might ask why he preferred instead to use the ambiguous παραφέρω (for 'subtract' cf. LSJ s.v. παραφέρω III 2).

[6] *HCT* 1.224–25. Steup in Classen–Steup (1919) 1.430–31 saw the point: 'Auch hätte, wenn als Ergebnis der Ποτειδαιατικά ein Sonderkrieg zwischen Athen und Korinth hätte hingestellt werden sollen, der Ausbruch dieses Sonderkrieges ganz deutlich hervorgehoben, und der Sonderkrieg dem noch nicht ausgebrochenen allgemeinen Kriege bestimmt und ausdrücklich entgegengesetzt werden müssen. Eine solche nähere Auseinandersetzung müsste man um so mehr erwarten, als Th. den peloponnesischen Krieg mit dem Überfalle von Platäa, der lediglich ein Unternehmen der Thebaner war, hat beginnen lassen.' See further Kagan (1969) 282–83, 285.

[7] De Ste Croix (1972) 82–85.

as later at 5.30.2, that at Potidaea the Corinthians were acting in a public capacity but 'on their own initiative' and independently of the League, so that hostilities so far did not yet constitute a war between Athens and the Peloponnesian alliance.

(3) At 2.19.1 the Peloponnesian army invades Attica. The full description of its leader, Archidamus, gives the event a formal significance. Elsewhere, most clearly at 1.125.2, but also at 2.13.9, Thucydides acknowledges the invasion of Attica as the *open* outbreak of war; but, as the chronological indication at 2.19.1 shows, he wishes clearly to distinguish it from the *actual* outbreak of war constituted by the Theban attack on Plataea.[8]

All three of these events, rejected by Thucydides, were acceptable to his contemporaries as the beginning of war. Aristophanes, *Peace* 990 (τρία καὶ δέκ' ἔτη),[9] presumes the Sybota campaign of 433 as its commencement; Andocides 3.4 (καὶ ἐνεμείναμεν ἀμφότεροι ταύταις ταῖς σπονδαῖς ἔτη τριακαίδεκα)[10] presumes the Potidaea campaign of 432; and Aristophanes, *Acharnians* 266 and 890 (ἕκτῳ ἔτει) with *Knights* 793 (ἔτος ὄγδοον),[11] presumes the first invasion of Attica in 431. Thucydides chose instead as his own peculiar beginning the Theban attack on Plataea, and his reason was clearly because this event best suited the importance of the beginning of spring within his own seasonal chronological scheme:[12] the battle of Sybota fell in

[8] Gomme *HCT* 2.70, cf. *HCT* 3.683, believed that 'at one time at least Thucydides considered the moment of invasion to be the true beginning of the war and the Plataian episode only the last and the most provocative of the αἰτίαι καὶ διαφοραί which preceded it'. Lendle (1964) agreed. However, 1.125.2 can be otherwise explained (see below pp. 26–27) and 2.13.9 is probably part of an extended interpolation (see Smart (1977a) 42).

[9] See Platnauer (1964) 150. Inclusive reckoning of archon-years puts the disappearance of peace in 434/3, the date of the Athenian alliance with Corcyra. Platnauer prefers the interpretation of thirteen as 'an indefinite number with a sinister tinge', but see Rogers (1913) 122–23.

[10] Thuc. 2.2.1, τέσσαρα μὲν γὰρ καὶ δέκα ἔτη ἐνέμειναν αἱ τριακοντούτεις σπονδαί, seems to be deliberately directed against this view.

[11] ἕκτῳ ἔτει (*Acharnians* 266 and 890) represents inclusive reckoning of archon-years from the Peloponnesian invasion of Attica in 431/30. ὄγδοον ἔτος (*Knights* 793) represents, as the context shows, inclusive reckoning of summers of deprivation consequential upon Peloponnesian invasions and includes the coming summer of 424. At the Lenaea of 425 the war is over for Dicaeopolis 'in the sixth year', but Demos at the Lenaea of 424 faces, thanks to Cleon, the certainty of another, 'eighth', year of war. See further Starkie (1909) 64.

[12] See Gomme *HCT* 2.70: 'Thucydides decided [...] to put the attack on Plataia among the events of the war proper as fitting better with his chronological scheme, "year by year and by summers and winters"; by which scheme the attack was naturally taken as the first event of year 1.'

late summer,[13] the battle of Potidaea in autumn,[14] the Peloponnesian invasion of Attica in midsummer (2.19.1), and only the attack on Plataea at the beginning of spring (2.2.1). However, he found it very difficult to justify his choice independently of the requirements of his chronological scheme. The Theban attack on Plataea was taken on the Thebans' own initiative and directly involved neither Peloponnesians nor Athenians. It thus had even less right to be regarded as the beginning of the war than did the battle of Potidaea, fought between a Peloponnesian state and the Athenians, but rejected by Thucydides at 1.66 on the grounds that it was a private Corinthian venture.[15] His addition of καὶ τῶν ἑκατέροις ξυμμάχων at 2.1 (cf. ἐς Πλάταιαν οὖσαν 'Αθηναίων ξυμμαχίδα at 2.2.1) does little to relieve his clear inconsistency. And yet he persisted in his choice and this persistence shows the deep importance he placed on his seasonal chronology and the necessity he felt to assert its validity by the identification, however otherwise perverse, of the beginning of the war with an event which occurred at the beginning of spring.

Alternative chronological schemes were current at the time when Thucydides wrote. The scholiast on Aristophanes, *Frogs* 694, commented (*FGrHist* 323a F 25): 'Hellanicus says that the slaves who fought in the sea battle were set free and, enrolled as Plataeans, joined in their [sc. the Athenians'] citizenship, when narrating the events in the archonship of the Antigenes who preceded Callias.' Hellanicus' *Atthis*, from which this quotation must certainly have been taken,[16] thus went down at least to 407/6, the archonship of Antigenes,[17] and

[13] For the date of the battle of Sybota in late August or early September 433, see Gomme *HCT* 1.196–97.

[14] The battle of Potidaea is variously dated from mid-June (Gomme *HCT* 1. 222–24, 421–25) to mid-October 432 (Thompson (1968) 200–24). Gomme's date of mid-June requires the emendation at 2.2.1 of μετὰ τὴν ἐν Ποτειδαίᾳ μάχην μηνὶ ἕκτῳ to μηνὶ δεκάτῳ as a necessary consequence of 1.125.2, ἐνιαυτὸς μὲν οὐ διετρίβη, ἔλασσον δέ (cf. *HCT* 1.421–23). However, 1.125.2 can be explained without emendation of μηνὶ ἕκτῳ (see below pp. 26–27) so that the battle can be dated to either mid-September or mid-October 432. See the clear summary of past discussions in De Ste Croix (1972) 319.

[15] Compare above pp. 20–21 on the meaning of ἰδίᾳ at 1.66. On the incongruity of Thucydides' choice of the attack on Plataea as the beginning of the war see Müller-Strübing (1883) 577–612, 657–713, with Rawlings (1981) 23–25.

[16] Jacoby (1913a) 109 and *FGrHist* IIIb (Supplement). 1.5 with 2.4–5 n. 44 rightly rejected attempts to expel the name of Hellanicus from the text; see further Pearson (1942) 2. But doubts persist. Lenardon (1981) 66 n. 27 would wish to revive the possibility of textual confusion and even suggests (67 n. 36) that the quotation might come not from the *Atthis* but from the *Priestesses*.

[17] Jacoby *FGrHist* IIIb (Supplement). 1.5 with 2.5 n. 45 quite properly dismissed 'speculation about a second edition of the *Atthis* published by his [sc. Hellanicus'] son, Skamon'. Gomme *HCT* 1.6–7 n. 3 with 362 n. 2, followed most recently by Lenardon (1981) 66 n. 28, was tempted into such speculation. No sound conclusion, however, about Hellanicus' life can be drawn from the ancient biographical evidence. See further Pelekidis (1974) 413.

in its treatment of the Peloponnesian War was ordered by archon-years.[18] It was probably published soon after the end of the war in 404.[19] A little earlier, perhaps soon after 421,[20] in a more general account of Greek history, Hellanicus had used a different chronological scheme based on a list of priestesses of Hera at Argos. Thucydides refers to both these schemes in his introduction to the Theban attack on Plataea at 2.2.1 as a prelude to his own dating ἅμα ἦρι ἀρχομένῳ. Later at 5.20, where he gives the length of his ten-year war as 'exactly ten years *minus* a few days',[21] he severely criticizes the accuracy of such schemes as those adopted by Hellanicus where names (ὀνόματα) are used to date events:[22] within the officials' terms of office an event may have occurred at the beginning, in the middle and 'as chance assigned it to any [sc. official]'.[23] His choice of words ὅπως ἔτυχέ τῳ rather than τελευτῶσι, as the scholiast paraphrases, is significant.[24] Thucydides wished thereby to indicate that the relationship between such eponymic schemes and the events they encompassed was contingent, rather than natural. In his own scheme the ten-year war, and indeed the twenty-seven-year war (5.26.3), began and ended almost precisely at the beginning and end of natural seasonal units. The chronological form thus matched its historical content. In an eponymic scheme, however, such as that based on the list of priestesses at Argos, there was no such natural match between form and content. Thucydides makes this beautifully clear at 4.133.2–3 in his description of the end of Chrysis' term as priestess in 423. Here

18 Jacoby in *FGrHist* IIIb (Supplement). 1.16 (cf. *FGrHist* I 473) believed that events were ordered by archon-years from 683/2 onwards. Pearson (1942) 14–15 doubted that the Pentekontaetia was so ordered, or even the early period of the Peloponnesian War. Such unwarranted scepticism is shared by Lenardon (1981) 68, who suggests that Hellanicus provided for the Pentekontaetia 'a terse narrative with some (a few?) archon dates and intervals of time'. More sensibly, Pelekidis (1974) 411.

19 See *FGrHist* IIIb (Supplement). 1.5: 'Here the inference is even more obvious that Hellanikos concluded with the epochal date of the end of the war in the last months of the year 404/3 B.C.' Jacoby clearly meant here 405/4 B.C.

20 See Jacoby (1913a) 144–48 and *FGrHist* IIIb (Supplement). 1.9. Dover (1953) 3 suggested that Thuc. 4.133.3 might mean that Hellanicus' *Priestesses* did not reach 423. For a different interpretation of 4.133.3 see below pp. 23–24, 32.

21 See above n. 5 for this interpretation of καὶ ἡμερῶν ὀλίγων παρενεγκουσῶν.

22 Lendle (1960) 35–38 proposes in place of the transmitted text at 5.20.2 the following: σκοπείτω δέ τις κατὰ τοὺς χρόνους καὶ μὴ τῶν ἑκασταχοῦ ἢ ἀρχόντων ἢ ἀπὸ τιμῆς τινος τῇ ἀπαριθμήσει τῶν ὀνόματα ἐς τὰ προγεγενημένα σημαινόντων πιστεύσας μᾶλλον. The emphasis thus given to ὀνόματα, rather than ἀπαρίθμησις, better expresses Thucydides' point here.

23 5.20.2, οὐ γὰρ ἀκριβές ἐστιν, οἷς καὶ ἀρχομένοις καὶ μεσοῦσι καὶ ὅπως ἔτυχέ τῳ ἐπεγένετό τι. Gomme *HCT* 3.687 describes the dative οἷς as ethic: it is surely better to take it more closely with ἐπεγένετο in the sense of 'to whom', i.e. 'in whose term of office'.

24 The scholiast's paraphrase reads: οὐ γὰρ ἀκριβῶς ἐντεῦθεν οἱ χρόνοι τῶν πράξεων λαμβάνονται, ἐπειδὴ καὶ κατὰ τοὺς πρώτους χρόνους τῶν ἀρχόντων καὶ κατὰ τοὺς μέσους καὶ κατὰ τοὺς τελευταίους πολλὰ ἐπράχθη (Gomme *HCT* 3.687).

the chance event of Chrysis' leaving a burning lamp near the garlands and falling asleep occurred in the middle of a natural seasonal unit (4.133.3, ἔτη δὲ ἡ Χρυσὶς τοῦ πολέμου τοῦδε ἐπέλαβεν ὀκτὼ καὶ ἔνατον ἐκ μέσου) and resulted in a ludicrous division of a naturally connected series of events, i.e. the ten-year war, between two priestesses and so between two chronological eras.

Thucydides' insistence on the fairly precise correspondence, to within a few days, between his own scheme and the war it encompassed presumes that he intended, and expected his readers to understand, a particular date for the beginning of his seasonal year, i.e. for the beginning of spring.[25] His words at 4.52.1 seem to indicate clearly enough that the date he intended was the spring equinox, 24 March. Here in 424 the beginning of summer, within which Thucydides included the spring,[26] is identified with the first decade of a lunar month extending from 21 March, the astronomical date for the solar eclipse, to *c.* 30 March, i.e. the period of about ten days surrounding the spring equinox of 24 March. The time of the spring equinox, if one allows a latitude of up to ten days before or after the equinox itself, say 15 March to 2 April, for the transitional period from the end of winter to the beginning of spring, will just satisfy the only other reliable indication of a date for the beginning of spring in Thucydides' narrative. At 8.60.3 the end of winter, 411, must fall after 29 March and not before the beginning of April. It comes after a Spartan treaty with the Persians, dated to the 13th year of Darius (8.58.1), which is known from Babylonian records to have begun on 29 March,[27] and not before the Peloponnesian return to Miletus (8.60.3) from an eighty-day stay at Rhodes (8.44.4),[28] which cannot have begun much earlier than mid-January.[29] It thus falls at the beginning of April, just within the allowed latitude of the period surrounding the spring equinox. Gomme, however, found it impossible to accept the spring equinox as the notional beginning of the Thucydidean spring because of his own date of the beginning of March for the Theban attack on Plataea ἅμα ἦρι ἀρχομένῳ in 431; he accordingly suggested instead the 'true' evening rising of Arcturus, 4 March.[30] The slightly earlier

[25] See Gomme *HCT* 3.702–3.

[26] See Gomme *HCT* 3.705.

[27] Parker–Dubberstein (1956) 33. Pritchett (1965) 259–61 doubts the date, but see Meritt (1966) 182–84 with Andrewes *HCT* 5.138.

[28] Proposed emendations of ὀγδοήκοντα at 8.44.4 (see Gomme *HCT* 3.711, Pritchett (1965) 260) are discussed and rejected by Andrewes *HCT* 5.147.

[29] The departure of Antisthenes from the Peloponnese for Ionia is dated to the time of the winter solstice, 24 December (8.39.1). It was only after his arrival at Cnidus (8.42.4) that the Peloponnesians went to Rhodes (8.44.2); see Andrewes *HCT* 5.93.

[30] Gomme *HCT* 3.709. Pritchett–Waerden (1961) 50 explain the difference between 'true' and 'visible' risings and correct Gomme's date to Euctemon's 6 March.

'visible' evening rising of Arcturus, *c.* 24 February, is found in Hesiod, *Works and Days* 564, as an acceptable date for the beginning of spring, but the whole matter is nowhere explained by Thucydides to his readers and 4 March is in any case much too early for the indisputable beginning of spring at the beginning of April in 411. Accordingly Andrewes in the most recent contribution to the controversy has reverted to Meritt's view that Thucydides intended no definite astronomical date for the beginning of spring.[31] Such imprecision would, however, be intolerable in a scheme which claimed to give the exact limits of the war to within a few days. The problem, then, has so far remained unsolved with present scholarly opinion forced in some embarrassment into an untenable position.

The central difficulty lies in Gomme's date of the beginning of March for the Theban attack on Plataea ἅμα ἦρι ἀρχομένῳ in 431. The attack occurred at the end of a month (2.4.2) just before the new moon (3.56.2, cf. 65.1) and this new moon can be either that of 8 March[32] or that of 7 April.[33] The Peloponnesian invasion took place about eighty days after the attack (2.19.1, ἡμέρᾳ ὀγδοηκοστῇ μάλιστα), and so by our calendar either *c.* 20 May or *c.* 20 June. Gomme regarded *c.* 20 June as impossible because of the indication θέρους καὶ τοῦ σίτου ἀκμάζοντος (2.19.1): 'the Attic harvest begins about the last week of May, not of June'.[34] He was thus obliged to accept that the Theban attack took place *c.* 6/7 March and so to emend with Krüger δύο to τέσσαρας at 2.2.1, Πυθοδώρου ἔτι δύο μῆνας ἄρχοντος, and to end Pythodorus' archonship *c.* 10 July rather than *c.* 10 June. In 1968, however, W. E. Thompson[35] went back to Busolt[36] to show that a date for the Peloponnesian invasion in the

[31] Andrewes *HCT* 5.148–49. The imprecision which Meritt conceives in Thucydides appears most clearly in Meritt (1962) 438: 'I have in mind a man who measures the beginning of spring not by the vernal equinox, not by any specific calendar date, but by the date on which he spades his garden'; or again in Meritt–McGregor (1967) 88, 'Thucydides did not reckon the end of winter and the beginning of spring by any fixed calendar, but by the *accident* [my italics] of the season's climate, whether it was still cold, or commencing to be warm.' De Ste Croix (1972) 317–28 in his useful Appendix 12 is wrong to maintain (325) that 'He [sc. Thucydides] does *not* argue "that his system of dating by seasons enables him to state the length of the ten years' war *exactly*" [De Ste Croix's italics], as Gomme has it (*HCT* 3.703)'. Exactness *is* claimed in αὐτόδεκα at 5.20.1 and its limits then qualified, in the further interest of exactness, by the addition of καὶ ἡμερῶν ὀλίγων παρενεγκουσῶν. Meritt (1979) 107–10 has most recently accepted Thucydides' assertion of precision at 5.20.1, but argues that Thucydides himself would have recognized it as a chance occurrence within a generally imprecise chronological scheme.

[32] Gomme *HCT* 1.422, corrected in *HCT* 3.705 to 10 March.

[33] Gomme *HCT* 1.422 n. 3, corrected in *HCT* 3.705 to 8 April.

[34] Gomme *HCT* 3.705, cf. *HCT* 2.70.

[35] Thompson (1968) 219–20.

[36] Busolt (1904) 909–15.

second half of June is not incompatible with τοῦ σίτου ἀκμάζοντος: corn in ancient Attica could quite well have continued to ripen until the end of June. Archidamus had wasted much time on the unsuccessful siege of Oenoe (2.18–19.1) and part of Thucydides' intention in writing ἡμέρᾳ ὀγδοηκοστῇ μάλιστα and θέρους καὶ τοῦ σίτου ἀκμάζοντος may well have been precisely to emphasize the lateness of the invasion. Thompson retained δύο at 2.2.1 (Πυθοδώρου ἔτι δύο μῆνας ἄρχοντος) and ended Pythodorus' archonship *c.* 10 June rather than *c.* 10 July. The Peloponnesian invasion of Attica thus occurred at the beginning of the archonship of Euthydemus.

Thompson's scheme has much to recommend it. First, it enables acceptance of the spring equinox, 24 March, as the beginning of Thucydides' spring. Second, it provides an explanation of the otherwise inexplicable comment by Thucydides at 1.125.1–2. Here Thucydides ends his account of the conference of the Peloponnesian League in winter 432/1 as follows:

καὶ τὸ πλῆθος ἐψηφίσαντο πολεμεῖν. δεδογμένον δὲ αὐτοῖς εὐθὺς μὲν ἀδύνατα ἦν ἐπιχειρεῖν ἀπαρασκεύοις οὖσιν, ἐκπορίζεσθαι δὲ ἐδόκει ἑκάστοις ἃ πρόσφορα ἦν καὶ μὴ εἶναι μέλλησιν. ὅμως δὲ καθισταμένοις ὧν ἔδει ἐνιαυτὸς μὲν οὐ διετρίβη, ἔλασσον δέ, πρὶν ἐσβαλεῖν ἐς τὴν Ἀττικὴν καὶ τὸν πόλεμον ἄρασθαι φανερῶς.
(The majority voted for war. Although they had so decided, it was impossible to start war immediately as they were unprepared, but they decided that each state should prepare what was required and that there should be no delay. Even so, while they were arranging what was necessary, not a year passed, but less, before they invaded Attica and put the war into open effect.)

This is very oddly expressed. As most editors believe, ὅμως must mean 'even so'.[37] Thucydides certainly wishes to point to the fact of Peloponnesian delay, despite their resolution to the contrary, and one suspects that his motive is thereby to remove yet another possible beginning of the war, i.e. this decision of the Peloponnesian League, in favour of his own choice of the Theban attack on Plataea. However, at the same time he wishes to insist that, although there *was* delay, it was not as much as a year, but less. 'Not a year, but less' is no more in Greek than in English an acceptable idiomatic expression for 'not much less than a year'.[38] A closer look at Thompson's chronology, however, explains Thucydides' strange choice of words. According to Thompson's

[37] See Gomme *HCT* 1.420. Thompson (1968) 221–22 disagrees.

[38] Gomme *HCT* 1.421 thought Hdt. 7.39.2, τὴν μὲν ἀξίην οὐ λάμψεαι, ἐλάσσω δὲ τῆς ἀξίης, very similar, but Wade-Gery (1949) 85 rightly disagreed. See Thompson (1968) 221.

scheme, the Peloponnesian conference took place in the archonship of Pythodorus, whereas their invasion fell in the following archonship of Euthydemus. If Thompson's scheme is right, Hellanicus will have dated the conference and the invasion to consecutive, but different, archon-years and, as Thucydides later insists at 5.20, an uninformed reader of Hellanicus' *Atthis*, unaware of where within each archon-year each event occurred, would conclude by counting names that one year separated the two events. Thucydides is thus at 1.125.2 correcting the misleading implications of Hellanicus' eponymic chronological scheme.

We may accept, then, with Thompson that the Peloponnesian invasion of Attica occurred at the beginning of the archonship of Euthydemus. This fact caused Thucydides considerable embarrassment as the coincidence of this invasion, which constituted an acceptable, indeed obvious, beginning of the war, with the beginning of an archon-year could be seen as validation of Hellanicus' chronological system. That Hellanicus exploited this coincidence and did in fact begin his war at the beginning of the archonship of Euthydemus with the Peloponnesian invasion of Attica is shown by later evidence derived ultimately from Hellanicus' *Atthis*:

(1) At 5.20.1 the interpolator quite unthinkingly glossed ἡ ἀρχὴ τοῦ πολέμου τοῦδε as ἡ ἐσβολὴ ἡ ἐς τὴν Ἀττικήν[39] and, as he was probably dependent upon the Atthidographical tradition and so ultimately upon Hellanicus, one may presume that Hellanicus likewise made the war begin with the Peloponnesian invasion.

(2) Diodorus 12.38.1 dates the beginning of war to the archonship of Euthydemus and one possible explanation is that he here faithfully follows his list of dates derived ultimately from Hellanicus.

(3) The commentator on Demosthenes 22.13–14 (*Anonymus*

[39] See Müller (1852) 33 n. 5, followed by Stahl, Classen, Steup, and Gomme, *HCT* 3.683–85. Interpolation is not accepted by e.g. Jacoby in *FGrHist* IIIb (Supplement). 1.18, 2.15 n. 142, Meritt (1962) 437–38 and Rawlings (1981) 20, 35–36. Jacoby's incredible suggestion that Thucydides at 5.20.1 revised his earlier view of the *archē* of the war given at 2.2.1 without alteration of this earlier text has been adequately dealt with by Lendle (1964) 129f. Meritt's view that ὡς τὸ πρῶτον ἡ ἐσβολὴ ἡ ἐς τὴν Ἀττικήν referred to the beginning of the siege of Oenoe at 2.18.1 ignored the clear implication of ᾗπερ ἔμελλον ἐσβαλεῖν there and ἐσέβαλον ἐς τὴν Ἀττικήν at 2.19.1. More recently Meritt (1979) 107 n. 2 has preferred the already discredited view of Jacoby. Rawlings' retention of the full MS text and interpretation as 'decision to invade' made at 1.125 and finalized at 1.145 depends ultimately upon his interpretation of ἐνθένδε ἤδη at 2.1. See above n. 5 for the basic improbability of this interpretation. There is no alternative to acceptance of interpolation.

Argentinensis 5) in dating to the archonship of Euthydemus the Athenian decision to expend on the war 5,000 of the 6,000 talents on the Acropolis (cf. 2.24.1 with 2.13.3) was probably likewise following the standard date from the Atthidographical tradition for the beginning of war.[40]

We can now see why Thucydides insists so strongly on the validity of his own choice to begin the war with the Theban attack on Plataea. In defence of his own seasonal chronological system he was obliged to assert the attack on Plataea as the *archē* of the war not merely against Hellanicus' particular choice of the Peloponnesian invasion of Attica, but also against the popular alternatives of the Sybota and Potidaea campaigns, both of which also occurred at the beginning of an archon-year.[41] At 1.125.2 he needed to stress the delay between the Peloponnesian decision on war and their actual invasion in order to impart added significance to the intervening Theban attack on Plataea; but at the same time, as we have seen, he could not resist criticism of a chronological scheme which artificially separated the decision on war from its consequence. At 2.2.1 (μετὰ τὴν ἐν Ποτειδαίᾳ μάχην μηνὶ ἕκτῳ) and 2.19.1 (μετὰ τὰ ἐν Πλαταίᾳ γενόμενα ἡμέρᾳ ὀγδοηκοστῇ μάλιστα) he carefully and precisely located his own beginning between its two greatest rivals, the battle of Potidaea and the Peloponnesian invasion; and likewise at 2.2.1 (Πυθοδώρου ἔτι δύο μῆνας ἄρχοντος) he emphasized that the war in fact broke out two months before the archonship of Euthydemus began. Finally, by the use of εὐθύς at 2.10.1 he connected the Spartan preparations for invasion directly to the Plataean affair and thus, as he intended by his similar use of εὐθύς elsewhere (1.56.1, 57.1, 61.1), he wove the whole series of events from the battle of Sybota to the Peloponnesian invasion of Attica into a single, connected whole with the Theban attack on Plataea as its crucial turning point ἅμα ἦρι ἀρχομένῳ (2.2.1). Wherever Hellanicus' scheme suggested discontinuity, Thucydides made a correction. For instance, the Athenian alliance with Corcyra (1.44.1) and their consequential dispatch of the ships which fought at Sybota fell in two separate archon-years, 434/3 and 433/2,[42] and so Thucydides at 1.45.1

[40] See Hill (1951) 51 with Meiggs (1972) 515–18. I follow the interpretation of Wilcken (1907) 387–403; cf. Gomme *HCT* 2.28–30.

[41] For the dates of the battles of Sybota and Potidaea see above nn. 13 and 14. On Thompson's scheme, which I adopt, the battle of Potidaea was fought in October 432, but the dispatch of Callias (1.61.1), and so the beginning of the campaign, fell at the beginning of 432/1; see Thompson (1968) 230–31.

[42] For the date of the battle of Sybota see above n. 13. The alliance with Corcyra would be reasonably dated to May/June 433, i.e. towards the end of the archon-year 434/3. De Ste Croix (1972) 319 prefers a date in early July, i.e. possibly in 433/2, but one cannot believe that the Corcyraeans left their approach to the Athenians so late.

significantly indicates the interval as οὐ πολὺ ὕστερον. Similarly the revolt of Potidaea, followed by the Corinthian dispatch of Aristeus, fell in 433/2, whereas Aristeus' arrival in Potidaea and the consequential dispatch of the Athenian force under Callias fell in 432/1;[43] and so Thucydides significantly at 1.60.3 dates Aristeus' arrival in Potidaea on the fortieth day after its revolt, and at 1.61.1 (εὐθύς) insists that the dispatch of Callias follows immediately after Potidaea's revolt. The whole underlying purpose of his chronological indications from the beginning of the Corcyraean affair to the Peloponnesian invasion of Attica is to remove from the course of events the distortions of Hellanicus' chronological scheme and to throw into prominence the crucial significance of the Theban attack on Plataea as the true *archē* of the war.

There are many other points in the *History* where Thucydides shows his obsessive concern to undermine the validity of Hellanicus' chronological system. In the introduction to his Pentekontaetia excursus at 1.97.2 he makes a beautifully dismissive reference to Hellanicus' *Atthis*:

ἔγραψα δὲ αὐτὰ καὶ τὴν ἐκβολὴν τοῦ λόγου ἐποιησάμην διὰ τόδε, ὅτι τοῖς πρὸ ἐμοῦ ἅπασιν ἐκλιπὲς τοῦτο ἦν τὸ χωρίον καὶ ἢ τὰ πρὸ τῶν Μηδικῶν Ἑλληνικὰ ξυνετίθεσαν ἢ αὐτὰ τὰ Μηδικά· τούτων δὲ ὅσπερ καὶ ἥψατο ἐν τῇ Ἀττικῇ ξυγγραφῇ Ἑλλάνικος, βραχέως τε καὶ τοῖς χρόνοις οὐκ ἀκριβῶς ἐπεμνήσθη.

(I wrote it and made the excursus in my account, because this period was omitted by all my predecessors and they were writing up either Greek history before the Persian Wars or the Persian Wars themselves; and the writer who in fact *touched* upon these events in his Attic history, Hellanicus, made mention of them briefly and with no chronological accuracy.)

Ziegler[44] and others have quite misunderstood the contempt[45] that Thucydides shows here for Hellanicus and have regarded τούτων δὲ ὅσπερ [...] ἐπεμνήσθη as a later addition, imperfectly adapted to its context, made by Thucydides to an introduction originally written,

[43] For the date of the dispatch of Callias see above n. 41. The Potidaeans paid fifteen talents tribute in spring 432 (cf. Meiggs (1972) 202, 528 with De Ste Croix (1972) 329), and so their revolt should be dated sometime between March and June 432. Thompson (1968) 223 n. 3, 232 suggests *c.* 1 June.

[44] Ziegler (1929) 66 n. 2. See further Adcock (1951) 11 and (1963) 22, 122, Jacoby *FGrHist* IIIb (Supplement). 1.5f., Westlake (1955) 53f. and (1977) 108 n. 72, Lendle (1960) 38 n. 5 and (1964) 141 n. 1, Luschnat (1970) 1145, De Ste Croix (1972) 314–15, Pelekidis (1974) 410.

[45] The contempt is self-evident. Lenardon (1981) 59–70 argues well against taking τούτων δὲ ὅσπερ [...] ἐπεμνήσθη as a later addition and accepts that Thucydides was critical of Hellanicus, but interprets this criticism as a veiled apology for the 'brevity and chronological imprecision' of his own excursus, which necessarily was heavily dependent upon Hellanicus' work and so reflected its qualities.

like the excursus itself, before the publication of Hellanicus' *Atthis*. In fact the excursus was certainly written in response to Hellanicus' *Atthis*[46] and a desire to correct the misleading implications of Hellanicus' 'imprecise' chronological scheme[47] can be detected throughout. At 1.108.2, for example, Thucydides dates the battle of Oenophyta to the sixty-second day after the battle of Tanagra. Hellanicus had probably dated Tanagra to 458/7 and Oenophyta to 457/6; these, at any rate, are Diodorus' dates (11.80 and 81–83) and Diodorus may here, as occasionally elsewhere, preserve the Atthidographical tradition.[48] Hellanicus' system had thus separated two battles which belonged together and Thucydides at 1.108.2 restores the connexion. A similar motivation probably explains the specific ἡμέρας ὕστερον δώδεκα μάλιστα, separating the two battles in the Megarid at 1.105.6, and ἡμέρας περὶ τέσσαρας καὶ δέκα at 1.117.1, separating a Samian victory during the Athenian siege of Samos from the re-establishment of the Athenian blockade. The use of οὐ πολλῷ ὕστερον (1.111.2, 114.1, 115.1) and εὐθύς (1.102.4, 111.3) in the excursus may have the same significance as in the αἰτίαι καὶ διαφοραί section at 1.45.1 and 61.1 respectively (see above pp. 28–29); and a similar explanation may be found for the other precise chronological indications in the excursus.[49]

A particularly perverse instance of Thucydides' obsessive concern to undermine Hellanicus' system occurs at 5.25.3. Here he states that after the Peace of 421 each side held back from invading the other's territory for six years and ten months. Hellanicus probably ended the Peace of Nicias and began his separate Decelean War[50] with the Spartan fortification of Decelea at the beginning of the archon-year 413/12; this, at any rate, is where Diodorus 13.9.1–2 dates it. Once again the beginning of a war seemed to coincide with the beginning of an archon-year. This explains why at 7.19.1 Thucydides, who in

[46] See Gomme *HCT* 1.363 n. 1, 369, Meiggs (1972) 444–46.

[47] Meritt–Wade-Gery–McGregor (1950) 162 believed that Hellanicus' 'imprecision' consisted in recording events in what Thucydides held to be the wrong order. However, Jacoby in *FGrHist* IIIb (Supplement). 1.17–18 rightly followed Niese (1888) 81f. in explaining οὐκ ἀκριβῶς at 1.97.2 by reference to οὐκ ἀκριβές at 5.20.2.

[48] See Gomme *HCT* 1.317.

[49] E.g. for τρίτῳ ἔτει (1.101.3), δεκάτῳ ἔτει (1.103.1), ἐνιαυτὸν καὶ ἓξ μῆνας (1.109.4), ἓξ ἔτη (1.110.1), διαλιπόντων ἐτῶν τριῶν (1.112.1), ἕκτῳ ἔτει (1.115.2) and ἐνάτῳ μηνί (1.117.3). All of these precise indications need careful and detailed examination as possible corrections by Thucydides of the misleading implications of Hellanicus' chronological division by archon-years. In every case, with the exception of the possibly interpolated διαλιπόντων ἐτῶν τριῶν (1.112.1), ἔτος must be interpreted as a seasonal year (i.e. campaigning season), rather than an archon-year. See further Smart (1977b) 249.

[50] For the later conception of the Decelean War as a separate entity see De Ste Croix (1972) 295. Jacoby in *FGrHist* IIIb (Supplement). 2.16 n. 147 rightly suggested that Hellanicus probably treated the Peloponnesian War as two distinct wars.

any case denied the existence of separate Archidamian and Decelean Wars (5.26), nevertheless chose to emphasize that the Spartan invasion which ended with the fortification of Decelea started in fact at the very beginning of spring (7.19.1, τοῦ δ' ἐπιγιγνομένου ἦρος εὐθὺς ἀρχομένου πρωίτατα δή); a little later at 7.20.1 (ἅμα τῆς Δεκελείας τῷ τειχισμῷ καὶ τοῦ ἦρος εὐθὺς ἀρχομένου) he indicates that the fortification itself was begun already in the spring of 413, even if it was not completed and operational until after the beginning of the archon-year 413/12. At 6.93.1–2 he went even further in suggesting that the Spartan plan to fortify Decelea dated from as early as Alcibiades' advice in winter, 415/14 (6.93.2, ὥστε τῇ ἐπιτειχίσει τῆς Δεκελείας προσεῖχον ἤδη τὸν νοῦν), and that this intention in itself, rather than the subsequent reality, constituted on the Spartan side after only six years and ten months the effective end of the ὕποπτος ἀνοκωχή (5.26.3) characterized by 'holding back from making an expedition against one another's territory' (5.25.3, ἀπέσχοντο μὴ ἐπὶ τὴν ἑκατέρων γῆν στρατεῦσαι).[51] He thus reduced Hellanicus' eight years between the Archidamian and Decelean Wars to less than seven.

Thucydides, then, was obsessed with the superiority of his own seasonal chronology over the eponymic chronology of Hellanicus. If one can explain this obsession, one can penetrate to the heart of his conception of his task as a historian. One reason was clearly his concern with accuracy: as he states explicitly at 5.20, a simple eponymic scheme did not distinguish between events at the beginning, middle and end of a year of office. Accordingly he took care himself to add to his winters and summers such qualifications as ἀρχομένου, μεσοῦντος and τελευτῶντος, or their equivalents.[52] He occasionally used other more precise seasonal and astronomical indications[53] and in general maintained a strict chronological order in his narration of

[51] This view has been well argued by Rawlings (1981) 13–18, 36–38 with full reference to previous discussions.

[52] The beginning of summer/winter is specifically indicated at 2.2.1 (ἅμα ἦρι ἀρχομένῳ), 2.47.2, 2.93.1, 4.1.1 (περὶ σίτου ἐκβολήν), 4.2.1 (ὑπὸ τοὺς αὐτοὺς χρόνους τοῦ ἦρος πρὶν τὸν σῖτον ἐν ἀκμῇ εἶναι), 4.52.1, 4.89.1, 4.117.1 (ἅμα ἦρι εὐθύς), 5.40.1 (ἅμα τῷ ἦρι εὐθύς), 5.52.1, 5.76.1, 6.8.1 (ἅμα ἦρι), 6.94 (ἅμα τῷ ἦρι εὐθὺς ἀρχομένῳ), 7.19.1 (τοῦ ἐπιγιγνομένου ἦρος εὐθὺς ἀρχομένου πρωίτατα δή), 7.20.1 (τοῦ ἦρος εὐθὺς ἀρχομένου), 8.2.1 and 8.61 (ἅμα τῷ ἦρι εὐθὺς ἀρχομένῳ). The middle is indicated at 2.19.1 (θέρους καὶ τοῦ σίτου ἀκμάζοντος), 2.79.1 (ἀκμάζοντος τοῦ σίτου), 3.1.1 (ἅμα τῷ σίτῳ ἀκμάζοντι), 5.57.1 and 6.30.1 (μεσοῦντος ἤδη). And the end is indicated at 2.31.1 (περὶ τὸ φθινόπωρον), 2.32, 2.67.1, 3.18.3 (περὶ τὸ φθινόπωρον ἤδη ἀρχόμενον), 3.86.1, 3.100.2 (περὶ τὸ φθινόπωρον), 3.115.6, 4.133.4, 4.135.1 (καὶ πρὸς ἔαρ ἤδη), 5.20.1 (ἅμα ἦρι), 5.39.3 (τελευτῶντος ἤδη καὶ πρὸς ἔαρ), 7.9, 8.25.1 and 8.60.1.

[53] Compare the employment of ἔαρ and φθινόπωρον above and add 2.78.2 (περὶ ἀρκτούρου ἐπιτολάς), 7.16.2 (περὶ ἡλίου τροπὰς τὰς χειμερινάς) and 8.39.1 (περὶ ἡλίου τροπάς).

events.[54] However, a more significant explanation of his obsession is indicated at 4.133.3: after the flight of Chrysis to Phlius, the Argives ἄλλην ἱέρειαν ἐκ τοῦ νόμου τοῦ προκειμένου κατεστήσαντο Φαεινίδα ὄνομα. The words ἐκ τοῦ νόμου τοῦ προκειμένου are contextually redundant and seem intended simply to show the basis of eponymic schemes in *nomos*. Thucydides in general adopts a consistently negative attitude towards *nomos* throughout his *History*. It is unable to survive the natural phenomenon of the plague (2.52.4, νόμοι τε πάντες ξυνεταράχθησαν οἷς ἐχρῶντο πρότερον περὶ τὰς ταφάς, cf. 53.4, θεῶν δὲ φόβος ἢ ἀνθρώπων νόμος οὐδεὶς ἀπεῖργε) and within the process of *stasis*, which is wholly conditioned by human *phusis* (3.82.2, καὶ ἐπέπεσε πολλὰ καὶ χαλεπὰ κατὰ στάσιν ταῖς πόλεσι, γιγνόμενα μὲν καὶ αἰεὶ ἐσόμενα, ἕως ἂν ἡ αὐτὴ φύσις ἀνθρώπων ᾖ), *nomos* is without effect (3.82.6, οὐ γὰρ μετὰ τῶν κειμένων νόμων ὠφελίᾳ αἱ τοιαῦται ξύνοδοι, ἀλλὰ παρὰ τοὺς καθεστῶτας πλεονεξίᾳ. καὶ τὰς ἐς σφᾶς αὐτοὺς πίστεις οὐ τῷ θείῳ νόμῳ μᾶλλον ἐκρατύνοντο ἢ τῷ κοινῇ τι παρανομῆσαι). This inefficacy of *nomos* explains its unreliability as a basis for εὐβουλία. The Melians in 416 put their trust in *nomos*, manifest in τὸ ὅσιον and τὸ δίκαιον, against the reality of *phusis*, embodied in Athenian δύναμις (5.104, ὅσιοι πρὸς οὐ δικαίους, cf. 89), and the result is their destruction. Similarly Nicias trusts in *nomos* (7.77.2, καίτοι πολλὰ μὲν ἐς θεοὺς νόμιμα δεδιῄτημαι, πολλὰ δὲ ἐς ἀνθρώπους δίκαια καὶ ἀνεπίφθονα, cf. 86.5, διὰ τὴν πᾶσαν ἐς ἀρετὴν νενομισμένην ἐπιτήδευσιν) with disastrous consequences both for himself and for his army.

The first and most elaborate statement in the *History* of the inefficacy and unreliability of *nomos* is precisely the account of the Plataean affair from 2.2–6 through 2.71–78 and 3.20–24 to 3.52–68. In the middle (2.71–74) and the end (3.53–59, 61–67) of the account the irrelevance of *nomos* to the reality of the action is clearly demonstrated. At 2.71–74 the Spartan attack on Plataea is presented as both contrary to *nomos* by the Plataeans (2.71.2–4, οὐ δίκαια ποιεῖτε [...] ἐᾶν δὲ οἰκεῖν αὐτονόμους καθάπερ Παυσανίας ἐδικαίωσεν) and at the same time in accordance with *nomos* by Archidamus (2.74.2 (to the gods), ξυγγνώμονες δὲ ἔστε τῆς μὲν ἀδικίας κολάζεσθαι τοῖς ὑπάρχουσι προτέροις, τῆς δὲ τιμωρίας τυγχάνειν τοῖς ἐπιφέρουσι νομίμως). And at 3.53–59, 61–67 the Plataean Debate is conducted throughout in terms of *nomos* and constitutes a most careful and elaborate demonstration of the effective neutralization of moral argument through antilogy.[55] The reality of what happened at Plataea

[54] Occasionally there is explicit overlap, as at 2.79.1, 8.45 and 8.63.3, and sometimes Thucydides passes over an event when it happened and refers back to it later, as at 3.34.1, 3.70.1, 3.86.2–3, 5.4.2–4, 5.75.4, 6.6.2 (see Smart (1972) 136) and 6.46.3.

[55] See Macleod (1977) 239–40: 'What matters is not that the reader condemn or acquit either side, but that he see the historical meaning of the rhetorical contradictions.'

was determined by Spartan and Theban strength, Plataean weakness and Athenian inability to intervene, and it was these natural factors of power, realized in the natural human propensity to win, preserve and fear power, which occasioned the resort to *nomos* at 3.52.2 (γνοὺς δὲ ὁ Λακεδαιμόνιος ἄρχων τὴν ἀσθένειαν αὐτῶν), conditioned the course of events at 3.60 (οἱ δὲ Θηβαῖοι δείσαντες) and determined their outcome at 3.68.4 (νομίζοντες ἐς τὸν πόλεμον αὐτοὺς ἄρτι τότε καθιστάμενον ὠφελίμους εἶναι). At 2.73.2–74.1 (ἐβουλεύσαντο Ἀθηναίους μὴ προδιδόναι) the Plataeans, like the Melians later, chose to base their deliberation on τὸ ὅσιον and τὸ δίκαιον and at 3.52.2–3 to put their trust in *nomos* (cf. 3.53.1, πιστεύσαντες, with the Melians at 5.104, πιστεύομεν, and 113, πιστεύσαντες), and the result was disaster. If one turns from the middle and end of the affair to its beginning at 2.2–6 one can see likewise here, as one would expect, the same concern with *nomos* and *phusis*. Now it is rather the Thebans at 2.2.4–3.1 (γνώμην δ' ἐποιοῦντο κηρύγμασί τε χρήσασθαι ἐπιτηδείοις καὶ ἐς ξύμβασιν μᾶλλον καὶ φιλίαν τὴν πόλιν ἀγαγεῖν) and 2.5.4–7 (ἐκ δ' οὖν τῆς γῆς ἀνεχώρησαν οἱ Θηβαῖοι οὐδὲν ἀδικήσαντες) whose trust in *nomos* leads them astray. The failure of their original plan for the seizure of Plataea is not presented, as Stahl suggests, as necessary inevitability, but as avoidable error. There is rather a close, and surely intentional, parallel drawn between the Thebans at 2.2–6, who both at 2.4 and 2.5.4–7 are seduced into δυσβουλία by considerations based on *nomos*, and the Plataeans at 2.73–74.1, who suffer a similar seduction. At 2.73–74.1 the process of Plataean deliberation is emphasized (βουλευσάμενοι μετὰ τοῦ πλήθους [...] βουλευσάμενοι μετ' αὐτῶν [...] ἐβουλεύσαντο Ἀθηναίους μὴ προδιδόναι) and what determines their decision is the Athenian insistence (ἐπισκήπτουσι) upon the moral obligation of alliance and oaths (ἀφ' οὗ ξύμμαχοι ἐγενόμεθα [...] πρὸς τῶν ὅρκων [...] μηδὲν νεωτερίζειν περὶ τὴν ξυμμαχίαν).[56] Similarly, both at 2.2.4 (τοῖς μὲν ἐπαγαγομένοις οὐκ ἐπείθοντο ὥστε εὐθὺς ἔργου ἔχεσθαι καὶ ἰέναι ἐπὶ τὰς οἰκίας τῶν ἐχθρῶν, γνώμην δ' ἐποιοῦντο) and at 2.5.4–7 (ἐπεβούλευον [...] ἐβούλοντο [...] διενοοῦντο [...] ἔτι διαβουλευομένων αὐτῶν), the narrative is concerned with the Thebans' conscious choice to act in accordance with, rather than contrary to, *nomos* to achieve their purpose.

From beginning to end, then, the Plataean affair is concerned with the avoidable consequences of *gnōmē* based on a misconception of history as a process determined by *nomos*. History was, on the

[56] At 3.68.5, καὶ τὰ μὲν κατὰ Πλάταιαν ἔτει τρίτῳ καὶ ἐνενηκοστῷ ἐπειδὴ Ἀθηναίων ξύμμαχοι ἐγένοντο οὕτως ἐτελεύτησεν, Thucydides seems concerned to underline not Athenian betrayal of Plataea (see Stahl (1966) 116 and Macleod (1977) 231), nor even Plataean error in reliance upon the alliance, but simply the insufficiency of any alliance, howsoever long-standing, within the reality of war.

contrary, for Thucydides a process grounded in *phusis*. The Theban attack on Plataea at the beginning of spring thus provided a natural *archē* to a natural process. Such a process could only be obscured by eponymic chronological schemes, such as those of Hellanicus, based as they were on *nomos*. Only a natural chronological scheme, grounded in *phusis* through its employment of astronomically defined summers and winters,[57] could reveal the true nature of human history and so enable its beneficial comprehension.

APPENDIX

Chronological scheme

434/3	May/June	Corcyraean alliance	(1.45.1, οὐ πολὺ ὕστερον)
433/2	August	battle of Sybota	(1.48–51, ML 61.10, 22)
433/2	*c.* 1 June	revolt of Potidaea	(1.58.1) Thompson (1968) 232
433/2	June	dispatch of Aristeus	(1.60)

beginning of Pythodorus' archonship *c.* 18 June 432: Thompson (1968) 218 n. 1

432/1	*c.* 10 July	arrival of Aristeus	(1.60.3, τεσσαρακοστῇ ἡμέρᾳ)
432/1	August	dispatch of Callias	(1.61.1) Thompson (1968) 230–31
432/1	October	battle of Potidaea	(1.63, cf. 2.2.1) Thompson (1968) 232
432/1	Nov./Dec.	Peloponnesian conference	(1.119–125) Thompson (1968) 232
432/1	*c.* 1 April	Theban attack on Plataea	(2.2.1) Thompson (1968) 232

end of Pythodorus' archonship *c.* 8 June 431: Thompson (1968) 232

[57] A similar concern with astronomically defined summers and winters is significantly evident in the Hippocratic corpus. See περὶ διαίτης 3.1: τὸν μὲν οὖν ἐνιαυτὸν ἐς τέσσαρα μέρεα διαιρέω, ἅπερ μάλιστα γινώσκουσιν οἱ πολλοί, χειμῶνα, ἦρ, θέρος, φθινόπωρον· χειμῶνα μὲν ἀπὸ πλειάδων δύσιος (= *c.* 6 Nov.) ἄχρι ἰσημερίης ἠαρινῆς (= 24 March), ἦρ δὲ ἀπὸ ἰσημερίης μέχρι πλειάδων ἐπιτολῆς (= *c.* 12 May), θέρος δὲ ἀπὸ πλειάδων μέχρι ἀρκτούρου ἐπιτολῆς (= *c.* 20 Sept.), φθινόπωρον δὲ ἀπὸ ἀρκτούρου μέχρι πλειάδων δύσιος (quoted by Gomme *HCT* 3.707). These seasonal definitions, with the extension of summer to include spring and autumn, are precisely those adopted by Thucydides, and Weidauer (1954) 73–74 rightly suspected that Thucydides was influenced by Hippocratic methodology in his choice of chronological scheme: 'Vielleicht lässt sich auch in der Eigenart des Thukydides, die Zeit nicht nach Archontenjahren, sondern nach Sommer und Winter, zu messen eine Nähe wieder zu den Epidemien sehen.'

431/30 *c.* 20 June	Peloponnesian invasion of Attica	(2.19.1) Thompson (1968) 232
424/3 *c.* 28 March	One Year Truce	(4.117.1, ἅμα ἦρι τοῦ ἐπιγιγνομένου θέρους εὐθύς, cf. 118.12, Elaphebolion 14) Meritt–McGregor (1967) 88
422/1 *c.* 13 March	Peace of Nicias	(5.19.1, Elaphebolion 25, cf. 20.1, τελευτῶντος τοῦ χειμῶνος ἅμα ἦρι) Meritt–McGregor (1967) 88
415/14 January	end of ὕποπτος ἀνοκωχή	(5.25.3, ἓξ ἔτη καὶ δέκα μῆνας, 6.93.2) Rawlings (1981) 36–38
414/13 April	Peloponnesian invasion of Attica	(7.19.1, πρωίτατα δή)
413/12 August	fortification of Decelea complete	(Diod. 13.9.1–2)
405/4 *c.* 25 March	Lysander's entry into Piraeus	(Plut. *Lys.* 15.1, Mounichion 16) Lotze (1967) 44[58]

[58] Acceptance of Lotze's date of late March for Lysander's entry into Piraeus on Mounichion 16, 404, allows παρενεγκούσας at Thuc. 5.26.3, καὶ ἡμέρας ου πολλὰς παρενεγκούσας, to mean 'being subtracted'; see above n. 5 on παρενεγκουσῶν at 5.20.1, καὶ ἡμερῶν ὀλίγων παρενεγκουσῶν.

Military engagements in Xenophon's *Hellenica*

C. J. TUPLIN

There are (at least) two reasons why discussion of the military engagements in *Hellenica* requires little defence. Firstly, *Hellenica* is chiefly concerned with the political interaction of Greek *poleis*, which, given the ancients' propensity for warfare, means that much of it is devoted to military history. Although the military narrative has various components, particular interest is bound to attach to the moments of conflict *par excellence*, i.e. battles, great and small; and since *Hellenica* contains references to or reports of some 153 distinct military engagements the phenomenon is certainly well represented in the text.[1] Secondly, the credit of *Hellenica* is much under attack nowadays, a situation greatly encouraged by comparison between some of Xenophon's battle narratives and corresponding accounts elsewhere. This aspect of the text is therefore in the front line when it comes to estimates of Xenophon's performance.

It is, of course, obvious that Xenophon does not aim to provide large numbers of highly and systematically detailed narratives. (The contrast with Thucydides is clear, though it is fair, and important, to add that there is much even in Thucydides which does not depart far from the level of detail characteristic of Xenophon.) After all (to take some crude indications) over 25 % of the relevant passages fail to name any (immediate) commanding officers on either side, nearly 50 % of the accounts of land battles say nothing about the types of

[1] A full list of references can be compiled from nn. 22–24 (117 items) and the discussion of the other 36 in pp. 44–64. The computation ignores over 50 examples of action against property (often reported in quite general terms, but sometimes mentioning e.g. cut trees (4.5.10; 5.2.43, 3.3; 6.5.22,30), burnt houses/villages (1.2.4; 5.4.21; 6.2.6, 5.22,27,30), captured slaves/animals (1.2.4; 3.2.2,26; 4.6.6; 5.4.21; 6.2.6) and even looted wine-cellars (6.2.6); the most striking item is Teleutias' Piraeus raid, 5.1.21f.), 6 sieges mentioned without report of fighting (2.2.10, 3.6; 3.2.11; 5.1.7, 2.4; 7.4.18), passages which mention campaigns in summary or unspecific terms (1.4.9,23; 2.1.16, 2.5, 4.26; 3.1.5,7, 4.12; 4.1.1,27, 4.1,14,16,17, 5.19, 6.1,12, 8.1,10,21,24,33,35; 5.2.12 24,36,43,46, 3.22, 4.63; 6.1.1,5, 2.23,37, 3.1, 5.32,49; 7.1.43, 4.14) or where an engagement is only implied (2.4.26; 6.3.1, 4.27, 5.27; 7.4.26) or uncertain (2.4.26; 5.1.7; 7.1.41, 5.16).

Note: (i) all references otherwise unidentified in text or notes are to *Hellenica*, and engagement narratives may be identified only by reference to their first section; (ii) within this paper, and contrary to the practice elsewhere in *Past Perspectives*, identifying numbers of books in the works of ancient authors are not repeated when references contain more than a single passage from the same book.

troops in use (i.e. hoplites, peltasts, etc.), and just over 60 % of the whole sample give no information about the sizes of forces involved. These crude figures are, of course, somewhat misleading. If one distinguishes between 24 naval engagements, 66 attacks on cities, towns or encampments, and 63 field battles, there turn out to be marked divergences.[2] One thing which emerges is the generally poor degree of detail in the middle group, and this is not contradicted if one looks at other characteristics, e.g. the amount of tactical information provided or the degree of topographical precision. Of the 66 items 36 consist of nothing more than a bald, almost formulaic, statement of the simple fact of attack/capture.[3] The remaining accounts say something more about the attack than that it happened, but, although 20 do give some notion of the tactical circumstances (as regards, e.g., the deployment of troops or the manner of attack – use of scaling ladders, siege machinery etc. – or the achievement of surprise),[4] only 13 provide topographical information more precise than the name of the place in question[5] and only 5 can be regarded as providing substantial descriptions.[6] This is, in short, a (common) type of military event in which Xenophon shows no particular interest. So far as topography is concerned the position is not indeed

[2] *Commanders.* (i) Naval: only once is there no information (1.6.19) and in 17 out of 23 we have names on both sides (in 1.1.4 the only named Athenian commander arrives in mid-battle; where there is only one named commander, 1.1.2,36; 4.4.19, 8.11; 5.1.2, 4.56, he is always Spartan). (ii) City attacks: in 33 cases the attacking commander is named, in 27 cases there are no names at all; names on both sides appear only in 1.2.6, 3.14,18; 3.2.27; 4.1.20; 7.5.10. (iii) Field battles: the commonest situation (35 times) is one named commander, and the other cases divide fairly evenly between both names (25 %) and neither (20 %). *Troop types.* Not really pertinent at sea, though X. does notice στρατιώτιδες in 1.1.36 and comments on crews at 1.6.15,26; 5.1.26. 80 % of city attacks offer no information. 80 % of field battles say something about at least one side, and full specification of both is the commonest single situation (though only found in 30 % of cases). *Troop numbers.* Nearly two-thirds of field battles lack information, better than city attacks (*c.* 80 %), worse than naval battles (only 3 cases, 4.4.19, 8.11; 5.4.60). In 27 of the 40 field battles where there is information it is non-numerical or relates to only part of one side's army and only 3 cases (4.1.17, 2.15; 5.3.1 (with 5.2.40)) approach a complete record for both sides, whereas 13 naval engagements have full figures and in only 3 (1.1.1,3; 4.3.11) is information vague or partial.

[3] 24 use combinations of προσβάλλειν, αἱρεῖν, αἱρεῖν κατὰ κράτος (1.2.2, 5.15 (2 items), 6.13; 2.1.19; 3.1.13 (3 items); 4.4.13 (2 items),19, 5.5,19 (3 items); 5.3.18; 6.4.3,27; 7.1.18 (2 items),22,28, 4.12,26), the remainder (almost all in books 6–7) other words ((κατα-/ἀνα)λαμβάνειν, κρατεῖν, ἁλίσκεσθαι: 2.4.2; 6.5.12; 7.3.4, 4.1 (2 items),12,14 (2 items),16,17,20,26). X. does not indicate what distinguished capture κατὰ κράτος; but the facts that victims of 'ordinary' capture do not include presumably well-fortified places like Methymna, Torone, Lampsacus, and that comment about P.O.W.s is found only with capture κατὰ κράτος may be noticed.

[4] 1.2.6, 3.14,18; 2.4.4,27; 3.2.3, 5.18; 4.4.13, 6.7; 5.4.11; 6.5.26,30; 7.1.15,18, 2.5,7, 20, 4.13,14, 5.10.

[5] 1.2.6, 3.18; 2.4.4,27; 3.5.18; 4.4.13, 6.7; 6.5.30; 7.1.18, 2.7, 4.13,14, 5.10.

[6] 3.2.3; 6.5.30; 7.1.18, 2.7, 5.10. (7.2.7 is the only narrated attack on a wall – an unusual situation of attack *from the inside*.)

a lot better with the other categories, the strong tendency being for events to be located in fairly imprecise terms;[7] and there is no shortage of items which are, tactically speaking, quite undetailed (i.e. we know something of their (general) context and their result but nothing of the tactical shape of the encounter; this is the position in about 20 % of cases).[8] But there are 10 naval engagements and some 37 field battles which can be called well-defined in the sense that one can discern separate concurrent or consecutive phases in the fighting or (put another way) in the sense that they are (in varying degrees) susceptible to diagrammatic representation of the sort beloved of military historians.[9]

All the same, one should not overestimate the extent to which Xenophon's narrative regularly takes us much beyond this. The most common categories of further information (not all confined to the tactically well-defined engagements) are observations about the attitude of those involved (anger, contempt, (over-)boldness, high or low morale, *aporia*, shame)[10] or their tactical thinking (but pre-battle speeches are very rare),[11] reports of the role of particular individuals

[7] Naval: Only 1.1.1 (a notorious problem) is totally unlocated. 5 items are located very vaguely ('in the Hellespont', 'in the Corinthian Gulf'), 8 by reference to the city/island from which one fleet started (generally without indication of distance), 4 occur 'around' a city or cape. The other 5 items report both sides' starting points or refer to parts of a city (Mytilene); the one use of figures (2.2.21) has them wrong. Field battles: 6 times there is either no toponymic localization (4.4.16) or it is very vague ('somewhere in Lydia', 1.2.5; cf. 4.3.14,22, 6.8, 8.18). (Such inexactitude is consistent with the presence of local topographic information: cf. 4.3.22.) 47 items are toponymically located in terms of cities, villages or a fortress, 2 'on Cithaeron' and one near the Pactolus. (In 30 of these cases there is no additional more precise information – e.g. distance from the named point – and only two of the remainder use figures, 4.5.11; 5.2.39.) Only 7 times does X. provide a more narrowly local toponym (1.1.33; 2.4.10, 32; 5.1.10, 4.49; 7.2.12, 4.28). In 32 cases there is comment about the terrain (generally only categorization as flat or otherwise).

[8] 1.1.1,36, 2.16, 4.22; 3.2.27; 4.8.11,21,28; 5.1.2, 4.10,60,63; 6.5.51; 7.1.22,25 (2 items), 2.10; also 1.2.5 (textually corrupt) and 4.4.16,7.6 (highlighted incidents without proper context). 19 items are only minimally particularized (i.e. we can class them as e.g. ambush rather than formal battle but no more than that): 1.1.33, 2.12, 5.19, 6.15, 19,22; 2.4.3; 3.1.7,18; 4.3.14, 4.15,19 (Teleutias), 8.24; 5.4.14,56,59; 7.2.4,18, 5.14.

[9] Naval: 4 arise from pursuit of one fleet by another (1.1.2, 4.11,18), 3 are attacks on moored ships (2.1.21; 5.1.8; 6.2.33), 2 are formal battles (1.6.26; 4.3.11), and 1 is an ambush (5.1.26). Land: 12 involve attacks on marching forces (2.4.32; 4.2.14, 3.3,22, 5.11, 6.8; 5.4.39,42,54; 6.5.14; 7.2.12), 10 are formal battles (1.3.2; 2.4.10; 4.2.15, 3.15, 4.9; 5.2.39; 6.4.4; 7.1.30, 4.28, 5.18), 8 arise from attacks on troops engaged in ravaging/foraging (1.2.3; 3.4.21; 4.1.17, 8.18; 5.3.1,3; 6.2.17; 7.1.21), 2 each involve chance encounters while marching (3.4.13; 7.4.26), assaults on a stationary force (7.2.14, 4.22) and an ambush (4.8.35; 5.1.10), and 1 involves a sortie (4.4.16).

[10] Anger: 2.4.32; 5.3.3,5. Contempt: 4.4.10, 5.12, 8.36; 5.3.1. (Over-)boldness: 2.4.2; 4.3.18, 5.16; 5.3.4, 4.43, 54, 65; 6.5.13; 7.2.8, 5.13. Morale: 3.5.21; 6.2.19; 7.1.30, 2.21, 4.24, 5.20, 22. *Aporia*: 4.5.17; 5.4.44. Shame: 7.4.13.

[11] 1.6.31,32; 3.4.23; 4.2.18,22, 3.5,6,19, 5.13, 6.9, 7.6,8, 8.18; 5.1.27, 2.39,42, 3.4, 4.43,44,50,51; 6.2.21, 4.12; 7.1.15, 5.21. Speeches: 2.4.13; 7.1.30.

(more often than not merely the fact of their being wounded or killed),[12] actual or effective first-person comments by Xenophon about the event he is describing (which is as much information about *Xenophon* as anything),[13] and references to the erection of trophies or the exchange of bodies (which is pretty incidental information).[14] By contrast other incidental matters, such as the time of day, the state of the weather, the noises of battle or the offering of pre-battle sacrifices,[15] and certain less incidental ones, such as the length of time required for the victors to get the upper hand or the number of casualties,[16] are only mentioned intermittently. There is little attempt to describe the fighting as such (at most we are told that an attack was made at the run or that the soldiers were using hand-held or thrown weapons or that two hoplite lines shoved against one another or that a ship was rammed),[17] and Xenophon only rarely says anything that brings a scene alive (it is somehow characteristic that his attempt in *Agesilaus* to evoke the noise during the second, murderous phase at Coronea is missing in the parallel account in *Hellenica*).[18] Moreover, the presence of any particular sort of detail is, as a general rule, no guarantee against the absence of other sorts.

Still, Xenophon's failure to indulge in systematic collection of information is paralleled by a not discreditable lack of system in other respects. His treatment of military engagements is actually remarkably varied, even when the same sort of event is in question (for example,

[12] Death: 1.1.18, 3.6, 6.33; 2.4.6,18,19,33; 4.3.8,12,23, 8.10,19,29; 5.1.12, 3.6, 4.39, 45,52; 6.2.23, 4.14, 5.14; 7.4.23,31, 5.25. Wounds: 4.3.20; 5.2.41; 6.4.13; 7.4.23. Other: 1.1.5; 2.1.28, 4.18; 4.3.17, 4.10; 5.2.41; 6.2.35.

[13] 4.3.19, 4.12, 5.14,16, 8.24; 5.3.7, 4.40,45,51,54; 6.2.19,34, 4.13, 5.51; 7.2.4,9,10, 4.32, 5.12,16,19. (At 6.5.51 and 7.5.19f. the narrative is largely formulated in terms of X.'s commentary.) The formula '*x* would have happened but for *y*' (4.3.23, 7.6; 5.2.41; 6.2.23, 5.14) is also a sort of authorial comment.

[14] Trophies: 1.2.3,10, 4.23, 5.14, 6.35; 2.4.7,35; 3.5.19; 4.2.23, 3.9,21, 5.10, 6.12; 5.2.43, 4.53,65,66; 6.2.24, 4.15; 7.1.19,32, 2.4,15, 4.14,24, 5.13,26. Bodies: 1.2.11; 2.4.19; 3.5.23; 4.3.21, 4.13; 6.2.24, 4.14; 7.1.19, 5.13,17,26.

[15] Time: 1.1.2,5, 2.16, 6.21,29; 2.1.27; 4.3.22, 8.18; 5.1.9, 4.39; 6.4.8; 7.2.14. Weather: 1.1.16; 2.4.3; 7.1.31. Noises: 4.2.19 (paean), 3.17 (*alalagē*); 5.1.9 (trumpet); 7.4.22 (κραυγὴ πολλή). Sacrifices: 3.1.17, 4.23; 4.2.18,20, 6.10; 7.4.30.

[16] Length: 1.1.5, 3.6, 6.33. Ship losses: 1.1.7,18,36, 2.12, 5.14, 19, 6.17,21,23,24; 2.1.28; 4.8.24; 5.1.9,27,4.56. Casualties: 1.2.3, 5.9; 2.4.19,32; 3.1.18, 5.20; 4.1.19, 6.11, 8.39; 5.1.12, 3.2, 4.10,14,59.

[17] Attack at run: 3.4.23; 4.3.17, 4.11, 8.37; 5.3.3. Weaponry: various combinations of παίειν, βάλλειν, (ἐξ-, κατ)ακοντίζειν, σφενδονᾶν, τοξεύειν, ἀκροβαλίζεσθαι in 1.3.14; 3.1.18, 2.3,4, 4.24, 5.20,24; 4.2.14,22, 3.14,22, 4.11,17, 5.13,14,15, 6.7,8,10,11, 7.6; 5.1.12, 3.5, 4.39,52; 6.2.20, 5.14,26; 7.1.16,19,21, 2.7,8,12, 4.31. Shoving: 4.3.19, 4.11; 6.4.14; 7.2.8, 4.31. Ramming: 1.6.33; 4.3.12.

[18] καὶ κραυγὴ μὲν οὐδεμία παρῆν, οὐ μὴν οὐδὲ σιγή, φωνὴ δέ τις ἦν τοιαύτη οἵαν ὀργή τε καὶ μάχη παράσχοιτ' ἄν (*Ag.* 2.12), missing in 4.3.19. There are occasional lively similes, e.g. 3.2.3; 4.4.12, 7.6.

no two of the formal land battles are really alike):[19] they resist neat topical analysis, lack prominent formulaic elements (of vocabulary, structure or substance),[20] and give little suggestion of lack of information being tackled with tired cliché or *a priori* guess-work. To the contrary, we may often suspect that Xenophon has allowed information to go by the board: for example, the text includes 10 engagements on land which develop from an attack on some sort of isolated enemy contingent (e.g. troops engaged in ravaging the land); these are all perfectly individual, even if not necessarily highly detailed.[21] There is no reason to suspect Xenophon of inventing permutations on a standard theme; his information was good enough for him to know the distinct tactical character of each event and will almost certainly have been good enough for him to know much more than he actually reports.

We have therefore the paradox of a historical work which is replete with battles but shows none of the enthusiasm for their systematic treatment which might be expected of an author who was, or had been, a professional military man. Appropriate technical interests do occasionally show in quasi-didactic comments (e.g. in 5.4.54, where some Olynthian cavalry pursue peltasts uphill and kill many of them, and Xenophon remarks ταχὺ γὰρ πρὸς ἄναντες εὐήλατον ἁλίσκονται πεζοὶ ὑφ' ἱππέων), and they may be relevant to the special attention given to some events (e.g. the Bithynian attack on a stockaded camp at 3.2.3–5 – where Xenophon was struck by the way in which the defenders were shot down 'like animals in a pen' – or the skilful tactics of the Celto-Iberian cavalry at 7.1.21). But I doubt that professional interest by itself often causes minor events to receive disproportionate space, and few of Xenophon's personal comments are purely technical or appropriate only to the *military* commentator (for example, the analysis of Epaminondas' tactics and strategy in 362 (7.5.8ff.) is there because Epaminondas failed despite his skill – which showed whose side the gods were on – not because Xenophon is engaging in objective technical assessment). Military instruction as such is certainly not a predominant specific purpose of *Hellenica*, nor, more generally, does the fact that Xenophon was a military man

[19] Cf. n. 9. There is, e.g., no consistency or stereotyping in the information provided in 8 cases (exceptions are 1.3.2; 7.1.28) about initial dispositions or in the pattern of separate tactical phases which characterize all except 7.1.28; and X.'s way of organizing the narrative can vary considerably.

[20] The big exception is the 36 items in n. 3. The permutations of παίειν/βάλλειν κτλ. (n. 17) might also be noted.

[21] 8 items in n. 9, plus 4.4.15; 7.5.15. The successive moves/countermoves by various contingents on each side are different in each case.

entitle us to make any assumptions about how battles in *Hellenica* ought to have been treated. The paradox I mentioned above is of our own making. Mere inspection of the end result in this area (as in others) does, of course, highlight the question of how best to describe his purpose in writing; but it provides no intrinsic grounds for impugning his credit.

What we *can* consider, without or (more often) with the help of alternative sources, is whether the information Xenophon does offer is demonstrably false or whether the additional information which, in the circumstances, we shall not be surprised to find in other sources shows him to have omitted details which could not on any view be appropriately missing – a category which can hardly include much more than essential tactical features of battles which Xenophon *does* purport to describe in some detail; at least, this is the area in which the prosecution has consistently felt itself able to bring damaging evidence to bear. In short, does the Xenophontic record display actual incoherences or misapprehensions or militarily significant lacunae? The rest of this paper aims at providing a rapid survey of some of the relevant material.

Rather over half of the 153 battles recorded in Xenophon (78 to be precise) are peculiar to him.[22] None of the accounts betrays obvious incoherence or error (though since two-thirds of them provided no more than minimal tactical details this is neither surprising nor particularly to Xenophon's credit), and in the absence of any alternative tradition it is futile to argue about whether there are significant lacunae. Our attention must therefore centre on the other half of the sample (75 items). More than half of these in turn (39 out of 75, about 60 % of them providing no more than minimal tactical details) are cases in which the non-Xenophontic sources produce no additional information at all (often less)[23] or none that is inconsistent

[22] 1.1.1,33,36, 2.2,3,5,12 (Cratipp. 64F2), 6.22; 2.1.15, 4.2 ([Arist.] *AP* 37, Aeschin. 3.187), 31,32; 3.1.7,13 (3 items: Polyaen. 8.54),18, 2.3, 4.13 (Plut. *Ag.* 9); 4.1.17, 2.14, 3.14,22, 4.4,13 (2 items),16 (2 items), 5.5, 6.7, 7.6 (2 items: Diod. 14.97.5), 8.11,21, 24; 5.1.2,9,10 (Polyaen. 3.11.9f., Front. 1.4.14 relate to a different event), 3.1,18, 4.10, 14,39,54,59; 6.4.27, 5.12,13,30,32; 7.1.18,21 (Diod. 15.70.1),22 (2 items: *ibid.*), 25 (2 items), 2.4,5,7,10,12,14,18 (Diod. 15.75.3),30 (*ibid.*), 3.4, 4.1,12,14 (2 items), 15,16,17,19,20,26(3 items),27. Bracketed references record passages which relate to the engagement's context but not specifically enough to count as sources on it.

[23] 1.3.2 (n. 29), 14 (Diod. 13.66), 4.22 (*id.* 13.69, Plut. *Alc.* 35 spell things out better), 5.19 (Paus. 6.7.4); 2.1.19 (Diod. 13.104, Plut. *Lys.* 9 spell things out better), 4.10 ([Arist.] *AP* 38, Diod. 14.33, Nep. *Thras.* 2.5; the latter two add another battle before or after X.'s),27 (Isoc. 16.13, 18.49); 3.2.29 (Paus. 3.8.4); 4.1.20 (Plut. *Ag.* 11), 4.19 (2 items: *ibid.* 21), 5.11 (numerous other undetailed refs.),19 (3 items: sch. Aristid. 282D), 8.28 (Diod. 14.94, not necessarily implying battle *at* Methymna in contradiction to X.),35 (Front. *Strat.* 2.5.42); 5.2.39 (Diod. 15.21); 7.4.12 (*id.* 15.77), 14 (*ibid.*).

with Xenophon,[24] though some of it provokes its own doubts, e.g. Diodorus' assertion that 10,000 Arcadians died at the Tearless Battle or (more arguably) the picture of the battle of Alyzeia which emerges from Polyaenus and Frontinus.[25] The details that are revealed as 'missing' in Xenophon do not constitute significant lacunae in the sense defined above (though if we had a complete text of the Oxyrhynchus historian's account of the battle of Ephesus we might find an example there; and there are striking lacunae or interpretative peculiarities in other senses, e.g. what comes close to the suppression of the great Athenian victories at Naxos and Alyzeia).[26] And there are few intrinsic problems in what *is* recorded. The account of Mnasippus' defeat at Corcyra is rather sloppily constructed at one point (some commentators have accordingly been misled) but a sensible picture emerges on careful reading;[27] similarly the location

[24] 1.2.6 (Diod. 13.64, *Hell. Oxy. apud* Koenen (1976) 55f.), 5.15 (2 items: Diod. 13.76), 6.13 (*ibid.*); 2.4.3 ([Arist.] *AP* 37, Diod. 14.32); 4.3.3 (Plut. *Ag.* 16, Paus. 3.9.12), 4.15 (Diod. 14.91, sch. Aristid. 282D; Polyaen. 3.9.49,54 is a different event, perhaps really in Thrace, cf. Front. *Strat.* 1.6.3), 8.18 (Diod. 14.99); 5.3.3 (*id.* 15.21), 4.11 (Plut. *Pel.* 13, Diod. 15.25), 56 (Front. *Strat.* 4.7.19, Polyaen. 2.7),60 (cf. n. 26),63 (cf. n. 25); 6.2.17 (Diod. 15.47 – assuming the killing of 200 Spartans corresponds to the first phase of X.'s battle rather than a separate earlier one); 7.1.18 (Sicyon: *id.* 15.69, Front. *Strat.* 3.2.10, Polyaen. 5.16.3, ? Paus. 6.3.3),28 (Polyaen. 1.41.5),30 (Diod. 15.72, Plut. *Ag.* 33), 4.1 (Diod. 15.76, Dem. 18.99, Aeschin. 2.164, 3.85),13 (Diod. 15.77). The extra information includes identification of attackers, sizes/types of contingents, commanders' names, tactical/topographical details, preparation of surprise attack, panic among defeated troops, estimates of losses, capture of P.O.W.s, omens.

[25] Polyaen. 3.10.2 (= Front. *Strat.* 1.2.11),4,6,12,13,16 (= Front. *Strat.* 2.5.47),17. Timotheus' first response to Nicolochus' challenge is to launch 20 ships which sail about near the enemy, teasing them but keeping out of range. The Spartans tire, and Timotheus attacks in force and wins. His fleet, arranged in a crescent around some damaged ships, then returns backwards to base, protected from attack by 10 newly arrived Spartan ships. T.'s opening stratagem is unconvincing; if the Athenians kept out of range their activities ought not to have tired the enemy particularly and if they actually fought the enemy (Polyaen. 3.10.16) they were behaving improbably foolhardily. T.'s retreat implies a battle near his base, i.e. (as X. reveals) Alyzeia (which corrects the other sources' location περὶ Λευκάδα); N. evidently placed his ships across the mouth of Alyzeia bay: but this leaves little space north of Karnos (mod. Kalamos) island for the 20 ships' manoeuvres.

[26] Naxos: Diod. 15.34, Polyaen. 3.11.2,11, Plut. *Phoc.* 6, Dem. 20.77, 23.198, 24.180, Aeschin. 3.222,243, Din. 1.75, sch. Aristid. 282D (these sources contradict one another about ship losses and about the commander and fortunes of the Athenian left). Diodorus distinguished the convoying of corn ships (near Attica) from a later battle at Naxos. X. mentions only 'the battle' which enabled corn ships to reach Athens. Either he has dramatically foreshortened or he omits Naxos altogether. Alyzeia: cf. n. 25. X. makes it a rather equivocal victory.

[27] 6.2.20f. Mnasippus' line ran from one city gate to another (on topography cf. Dontas (1967), Kalligas (1980)) and each wing (Mnasippus at one end, the ἔσχατοι at the other) is under heavy attack. X. then mentions some Spartans drawn up 8 deep who attempt *anastrophē* (variously understood: contrast Hatzfeld (1939) 125, Warner (1978) 312 with Breitenbach (1876) 113f., Underhill (1900) 231) but suffer severe assault in mid-manoeuvre, causing those next to them to flee. Some identify this section with the ἔσχατοι (Breitenbach, Warner ll.cc.); this is understandable, but wrong because it

of Agesilaus' cavalry victory in 4.3.4f. 'between Pras and Narthakion' need not be the problem that some modern topographers have made it.[28] More puzzling is the battle of Chalcedon.[29] The Athenians build a wooden wall, cutting off the city's isthmus site; Hippocrates comes out to fight, the Athenians draw up facing him, and Pharnabazus appears outside the stockade to help Hippocrates. Thrasyllus and the latter fight for a long time, until Alcibiades (who has evidently, as Plutarch explicitly says, been fighting and defeating Pharnabazus) comes to the rescue, whereupon Hippocrates is killed and his army routed. Pharnabazus cannot join him and retires to a nearby Herakleion. The problem is Xenophon's observation that Pharnabazus was unable to join his ally διὰ τὴν στενοπορίαν, τοῦ ποταμοῦ καὶ τῶν ἀποτειχισμάτων ἐγγὺς ὄντων. This is obscure, not so much because the earlier description of the wall as ἀπὸ θαλάττης εἰς θάλατταν καὶ τοῦ ποταμοῦ ὅσον οἷόν τ' ἦν seems unintelligible (we can be fairly sure that it ought to mean that the wall crossed the river)[30] as because it was surely the wall's *existence* which hampered Pharnabazus. Perhaps the wall was incomplete (Xenophon and Plutarch, though not Diodorus, could be read as saying only that the Athenians *started* to build the wall) and there was still a gap (though not a wide one) near the river. But it is hard to feel sure.

There remain 36 cases where, although the other sources may provide extra information that is not inconsistent with Xenophon, there is also some degree of conflict. Apart from 3 cases to be mentioned in due course (pp. 48–51), the extra consistent information merely illustrates what we knew already, that Xenophon is not a very detailed source, without raising any major issues of credibility. Our chief interest will rather be with cases of conflict. In 1 instance the conflict is probably illusory, which is as well, since it is between two Xenophontic works. In 4.6.8f. Agesilaus' hoplites and cavalry defeat some Acarnanian peltasts and hoplites on hills above their line of

attempts its manoeuvre in order to help a wing (ἄκρον τῆς φάλαγγος) and could only contemplate it if (unlike the wings) it was not under attack. The reference is to the *centre*.

28 Narthakion is fixed by the find-spot of *IG* IX.2.89. Ag. was marching south, so one naturally assumes Pras was north of Narthakion (with the battlefield between) and a site seven km away has been suggested (Stählin (1935) 1760, Béquignon (1937) 284, Meyer (1965) 651). But the defeated Thessalians' flight, presumably northwards, took them to 'Mt Narthakion'. Stählin l.c. compounded the problem by placing the latter north of Pras, an unexplained ten km from the homonymous town. We must either abandon our initial assumption and locate Pras *south* of Narthakion or suppose that the Thessalians moved in a wide arc to the hills west of Narthakion.

29 1.3.2, Plut. *Alc.* 30, Diod. 13.66.1f.

30 Breitenbach (1873) 23, Warner (1978) 65 make the wall cross the river, Hatzfeld (1936) 40 makes it run along the riverbank. The proximity of the R. Chalcedon (Kurbaya Dere) to the south and east sides of the town tells against the latter. The text may be corrupt.

march. In *Agesilaus* (2.20) the situation is reversed: [Agesilaus] ἐπιθεμένων ἐν στενοῖς τῶν Ἀκαρνάνων καταλαβὼν τοῖς ψιλοῖς τὰ ὑπὲρ κεφαλῆς αὐτῶν μάχην συνάπτει καὶ πολλοὺς ἀποκτείνας αὐτῶν τρόπαιον ἐστήσατο. The answer is emendation: read ⟨καὶ⟩ καταλαβ⟨όντ⟩ων for καταλαβὼν and concord is restored.[31] Xenophon's credit, as measured by comparison with alternative traditions, therefore depends on our judgement of 35 cases. The prosecution has tended to concentrate on only a portion of these, and we shall have to follow suit. But although some of the generally undiscussed items are indeed trivial[32] or unproblematic (i.e. nobody would dream of preferring the non-Xenophontic version),[33] others merit a little space. Occasionally they actually tell against Xenophon. In 369 some Thebans unsuccessfully assaulted the Phliasian gate at Corinth.[34] According to Xenophon they ran up intending to burst in 'should the gates be open' but were thwarted by *psiloi* who met them four *plethra* from the wall and drove them back. But why should they have expected the gate to be open, with an enemy army in the vicinity (marching from Epidaurus to Sicyon), and why could it not be closed in time (the local topography should not have denied the Corinthians a clear view)? In Diodorus the attack follows the defeat of a Corinthian sortie and some Thebans manage to enter the city, only to be driven out – after which we arrive at Xenophon's battle. This answers the problem raised in Xenophon and may well be preferable, although Xenophon (a Corinthian resident) ought to have known the truth and had no discernible reason for misrepresentation (the point he is making about the punishment of Theban over-confidence could stand on the Diodoran version as well as on his own). One can only suppose that his interest in the effectiveness of the *psiloi* overwhelmed accurate recollection of the circumstances.

But there is also evidence for the defence which is normally

[31] I assume a lacuna before ἐπιθεμένων (cf. Marchant (1920)), where the reference of αὐτῶν will have been clarified.

[32] Disagreement about the number of ships captured at Creusis (6.4.3 (12), Diod. 15.53 (10)), the size of the force which seized Phyle (2.4.2 (70), Paus. 1.29. (60), Nep. *Thras.* 1 (30), Aeschin. 3.187 (100), sch. Ar. *Pl.* 1146 (800 – certainly wrong)), or Pharnabazus' army in 409 (1.2.16 (cavalry), Plut. *Alc.* 29 (cavalry and infantry): the fact that he was pursued by cavalry and hoplites (Xen. l.c.) may support Plutarch).

[33] Polyaenus' denial (1.4.84) that one of Conon's blockade-runners was captured (Xen. 1.6.19), Diodorus' inversion of events at Olympia in 364 (Xen. 7.4.28f.), Justin's and Frontinus' mention of a *kērux* at Cromnus (Just. 6.6.6., Front. *Strat.* 1.14.4, Xen. 7.4.22), Polyaenus' apparent amalgamation (2.2.4) of two separate naval battles in Xen. 5.1.25f. into a single one in a quite different place.

[34] 7.1.18f., Diod. 15.69.1f., Plut. *Mor.* 193F. The gate was near Anaploga (Carpenter–Bon (1936) 74f., Wiseman (1978) 80 – who fail to note that according to Plut. l.c. 2 roads met outside the gate, one from Phlius, the other (presumably) from the plain).

unaired. Consider, for example, the Thebans' penetration into the Peloponnese in 369.[35] In Xenophon they attack Spartan and Pellenean guards at an accessible spot on the Oneion ridge near Cenchreae: this involves a thirty-stade march timed to reach the enemy at dawn and catch them unawares. Most of the Spartans and Pelleneans surrender and withdraw under a truce. One alternative to this (divergently reported in Polyaenus and Frontinus) also involves dawn attack on tired defenders but has no particular claim to preference.[36] The interesting contrast is with Diodorus, where the Boeotian army launches frontal attacks in several sectors of a stockade-and-ditch fortification and at one easily accessible and ill-defended spot the Theban *aristoi* just manage to break through, though there is no great carnage. There is some self-contradiction here (for the notion of attacks on a long front consorts ill with Diodorus' own report that Epaminondas was outnumbered three to one and that he selected a εὐεφοδώτατος τόπος for attack). But the account is chiefly discredited by the statement that the fortifications stretched from Cenchreae to Lechaeum, which is simply ridiculous (why build field-works of such length when the Isthmus itself was available as an alternative?) and represents a grotesque caricature of the real situation, viz. the Theban advance blocked by defenders on the Oneion ridge, which runs from Cenchreae to Corinth, and by the Long Walls from Corinth to Lechaeum.

A principle sometimes invoked against Xenophon is that circumstantiality confers credibility. This may or may not be sound, but can certainly work both ways. For instance, Diodorus' vague assertion that Iphicrates 'chanced upon' some Syracusan ships near Corcyra and captured all of them will hardly stand against Xenophon's account of a deliberate surprise attack in which one enemy ship escaped (further details appear in Polyaenus);[37] his conventional picture of Agesilaus' attack on a position near Thebes in 377 is obviously less good than Xenophon's more individual presentation

[35] 7.1.15f., Diod. 15.68.2f., 72.1, Polyaen. 2.3.9, Front. *Strat.* 2.5.26. Location: Stroud (1971).

[36] They differ as to why they were tired and where they were (Oneion (Polyaen.), behind a *vallum* 'at the Isthmus' (Front. *Strat.*)), but essentially represent a single tradition distinct from Diodorus and X. X.'s unnoticed 30-stade (5.3 km) approach march against an elevated position may seem surprising (even at night): but the lie of the land (including tree cover) makes it plausible.

[37] 6.2.33f., Diod. 15.47.7, Polyaen. 3.9.55, Ephor. 70F211, sch. Aristid. 282D. Polyaenus adds that Iphicrates used a fake signal to give the impression that Corcyra was still in Spartan hands, that the Syracusans moored at an island (circumstantially good, since there *are* islets north of Corfu on the shortest approach from Italy), and that the attack was at night.

of the circumstances (even though the latter raises a topographical problem);[38] his assertion that the battle of Elymia involved 5,000 Arcadian *epilektoi* (i.e. the federal *eparitoi*?) against 1,500 Spartan hoplites and Boeotian/Argive exiles clashes with Xenophon, where the forces are Mantineans and a Spartan *xenikon*, and is worthless in view of Xenophon's clear indication of the real whereabouts of the Arcadians (Asea) and the Lacedaemonian levy (Eutaea);[39] his casual statement that the camp near Acharnae which Thrasybulus attacked contained all the troops the Thirty could muster is unimpressive compared with Xenophon's exclusion of all the Athenian hoplites and most of their cavalry.[40] A more interesting example is provided by the fighting near the Isthmus as the Thebans returned home from Messenia in 369.[41] According to Xenophon Iphicrates sent a large cavalry squadron to see whether the enemy had passed Cenchreae and over 20 *hippeis* were lost when the (stronger) Theban cavalry challenged them. In the alternative tradition we have a more 'normal' situation, with Iphicrates on the offensive and (in Pausanias' version) using 'peltasts and the rest of the Athenian force' (not just cavalry). Buckler (1980a) 295 n. 30 accepts this to the extent of thinking that Iphicrates was using his cavalry to harass the Theban march, and accuses Xenophon of misunderstanding or misrepresenting the situation. But on Xenophon's view (as expressed in *Hipparchicus* 8.10ff.) the principle, which he states in the present context and which appears to be his chief interest in it, that one should not commit large forces if the enemy is going to be numerically superior anyway applies both to *skopoi* and to offensive action; so he certainly had no doctrinal need to misrepresent in order to criticize Iphicrates, and I fancy his account is perfectly reliable.

Often enough, of course, such decisions must remain a matter of faith. When Diodorus tells us that the casualties in a battle were 500, whereas Xenophon reports that the victorious Theban cavalry did not pursue very energetically and killed only a few of the enemy, we can perceive a contradiction but really have no way of knowing the truth. (Xenophon might be lying, in order to enhance his picture of

[38] 15.34.1f., Xen. 5.4.49 (ἐν ἀριστερᾷ ἔχων τὸ τεῖχος (sc. of Thebes) is hardly consistent with ref. to the Potniae road in 51), Polyaen. 2.1.12,24, Front. *Strat.* 1.4.3.

[39] 15.62.1f., Xen. 6.5.13. Diodorus' 1,500 'Spartans' is a possible figure for Polytropus' *xenikon*, but 5,000 *epilektoi* (a figure recurring at 15.67.2) is too much for the Mantineans (Hodkinson (1981) 271f.) and perhaps for the *eparitoi* (Dušanić (1970) 343).

[40] 14.32.6, Xen. 2.4.4f. Thrasybulus' claim of a large numerical discrepancy (2.4.14) need not encourage us to accept Diodorus: protection against insurgents (the Thirty's purpose according to X.) did not require every last soldier. (X. and Diodorus diverge on Thrasybulus' numbers too, 700 and 1,200 respectively.)

[41] 6.5.51, Plut. *Pel.* 24, Paus. 9.14.6f.

Thespian cowardice – they run away even when not under pressure. But how can we know?)[42] Again, how do we choose between Xenophon's assertion that Ischolaus defended Oion in 369 with 400 young Tegean exiles and an unnumbered contingent of *neodamōdeis* and Diodorus' assertion that he had a few elderly troops, having dismissed the majority of his original garrison in imitation of King Leonidas?[43] The two views are only reconcilable on the assumption that Xenophon's description properly refers to the original complement. But this would be odd, for Xenophon indicates that the circumstances of Ischolaus' defeat were controversial, and any deliberate reduction of his forces would have been relevant to the controversy. Moreover he had an interest in minimizing the numbers, since he is clearly concerned in the context to show that the Thebans were unreasonably afraid to invade Laconia. If, then, there was any reduction, it left the force as Xenophon describes it (Diodorus' πρεσβύτεροι will be a product of the Leonidas parallel – itself induced by the fact that Ischolaus' men were surrounded and killed – since the 300 at Thermopylae were also older men); but I should be inclined to suspect the whole Diodoran story.

The battles mentioned so far are for the most part minor affairs (in terms of space in the sources and/or historical importance). In the remainder of this paper I shall examine some of the 16 contexts which involve what are by either criterion major engagements.

There are certainly some cases in which the alternative tradition contains information which is intrinsically acceptable, consistent with Xenophon and sufficiently important to make one speak of significant lacunae. A remarkable example is the Athenian capture of Byzantium in 408.[44] In the non-Xenophontic version Alcibiades is let into the city during a diversionary attack on the harbour; the defenders eventually hear of this and move against him, whereupon a battle is fought issuing in Athenian victory. In Xenophon Alcibiades enters the so-called Thrakion gates (somewhere just west of the site later occupied by Ag. Sophia). Helixos and Koiratadas οὐδὲν τούτων εἰδότες ἐβοήθουν μετὰ πάντων εἰς τὴν ἀγοράν (somewhere just south of Ag. Sophia), but since the Athenians were in possession everywhere they could do nothing and surrendered. This appears to be a lacunose version of the other tradition's story, composed by someone whose

[42] 5.4.42f., Diod. 15.33.5f., Plut. *Pel.* 15. Buckler (1979) 53f. (and others) regard Polyaen. 2.5.2 as another account. But the topographical setting is different, the central notion of feigned retreat contradicts X., the hoplites are missing and Phoebidas appears not to be killed. The passage should perhaps be associated with Phoebidas' earlier attacks on Theban territory (Xen. 5.4.42).

[43] 6.5.26, Diod. 15.64.3f.

[44] 1.3.20f., Diod. 13.67, Plut. *Alc.* 31, Polyaen. 1.47.2, Front. *Strat.* 3.11.3, Nep. *Alc.* 5.6. On Byzantine topography cf. Oberhummer (1897) 1119f., Janin (1964).

overriding interest was the fact of treachery. That this *was* Xenophon's position is shown by his immediately preceding remarks about the traitors' justification of their action (1.3.18–19) and it will account for the absence of the naval attack, the virtual suppression of the battle and for the awkward wording which makes it appear that Helixos and Koiratadas went to the rescue when they did not know of any circumstances which called for such action. What they did not know was actually that treason was involved (so reports of an attack in the area of the Thrakion gates did not prepare them to find the attackers inside the city and well entrenched). Xenophon's performance is certainly inadequate here;[45] but we may allow that his indication that the final battle occurred in the *agora* (close to the Thrakion gates, and on the way to the acropolis) is a useful supplement to the other tradition.

More notorious cases of Xenophontic inadequacy are provided by Notium and Leuctra.[46] In both cases contradictions are relatively unimportant (at least do not certainly impugn Xenophon's credit);[47] what matters is supplementary information. At Notium this amounts to the explanation provided by the Oxyrhynchus historian of what Antiochus (the temporary Athenian commander) had in mind when he took two ships into the Bay of Ephesus, viz. that he was trying to lure some of Lysander's ships into an ambush outside the bay.[48] (Some claim that the tradition stemming from the Oxyrhynchus historian also indicated that Lysander had used some stratagem to induce Antiochus to behave thus; but this seems uncertain to me.[49]) Xenophon's failure to provide any explanation is certainly curious, and there is little to be gained by trying to explain it in terms of the nature or identity of his sources.[50] Given what he shows that he did

[45] Hardly because of poverty of sources, however. As a one-time companion of Clearchus (governor of Byzantium in 408 (though absent during Alcibiades' capture) and later) he will have heard the facts. (Clearchus might have stressed the treachery.)

[46] Notium: 1.5.10f., Diod. 13.71ff., Plut. *Alc.* 35, *Lys.* 5, *Hell.Oxy.* 4, Paus. 3.17.4, 9.32.6, Just. 5.5, Nep. *Alc.* 7. Leuctra: 6.4.4f., Diod. 15.52ff., Plut. *Pel.* 18f., Nep. *Pel.* 4.2, Din. 1.73, Dio Chrys. 22.3, Plb. 12.25f.3f.

[47] Notium: the Athenians (a) lose 22 ships in Diodorus, 15 in X. and (b) remain at Notium until Alcibiades' return in Diodorus but go to Samos in X. On (b) Diodorus is perhaps right, on (a) it is anybody's guess. Leuctra: Diodorus' assertions that 4,000 Lacedaemonians died and that Archidamus was present will not stand against X.'s contrary indications.

[48] *Hell.Oxy.* is of course needed to disentangle Diodoran incoherence (Andrewes (1982) 16f.). De Sanctis' description of Diodorus as 'in se pienamente coerente' is remarkable ((1931) 226).

[49] Cf. Andrewes (1982) 17f. Paus. 9.32.6 claims that L., aware of Alcibiades' absence, cleverly tempted Antiochus to attack; what survives of *Hell.Oxy.* shows no certain trace of this (the three ships of 4.2 can hardly be claimed as such).

[50] Disagreement about Athenian losses (n. 47) is variously held to show that Diodorus represents the Athenian generals' official report and X. a Spartan source (De Sanctis

know of the circumstances (i.e. the three stages of the engagement, also visible in *Hellenica Oxyrhynchia* and Diodorus, and the fact that Antiochus sailed right into the Bay of Ephesus),[51] it is hard to believe that Antiochus' plan had never come to his attention. He is simply more interested in Antiochus' initial disobedience of Alcibiades' orders and in the end result (Athenian defeat and Alcibiades' disgrace). It remains true that Xenophon is an indispensable, even if not sufficient, source for the train of events.

As for Leuctra, Xenophon clearly appreciated the central fact, viz. the Thebans' successful strategy of fighting the battle on one wing, but we need other sources (especially Plutarch) to tell us something of how this was managed and of the redeployment ordered by Cleombrotus in a vain attempt to counter it.[52] (We could, however, do without Diodorus' bizarre and erroneous notion that the Spartans were drawn up in a convex crescent.) Xenophon surely knew more than he chose to record, but his preoccupying interest is the argument that, although all luck and judgement favoured the Thebans, their victory was not a complete walkover (cf. 6.4.13). He does, however, record at least one major feature ignored elsewhere. Cleombrotus placed his cavalry in front of the infantry, causing the Thebans to follow suit; the two units clashed just as Cleombrotus advanced, and the Spartans were rapidly defeated, some of their men falling back on the infantry behind. This is somewhat problematic, since it was unusual to locate cavalry contingents at formal battles anywhere but on the two wings, where their purpose (rarely fulfilled in classical battles) was to defeat their counterparts and disturb the coherence of the adjacent infantry, rendering them more vulnerable to frontal infantry attack;[53] yet Xenophon's only explanation of Cleombrotus'

(1931) 226f., Bruce (1967) 37, Lanzillotta (1975) 151) or vice versa (Breitenbach (1971) 168, 170)! Andrewes (1982) 18 postulates for X. a Spartan source remote from Lysander's entourage and unaware both of Antiochus' plan and Lysander's hypothetical stratagem (cf. n. 49). But all Spartans at Notium surely eventually knew what Antiochus intended.

[51] Only in X. (followed by Plutarch). There can be no doubt X. meant what he said, remarkable though it is: he had been to Ephesus and (cf. 1.5.15) knew that there was a distinction between entering the bay and parading outside. For the 5th-century shore line cf. Miltner (1958) map 1.

[52] On Plutarch see now Buckler (1980b).

[53] Ordinary position: Thuc. 4.93.4, 5.67.1, 6.67.2, Xen. 3.2.15, 5.4.20, 7.5.23. Purpose: cf. Thuc. 2.79.3, 4.96.1, 6.66.1, Xen. 5.2.41. (Epaminondas' tactics in Xen. 7.5.24, Philip's in Diod. 16.4.5f. and Pammenes' in Front. *Strat.* 2.3.3 are developments of this.) Cavalry could also play an important role late in the battle: cf. Thuc. 4.44.1, 96.8, 5.10.9, 73.1, 76.2, Xen. 1.3.6. Pre-battle skirmishing is not often attested: Kromayer–Veith (1928) 92 and Cawkwell (1972) 262 adduce Leuctra and Xen. 3.2.16 only; cf. also Diod. 12.70.2 (*contra* Thuc. 4.96), 15.85.3 (*contra* 7.5.24f.). Cavalry fight between two lines in Xen. *Hipp.* 8.23, *Eq.* 8.12 (not necessarily the first stage of a formal battle), Thuc. 4.72 (no infantry battle follows), 124.3f.(Macedonian rather than classical Greek tactics), Diod. 18.17.3f. (Crannon, 322 – far in the future).

act (that the land between the lines was flat) is insufficient.[54] Historians tend to assume either that Xenophon is wrong to represent Cleombrotus as taking the lead in this or that Plutarch is wrong to suggest that Cleombrotus only attempted redeployment in response to the Thebans' oblique advance, and to explain the siting of the cavalry as a ploy by Epaminondas or Cleombrotus to mask his manoeuvres behind a dust cloud. But there is no good reason for such rewriting of the data. Xenophon certainly had no need to misrepresent the truth. Since he does not pretend that the Theban victory was solely due to τύχη,[55] the cavalry's fouling of infantry lines does not have to be Cleombrotus' fault. In seeking an answer one should perhaps remember that the Theban left wing started its final advance well to the left of Cleombrotus' right wing and that its unusually deep formation will have been quite evident from the beginning. Cleombrotus may have thought it more useful to put his cavalry in the way of their apparent line of advance rather than leaving them in the ordinary position beyond his right wing. In any event, reconstruction of Leuctra must pay serious attention to the cavalry, and Xenophon is an indispensable, if insufficient, source.

In a number of cases Xenophon's account presents intrinsic problems, for which, however, the alternative tradition provides no satisfactory resolution:

1. *Corinth* (*Nemea*).[56] At 4.2.15–23 he produces a generally lucid account of the Spartan victory near Corinth in 394, which he rightly locates near the R. Longopotamos (rather than the R. Nemea, as Diodorus has it).[57] The problem is that his list of combatants and contingent sizes omits from the Spartan side Tegean, Mantinean and Achaean contingents mentioned elsewhere in the narrative.[58] His total of 13,500 infantry and 600 cavalry on the Spartan side (facing a confederate army of 24,000 infantry and 1,550 cavalry) is therefore wrong. But Diodorus only compounds the problem by giving much higher figures for the Spartan infantry (23,000; his 500 cavalry can pass as roughly equal to Xenophon's estimate) and much lower ones for the confederate forces (15,000 infantry, 500 cavalry). There are two ways of tackling this difficulty. One is to make the figures 'agree'

[54] Strictly a supplementary explanation, since ἅτε καὶ πεδίου ὄντος τοῦ μεταξύ implies there were other (unstated) reasons (cf. Xen. 2.3.15; 5.2.37; 6.2.16, 4.6; *Cyr* 4.1.8; 6.4.4; Plat. *Rep*. 350D for ἅτε καί).

[55] 6.4.8: τοῖς μὲν Λακεδαιμονίοις πάντα ἐναντία ἐγίγνετο, τοῖς δὲ πάντα καὶ ὑπὸ τῆς τύχης κατωρθοῦτο – but also by rational calculation (6.4.12).

[56] 4.2.15f., Diod. 14.82.9f., Dem. 20.52f., Xen. *Ag*. 7.5, Plut. *Ag*. 16, *Mor*. 191F, 211F, Andoc. 3.18, Paus. 1.29.11, 3.5.7.

[57] Pritchett (1969) 82.

[58] 4.2.16f. Tegeans: 13, 19, 21. Mantineans: 13. Achaeans (Pelleneans): 18, 20.

either by finding 9,500 extra infantry to add to Xenophon's Spartan figure (rather a lot for Tegeans, Mantineans and Achaeans alone) and 9,000 infantry and 1,000 cavalry to add to Diodorus' confederate figures (with no explanation of how he came to omit them) *or* by switching the attribution of the figures in Diodorus, putting the confederates at 23,000 infantry and 500 cavalry (still 1,000 adrift from Xenophon's figures in both categories) and the Spartans at 15,000 infantry and 500 cavalry (leaving only 1,500 Tegeans, Mantineans and Achaeans – surely too few). The other approach is to ignore Diodorus' figures and attempt a calculation of the Spartan army's true size based on Xenophon's report of the way in which the two armies overlapped in the eventual battle (4.2.18f.): this involves making trial assumptions about the depth of the Spartan line and of the Boeotian contingent in the confederate army, aimed at producing neither too many Tegeans nor too few Mantineans and Achaeans, and the results are probably too hypothetical to be taken very seriously.[59] Pritchett (1969) 74 claimed that 4.2.13 at least shows the two infantry forces to be roughly the same size. But this is false: what Xenophon says is that the confederates fixed on a maximum depth of line (later, 4.2.18, revealed as 16) in order to avoid *kuklōsis*. This is an odd passage, since 16 is only a limiting depth if the confederates are assuming (for no apparent reason) that the Spartans would in no circumstances have a front wider than that occupied by their own army drawn up 16 deep (i.e. 1,500 men).[60] It appears that Xenophon has manipulated the narrative to make the Boeotians (who eventually formed their contingent much more than 16 deep) wholly responsible for the confederate defeat, in which *kuklōsis* played a key role. But his representation of what actually happened in the battle remains (to all appearances) perfectly acceptable.

2. *Coronea*.[61] Again Xenophon's generally lucid account offers a few puzzles. (i) Neither the list of combatants nor the narrative mention the Peloponnesian allies whom one would expect to be present and some of whom, to judge by the account in *Agesilaus* (2.11), should have been among what is here called Herippidas'

[59] With a Boeotian depth of 26, the 'best' solutions are a Spartan depth of 12 or 14, putting Tegeans at 1,800 or 2,400 and leaving 5,300 or 6,600 (at most) for the Mantineans and Achaeans together. Cavaignac (1925) made similar calculations, but was starting from the assumption that the Spartan total was 15,000 and trying to prove that X.'s 6,000 'Lacedaemonians' included the Tegeans and Mantineans.

[60] A smaller Spartan army can always achieve a wider front at the expense of a smaller depth. For any given Spartan army total the disproportion in depths which they must concede to secure e.g. at least a 100-man overlap oscillates as the confederate depth increases; there is no increasing Spartan advantage with depths over 16.

[61] 4.3.15f., *Ag*. 2.6f., Diod. 14.84, Plut. *Ag*. 18, Front. *Strat*. 2.6.6, Polyaen. 2.1.4,5,19, Nep. *Ag*. 4.5.f., Paus. 3.9.13, 9.6.4.

xenikon (4.3.15, 17). (ii) The two armies met in the Coronea plain, coming from the R. Cephisus and Mt Helicon respectively.[62] But according to some modern maps the plain was enclosed on the north by a western spur of Lake Copais,[63] so it appears that Xenophon ought to have said ἀπὸ τῆς λίμνης not ἀπὸ τοῦ Κηφισοῦ. However this difficulty disappears if current re-examination of the Copais region is right in suggesting that the spur in question did not exist in antiquity.[64] (iii) Non-Xenophontic sources have nothing to say about either of the problems just mentioned. The third differs in this respect. The battle's most remarkable tactical feature was that Agesilaus chose to meet the retreating Thebans in a fierce head-on clash instead of attacking them in the side and rear; the upshot was that 'some Thebans got through to Helicon, but many died in the retreat' (4.3.19). But how did the survivors get through? Plutarch, Polyaenus and Frontinus offer an answer: Agesilaus ordered his troops to open ranks and let them through. But one might wonder how practical or prudent this parade-ground manoeuvre would have been in the circumstances.

3. *Haliartus.*[65] Here Xenophon explicitly presents us with a problem. Having arrived early for his rendezvous with King Pausanias and failed to get the Haliartians to surrender thanks to opposition from some Thebans in the city, Lysander attacked. 'Hearing this, the Thebans ran to the rescue, hoplites and cavalry. It is unclear whether they fell on Lysander unawares or he saw them coming and stood his ground in the expectation of victory. Anyway the battle occurred by the walls and the trophy stood by the Haliartians' gate.' And there is another problem: is Xenophon describing a Theban attack from inside or outside the city? '*Hearing* this' (not 'seeing this') suggests the latter (as does Lysander's initial attempt to encourage Haliartian surrender – rather pointless if the full Theban army was already in the place); but how could any question of surprise attack arise if the Thebans came into battle up the road from Thebes? Pausanias and Diodorus go opposite ways on this matter (neither says anything about surprise attack); Plutarch has it both ways, for in his account the Thebans reach Haliartus before Lysander but leave part of their army outside the walls, and Lysander is later attacked by both sections (though again there is nothing explicit about a surprise

[62] Near the Itonian sanctuary (Plut. l.c. (n. 61)), just north-east of Coronea (Spyropoulos (1973) 376f., *Ergon* (1975) 12f.; Pritchett (1969) 86f. put it further north).

[63] E.g. Kambanis (1892) pl. xii, Geiger (1922) 1354, Pritchett (1969) 86f.

[64] Information from Professor Snodgrass (letter 14.1.83), who stresses that as yet it is 'only a strong hunch, not a scientific finding'.

[65] 3.5.6f., 17f., Diod. 15.81, Plut. *Lys.* 28f., Paus. 3.5.4, Nep. *Lys.* 3.4, Dem. 4.17,18.96, Aristid. *Panath.* 266.

attack). Plutarch does not seem to display a clear grasp of what happened; he gives no reason for the division of forces, and in the narrative of the fighting the alleged attack from outside is suspiciously ill co-ordinated with what is presented as doing all the damage, viz. a sudden sortie from within the city.[66] I doubt therefore whether he provides a sound resolution of the second problem raised by Xenophon's account; and on the issue of whether Lysander was surprised or not he has nothing to say at all.

4. *Rhoiteion/Abydos.*[67] Xenophon's account runs thus: Dorieus enters the Hellespont with 14 ships; the Athenian generals, warned by a *hēmeroskopos*, launch 20 ships; Dorieus flees, beaches his ships περὶ τὸ Ῥοίτειον and fights off an Athenian attack; the Athenians rejoin the main fleet at Madytos. Meanwhile Mindarus has seen the fighting from Ilium, goes down to the sea, and sets off with his fleet to pick Dorieus up. The Athenians set sail too and a battle ensues περὶ Ἄβυδον. Alcibiades' fortuitous arrival causes the Peloponnesians to flee towards Abydos and there is fighting on shore, after which the Athenians sail off with 30 empty ships and some of their own which they have recovered. This raises three questions. (i) If Dorieus was noticed only when he entered the Hellespont, should he not have got further than Rhoiteion before the Athenians arrived? (This is an arguable point, however: he might have been spotted well out to sea off the Hellespont mouth by *hēmeroskopoi* around Elaeus.) (ii) Could Mindarus have seen the fighting, granted that Rhoiteion is some seven km from Ilium beyond high ground?[68] (iii) What happened to Dorieus? Did Mindarus pick him up before the second battle? Plutarch's version is no help, since it deals only with the second battle περὶ Ἄβυδον. In Diodorus' account Dorieus is pursued by the whole Athenian fleet and escapes to Dardanus (about halfway between Rhoiteion and Abydos), where he resists attacks. Mindarus hears

[66] Plutarch's account mentions a message from Lysander (at Lebadeia) to Pausanias (at Plataea) which was intercepted by the Thebans, who therefore reached Haliartus first. Bommelaer (1981) 193f. hypothesizes a stratagem of Lysander to catch the Thebans between his and Pausanias' armies, but his account is somewhat unclear (it rather looks as though Lysander is supposed both to have intended the message to be intercepted and to have behaved as though it had not been). Bommelaer also deduces from ἐν ἀριστερᾷ τὴν πόλιν λαβόντες (sc. the outside contingent attacking Lysander) that L.'s camp south of Haliartus was *east* of the Theban position. But the phrase could mean that they attacked 'on the left of' the city (from a base east of L.'s position): cf. Hdt. 7.42 with Bommelaer (1981) 48.

[67] 1.1.2–7, Diod. 13.45ff., Plut. *Alc.* 27.

[68] Assuming the location of Rhoiteion at Baba Kale (Cook (1972) 77f.). Xen. 1.1.3–4 is not discussed in Cook (1972); but Professor Cook reports in a letter (19.7.83) that he feels 'pretty sure that nothing east of the İn Tepe Azmağı could be seen' from Ilium. (The İn Tepe Azmağı is a creek *c.* three km inside the Dardanelles: cf. Cook (1972) 104 (fig. 5).)

what is happening and moves down from Abydos to the Dardanian promontory (Kepez Burnu, just east of Dardanus), whereupon a variant of Xenophon's battle περὶ Ἄβυδον is fought, the Athenian fleet having presumably temporarily backed off and Dorieus having joined Mindarus (Diodorus is somewhat hazy hereabouts). This version certainly alleviates our first and third problems. But these are not *in themselves* sufficiently serious to cast significant doubt on Xenophon's credibility, and the alleviation is achieved at the expense of fusing two battles in two places and on two days into one bipartite battle at one place (different from both those involved in Xenophon)[69] on one day. Our second problem, on the face of it much more serious, is unresolved: Dardanus was indisputably invisible from Ilium, so we gain nothing by simply substituting Dardanus for Rhoiteion in Xenophon's account. Leaving this aside we might compromise between the two accounts by supposing that Mindarus went to his fleet *via* Rhoiteion and told Dorieus to sail up to Dardanus to await him. But if we follow Xenophon this far, we must surely also accept that the Athenians were at Madytos before the main battle, and there is no reason why they should have engaged Mindarus anywhere but in the immediate vicinity of Abydos (well east of Dardanus, or even of Cynossema). The truth is that Dardanus only enters the picture if we substantially accept Diodorus' whole scenario; and that involves at least one major implausibility, viz. the claim that the Athenians launched their whole 74-ship fleet to deal with Dorieus' squadron of 14. We are left with the problem of the visibility of Rhoiteion from Ilium. This may perhaps be solved by stressing two facts, that the whole shore from Rhoiteion as far as and perhaps beyond the nearest point (*c.* six km away) at which a naval engagement would be visible from Ilium must have been Rhoiteian territory (Cook (1972) 87), and that Xenophon does only say that Dorieus beached περὶ τὸ Ῥοίτειον. Of course, unless we suppose that Xenophon deliberately used τὸ Ῥοίτειον as a name for the whole Rhoiteian shore rather than just for the actual town, this solution leaves him guilty of somewhat misleading vagueness. But this is a tolerable price to pay, and his narrative as a whole remains credible enough and not manifestly inferior to the Diodoran alternative.

Thus far we have been examining cases in which the Xenophontic account raises problems which are, however, not simply resolved by the alternative source. But the common situation is to be faced with

[69] Diodorus says the Athenians erected a trophy πρὸς τῷ προτέρῳ (at Cynossema, well north of the Dardanian promontory and on the other shore). If πρός = 'near' this is dubiously consistent with a battle site near Dardanus. But it may simply mean 'in addition to', with no geographical implications.

conflicting traditions, of which that in Xenophon contains no pressing difficulties in principle. Considerations of space compel me to mention some of these with more or less cavalier brevity. First, the battle inside the Corinthian Long Walls in 392.[70] In Xenophon's account the Spartans enter the Walls at night, construct a σταύρωμα to protect their position, defeat a confederate attack on the second day following and capture Lechaeum, having killed its Boeotian garrison. This is essentially credible[71] (its chief fault is that preoccupation with the Spartans' slaughter of their opponents (4.4.12) distracts Xenophon from proper exposition of the capture of Lechaeum) and certainly raises no problems which would make one prefer Diodorus' apparent belief that the capture of the port *preceded* the battle.[72] Second, the endlessly discussed battle of Sardis.[73] It seems clear that we have two quite distinct and irreconcilable versions, that neither is in itself manifestly unreasonable (though Diodorus introduced some errors into his retailing of the non-Xenophontic version), and that no utterly compelling grounds have ever been advanced for preferring one to the other.[74] The only further observation I would make is that any attempts to argue that Xenophon was not actually present (which is doubtless possible) and that *therefore* he did not really know what happened are simply silly: he was perfectly well placed to get good eye-witness information. Third, the battle of Cnidus (a major event only scantily recorded in the sources).[75] Notable points here are (i) that Diodorus perpetrates a majestic confusion in locating the battle near Physcus, over fifty km east of Cnidus, which is certainly false

[70] 4.4.9–13, Diod. 14.86.2f.

[71] I assume that the Spartans (? *c.* 3,000 strong) could erect a stockade of stakes across the 1,200 m gap between the walls by daybreak (not therefore a *very* solid wall) and that their initial position in the battle was behind the stockade. Hence, no immediate confederate attack and no disastrous results from the Spartans' numerical disadvantage. (The totality of their success is still remarkable.) On 4.4.11 (βοηθοῦσιν [...] σταύρωμα) cf. Breitenbach (1874) 143.

[72] (a) The Spartans storm Lechaeum at night and defeat Iphicrates next day. (b) Then μετὰ...ταῦτα, confederate forces enter the διατείχισμα but, again μετὰ...ταῦτα, are driven out. (The Isthmia of 390 follow immediately.) Contradictions can only be removed if X.'s narrative is regarded as grossly summarized in Diodorus' nocturnal storming of Lechaeum. But I suspect that (a) corresponds to X.'s narrative (with events inverted) and (b) is a (much) later event (the διατείχισμα being Lechaeum's south wall not X.'s stockade).

[73] 3.4.21f., *Hell.Oxy.* 11(6), Diod. 14.80, Plut. *Ag.* 10, Paus. 3.9.6, Polyaen. 2.19, Front. *Strat.* 1.8.12.

[74] Anderson (1974) and Gray (1979) are recent defences of X. (Anderson is certainly right to reject the supposed contradiction between X. and other sources on Agesilaus' route to Sardis: cf. already Mess (1909) 238.)

[75] 4.3.11f., Diod. 14.83.4, Philoch. 328 F 144–45, Nep. *Con.* 4.4, Paus. 6.3.16, Andoc. 3.22, Dem. 20.68, Din. 1.75, Isoc. 9.68, Lys. 19.28. Polyaen. 1.48.5 is sometimes associated with Cnidus: it contradicts X. in having the Spartan left fight vigorously, but its relevance is dubious (Barbieri (1955) 152).

(everyone else agrees it was around Cnidus)[76] and even self-contradictory (since he has already located the Persian fleet at Loryma, halfway between Cnidus and Physcus),[77] and (ii) that the apparent conflict between him and Xenophon on the relative sizes of the two fleets (the Persian is slightly bigger in Diodorus, very much bigger in Xenophon) might be mended by deleting τοῦ Ἑλληνικοῦ in Xenophon 4.3.12 as a gloss by someone who did not understand that Xenophon was now using τὸ μετὰ Κόνωνος to describe the whole Perso-Greek fleet.[78] Fourth, the Mantinea campaign,[79] which includes three battles (Xenophon, it happens, is the only source to provide a clearly articulated account of all three; Diodorus more or less amalgamates the second and third).[80] Three points of conflict stand out: the whereabouts of Agesilaus and the main Lacedaemonian levy at the beginning of Epaminondas' assault on Sparta (were they at Sparta (Xenophon) or still returning from Arcadia?); the context of the cavalry battle near Mantinea immediately after Epaminondas' return from Sparta (were the Theban cavalry merely about to cut up Mantinean βοσκήματα and agricultural workers (Xenophon) or part of a full-scale attack on the city?); and the tactical details of the final battle at Mantinea (Xenophon's general analytic picture, in which a co-ordinated cavalry and infantry assault by the Theban left wing is the key feature, is plainly fundamental (and preferable to Diodorus' separation of two phases, first cavalry, then infantry), but is Diodorus' apparently circumstantial account of a cavalry engagement on the Theban *right* wing an acceptable supplement, and, if so, is it preliminary to or concurrent with the main fighting?). On the first two issues I am sure that there is no reason to question Xenophon's authority (the alternative versions being virtually impossible);[81] on the third issue one may, I think, give Diodorus the benefit of the doubt (his reference to Theban infantry and cavalry on nearby hillocks does tie in with Epaminondas' dispositions as represented by Xenophon), but it is hard to judge how significant a lacuna is thereby revealed in Xenophon's account.

[76] Pausanias also mentions the 'so-called Dorian mountain', otherwise unknown.

[77] If we postulate another Physcus in the Cnidian peninsula (Barbieri (1955) 145), Diodorus' description τοῦ Χερρονήσου is no more accurate than it is of the famous Physcus (cf. Fraser–Bean (1954) 65f.).

[78] On fleet sizes at this time cf. Barbieri (1955) 120f.

[79] 7.5.9ff., Diod. 15.82ff., Ephor. 70 F 85, Plb. 9.8.2ff., Plut. *Ag.* 34f., Aen. Tact. 2.2, Just. 6.7, Polyaen. 2.3.10,14, Front. *Strat.* 2.2.12, 3.11.5, Paus. 1.3.4, 8.9.8, 11.5f., 9.15.5, Plut. *Mor.* 345DE, Suda s.v. Κηφισόδωρος, Harpoc. s.vv. Γρύλλος, Κηφισόδωρος.

[80] Diogenes' view (D.L. 2.53) of what Ephorus said about the circumstances of Gryllus' death suggests that Diodorus' foreshortening merely reflected his source.

[81] Could Epaminondas have failed to capture Sparta in the circumstances envisaged by the non-Xenophontic sources? And would he really have attempted a full-scale assault on Mantinea's walls straight after the return march from Sparta?

We are left finally with four naval battles during the Ionian War which I want to examine in more detail (though still with rather indecent haste):

1. *Arginusae.*[82] There are two notable areas of dispute. First, the circumstances of Callicratidas' death: in Xenophon the shock of ramming an enemy ship causes him to fall overboard and he is never seen again; in Diodorus he is killed trying to repel boarders. The latter version is certainly more 'conventional' (and Callicratidas is not the only Diodoran general to die λαμπρῶς ἀγωνισάμενος), and I should prefer to follow Xenophon. Second, the initial disposition of the two fleets. In Xenophon the 120 Spartan ships are in a single line with Callicratidas on the left wing, while the 150 Athenian ships are in two parallel lines, with a front of some 80 ships.[83] These arrangements are, quite reasonably, explained in terms of the Spartan intention to attempt *periplous* and *diekplous* and the Athenian need to thwart this with a larger but less well-trained fleet.[84] For Diodorus, however, the key fact is that the Athenians included the Arginusae Islands in their line in order to extend it as far as possible, and that Callicratidas, unable to match this extended line, fought the battle with two separate squadrons. This has no place in Xenophon, where the Athenians are not particularly concerned to maximize the length of their line, and where they ἀντανήγοντο εἰς τὸ πέλαγος τῷ εὐωνύμῳ, presumably implying a position well out to sea and very largely to the south of the islands, since the Spartan attack was coming from the west. (This incidentally helps to explain why the Spartan ships which escaped all fled south to Chios/Phocaea (Cyme in Diodorus), rather than back to Lesbos.) No doubt either view might be correct, but I am not especially impressed by Diodorus, partly because he contradicts himself about the position of the Athenian general Pericles (successively put on the right (13.98.3) and left (13.99.4)), partly because the Athenian dispositions are poorly explained. Placing their ships either side of the Arginusae increased the area covered by the battle but did not extend their line to any great purpose, since Callicratidas would obviously follow suit (as he is indeed said to have done), producing two battles in which the Athenians had no more

[82] 1.6.26f., Diod. 13.97ff., Plut. *Lys.* 7, Cic. *de off.* 1.84, Pliny *NH* 5.140, Str. 13.2.2.

[83] Assuming (i) that all the Athenian generals had contingents of *c.* 15 ships and (ii) that the statement that the Samians and taxiarchs' ships were ἐπὶ μιᾶς (τεταγμέναι) does not imply that those contingents were not in single lines.

[84] διέκπλους: Hdt. 6.12.1, 15.2, 8.9, Thuc. 1.49.8, 2.83.5, 89.8, 7.36.4, 70.4, Plb. 1.51.9, 16.4.4,10, Sosyl. 176 F 1(II). περίπλους: Thuc. 7.36.3,4, Plb. 1.23.9, 27.11, 16.4.14. The Athenian rear line will impede the Spartan manoeuvres, a gain for which they are prepared to concede an overlap.

advantage than they would have done in one.[85] (On Diodorus' figures they had a slight numerical advantage anyway (150 against 140), on Xenophon's a marked one (150 plus against 120).) Perhaps, indeed, some other explanation could be envisaged; but as things stand Diodorus is not a manifest improvement on Xenophon.

2. *Aegospotami*.[86] Some of the disagreements in this case (e.g. about Alcibiades' precise comments to the Athenian generals or the number of Athenian prisoners who were executed)[87] do not immediately concern us here, but two matters require comment. First, the number of Athenian ships which escaped to Athens. Xenophon says 9 got away, of which 8 went to Cyprus (possibly confirmed by *IG* II^2.1951)[88] and 1 (the *Paralos*) went to Athens. But according to Isocrates (18.59f.) several Athenian ships reached the city,[89] and Lysias (21.11) puts their number at 12, Diodorus at 9. The contemporary evidence makes it likely (if not certain) that Xenophon is in error (though *Paralos* was surely the *first* ship home), but the point is irrelevant to reconstruction of the battle, since a figure of 20-plus escaping ships is not clearly better suited to the alternative tradition than to Xenophon. Certainly Diodorus (the only important other source) is not vindicated, since he has only 10 ships escaping (just 1 more than Xenophon) and simply differs as to their destination (9 to Athens, 1 to Cyprus). Second, the circumstances of the battle. Xenophon and Diodorus agree that there was a period (four days in Xenophon) during which the Athenians daily challenged Lysander to fight, and that the end result (on Day Five) was Lysander's descent on a virtually unmanned Athenian fleet. According to Xenophon this happened because Lysander launched a sudden attack when the Athenians had returned to base and scattered in search of food, this being the dénouement he had been planning all along. According to Diodorus it happened because the Athenian *stratēgos* Philocles sailed out with 30 ships, ordering the trierarchs to man their triremes and follow, whereupon Lysander, who 'heard of this' through deserters, drove him back towards the Athenian shore and reached the bulk of the fleet before it was ready.

Various reasons are advanced for favouring Diodorus. (i) The

[85] The ships of the Athenian centre survived intact (1.7.30), which may confirm that the engagement was most heavily fought on the wings.

[86] 2.1.16f., Diod. 13.104.7f., Plut. *Alc.* 36f., Nep. *Lys.* 1, *Alc.* 8, Polyaen. 1.45.2, Front. *Strat.* 2.1.18, Paus. 3.17.4, 9.32.7f., 10.9.11, Dem. 23.212; other sources are mentioned below. Recent discussions: Ehrhardt (1970), Bommelaer (1981) 163f., Strauss (1983).

[87] Only Philocles (Diod.) or 3,000 (Plut.) or 4,000 (Paus.) others too? X. reports the *decision* to execute all Athenian P.O.W.s, but only mentions Philocles' actual death.

[88] Cf. Laing (1964). (Paus. 3.11.5 says 10 escaped to Cyprus.)

[89] Cf. perhaps Lys. *apud* P.Ryl. 3.489, ll. 100f.

Peloponnesian ships which followed the retreating Athenians each day to see what they did on landing could not have been persistently unnoticed. – But they did not need to be: indeed there was an advantage in their being seen, for on Day Five Lysander had to be sure that the Athenians had disembarked and scattered and would not want to alert them by sending spy ships for the first time. (ii) It was appropriate that Philocles should attempt to force battle, since the Athenians were under severe logistical pressure. – True: but it is agreed that they wanted to fight; the issue is the credibility of Philocles' fresh plan for producing this result. (iii) It is preferable to believe that the battle was lost through failure of Philocles' plan rather than for reasons of negligence and indiscipline. – But battles can be lost for such reasons: and Philocles' plan is rather unimpressive, indeed unexplained. Ehrhardt says that he was repeating Antiochus' plan at Notium and that he failed for the same reason, the unpreparedness of the main Athenian fleet. The analogy is false. Firstly, the idea of a sea ambush (credible in principle at Notium because of the peculiar topographic setting of the Bay of Ephesus) is not manifestly appropriate in the conditions at Lampsacus/Aegospotami. Secondly, the Athenians who fought unprepared at Notium had not *expected* to fight at all. But the plan at Aegospotami *did* (apparently) involve the whole fleet; yet most of it was still unprepared, and this although the enemy was virtually in sight to start with, not (as at Notium) sixteen km away. This fact remains unexplained. (The alleged deserter's information does not alter the situation, of course, for the logical reaction to the message would *not* have been to act on the assumption that the Athenian fleet would still be unmanned when Philocles set out.) (iv) The accusations of treason against various *stratēgoi* and the general public anger with the trierarchs could reflect their failure to support Philocles. – True, but they may as well derive from the fact that Adeimantos was not executed (cf. Xenophon 2.1.32), from partisan views of Alcibiades' conversation with Tydeus (hence, other partisan views accuse *Alcibiades* of treason) and from the undoubted fact (on either version) that the fleet was ill-disciplined (easily, perhaps justly, represented as the trierarchs' fault). In short, the prosecution case does not strike me as proven.

3. *Cyzicus.*[90] Xenophon's account (with some interjected comments) runs as follows: Alcibiades sails from Proconnesus towards Cyzicus in a rainstorm, ready for a ναυμαχία. [Nothing surprising in that: he did not *know* that Mindarus was unaware of his approach or what circumstances would confront him as he approached his target.

[90] 1.1.11f., Diod. 13.49ff., Plut. *Alc.* 28, Polyaen. 1.40.9, Front. *Strat.* 2.5.44. Map in Andrewes (1982) 21.

We do not have to infer that he had some undisclosed plan for forcing a battle.] Near Cyzicus the rain stops and Alcibiades sees Mindarus' ships at sea well away from the harbour and cut off from it by his own ships.[91] Mindarus in turn sees that the Athenians are present in large numbers and are πρὸς τῷ λιμένι. [That is, they were closer to it than he was and able to block his return there. He was thus some five or six km out at sea, with his view north impeded by the Artake headland and/or (?) Polydorus' island, and perhaps not helped by weather conditions.] He flees to the land. [This must be somewhere on the mainland south-west of Cyzicus.] The Athenians follow, some attacking from the sea, while Alcibiades sails round and lands with 'the twenty ships'. [Nothing in Xenophon or elsewhere explains this description.[92]] Mindarus is killed and all his ships captured. This version makes Alcibiades rather lucky, but is not therefore incredible. The alternative tradition (Diodorus, Polyaenus, Frontinus and parts of Plutarch) reduces the element of luck, however. Here the Athenians on leaving Proconnesus first put an infantry force under Chaereas on shore with orders to advance towards Cyzicus. Alcibiades then sails on ahead, leaving Theramenes and Thrasybulus with the rest of the fleet hidden behind the Artake headland.[93] This successfully tempts Mindarus out of Cyzicus to attack him, and an engagement has virtually started when the other Athenians appear and get between him and the harbour. After some fighting (later celebrated by a trophy on Polydorus' island: Diod. 13.51.7) the Peloponnesians take refuge on land (i.e., as in Xenophon, the mainland south-west of Cyzicus). The Athenians make some attempt to drag their ships away with grappling irons but then first Alcibiades and afterwards Theramenes and Thrasybulus disembark their marines and a land battle ensues with a similar end result to that in Xenophon.[94] All this looks very fine and it certainly does not merely supplement Xenophon's account (since it contradicts him not only as regards the element of stratagem, but also in asserting that there was fighting at sea before Mindarus' flight). It is not, however, intrinsically more plausible, and there is

[91] Accepting the majority MS reading ἀπειλημμένας ὑπ' αὐτοῦ ('by himself'); but recent discussion of reflexive pronouns in X. would make one expect ὑφ' αὑτοῦ (Goodall (1976) 50), so the reading of Urbin. 117, Parisin. 1739, ἀπ' αὐτοῦ ('from it' (sc. the harbour)), may be preferable (so Hude (1930) and some older edd.).

[92] The 20 ships in modern texts of Diod. 13.50.2 are Vogel's uncertain supplement after Xen. 1.1.18. If anything the figure should be 40 (Andrewes (1982) 20 n. 14).

[93] For the location of the ambush cf. Andrewes (1982) 20f.

[94] Andrewes (1982) 22 connects X.'s statement that Alcibiades 'sailed around' and landed (1.1.18) with Diodorus' indication of a change of relative position of Alcibiades and the other generals between the fighting at sea and on land. But it need not be a trace of the alternative version surviving in X.; Alcibiades would anyway have to sail around the mêlée of Spartan ships to effect a landing.

a problem. One of the participants in the land battle is Chaereas. How does he come to be somewhere south-west of Cyzicus? If he had been landed on Arctonnesus[95] he cannot have got there by land (this would involve going through Cyzicus)[96] so we must imagine that Theramenes (whom Diodorus represents as instructed by Thrasybulus to join up with him) sailed back to pick him up – which is not what Diodorus says and is unconvincing for reasons of time. Alternatively we must suppose (as Andrewes (1982) 22 does, without making the point explicit) that he had been landed on the mainland. Again this is not what Diodorus would naturally be taken to say, and it materially complicates the whole enterprise: for part of the Athenian fleet will have to make a lengthy return trip from Proconnesus or Arctonnesus to the mainland while the rest sits about doing nothing, with an attendant increased risk that the element of surprise will be lost and no guarantee anyway that Mindarus would extricate himself and escape southwards, the only circumstances making it worth landing Chaereas on the mainland in the first place. I should hesitate to call this problem a fatal objection to Diodorus' whole account; but the case against Xenophon is perhaps not open-and-shut. (I would add that, if we *do* prefer Diodorus, Andrewes' identification of Xenophon's source as a partisan of Alcibiades on one of Thrasybulus' ships hardly accounts for his failure to report the supposed ambush.)

4. *Mytilene.*[97] Xenophon's account begins abruptly with Callicratidas in pursuit of Conon. Conon has sufficient extra speed to take refuge in Mytilene (καταφεύγει εἰς Μυτιλήνην), but Callicratidas sails into the λιμήν with him with 170 ships (this is admittedly an error for 140) and Conon is forced to fight πρὸς τῷ λιμένι. 30 ships are lost (their crews escaping by land), the remaining 40 Conon manages to draw up ὑπὸ τῷ τείχει. Callicratidas then moors in the λιμήν and blockades the Athenians by controlling the ἔκπλους. Subsequent events tell us more about the topography. (i) The circumstances in which two Athenian ships managed to run the blockade (1.6.19) show that Conon's position was close to and visible from some of the Peloponnesian ships and suggest that the *ekplous* is relatively spacious. Moreover, since those of Callicratidas' ships which put to sea to chase the Athenians elected to follow the ship which turned south, it might be inferred that they were moored south of Conon's position. (ii) Later on (1.6.22) Diomedon came to help Conon and moored in the

[95] So Hatzfeld (1940) 271, Bloedow (1973) 51 n. 304.

[96] Even assuming Arctonnesos was not a true island in 410. On Cyzicene topography cf. Hasluk (1902) 132f., Hasluk (1910), Hasluk–Henderson (1904) 135f., Lehmann-Hartleben (1923) 63f., 100f., 261f.

[97] 1.6.15f., Diod. 13.77ff., Polyaen. 1.48.2 (summarizing part of the Diodoran version). For topography cf. *IG* XII.2 pl. 1, British Admiralty Handbook, *Greece* 3.502f.

εὔριπος (i.e. the channel through the Mytilene isthmus).[98] Clearly he did not simply run in through the blockade and join Conon's ships, and must have approached from the other side of the city. But even so he did not join Conon, and remained exposed to separate attack by the Spartans. Therefore the εὔριπος was not navigable. Moreover, Callicratidas was willing and able to launch a successful attack on Diomedon, which means that his position was not protected to the same degree by the city walls as was Conon's. Since both ends of the εὔριπος must have been at least partly adjacent to walls, we must conclude that Conon's refuge was actually inside them.

Conon's battle with Callicratidas requires two further comments. (i) Xenophon explains his being compelled to fight πρὸς τῷ λιμένι with the words ὡς ἔφθη ὑπὸ τῶν πολεμίων κατακωλυθείς, which is taken to mean that the enemy arrived too quickly for Conon to draw up his ships unimpeded. The formulation is rather strained and there may be corruption (especially since πολεμίων is already an emendation of MSS πολιτῶν). However, it is clear anyway that the pursuers got too close and that Conon had to turn and halt them. Since he none the less managed to extricate over half his ships we must conclude that not all of Callicratidas' 140 ships were involved – which is hardly surprising in view of the long preceding chase. Nor on the other hand will it be surprising that Conon lost as many as 30 out of 70. (ii) Callicratidas and Conon are both said to sail into the λιμήν, but the battle is πρὸς τῷ λιμένι and is followed by Callicratidas' mooring in the λιμήν, while Conon retires ὑπὸ τῷ τείχει. Perhaps Xenophon is actually referring to two interconnected λιμένες, one within the walls, one not, without making clear that he is applying the term to two different places. But it seems more likely that he merely anticipates a little in saying Callicratidas entered the harbour before fighting. However, we shall still have to distinguish between Xenophon's λιμήν, a relatively large area outside the walls, and what must amount to a smaller internal λιμήν, the place where Conon takes refuge ὑπὸ τῷ τείχει.

The conflict must therefore be played out wholly on one side of Mytilene, and we are looking for an area which can legitimately be said to consist of an inner and outer harbour. This requirement appears to be better fulfilled on the south side, where we can distinguish between the modern south harbour and the rest of the bay to its south. This is, of course, the direction in which other indications have already suggested that we look. To the north, by contrast, the area of the modern north harbour (now marked off by moles) is the

[98] The εὔριπος is thought to have been roughly on the line of the main north–south road running from the Turkish Cemetery towards Ag. Apostoloi.

most that could ever have been called a harbour (there is no larger harbour from which it can be distinguished), and on current views its shores were largely adjacent to the city walls and therefore not available as a base for Peloponnesian ships.[99]

So much for Xenophon. Diodorus' account is markedly different. Conon is at Hekatonnesoi when he sees the Spartans approaching from Methymna. He sails south deliberately drawing the enemy after him with the intention of engaging near Mytilene, a strategy permitting him the option of withdrawal into the harbour in the event of defeat. (Actually it is hard to see that there could be any other ultimate outcome, given numerical disparity.) The Peloponnesian fleet becomes strung out (in Diodorus, as in Xenophon, Conon has much the better crews) and, once near Mytilene, the Athenians turn on them. The upshot is that Conon (on the right wing) escapes into Mytilene with 40 ships, while 30 ships on the left wing, becoming separated from their companions, are compelled to flee to the land (where the crews escape). This corresponds to the result of Xenophon's battle, but the accounts are already inconsistent: there is no place for Conon's stratagem in Xenophon, and it is not clear that Diodorus' battle is πρὸς τῷ λιμένι. The inconsistency is compounded in what follows. Callicratidas camps overnight near the city while Conon prepares to block the harbour entrance (this involves sinking ships in the shallows, anchoring merchantmen with stone-throwing artillery elsewhere, putting soldiers on the harbour χηλαί, and stationing the triremes in the remaining διέκπλους). Next day there is fierce fighting and at a second attempt the Athenian triremes are driven back: Callicratidas enters the harbour and anchors near the city, while the Athenians flee into *another* harbour, ὁ ἐν τῇ πόλει λιμήν; the harbour at whose entrance the battles were fought was, by contrast, outside the city. It is possible that Diodorus' source imagined this city harbour as being at the other end of the εὔριπος (which Diodorus certainly mentions as though it explained the distinction between the harbours). This totally contradicts Xenophon, of course, and compounds another problem. According to Diodorus Conon lost no ships in the defence of the outer harbour. This defies belief anyway, and especially if his fleet had to retire down a narrow channel, with the victorious enemy behind. But if Diodorus does not mean to place the city harbour at the other end of the εὔριπος, we are being asked to believe that, having

[99] Koldewey (1890) 1ff., *IG* l.c. (n. 97), Lehmann-Hartleben (1923) 88f., plus new information about walls in *AAA* 5 (1972) 39f., 7 (1974) 199f. (south sector), *AD* 28 (1976) Chron. 509f. (south harbour jetty), *AD* 17 (1961/2) Chron. 261, *PAAH* (1961) 211 (north sector). We may apparently believe the (inner) south harbour to have been within the walls, the north harbour outside them (i.e. the walls ran along its west and south shore, and there were no fortified moles).

just lost nearly half his fleet, Conon did not simply take grateful refuge in the secure city harbour but set about blocking the entrance of the larger southern harbour area; that in less than twenty-four hours he achieved enough to give Callicratidas a hard fight; and that he still lost no ships. I confess that I do not feel impelled to prefer Diodorus' two battles to Xenophon's one.

There is no call for a lengthy summary, since my overall case, or *idée fixe*, will be clear enough. Although it is not uncommon for the non-Xenophontic tradition to be able to supply us with additional information about particular battles, it is rare for the Xenophontic tradition to be of negligible importance (i.e. for the situation to be that non-Xenophontic sources provide all the information found in Xenophon and more besides) and rare for the novel information from other sources to be both divergent from Xenophon and demonstrably preferable to him. In short, I am not (yet) convinced that actual error or really serious omission is a frequent feature of Xenophon's treatment of military engagements. This may, no doubt, be wrong-headed obstinacy; and it is certainly true that the arguments at my disposal are not as satisfying as one could wish. But what of the other side's arguments? It seems to me that in the huge majority of cases Xenophon's credit is not seriously questionable (and has not been seriously questioned), and that in the few major exhibits for the prosecution we are faced with a choice between one author (Xenophon) whose credentials are at least to some extent clear and who does not normally say things which are manifestly silly and another (the Oxyrhynchus historian or later representatives of his tradition) whose credentials are not clear (except perhaps to those who feel sure they know his name) and for whom the chief argument in principle is that he writes long and complexly detailed accounts (a version, that is, of the argument from circumstantiality). In those cases where actual contradiction is involved, a decision in Xenophon's favour will mean that the Oxyrhynchus historian has been guilty in some degree of 'creative writing', and it is therefore understandable if historians prefer what looks like the 'easier' option of deciding in his favour and regarding Xenophon's versions either as extreme examples of a general lack of concern for detail or as inventions indeed, but inventions on a smaller (because less detailed) scale – almost 'invention by omission'. But I am inclined to reject the simple equation of lack of interest in detail with uninterestedness in accuracy, and I should like to see better explanations – in fact, any serious explanations – of the supposed inventions. This is not to say that I have an explanation to offer of any creative writing in which the

Oxyrhynchus historian may have indulged. But I would insist on the possibility that *that* is the explanation for which we need to search. At any rate, a clear issue of principle is raised, and can be summed up in a question which this paper may by now seem to provoke in its own right: are length and complexity reliable signs of credibility?

The formation of the historical tradition of early Rome

T. J. CORNELL

This paper is divided into three sections. The first part aims to give a résumé of what I take to be the generally agreed view of how the Roman historical tradition came into being. In the second section I shall focus on certain problems that seem to me to be inherent in the received view, and to indicate why I consider it to be an inadequate explanation of the origin of the historical information we find in the surviving literary sources. In the third section I have tentatively outlined a different and, I hope, more satisfactory model of the growth and development of the historical tradition about the archaic age of Rome.

Before proceeding I ought briefly to recapitulate the nature of the problem that surrounds the study of early Roman history. The surviving literary accounts, which date at the earliest from the second half of the first century B.C., and which include the works of (among others) Cicero, Diodorus Siculus, Livy and Dionysius of Halicarnassus, give us what appears to be a very full and very detailed account of the political and military history of the Roman people from the earliest times. Admittedly the story of the origins of the city has the character of legend, but the narrative takes on a truly historical appearance with the arrival of the dynasty of the Tarquins, towards the end of the seventh century B.C. according to the traditional chronology. From the beginning of the Republic (traditionally 509 B.C.) we have a complete list of eponymous magistrates (the *fasti*), and a regular and systematic record of political and military events.[1]

The problem is that we do not know how historical information about the events of the sixth, fifth and fourth centuries came to be transmitted to the historians who were writing at the end of the Republic, and consequently we cannot be certain that the information

[1] The problem of the sources for early Roman history has been endlessly discussed, and it is not possible here to give a representative bibliography. I would simply mention, apart from the works cited in the following notes, the lucid and rigorous account in English by Lewis (1855), and the comprehensive critical discussions of De Sanctis (1907) and Beloch (1926). An admirable recent summary of the main issues is given by Heurgon (1973) 244–50, with full bibliography. On the history of the question in the eighteenth and nineteenth centuries see Barbagallo (1926).

is, in fact, historical. We should not lose sight of what an extraordinary situation this is. It is sometimes said that little is known about early Roman history. Such a statement is however the product of a secondary historical judgement. On the face of it the period is extremely well documented. For the archaic age down to the end of the fourth century B.C. we have no fewer than ten complete books of Livy and four Lives of Plutarch. We possess the complete text of the eleven books Dionysius of Halicarnassus needed to bring his account down to the time of the Twelve Tables, and numerous other sources besides. The contrast with the scrappy and exiguous evidence that exists for the political history of the Greek archaic age is very striking. For example we know far less about Pisistratus, who lived less than a century before Herodotus, than we do about Servius Tullius, who lived more than three hundred years before Fabius Pictor.

The Romans thus seem to have been unusual in preserving a very detailed account of their archaic age. It is natural to relate this to their remarkable obsession with tradition, the *mos maiorum*, and the question of their own origins. Scholars often contend that the Romans were unlike the Greeks in that they had no native myths to speak of, but compensated for this by constructing a historicized ideology.[2] What we need to know is whether the Romans' claim to a detailed knowledge of their archaic past is well founded; for it seems obvious that they were either very good at remembering things, or very good at concocting them.

I

Let me now turn to the first of the three sections outlined at the start of this paper.

It is conventional for an analysis of the Roman historical tradition to begin with Fabius Pictor. Fabius is normally seen as a pioneer who put together a basic account drawn from a variety of sources. These probably included: a list of eponymous magistrates going back to the beginning of the Republic; the texts of ancient laws and treaties (for example the Twelve Tables and the *foedus Cassianum*); some kind of oral tradition, including for example the stories of Horatius and the bridge, Coriolanus, and Cincinnatus at the plough; the records of the great noble families who preserved the memory of their ancestors' achievements; and probably also the *Annales Maximi*, a chronicle kept by the *pontifex maximus* which apparently contained some sort of record of historical events. Finally, Fabius must have

[2] See Grant (1971) *passim* esp. 239ff.

made use of whatever earlier Greek writers had had to say about Rome.[3]

Naturally scholars disagree about the particular contributions of these different types of sources, and about the form and literary character of the work that Fabius eventually produced. Did it, for example, follow an annalistic structure, listing events under the eponymous magistrates for each year? We do not know, and scholarly opinion is divided.[4] Again, although we know that Fabius wrote in Greek, we cannot tell how far he adopted the more sophisticated techniques of contemporary Hellenistic writing. Some scholars have suggested that he wrote fairly elaborate 'tragic' history, others that he had no stylistic pretensions and was little more than a chronicler.[5] The evidence on this matter is ambiguous and very difficult. But there does seem to be fairly general agreement that Fabius created the Roman historical tradition almost out of nothing. Thus it is assumed that Fabius put together the first continuous and articulated account on the basis of widely scattered scraps of information drawn from haphazard sources. For instance it is said that 'he faced an almost overwhelming task in organising what sources he had into a coherent historical narrative [...] the Romans had neither the benefit of a complete Greek history of Rome nor of a local historical tradition of their own'.[6] Or, as T. P. Wiseman has put it in a recent book: 'For the first Roman historians [...] there was simply nothing to go on – except for a haphazard collection of traditional stories, only roughly dateable at best – until they reached a period about which reliable information was available from their older contemporaries [...]'.[7]

On this view Fabius' narrative was the basis of all subsequent accounts. Later historians such as Cincius Alimentus, Cato the Censor and Cassius Hemina made minimal additions to it. Although Cato broke new ground by incorporating the history of the other peoples of Italy, his initiative was not taken up by subsequent historians; Cassius Hemina may have been the first to include antiquarian details on any significant scale; but the basic structure

[3] The fragments of Fabius Pictor are assembled in Peter (1914) 5–39, and in *FGrHist* 809. For some basic discussions of Pictor and his work see Momigliano (1960b), Badian (1966) 2–7, Timpe (1972), Frier (1979) 255–84. On the sources that might have been available to the first historians see De Sanctis (1907) 1–49, Momigliano (1963) 547–48, Fraccaro (1957).

[4] Fabius an annalist: Bömer (1953), Walbank (1945) 15–18; Fabius not an annalist: Gelzer (1934 and 1954), Timpe (1972) 952–53.

[5] 'Tragic' history in Pictor: Walbank (1945) 12–13, Flach (1973) 24–26, Alföldi (1965) 147–59. *Contra* Bömer (1953) 208, Frier (1979) 278–79. On 'tragic' history in general see Ullmann (1942) and Walbank (1960), and (1972) 34–40.

[6] Frier (1979) 60.

[7] Wiseman (1979) 9–10.

was not affected. By the time of the Gracchi a rough and ready tradition of historiography had been established. The results were encapsulated in the work of L. Calpurnius Piso Frugi (*cos.* 133, *censor* 120 B.C.), who wrote a history of Rome from its origins in at least seven books. Piso's work was characterized by a strong moralizing tone; perhaps he was the first to draw moral lessons from the past, since in spite of what one might have expected there is no evidence that Cato did so.[8] It has also been suggested that Piso was the first historian to arrange his material annalistically and to call his work *Annales*.[9] The evidence on this point is however very uncertain. As far as the title *Annales* is concerned, Piso was certainly preceded by Ennius, whose use of it would have been very strange if annalistic history had not yet been invented.

Piso is referred to by Cicero[10] as one of the three founding fathers of Roman historiography, along with Fabius Pictor and Cato. From the little we know of the economy of their works, these early historians dealt very briefly with the archaic period. Cicero comments on their meagre narrative style, and regards brevity as their only commendable quality; and Dionysius of Halicarnassus noted that Fabius and Cincius Alimentus covered the early events after the founding of the city 'in a summary fashion', and only wrote at length on the period in which they themselves lived.[11]

A later generation of historians, however, treated the archaic age much more generously; writers such as Cn. Gellius, writing around 100 B.C., and the first century annalists C. Licinius Macer, Valerius Antias and Q. Aelius Tubero, all seem to have treated the early history of the city much more extensively than their predecessors.[12] It is difficult to be more specific, since the evidence, which consists mainly of fragments quoted with book numbers, is very thin and often unreliable.

The facts, such as they are, can be briefly summarized: Cn. Gellius needed at least fourteen books to reach the Gallic sack, and dealt with events of 216 B.C. in his thirtieth or thirty-third book.[13] His work is said to have comprised ninety-seven books in all.[14] Licinius Macer probably did not get as far as the Second Punic War, since he is not quoted by Livy in the third and subsequent decades; but he

[8] On this point see Rawson (1976). Rawson's whole paper is an important study of Hemina, Piso and Gellius. On Cato see further Timpe (1970–71) and Astin (1978) 211–39.

[9] Wiseman (1979) 12–20.

[10] Cic. *de or.* 2.51–53; cf. *de leg.* 1.6.

[11] Dion. Hal. *AR* 1.6.2. On this important text see Gabba (1967), Timpe (1972) 932–40, Frier (1979) 255–58, Cornell (1980) 19–22.

[12] On the 'expansion of the past' see Badian (1966) 11–13.

[13] Cn. Gellius frs. 25 and 26 Peter.

[14] Cn. Gellius fr. 29P.

nevertheless managed to complete at least sixteen books.[15] Valerius Antias' work contained at least seventy-five books,[16] although if we are to believe a statement of Aulus Gellius[17] the affair of C. Hostilius Mancinus (136 B.C.) was treated in Book 22, which would mean that Antias' work was mainly concerned with contemporary history. Finally, we know that the work of the obscure Q. Aelius Tubero treated events of the First Punic War in Book 9.[18]

From this very unsatisfactory jumble of insecure evidence it is possible to infer that the annalists of the first century B.C. were somehow able to say more about the archaic period than their second-century predecessors. Their efforts made it possible for Livy and Dionysius of Halicarnassus to construct their full-length narratives. The question is, where did they obtain the necessary raw materials for their expanded accounts? Modern scholars are agreed that there are only two possible explanations: either new information became available at the end of the second century B.C. which had not been exploited by the earliest historians, or the later annalists simply drew upon their own imaginations to supplement the meagre supply of facts.

The first of these possibilities – that the later annalists had access to new information which had not previously been available – has been taken up by those scholars who believe that the pontifical chronicle was published in book form towards the end of the second century B.C. by the *pontifex maximus* P. Mucius Scaevola (who held office from *c.* 130 to *c.* 115), and that the resulting compilation, called the *Annales Maximi*, formed the basis of the expanded accounts of Cn. Gellius and his successors.[19]

This theory is open to two serious objections. In the first place it is not at all clear that the compilation in eighty books known as the *Annales Maximi* was in fact published by Scaevola. The only thing we know about Scaevola in relation to the chronicle is that the practice of keeping it came to an end during his term of office.[20] That fact might seem to be evidence, not of Scaevola's enthusiasm for the chronicle, but rather of his indifference to it. In a recent book on the subject B. W. Frier has argued that the *Annales Maximi* were published, not by Mucius Scaevola in the second century B.C., but by the emperor Augustus shortly after he became *pontifex maximus* in 12 B.C.[21] Frier is surely right about Scaevola, but his theory of an Augustan edition is both fragile and unnecessary. In fact there is no

[15] Licinius Macer fr. 22P.
[16] Valerius Antias fr. 62P.
[17] A. Gellius *NA* 6.9.12 = Antias fr. 57P.
[18] Tubero fr. 8P.
[19] Thus, e.g. Badian (1966) 12, Ogilvie (1976) 18. *Contra*, Wiseman (1979) 17.
[20] Cic. *de or.* 2.52.
[21] Frier (1979) 197–98.

evidence that the work was ever published at all, and the most sensible reconstruction seems to be that the eighty books of the *Annales Maximi* were identical with the chronicle that was kept by the *pontifices* until the time of Scaevola.

The second objection is that the earliest historians surely could have availed themselves of the *Annales Maximi*, whether published or not, and it seems certain that they did so. In a famous passage of the *de oratore*[22] Cicero argues that Pictor, Cato and Piso wrote in the manner of the chronicle. The same passage partly states and partly implies that these same historians used the chronicle as a principal source. This conclusion is confirmed by a fragment of Cato's *Origines*,[23] in which the old man declares that he does not wish to clutter up his account with trivia taken from the chronicle – he refers specifically to celestial phenomena and increases in the price of grain. It seems clear that Cato's statement would have had very little point if the chronicle had not already been a recognized source for historians, and if such trivia had not been included by them in their accounts.[24] It is important to note that Cato does not say that the pontifical records consisted *entirely* of trivia, nor that he had spurned the chronicle as a source of historical information. Rather he should be seen as criticizing those who had indiscriminately reproduced everything that the chronicle contained, including trivial items unsuitable to serious history.[25]

For most scholars, where documentary evidence ends, forgery begins; and it is widely assumed that, if the publication of the *Annales Maximi* does not explain the bulk of the work of Cn. Gellius and his successors, then the only alternative is that they filled out their narratives with fictitious inventions.[26] The process of annalistic invention can be understood in two distinct ways. In the first place we can be fairly certain that the later annalists felt entitled to add rhetorical colour and incidental detail to a traditional story in order to make the narrative more dramatic or moving. Thus the bare record of a battle or campaign could be embellished with all sorts of fictitious but plausible details supplied by the historian's own imagination or drawn from some pre-existing literary model. Consider for example the battle between the Horatii and the Curiatii, an ancient legend in which three Roman brothers fought as champions against three Alban brothers in order to decide the outcome of the war between their

[22] Cic. *de or.* 2.51–53.

[23] Cato *Origines* fr. 77P.

[24] Cf. Walbank (1945) 17.

[25] I owe this important point to John R. Wood, whose account of the pontifical chronicle in his unpublished Ph.D. thesis (London, 1982) is the best discussion of the subject known to me.

[26] This is the principal thesis of Wiseman (1979); see esp. 16–26, 113–39.

respective cities. The combat is described in great detail in the surviving sources, and an assessment is given of the feelings of the armies on both sides as they watched their champions fight it out;[27] the changes from elation to despair as the contest seemed to go first one way and then the other are directly modelled on the celebrated passage of Thucydides in which the Athenians and Syracusans watch from the shore as their respective fleets struggle in the Great Harbour.[28] In the same way historians were expected to compose imaginary speeches to put into the mouths of leading historical figures, regardless of whether or not there was any real historical evidence of what was actually said, or even whether any speech was actually delivered.

These relatively harmless literary devices were an accepted feature of the Hellenistic style of historical writing that was fashionable in Rome in the late Republic. The convention surely was that such rhetorical padding was harmless enough provided that it did not do violence to the traditional facts.[29] It is often supposed, however, that Roman historians habitually abused the accepted conventions by consciously distorting the historical facts at their disposal and giving free rein to their imaginations when the facts were lacking. The villains are usually identified as the annalists of the first century B.C., men such as Licinius Macer and Valerius Antias, who are alleged to have perpetrated lies and distortions on a large scale, not only for frivolous reasons (e.g. to entertain their readers), but also, more mischievously, to promote political causes and to glorify the achievements of their own real or supposed ancestors. On this view the surviving accounts of early Roman history represent a bogus tradition, consisting largely of mendacious annalistic fabrications.

Part of the reason for this deterioration in standards is thought to have been a change in the social status of the men who wrote annalistic history.[30] In the early days the leading historians had been senators who had been actively involved in political life. But by the end of the second century B.C. such men had abandoned the annalistic tradition and had committed themselves instead to the study of contemporary history. The earliest known practitioners of this new form were C. Fannius and Sempronius Asellio; their successors were Sisenna and Sallust. The writing of annals now became the preserve of literary men outside the senatorial class who had no direct experience of politics and had probably never raised a sword or shield. Proponents

[27] Livy 1.25, Dion. Hal. *AR* 3.19–20. Cf. Solodow (1979).
[28] Thuc. 7.71; cf. Ogilvie (1965) on Livy 1.25.2.
[29] This seems to have been Cicero's view. See Brunt (1979).
[30] For this and what follows see Badian (1966) 18–26.

of this view tend to point the finger at Valerius Antias, supposedly a shameless liar and a man of low birth, who nevertheless had the effrontery to invent an ancestor for himself (serving as a prefect in the Hannibalic War) and to attach himself to the patrician Valerii, whose fame and achievements he exaggerated to an extravagant degree. The very prominent role played by the Valerii in the early centuries of the Republic is the result of Antias' self-important fabrications. In his account of the struggle of the Orders Valerius Antias is thought to have been strongly biased in favour of the patricians, whereas his rival, Licinius Macer, favoured the plebs, whose leaders include suspicious numbers of Licinii. A particular feature of these late annalistic accounts is that they discussed the struggle of the Orders in terms of the politics of their own day; thus the measures and policies of the Gracchi and Saturninus were arbitrarily ascribed to early popular figures such as Sp. Cassius.[31]

The first-century annalists are also generally thought to have been crassly chauvinistic in their accounts of Rome's foreign relations. They minimized Roman defeats – or else completely concealed them. Thus the capture of Rome by Lars Porsenna, of which a memory survived and is preserved in later sources,[32] was hushed up and replaced by the edifying tale of the defence of the city by Horatius, Cloelia and Mucius Scaevola. Disasters such as the Gallic sack or the Caudine Forks could not be denied, but unscrupulous annalists did not hesitate to invent a series of face-saving victories in the immediate aftermath of these defeats.[33] In foreign affairs Rome was always in the right, and fought wars only in defence of her legitimate interests against enemy aggression; the notion of the 'just war' is regarded by some scholars as an annalistic fiction. 'It may be regarded as certain', writes E. Badian, 'that Claudius [Quadrigarius] and Valerius [Antias] (two of Livy's main sources) are responsible, in elaboration of what had been done by their predecessors, for the presentation of all Roman wars as just and all Roman dealings as honourable (even where the reverse is clear to us) that marks so much of Livy; [...] where earlier annalists, for serious moral and political reasons, had prepared the way, the entertainers followed without scruple, converting history into romance.'[34]

The annalists of the first century B.C. are thus seen principally as entertainers, devoid of any serious political or moral purpose; it is said that they were more concerned with plausibility than truth, and that if the facts did not precisely fit their dramatic needs they altered

[31] Thus e.g. Ogilvie (1976) 20, Wiseman (1979) 24–25.
[32] Tacitus *Hist.* 3.72.1, Pliny *NH* 34.139.
[33] Toynbee (1965) 1.373–74.
[34] Badian (1966) 19.

them without scruple and fabricated them whenever necessary. For many years in the early Republic, so it is said, tradition recorded nothing but the names of the magistrates; but this presented no problem to the likes of Claudius Quadrigarius and Valerius Antias, who simply inserted plausible fictions modelled on the genuine notices recorded in other years.[35]

Unfortunately these later writers were the principal sources of Livy, who found them congenial because of their plausibility and breadth of treatment. The usual view of Livy is that he drew upon only a very few late authorities, and that he knew of early writers like Fabius and Piso only through quotations in secondary authorities. For each section Livy is supposed to have followed whichever of his few main sources seemed most suitable, without inquiring, perhaps without caring, whether the information it contained was historically true.[36]

Livy's work was such an artistic masterpiece that it deterred all competition; after Livy no one ever again attempted to go back to the origins of the city and trace its entire history from an independent point of view. Later hacks and epitomators simply followed Livy. His achievement also overshadowed all its predecessors, which inevitably failed to survive. The result is that we are left with a second-hand and – from a historical point of view – second-rate literary source. What we read in the surviving literary accounts is therefore thoroughly contaminated and untrustworthy, and to be treated with extreme suspicion by the modern historian. This is the basis of the approach that has been labelled 'hypercriticism', and is described by J. Heurgon as follows: 'For a long time it has seemed that, when faced with any statement by a Roman historian, sound method demands that one should *a priori* reckon it false, work out in what circumstances it was invented, of what later events it was a deliberate anticipation, and what public or private interest it was intended to serve.'[37]

II

The foregoing remarks represent a summary of a general theory about the origin and development of the annalistic tradition which can be found (expressed in different ways and with many variations in detail)

[35] Thus for example Badian (1966) 21 writes: 'The tradition of Roman historiography made plausible lying easy: its true content was to some extent based on archival material, written in simple and archaic style and *clamouring for imitation*' (my italics).

[36] This view of Livy's working methods is to be found in the majority of standard accounts, e.g. Klotz (1940), Walsh (1961) 110–37, Ogilvie (1965) 5–17 and *passim*. See below n. 51 for some critical reappraisals of this standard view.

[37] Heurgon (1973) 247.

in a number of modern accounts.[38] But in spite of its wide currency, this scholarly construction seems to me to have certain basic weaknesses in general and to be quite wrong in some of its particulars. Let me begin by making two general points.

In the first place, the received view seems to me to be over-optimistic in its attitude to the evidence. It is in fact riddled with conjectures and assumptions about literary figures of whom we know almost nothing and about works which are represented only by the most meagre and haphazard fragments. It is paradoxical that this farrago of uncertain and fragmentary evidence should serve as the foundation of a fundamentally negative approach to the historical problem of archaic Rome. That is to say, the supposed character of the sources of the surviving accounts is invoked as a reason for rejecting much of the tradition as false. The weakness of the case is that there is not enough evidence to allow us to judge the reliability of the late-republican annalists (let alone their honesty, which is a different matter). More important still is the fact that we cannot know how far the information that is now available to us has been distorted by their supposed shortcomings. The irony is that those who deny the possibility of knowledge of archaic Roman history are themselves claiming to know too much.

Secondly, the received view places far too much emphasis on the contributions of individual annalists, and in my opinion grossly exaggerates the role of the annalists in shaping the Romans' view of their own past. It is sometimes supposed that the annalists were free to invent anything they liked, and that Livy, being not very bright and not very conscientious, has unwittingly passed on their lies to us. Once it is admitted that almost anything we read in Livy might be the capricious fabrication of some annalist, the historian's task becomes hopeless. But there is no need to assume any of these things, and I hope to show that we can approach Livy with a far greater degree of confidence. Naturally I am not saying that everything in Livy is true. But I am saying that fabrications and falsehoods are not necessarily to be ascribed to the annalists. For instance, the story of Horatius and the bridge is not only legendary, but also a patriotic fiction, if we are to believe (as we probably should) the variant tradition that Lars Porsenna actually captured Rome. But the suggestion that the saga of Horatius was an annalistic fabrication would barely merit discussion.

More controversial is the question of the 'just war'. As we have seen, many scholars believe that the late annalists were responsible

[38] As a representative example I would cite the important and influential article of Badian (1966), which has come to be seen as the standard treatment.

for the presentation of all Rome's wars as 'just' wars. But it is surely much more likely that the idea of the 'just war', sanctioned by the gods and enshrined in the ritual of the *fetiales*, was a genuine feature of Roman attitudes and behaviour in foreign relations from the earliest times. By this I do not mean to suggest that Roman foreign policy really was just according to some objective standard of equity, but rather that the Romans, like all other civilized peoples known to history, convinced *themselves* that their interests were legitimate and that their actions and policies were just. Equally I do not wish to challenge W. V. Harris' convincing demonstration that the Romans were in fact aggressive imperialists and that many of their wars were far from defensive in character.[39] I am only saying that the Romans did not see themselves as aggressive imperialists. Moreover, the Romans never claimed that their wars were defensive, but only that their wars were just. This seems to me far more likely than that the concept of the 'just war' was a cynical pretence designed to give respectability to deliberate acts of aggression. Leaving this problem to the reader, I shall now pass on in the hope that I have made it clear what I mean by the statement that too much is being attributed to the annalists.

Regarding the specific criticisms that have been levelled at individual annalists, it hardly needs saying that for the most part they go way beyond the evidence. For example there is no warrant for the contention that Valerius Antias exaggerated the part played by the Valerii in the early history of Rome. On this matter scholars conventionally refer to F. Münzer's 1891 dissertation *De Gente Valeria* as having proved the point beyond doubt; but Münzer's many pages of affirmation cannot compensate for the fact that the theory is not based on any evidence. And even Münzer was not prepared to condemn as fictitious the Valerius Antias whom Livy records as serving as a prefect in 215 B.C.[40] The modern assertion that this person was a figment of the annalist's imagination, rather than a genuine ancestor, is entirely arbitrary. It would not be at all surprising if Valerius Antias' account was favourable to the Valerii; after all, other historians certainly were, and Antias may well have felt a vicarious pleasure in recounting the good deeds of the great patrician clan whose name he shared. But nothing proves that he invented any of the Valerian material, or even that it was invented by anyone. It might after all be substantially true. For instance there is no good reason to reject *a priori* the law of Valerius Publicola on *provocatio*, supposedly enacted at the beginning of the Republic; in

[39] Harris (1979).
[40] Livy 23.34.9, with Münzer (1891) 60.

fact the existence of the right of *provocatio* is presupposed in the Twelve Tables. Finally the newly discovered Satricum inscription, dating from the early fifth century B.C. and recording a dedication by the companions of a certain Publius Valerius, surely helps to strengthen the traditional belief in the importance of the *gens Valeria* at the beginning of the Republic.[41]

Again there is no good evidence that Antias favoured the patricians, or indeed that he had any kind of political bias. In Livy and Dionysius of Halicarnassus we find both pro-patrician and pro-plebeian passages. It is often suggested that this resulted from their use of different sources, each of which had its own pronounced bias. But this argument is double-edged; for obviously if Livy and Dionysius could combine different and opposing points of view, it follows logically that their sources, including Valerius Antias, could have done the same.[42]

The implication of much modern research, however, is that the lost works of the late-republican annalists were totally different from the surviving accounts that we are actually able to read. In fact this constitutes a serious weakness for the modern theory. Many harsh things have been said, rightly or wrongly, about Livy and Dionysius of Halicarnassus. They have been variously described as tedious, naïve, prejudiced, ignorant and foolish; but no one has seriously suggested that they were downright dishonest. The theory that the Roman historical tradition consists largely of annalistic fabrications is thus undermined by the fact that there are no surviving examples of the kind of historical writing the theory necessarily presupposes.

Livy and Dionysius were not senators and had no direct experience of politics or warfare. This at least may have been something they had in common with their annalistic predecessors. According to the standard view, the earliest historians were senators writing serious political history. But the later annalists came from outside the political class. They were professional scribblers, devoid of serious purpose, who aimed to please and entertain their readers at all costs. But let us consider the facts for a moment. Of the historians we have discussed, the following are known to have been senators and are attested in independent historical sources as playing an active part in public life: Fabius Pictor, Cincius Alimentus, Cato, Piso, Licinius Macer and Aelius Tubero. The status of the others is not known. It is usually assumed that Valerius Antias and Claudius Quadrigarius

41 Stibbe (1980), Versnel (1982).

42 I follow Briscoe (1981) 50: 'There is of course the logical point that, if Livy and Dionysius felt no difficulty in combining both versions, there is no reason why one of their predecessors should not have done the same.' Cf. Briscoe (1973) 3–4.

were not senators, but that Cn. Gellius probably was.[43] But it is hard to see what can be proved by a distinction that places Licinius Macer, Aelius Tubero and probably Cn. Gellius on one side in opposition to Valerius Antias and Claudius Quadrigarius on the other. In any case the construction is founded on quicksand. Since we know nothing about Gellius, Quadrigarius and Antias beyond the fact that they wrote annalistic histories, it follows that we cannot know whether they were senators or not. This elementary point is seen by Wiseman, who rightly entertains the possibility that Antias might have been a senator;[44] but for the most part scholars confer upon themselves the censorial privilege of excluding Valerius Antias and Claudius Quadrigarius from the senate.

Finally, it is not clear why the senatorial status of the annalists is so important. In these days of Ronald Reagan's presidency we have become aware of the possibility of marginality between the world of politics and the world of entertainment. But in the past scholars seem to have assumed that senatorial historians were serious, whereas non-senators were *ipso facto* mere entertainers and up to no good. The dissemination of this idea probably has something to do with Sir Ronald Syme, who constantly harps upon it: 'The senator came to his task in mature years, with a proper knowledge of men and government, a sharp and merciless insight. Taking up the pen, he fought again the old battles of Forum and Curia.'[45] '[...] the non-political classes acclaimed the new order everywhere, with enthusiasm, but no senator could bring himself to confess a joyous acceptance [...] the senator will be alert for the contrasts of name and fact, contemptuous of sporadic subservience or the manifestation of organised loyalty.'[46]

As far as the Republic is concerned, the suggestion is that the practice of historical writing deteriorated intellectually as it became 'socially degraded'; that the intellectual honesty, seriousness of purpose and competence in research of a historian were commensurate with his social standing. This is surely a classic case of modern scholars adopting the prejudices of their ancient sources. The theory is in any case contradicted by the fact that the surviving examples of non-senatorial historiography clearly fail to show the required degree of worthlessness. Once again it will not do to assert that Livy and Dionysius are somehow 'different'.

43 That Gellius was a senator is asserted by Badian (1966) 12. The few known facts are set out by Rawson (1976) 713ff. and Wiseman (1979) 20. Cn. Gellius may be identical with the *monetalis* of 138 B.C.; thus Crawford *RRC* 265; but that would still not necessarily make him a senator.

44 Wiseman (1979) 135.

45 Syme (1970) 2; cf. 11.

46 Syme (1970) 8–9.

Two final points can be made on the subject of supposed annalistic inventions. As far as we can see, the Roman annalists were not in a position to impose a fraudulent version of Rome's history on their contemporaries and on succeeding generations of historians.[47] The main outline of political and military events was a matter of public knowledge in the late Republic; it was clearly set out in the works of the early historians, and the constituent elements of the narrative were based securely on the *fasti* and other documents. It is simply inconceivable that relatively late writers such as Valerius Antias could have departed radically from the received tradition and hoped to get away with it. I am not suggesting that Antias was entirely truthful, but only that the influence of his supposed lies and distortions should not be exaggerated. We cannot get around this by saying that he might none the less have been able to deceive the gullible Livy, because it was precisely Livy who caught him out on several occasions by comparing his account with those of other sources, and it is only from Livy that we gain the impression that Antias was not altogether reliable.[48]

The elementary point that republican historians could be tested by checking their versions against other sources was made already by Cassius Dio in his famous comment on the difficulties of writing imperial history: 'In former times, as we know, all matters were reported to the senate and people, even if they happened at a distance; hence all learned of them and many recorded them. Although sometimes the facts might be distorted by fear or favour, friendship or hostility, the truth could always be found in the works of other writers who recorded the same events or in the public records.'[49]

Moreover we should not forget that we are not only dealing with Livy; there are other sources too. The fact that the surviving accounts of Cicero, Diodorus, Livy and Dionysius of Halicarnassus agree closely with one another on all fundamental points (and often in matters of fine detail) can only mean that there was a basic common tradition reflected in all of them.[50] This received tradition must have been more or less faithfully reproduced in the works of earlier annalists, whose individual contributions were therefore effectively negligible and whose peculiar eccentricities could be ignored. This conclusion is further borne out by the fact that Livy and Dionysius record only minor discrepancies between their sources. Naturally I am assuming that Livy and Dionysius had actually read the sources to which they refer; the once standard view that Livy knew of the works of early writers like Fabius Pictor only from quotations in

[47] Cornell (1982) 206.
[48] Luce (1977) 148, 162.
[49] Dio 53.19.
[50] In general see Fraccaro (1952).

secondary authorities has rightly been challenged in recent studies and is almost certainly wrong.[51] As for Dionysius, his erudition is generally acknowledged.

Comparison of Livy and Dionysius can provide a possible solution to another problem, namely the 'expansion of the past'. This phrase is conventionally used to denote the process whereby the late annalists were able to write at greater length than their predecessors. Here we should note that mere 'length' is an unsatisfactory criterion for judging the character of a lost historical work.[52] Moreover the precise facts are not clear. It is not absolutely certain that the accounts of the later annalists were necessarily voluminous (with the exception, probably, of Cn. Gellius), or that those of the early annalists were invariably short. There are for example second-century annalists, such as Vennonius and Sempronius Tuditanus, of whom we know almost nothing.[53] And Fabius Pictor, although not necessarily very expansive by Dionysius' standards, did not skimp the early period, since we know that he dealt with events of 366 B.C. in his fourth book.[54] It is often assumed that the Latin text of Fabius Pictor, from which this reference is taken, was a separate work by a different man of the same name;[55] but that would not affect the point being made here, since the 'Latin Fabius' was clearly a work of the second century B.C.

However that may be, it is clear that empty rhetorical elaboration is in itself quite adequate to explain an inordinate amount of lengthening. There is no need to suppose that the long-winded historian necessarily had to invent new 'facts'. The classic illustration is the story of Coriolanus, which a modern historian could narrate in full in a couple of paragraphs, but which occupies six dramatic chapters in Livy, and over one hundred and six chapters (the bulk of Books 7 and 8) in Dionysius.[56] Amid all the rhetoric and the philosophical platitudes Dionysius nevertheless contrives to introduce no new 'facts' of any substance whatsoever.

[51] On the standard view see above n. 36. The opinion expressed in the text is derived from Laistner (1947) 83–88, Traenkle (1965), Briscoe (1973) 9, and (especially) Luce (1977) 161–81.

[52] Cf. Frier (1979) 187: 'Length is not an easy criterion to apply in discussing sources.'

[53] Peter (1914) cc–cciii; 142–47.

[54] A. Gellius *NA* 5.4.3 = Fabius (Latinus) fr. 6P. For a tentative reconstruction of the economy of Fabius' work see Beloch (1926) 99–100.

[55] Peter (1914) clxxiv–clxxvi; 112–13 (although Peter himself believed that the Latin annals were a translation of the original Greek text [lxxvii–lxxxi]). The principal arguments are outlined by Frier (1979) 246–53, listing the bibliography. I am not personally convinced by the theory of two Fabii Pictores. The Latin text of Fabius is surely more economically explained as a translation of the first Roman history.

[56] Livy 2.36–41, Dion. Hal. *AR* 7.21–8.62.

III

My contention is that the annalists had only limited scope for tampering with the received facts, and that they did not, in fact, greatly alter the basic outline of events that had been handed down to them. The same argument applies even to earlier historians like Fabius Pictor. One should not assume that because Fabius was the first Roman historian he had *carte blanche* on which to scribble anything he pleased. Rather it is probable that educated Romans of the third century B.C. were already familiar with the main elements of their historical tradition, and that Fabius broke new ground only in that he was the first of them to set it down in writing. It seems inconceivable that before Fabius no Roman had ever formulated a serious thought about the past, or that the only evidence was some scattered documents and a few haphazard stories, 'only roughly dateable at best'. In fact the chronological framework was already in existence, and it may be that the pontifical chronicle contained a systematic record of annual events. The Romans were surrounded by monuments and relics of the archaic age, regularly practised age-old cults, and were constantly reminded of the elaborate rigmarole of archaic official formulae and obsolete institutional survivals that made republican Rome a kind of living museum.

It is most unlikely that the Romans of the third century would not have been able to give some explanation of the origins of these features, to describe the development of the constitution and the main stages of the conquest of the Italian peninsula, and to recount stories of great men and noble deeds. In fact the existence of some such rudimentary historical tradition is the only reasonable explanation of the fact that extensive information about Rome's history had already found its way into the works of Greek writers such as Theophrastus, Timaeus and Hieronymus of Cardia (among others). We have the testimony of Plutarch that Fabius' version of the saga of Romulus and Remus was similar to an account that had previously been given by Diocles of Peparethos.[57] What I am suggesting is that, when the learned men of Rome first read the work of Fabius Pictor, they probably nodded their heads in agreement, rather than that they fell off their chairs in amazement.

It is important to note that what I have called the historical tradition is not the same as the tradition of literary historiography. In the Republic the story of the city's past was not confined to history

[57] Plut. *Rom.* 3. The evidence for Greek accounts of early Roman history is assembled by F. Jacoby *FGrHist* 840. General discussions of the subject include Fraser (1972) 763–69, Cornell (1975).

books, but was rather a living tradition that formed part of the consciousness of the entire community of Roman citizens. In this sense the Roman historical tradition can be defined as the sum of what successive generations of Roman citizens believed about their own past; and in a society in which tradition – the *mos maiorum* – provided the standard by which all political and moral actions were judged, the living past had an importance that is difficult for us now to appreciate. Moreover the record of past events was a matter of direct concern to the ruling class, whose position was sustained by it and whose members based their claim to high office on the historic achievements of their ancestors. The historical tradition of the Roman Republic was not an authenticated official record or an objective critical reconstruction; rather, it was an ideological construct, designed to control, to justify and to inspire.[58]

The functional role of the historical tradition in the political and social life of the Republic meant that the accepted picture of Rome's history was subject to a process of constant interpretation and reappraisal, as succeeding generations attempted to make sense of their past and to harness it to their own present needs. To my mind there is not the slightest doubt that the Romans of the last two centuries of the Republic were able to dispose of a great deal of authentic historical information, preserved and transmitted from the remote past in ways that we are not now able to reconstruct with any precision. The problem is that the Romans themselves did not necessarily comprehend the difficulties of interpretation that faced them, and were not always able to account adequately for the data at their disposal.

This happened not so much because they were not trained in the techniques of historical criticism, as because they were not in fact engaged in the process of historical research at all. The Romans' approach to their early history was uncritical because it was not founded on the basic principle of historical criticism, which is that the past is different from the present. The transmission and preservation of traditional stories of the city's history should in no sense be seen as an attempt to understand the archaic period as it really was. Rather, the Romans of the late Republic saw the remote past as an idealized model of the society in which they themselves lived. It is not therefore in any way surprising that the traditional data should have been systematically modernized in the light of contemporary experience, or that the political and social conditions of the late Republic should have been imposed upon the events of the distant past. The assimilation of political convulsions in the fifth and fourth

[58] For the idea of historical tradition as a form of social control see Plumb (1969).

centuries B.C. to the tribunates of the Gracchi and the conspiracy of Catiline is only the most obvious and easily detected sign of a much more general and pervasive tendency.[59]

It is important to note, however, that this modernizing process should not be regarded as the operation of a purely literary technique, consciously adopted by scribblers who introduced anachronistic details in order to fill gaps in the narrative or to make it more entertaining for their readers. Rather it naturally resulted from the Romans' attempts to make sense of their own past and to draw lessons from it. Inevitably they tended to emphasize the similarities, and to overlook the differences, between the conditions of the archaic period and those of their own age. The result was that they unwittingly distorted the truth; having no conception of the structural changes that had taken place, they assumed a false continuity of institutional function and mental outlook from the earliest days of the Republic. The consequence was that they completely failed to appreciate the peculiar character of the archaic age.

The point can be illustrated by an example. The sources preserve a vivid memory of plebeian agitation against the *nexum*, a form of contract by which the poor were placed in bondage and compelled to give their services to the rich in perpetuity.[60] The *nexum* was abolished by statute at the end of the fourth century B.C., and it is clear that the later jurists who tried to define it had no precise idea of its true character. In the historical tradition the *nexum* is described in terms of debt and credit, and assimilated to the debt servitude that persisted in the late Republic.[61] There is much disagreement on the nature of the *nexum*, but it is generally acknowledged that it is to be distinguished from the harsh debt procedures that were laid down in the Twelve Tables. Its connexion with debt was probably artificial, the payment of a nominal 'loan' being merely the formal means of making the contract. Here we see an example of how the tradition preserved a record of authentic historical facts, but gave an erroneous and misleading account of them. The modern historian must base his reconstruction of the historical reality on the evidence of the sources, but at the same time he must also attempt to go beyond them, by ignoring the conscious assumptions of the literary narratives and constructing hypothetical models, derived for example from comparisons with other archaic societies, which will give a better

[59] Momigliano (1967) 438–39. Cf. Crawford (1976) 198f., who refers to the 'relentless modernising' of the sources when dealing with economic facts.

[60] For a recent discussion of the *nexum* see Watson (1975) 111–24, with bibliography.

[61] Brunt (1971b) 57.

account of the traditional data and help to uncover something of the real nature of archaic Roman society.[62]

The principal conclusions of this paper can be summarized as follows:

(1) The Roman historical tradition was ultimately founded upon a sound body of authentic historical information. The basic structural data consisted of a record of events set against a background of political, military and social institutions of which many decayed relics still survived in the late Republic. We do not know precisely how the memory of historical events of the archaic age was preserved, but many explanations are possible in theory. It is an elementary point that our ignorance in this matter demands caution, not scepticism.

(2) We should be careful to distinguish between the structural data on which the surviving accounts are ultimately based and the narrative superstructure within which those data are recounted, interpreted and explained.[63] This not only means that the literary accounts of the Roman historians and annalists were secondary; as far as the archaic period is concerned that is a truism. Rather, the point is that the combination of structural facts and narrative superstructure was an inherent feature of the tradition from the very beginning, since the narrative form comes naturally to all conscious attempts to transmit information about the past. The formation of a narrative tradition about Rome's past began long before Fabius Pictor, and its development continued until the end of the Republic. Inevitably as time went on the part played by historiography became increasingly important in the preservation of information about the past and in shaping people's attitudes to it; and by the time of Augustus, when Livy and Dionysius were writing, the living historical tradition of the Republic was dying fast. It is surely for this reason, and not because of his artistic perfection, that Livy found no imitators.[64] For the Romans of the Empire the early history of the Republic was a matter of antiquarian interest, retrievable only from books. The explanation is that with the establishment of the Principate the Romans became conscious of the fact that a historical transformation had taken place which cut them off from their past. When in A.D. 14 there was hardly anyone left who remembered the Republic, the immediacy and vitality of the old historical tradition had been completely extinguished.

[62] Note for example the attempt by Finley (1981) 156–61 to reconstruct the nature of the *nexum* by setting it in the wider context of archaic forms of personal dependence attested in the Greek world.

[63] On this distinction see Momigliano (1977) 484–85.

[64] Momigliano (1961) 4.

(3) The introduction of rhetorical elaboration and philosophical moralizing, which came at a relatively late stage, had only a superficial effect on the development of the tradition. According to the view that has been outlined in this paper, the several annalists gave different versions of the same story, and their alleged shortcomings cannot in themselves justify a sceptical and hypercritical approach to the study of early Roman history. Modern accounts which lay particular emphasis on the late-republican annalists are in a sense the heirs to the old tradition of *Quellenkritik*. The methods of the *Quellenforscher* have largely been discredited for practical reasons. In the present state of the evidence it is simply not possible to identify the individual sources that lie behind the surviving narratives. But there is also a basic theoretical objection, in that the identification of particular sources would not in itself explain anything. Even if it were possible to distinguish with certainty between those parts of Livy and Dionysius that derive from (e.g.) Licinius Macer and those that come from Valerius Antias, we should gain little, partly because of our general ignorance of those writers, but more particularly because their contributions are unlikely to have had a decisive effect on the character of the tradition.

(4) The modern historian of early Rome is obliged to work with the texts that happen to have survived. That is a fact of life, and there is little point in speculating about the content of literary sources that do not survive. The loss of so many texts is obviously serious, but it is not completely disastrous if, as I have tried to argue in this paper, the basic outline of the story of archaic Rome is traditional and relatively free from conscious distortions and fabrications of literary origin. There seems no reason to doubt that the surviving accounts are fairly representative of what educated Romans believed about their own past in the last decades of the first century B.C. Obviously they thought they knew a great deal, a claim which would be hard to understand if there were not some sound basis for it. On the other hand it is clear that they were not very good at interpreting the traditional facts, and that the developed narratives give a distorted version of the truth.

We must therefore endeavour to free ourselves from the conscious presuppositions of the literary sources, and to provide a more satisfactory explanation of the information they provide. It may seem presumptuous to attempt to improve on Livy and Dionysius by reinterpreting their data; but it is surely an unjustifiable arrogance to attempt to improve on them by rejecting their evidence entirely, on the grounds that it is not demonstrably based on reliable sources.

Monuments and the Roman annalists

T. P. WISEMAN

I

In Book 6 of Apuleius' *Metamorphoses*, the girl kidnapped by robbers – who has just listened to the old woman telling the Cupid and Psyche story – makes a desperate attempt to escape by leaping on to the back of the ass and galloping off. Unaware that Lucius can understand her words, she rehearses aloud the rewards she will give him if he brings her to safety. Among these *honores* will be a sort of triumphal procession before cheering crowds, and a *dignitas gloriosa* which she defines as follows:[1]

I shall preserve the memory of my present fortune and the divine providence in a permanent record, and dedicate a painted picture of this escape in the *atrium* of my house. It will be looked at, and heard in stories, and perpetuated by the pens of learned authors – the simple history of 'The Princess who fled Captivity on Ass-back'.

This little episode seems to me to offer a useful model for our understanding of the annalists of the second and first centuries B.C., and for the place of historiography in the value system of the Roman Republic. First comes the *res gesta*, the exploit worthy of record;[2] then the rewards for achievement, *honores* and the triumph;[3] then the *monumentum* to preserve the memory of the deed;[4] then the celebration

[1] Apul. *Met.* 6.28.4 ('honores'), 28.6 ('gaudiis popularium pomparum ovantem'), 29.2: 'nam memoriam praesentis fortunae meae divinaeque providentiae perpetua testatione signabo, et depictam in tabula fugae praesentis imaginem meae domus atrio dedicabo. Visetur et in fabulis audietur doctorumque stilis rudis perpetuabitur historia "Asino vectore virgo regia fugiens captivitatem".'

[2] Cf. Cic. *de or.* 2.63 on the subject-matter of history 'in rebus magnis memoriaque dignis'; for *res gestae* and *res Romanae* as history-book titles, cf. Nonius 835L, Gell. *NA* 11.8.2, Diod. 7.5.4, etc.

[3] On triumphs as the annalist's subject-matter, cf. Asellio fr. 2P (Gell. *NA* 6.18.9): 'scribere autem bellum initum quo consule et quo confectum sit et quis triumphans introierit ex eo [...]'.

[4] Cf. Cic. *II Verr.* 4.69 on *monumenta* and the *nominis aeterna memoria*; Pliny *NH* 35.22f. on the *tabula Valeria* and other painted records of *res gestae*. For paintings in the *atria* of private houses, cf. Bonfante (1978) 139 on the François tomb, and the bibliography cited by her in n. 19. Trimalchio's *atrium* featured a painted record of his life, including a quasi-triumphal entry ('Minerva ducente Romam intrabat'): Petr. *Sat.* 29.3–6.

of it by story-tellers and learned historians, for the unlettered multitude and the literate élite respectively.

The role of the professional story-teller and the proximity of history-writing to fiction and the novel are important subjects which are now at last receiving proper attention,[5] but the point I want to explore here is a different one – the relation to both *fabulator* and historian alike of the *monumentum* which provided them with their material. It is clear from the train of thought in Apuleius that the primary record of the exploit would be the painting, logically prior to the *fabulae* and the *historia*. They would be interpretations of it, and not necessarily accurate interpretations either. The girl was not, after all, a princess. Her family was rich, and of high aristocracy in the locality – *domi nobilis*, certainly, but not royal.[6] The learned authors' history of the *virgo regia* would evidently be based on a misinterpretation of the pictorial record, the *monumentum*.

Monuments formed an important part of the early Roman historians' material, from the so-called tomb of Romulus in the *comitium* to the *tabulae triumphales* of victorious second-century proconsuls.[7] For the regal and early-republican periods, of course, we may suspect that they were used as foundations for whatever aetiological stories they could be made to fit. The monument under the black paving-stones in the *comitium* is itself a good example: the tomb of Romulus (though not if you believed that Romulus miraculously disappeared at the *palus Capreae*); or the tomb of Faustulus, killed in the faction-fight between the supporters of Remus and Romulus; or the tomb of Hostus Hostilius, killed in the battle against the Sabines.[8] Similarly, there was a monument under white paving-stones somewhere near the Circus which was known as the Pyre of the Nine Tribunes: nine patrician ex-consuls, killed as *tribuni militum* in battle against the Volsci; or nine tribunes of the *plebs* burnt alive by their colleague P. Mucius for complicity in Sp. Cassius' attempted *coup d'état*; or nine bold tribunes 'delivered to the flames' by the populace at the secret instigation of the patricians.[9]

[5] See esp. Scobie (1979) 229–59, and Salles (1981) 3–20. For history and the novel, cf. Momigliano (1978) 74 (= (1980) 375), and Gabba (1981) 53; for an example of fiction becoming 'history', see Winkler (1980) 175–81. There is a lively polemic on the subject in Woodman (1983b) 24–27.

[6] Apul. *Met.* 4.23.3 'virginem filo liberalem et, ut matronatus eius indicabat, summatem regionis'; cf. 23.5 (wealth), 24.4 ('tanta familia'), 7.13.1 ('clientes', etc.).

[7] *Comitium* 'tomb': schol. Hor. *Epod.* 16.13 (quoting Varro), Festus 184L, Dion. Hal. *AR* 1.87.2, 3.1.2. *Tabulae triumphales*: Livy 40.52.4–6 (L. Aemilius Regillus), 41.28. 8–9 (Ti. Gracchus), cf. Keil *Grammatici Latini* 6.265, 293.

[8] See previous note; Coarelli (1977) 215–29, esp. 221f.

[9] Respectively Festus 180L, Val. Max. 6.3.2, Dio 5.22.1 = Zon. 7.17.

We cannot simply assume that accurate knowledge of the true nature of such monuments survived till the beginning of the Roman historiographical tradition – and the same may be said of such other 'documents' of early history as the tombs of the Horatii, the *tigillum sororium*, the statues of Horatius Cocles and Cloelia (or Valeria), the Column of Minucius and the *busta Gallica*.[10] The stories that accounted for them were part of the 'expansion of the past' (to borrow Badian's expressive phrase) – the elaboration into satisfying detailed 'history' of the meagre record of Rome's early past that was available to Fabius Pictor and Cincius Alimentus at the end of the third century.[11]

For events after about the time of the Samnite wars, however, the situation is different. In general, more reliable information was available, since what happened was within the memory of the fathers and grandfathers of men Fabius and Cincius could have talked to. And, in particular, the *monumenta* of the period were of a kind with which the first historians were wholly familiar. It is precisely in the generation around 300 B.C. – that heroic age of Roman conquest and expansion – that we see reliably manifested for the first time the familiar self-glorifying ethos of the Roman republican ruling class: in 312, with Ap. Claudius, the first road and aqueduct to be named after their originator; in 293, with Sp. Carvilius, the first self-portrait statue dedicated by a *triumphator*; in 272, with L. Papirius Cursor, the first known pictorial representation of a triumph; and so on.[12] Fabius, Cincius and their senatorial successors understood that ethos at first hand. Indeed, their own works were a part of it – *monumenta litterarum* designed, like other *monumenta*, to preserve *res gestae* from oblivion.[13]

[10] Tombs of Horatii: Livy 1.25.14, Dion. Hal. *AR* 3.22.1, Mart. 3.47.3. *Tigillum sororium*: Livy 1.26.13, Dion. Hal. *AR* 3.22.8, Festus 380L. Cocles statue: Livy 2.10.12, Dion. Hal. *AR* 5.25.2, Plut. *Popl.* 16.7, Plin. *NH* 34.29, Gell. *NA* 4.5.1–4. Cloelia statue: Piso fr. 20P (Plin. *NH* 34.29), Livy 2.13.11, Dion. Hal. *AR* 5.35.2, Plut. *Popl.* 19.5 and 8 (Valeria). Column of Minucius: Dion. Hal. *AR* 12.4.6, Plin. *NH* 18.15, 34.21, cf. Livy 4.16.2 (where read 'bove aurato ⟨et statua⟩ extra portam Trigeminam' with Crévier); *RRC* 273, 275. *Busta Gallica*: *ILLRP* 464.6, Varro *LL* 5.157, Livy 5.48.3, 22.14.11.

[11] Dion. Hal. *AR* 1.6.2 (with Balsdon (1953) 158–64, and Gabba (1967) 135–69), Badian (1966) 11f.

[12] Diod. 20.36.2 etc. (see also Cic. *Mil.* 37 for the Via Appia as a *monumentum*); Plin. *NH* 34.43; Festus 228L, cf. Degrassi (1947) 546. The first coffin in the *sepulcrum Scipionum* is that of L. Scipio Barbatus, *cos.* 298, though his *elogium* was evidently not carved on it until two or three generations later (*ILLRP* 309). For the significance of the late-fourth-century 'Anfänge römischen Repräsentationskunst', see Hölscher (1978) 315–57.

[13] Cato fr. 83P (Gell. *NA* 3.7.19) on Leonidas: 'virtutes decoravere monumentis: signis, statuis, elogiis, historiis aliisque rebus.' Cf. Festus (Paulus) 123L: 'monimentum est [...] quicquid ob memoriam alicuius factum est, ut fana, porticus, scripta et carmina.'

But Fabius, Cincius and their senatorial successors are one thing; first-century, non-senatorial historians like Quadrigarius, Antias and Livy himself are quite another. *They* could quite easily make mistakes in the interpretation of monuments from the middle Republic. For instance, the existence of a statue of Africanus on the façade of the tomb of the Scipiones gave rise to the false tradition that he was buried there, and not at Liternum.[14] Inscriptions below honorific *imagines* were notoriously unreliable, as Livy complained; and we know from Cicero's correspondence that any historian who relied on the *tituli* of Q. Metellus Scipio's statues of his ancestors on the Capitol would be misled by the aristocratic dedicator's own ignorance of his family history.[15] On top of honest errors of that sort is the suspicion that the later annalists continued to use for third- and even second-century history the technique that enabled them to fill the wide open spaces of the early Republic,[16] with the result that third-century monuments which Fabius and Cincius would have understood correctly could be interpreted as 'evidence' for the late-republican historian's own irresponsible inventions.

It is against that background that I want to consider two unhistorical episodes from that important and ill-documented decade, the 260s B.C. In one case the historian's invention was based, like the 'Princess on Ass-back', on a misinterpreted monument; in the other, it was only made possible by the disappearance of the monument that proved it false.

II

Suetonius opens his *Tiberius* with examples (three each) of the good and bad deeds of the emperor's Claudian ancestors.[17] The *egregia merita* are: first, Ap. Caecus' speech against making peace with Pyrrhus; second, Ap. Caudex's command of the first Roman army to cross to Sicily; and third, C. Nero's defeat of Hasdrubal at the Metaurus. The *sequius admissa* begin with Appius the Decemvir's attempt to make Verginia his slave, and conclude with P. Claudius Pulcher's treatment of the sacred chickens; between those two, however, comes a very mysterious item:

> Claudius †Drusus statua sibi diademata ad Appi Forum posita Italiam per clientes occupare temptavit.
>
> Caecus, *Mommsen*; Crassus, *Hirschfeld*; Rusus, *Fruin* (*potius* Russus, *Ihm*).

[14] Livy 38.56.2–4, with Coarelli (1972) 72f.

[15] *Tituli imaginum*: Livy 8.40.4, cf. 4.16.3–4. Metellus Scipio's ἀνιστορησία: Cic. *ad Att.* 6.1.17 (q.v. also for the possibility of masons' errors).

[16] For some possible examples see Wiseman (1979) 90–103.

[17] Suet. *Tib.* 2.1–2: dates 279/8, 264, 207; 449, 268 (see below), 249.

Both lists are in chronological order, so 'Claudius Drusus' must antedate the consulship of P. Claudius Pulcher in 249. Mommsen's suggestion is surely ruled out by the presence of Caecus in the list of good Claudii, while that of Hirschfeld is hard to reconcile with the placing of the statue at Forum Appi: the 'Forum' presupposes the road on which it was founded (Via Appia, 312 B.C.), while the *cognomen* Crassus is only attested for Claudii of the fifth century and the first half of the fourth.[18] The Fruin/Ihm solution is clearly preferable: 'Russus' as the *cognomen* of Ap. Claudius (*cos.* 268), already attested by the 'Chronographer of A.D. 354', was confirmed in 1925 by the discovery of the relevant part of the Augustan consular *fasti*,[19] and the corruption to Drusus – a name which appears frequently in the *Tiberius* – is a particularly easy one to explain.

Ap. Claudius Russus was Appius Caecus' eldest son, consul in 268 with P. Sempronius Sophus. Both men celebrated triumphs over the Picentes (attested in the *fasti triumphales*), but Claudius died soon after – probably right at the end of the year, since no suffect was elected.[20] The defeat of the Picentes was practically the final stage in the Roman conquest of cis-Apennine Italy.[21] It is true that the Sallentini in the far south-east remained (they were dealt with the following year), but it must have been tempting for the consuls of 268 to claim the credit of having brought all of Italy under Roman control.

One of them at least evidently did so. Sempronius vowed the temple of Tellus during his campaign, and presumably built it *ex manubiis* after his triumph. In it, there was a map of Italy painted on the wall.[22] The known parallels – Ti. Gracchus' map of Sardinia in the Mater Matuta temple, and the plan of Carthage exhibited in the *forum Romanum* by L. Mancinus – strongly suggest that the map was not mere decoration, but meant as visual evidence of the founder's *gloria*.[23]

Claudius Russus died before he could create a similar *monumentum*, but his statue was set up where his father's memory lived on most strongly: Appius' *forum* on Appius' road. It is reasonable to suppose that he was portrayed in triumphal costume, and as certain as can be that the inscription on the base made the most of his achievements. We may compare the *elogium* of T. Annius on the base of the

[18] *Cos.* 451, *Xvir* 451/50; *tr. mil. cos. pot.* 424; *tr. mil. cos. pot.* 403; *dict.* 362, *cos.* 349: see Degrassi (1947) *sub annis*.

[19] Degrassi (1947) 5, 40 (fr. xix), 432f., Fruin (1894) 103–18, Ihm (1901) 303.

[20] Degrassi (1947) 547 (triumph), 40 (*in m. m. e.*).

[21] Livy *per.* 15, Eutrop. 2.16, Flor. 1.19.

[22] Flor. 1.19.2, Varro *RR* 1.2.1.

[23] Livy 41.28.10 (Ti. Gracchus), Pliny *NH* 35.23 (Mancinus); cf. also Plin. *NH* 35.22 (M'. Valerius Messalla), Festus 228L (M. Fulvius Flaccus, T. Papirius Cursor) for contemporary paintings – though not geographical in content – as triumphal *monumenta*.

statue set up at Forum Anni on *his* road, or that of Sempronius Tuditanus below his statue at Aquileia, presumably copied from the *tabula triumphalis* dedicated on the Capitol;[24] the tombs of Scipio Barbatus and his son show that a third-century version could be just as boastful as these second-century ones. It was only ten years since old Appius' speech of defiance to Pyrrhus' envoy; the Claudii had plenty to be proud about, and might well have emphasized the completion of the conquest of Italy by Russus' triumph, just as his colleague evidently did on the walls of the temple of Tellus. Did some such phrase as *tota Italia occupata* occur on the statue-base of Claudius Russus?

According to Suetonius, the statue was *diademata*. The *diadema*, a white head-band tied at the back, was the symbol of kingship in the Hellenistic world ever since Alexander took it over along with the rest of the apparatus of the Persian monarchy.[25] Most conspicuous, and clearly visible on the coins of all the rulers of the Successor kingdoms, were the two ends behind the knot, that hung, or floated like streamers, over the neck and shoulders of the king.[26]

By the time of the late Republic, the *diadema* was retrospectively attributed to the kings of Rome, but there is no evidence – or likelihood – that this idea predates the second century B.C.[27] Similarly, Dionysius I of Syracuse is credited with a *diadema* only in the context of the posturings of Hieronymus in 215 B.C.; a century earlier the worst that could be said of him was that he wore a golden *stephanos*.[28] So I am sure Weinstock was wrong to take Suetonius' report literally.[29] Even if one could believe in an early-third-century attempt at *regnum*, the symbol of that aspiration would not be a *diadema*. Whatever Claudius Russus' statue was crowned with, it wasn't that.

Crowns and wreaths could signify many things in the early and middle Republic,[30] but in the case of Claudius Russus there is no

24 *ILLRP* 454, with Wiseman (1964) 30–37 and (1969) 88–91; *ILLRP* 335, with Morgan (1973) 40–48.

25 Just. 12.3.8, etc. White: Curt. 6.6.4, Lucian *Dialogi mortuorum 13. Diogenis et Alexandri* 393, Apul. *Met.* 10.30, Val. Max. 6.2.7, Festus (Paulus) 28L, Tac. *Ann.* 6.37.2.

26 Duris in *FGrHist* 76 F 14 (Athen. 12.536A), on Demetrius Poliorcetes. Coins: Davis–Kraay (1973) *passim*; also *RRC* plates XL.293.1 (Philip V, 113/12 B.C.), LXIV.543.1 (Cleopatra, 32 B.C.).

27 *RRC* plates LI.425.1 (Ancus, 56 B.C.), LIII.446.1 (Numa, 49 B.C.); Juv. 8.259f. 'diadema Quirini'. *Pace* Alföldi (1935) 145, there is no reason to think that the statues of the kings on the Capitol were *diadematae*: cf. Hölscher (1978) 331f. for the irrelevance of the late-republican coins to the Capitol statues.

28 Livy 24.5.4; *contra*, Duris in *FGrHist* 76 F 14 (Athen. 12.535E).

29 Weinstock (1971) 334, cf. 320, attributing the statue (with Mommsen) to Ap. Caecus, and suggesting 'he could have done it under Sicilian influence' (i.e. Dionysius I; but see previous note).

30 Prizes at *ludi* (though not relevant to men of rank later than the fifth century B.C.): Plin. *NH* 21.5–7, with Rawson (1981) 1–5. Military decorations: Plin. *NH* 16.6–14, 22.4–14, Gell. *NA* 5.6, with Maxfield (1981) esp. c. 4.

need to look further than the symbols of the triumph. It was precisely in this period, as we should expect, that the ceremony and trappings of the triumph took on their classic form, as the glorification of the *triumphator* to an all but superhuman level.[31] Prominent among those trappings were the laurel-wreath worn by the *triumphator*, and the gold-leafed *corona Etrusca* held above his head by the slave whose duty it was to repeat the apotropaic formula 'hominem te esse memento'.[32] It would be reasonable to expect that Russus was portrayed wearing one or other of these.

Any wreath or garland could be made more honorific by the addition of *lemnisci*, coloured ribbons binding the leaves or flowers.[33] In particular, they were attached to the victor's laurel-wreath, hanging from it like streamers: the coins of the Roman Republic show many examples of the laurel-wreath, usually in the hands of Victory, with the two *lemnisci* fluttering below.[34] (The *corona Etrusca* was decorated in the same way, though for that the 'ribbons' were of gold leaf.)[35] The earliest representation we have is almost contemporary with Russus' statue, and an illustration of precisely the ideological value-system that caused it to be set up. At some date between 265 and 242 B.C. the Romans minted silver didrachms with a superb reverse design of Victory attaching a wreath to a palm-branch; the goddess is hanging the wreath by its *lemnisci*, two long ribbons which would be floating out behind the wearer's neck and shoulders if the wreath were on a *triumphator*'s head.[36]

We do not know what Russus' statue was made of (presumably

[31] For the development of the triumph see Warren (1970) 49–66. The classic form – which she attributes to Hellenistic influence – is first attested in 201 B.C. (triumph of Scipio Africanus, App. *Pun.* 66); but Festus' item on the *toga picta* (228L: the latest *toga sine pictura* he knew of was from 264 B.C.) shows that the development was under way two or three generations earlier. For the new ideology of victory in the late fourth and early third centuries (cf. n. 12 above), see Weinstock (1957) 211–47, *RE* 8A, cols. 2486–87, and Hölscher (1967) 136–72.

[32] Juv. 10.39f., Tertull. *Coron.* 13.1, Plin. *NH* 21.6, 33.11. Cf. Dion. Hal. *AR* 3.62.2: the golden crown was supposed to have been part of the regalia of the Etruscan kings of Rome. Pompey in 63 (Vell. 2.40.4; *RRC* 450) and Caesar in 45 (Dio 43.43.1, 44.6.3, 11.2) were given the right to wear it at *ludi*: see Kraft (1952–53) 7–97, with Versnel (1970) 74–77, and *RRC* 488 n. 1.

[33] Varro *apud* Serv. *Aen.* 5.269 ('magni honoris'), Plin. *NH* 16.65 ('antiquorum honore'); Plaut. *Pseud.* 1265 (convivial garlands).

[34] Plut. *Sulla* 27.4; cf. Serv. *Ecl.* 9.46 (*sidus Iulium*), Plb. 18.46.2 and Suet. *Nero* 25.2 (*lemnisci* alone as a sign of triumph). *RRC* plates XIV.71.1a (211–208 B.C.), XXXVI.246.1, XXXVII.247.1, 253.1, 253.3, XXXIX.280.1, XLIX.387.1, LI.419.1e, 419.2, 421.1, LIII.449.4, LXIV.545.1, 546.2a. Ennius *Trag.* fr. 23 Jocelyn ('volans de caelo cum corona et taeniis') has been plausibly attributed to a prologue spoken by Victory (cf. Plaut. *Amph.* 41f.): Skutsch (1968) 175–77.

[35] Plin. *NH* 21.6; *RRC* plates LI.426.4b, LII.435.1 (Pompey's crown, n. 32 above).

[36] *RRC* plate I.22.1; cf. Cic. *Rosc. Am.* 100 (*palma lemniscata*). Two laurel-wreaths hang in a similar way from a palm-branch carried by an eagle on the Sullan monument from the Capitol: Crawford (1978) plate 6.

bronze or terracotta); nor what condition it was in when it was seen by the historian that Suetonius used; nor how high it stood on its base, and how visible were the details of its headgear. But it is a natural and obvious conjecture that the unknown historian misinterpreted the ribbons of a triumphal crown or laurel-wreath as the ends of a *diadema*. The colour is important: a *diadema* was white, and *lemnisci* were brightly coloured (or gold).[37] If the statue was painted clay, the colours might well have faded away after two hundred years or so. If it was bronze, or if its crown at least was metal, there would be no way of distinguishing the type of ribbon intended.

But surely anyone could tell the difference between a wreath of laurels (or a crown of gilded leaves) and a plain headband? Perhaps it was not as simple as that. At the Lupercalia in 44 B.C., the *diadema* Antony offered Caesar was not just a plain headband, but 'a diadem twined in a wreath of laurel'.[38] Evidently you could have something that looked like an innocent laurel-wreath but incorporated a diadem, presumably in the form of white binding ribbons. A few days earlier, Caesar's statue had been crowned with a 'corona laurea *candida fascia* praeligata'; the tribunes Marullus and Flavus had no objection to the laurel-wreath itself, but demanded the removal of the white binding and imprisoned the man who had put it there.[39] People evidently looked with care at these symbolic objects, interpreting the significance of every detail. And that no doubt applied as much to Pompey in the fifties as to Caesar in the forties; then too honorific crowns and quasi-diadems were among the signs that might indicate a coming *regnum*.[40]

My guess is that at some time in the fifties or forties B.C., when such matters were much on people's minds, the old triumphal statue of Ap. Claudius Russus was misinterpreted – wilfully, I imagine – by a historian anxious to find one more episode in the brutal and arrogant story of the patrician Claudii. The abuse of *clientela* was a commonplace in that story;[41] with the help, perhaps, of an ambiguous phrase

[37] *Diadema*: n. 25 above. *Lemnisci*: Festus (Paulus) 102L, Serv. *Aen*. 5.269; Plin. *NH* 21.6 (gold).

[38] διάδημα στεφάνῳ δάφνης περιπεπλεγμένον (Plut. *Caes*. 61.3), διάδημα δὲ δάφνης στεφάνῳ περιελίξας (Plut. *Ant*. 12.2), δάφνινον ἔχων στέφανον, ἐντὸς δὲ διάδημα περιφαινόμενον (Nic. Dam. in *FGrHist* 90F 130.71).

[39] Suet. *DJ* 79.1, App. *BC* 2.108 (ἀναπεπλεγμένης ταινίας λευκῆς).

[40] See n. 32 above; Val. Max. 6.2.7 (Favonius on the *diadema*); *RRC* 457, plate LII.435.1 (Pompey's *corona* as a symbol of monarchy); Brutus *apud* Suet. *DJ* 49.2 (Octavius on Pompey as *rex*); Plut. *Pomp*. 67.3, *Caes*. 41.1 (Ahenobarbus on Pompey as king of kings).

[41] E.g. Dion. Hal. *AR* 8.90.1, 11.28.5, Livy 3.44.5, 56.2, 9.46.10f. (cf. Plin. *NH* 33.17), *per*. 19 (cf. Suet. *Tib*. 2.2). The origin of the theme is the arrival of the first Appius in Rome 'magna clientium comitatus manu' (Livy 2.16.4, cf. Suet. *Tib*. 1.1), the elaboration of what was probably a genuine event: for the historical context see Cornell in Cornell–Matthews (1982) 24f.

in the *elogium* beneath the statue, all he had to do was see the ends of a *diadema* in the *lemnisci* of Russus' wreath or crown, and he could produce the dramatic episode of which Suetonius' sentence is the one surviving echo.

I think it is likely that the whole tradition of *superbia Claudiana* was created by a historian writing at precisely that period.[42] Whether or not that is accepted, I hope at least to have shown that the *statua diademata* at Forum Appi is not a historical but a historiographical phenomenon. Like the girl in the story of the escape on ass-back, Russus is given royal rank through the misreading of his *monumentum*.

III

In 264 B.C., the consuls were Ap. Claudius C.f. Caudex and M. Fulvius Q.f. Flaccus. Claudius was famous in Roman history for being the first to lead a Roman army overseas, in the opening campaign of the First Punic War.[43] Fulvius continued the war against the 'slaves' of Volsinii after the previous Roman commander's death from wounds; he besieged the city and took it, bringing back 2,000 bronze statues in his booty.[44] He triumphed *de Vulsiniensibus* on 1 November, and the temple of Vertumnus was his triumphal *monumentum*.[45]

Excavation at the S. Omobono site in 1961 revealed the remains of a circular base in peperino, evidently intended to display some of the statues. The inscription on it reads 'M. FOLV[IO. Q.F. COS]OL. D. VOLSI[NIO. CAP]TO'.[46] Like the two peperino altars on either side of it, it originally stood on level 4 in the stratigraphic series, a pavement of thick blocks of Monteverde tufa, but was demolished and its pieces used in the laying of level 5, a pavement of thin slabs of the same stone.[47] The great podium that was raised after the destruction of the archaic temple(s) on the site – on which the twin temples of Fortuna and Mater Matuta were

[42] Wiseman (1979) 104–11. For doubts, Rawson (1980) 18, Briscoe (1981) 50f.

[43] Sen. *de brev. vit.* 13.4, Suet. *Tib.* 2.1, Flor. 1.18.5, Sil. 6.660, [Aurelius Victor] *de vir. ill.* 37.3; cf. Enn. *Ann.* 223V 'Appius indixit Karthaginiensibus bellum'.

[44] Volsinii war: Flor. 1.16, Zon. 8.7, Val. Max. 9.1 *externa* 2, [Aurelius Victor] *de vir. ill.* 36. Statues: Metrodorus of Scepsis in *FGrHist* 184F12 (Plin. *NH* 34.34).

[45] Degrassi (1947) 74f.; Festus 228L (painting in temple of Fulvius in triumphal dress); cf. Prop. 4.2.3f. (Vertumnus' origin from Volsinii).

[46] Torelli (1968) 71–75. The original publication was by Mercando–Ioppolo–Degrassi (1966) 35ff.

[47] I use the numeration of Sommella (1968) 63–70, followed by Sydow (1973) 580–85. Sommella's levels 4 and 5 are labelled respectively V and VI in Coarelli (1974) 282f., and on the diagram in Coarelli (1980) 315, though in the text of the latter (pp. 315–17) Coarelli refers to them as VI and VII respectively.

built – may have been paved first in *cappellaccio* (level 3), unless this was merely a foundation for the tufa-block pavement.[48] At any rate, Fulvius' inscription now gives 264 B.C. as a firm *terminus ante quem* for the latter.

Much more interesting is the fact that level 5, which buried the remains of Fulvius' monument, must be dated to the reconstruction programme begun in 212, after the disastrous fire the previous year which ravaged the whole area from Salinae to the Porta Carmentalis and destroyed the twin temples.[49] The consuls of 212 were Q. Fulvius Flaccus (for the third time) and Ap. Claudius Pulcher, respectively son and great-nephew of the consuls of 264; they had been elected under the dictatorship of C. Claudius Cento (*cos.* 240), who was Claudius' uncle and had just named Fulvius as his *magister equitum*; Fulvius' brother Gnaeus was elected praetor at the same time.[50] The stemmata in Fig. 1 show the essential relationships.

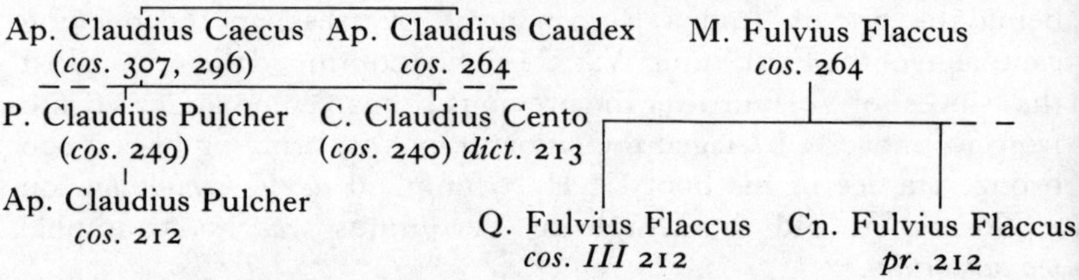

Fig. 1. Stemmata of consuls of 212 B.C.

The bronze statues on M. Flaccus' *monumentum* were presumably destroyed in the fire; all the same, it is striking that so powerful a figure as his eldest son, now in his third consulship, failed to replace it and allowed it to be completely dismantled and buried under the new pavement. It cannot have been anything but a blow to the *dignitas* of the Fulvian house. Perhaps the explanation lies in the defeat of the praetor Cn. Fulvius Flaccus by Hannibal in Apulia that year. His brother the consul was busy with the siege of Capua at the time – it was Appius who returned to conduct the elections – and in his absence the *triumviri* entrusted with the job of rebuilding the temples may not have felt it necessary to replace the Fulvian monument.[51]

'Heu quam difficilis gloriae custodia est!' That *sententia* of

[48] So Sommella (1968) 65; cf. Gjerstad (1960) 386, though his dating must be abandoned in the light of the new evidence. However, Coarelli (1974) 283 and (1980) 317, numbering the *cappellaccio* layer as IV in the former and as V in the latter, believes it to be a separate pavement of the early fourth century; cf. Sydow (1973) 581f.

[49] Livy 24.47.15 (fire), 25.7.6 (reconstruction begun); cf. Torelli (1968) 74.

[50] Livy 25.2.3–5.

[51] Livy 25.7.6 (*triumviri*), 21 (defeat), 41.10 (elections).

Publilius Syrus finds another such example, I think, in the *area sacra* of the Largo Argentina: A. Postumius Albinus' beautifully inscribed altar, erected in front of the temple of Feronia at some time in the second half of the second century B.C., was covered over by L. Minucius Rufus in 106 with the paving of his triumphal monument, the Porticus Minucia; four years earlier an A. Albinus had been humiliatingly defeated by Jugurtha, so the dedicator and his family were in no position to protest.[52] Later examples of the destruction of *monumenta* are more familiar: for instance Sulla's removal of the trophies of Marius from the Capitol, or Clodius' demolition of the Porticus Catuli on the Palatine in order to build a shrine to Libertas on the site, or the senatorial proposal in A.D. 41 to abolish the memory of the Iulii Caesares by pulling down their temples.[53]

It is a pity that we do not know who the *triumviri* were who dealt this blow to the prestige of the Fulvii in 212 B.C. Nor do we know what Q. Flaccus' consular colleague Ap. Claudius thought about it. There is no hint of rivalry between them in Livy's narrative on the campaigns of 212/11; on the other hand, there are indications that at some point in the annalistic tradition an attempt was made to exalt Appius at Flaccus' expense. Livy's story of the execution of the Campanian prisoners after the fall of Capua shows clearly that at least one of his sources had made a great melodramatic scene out of Flaccus' brutality, either contrasting it with Appius' moderation or making it happen only after Appius' death from his wound.[54] (It is also clear from Silius Italicus – and an echo in Livy – that there was one version which emphasized Appius' heroism in the engagement that led to his death.)[55] In the light of these indications it is worth looking at a curious passage in the anonymous work *de viris illustribus* on the war against the Volsinian 'slaves' in 264:

36 Vulsinii, Etruriae nobile oppidum, luxuria paene perierunt. Nam cum temere servos manumitterent, dein in curiam legerent, consensu eorum oppressi. Cum multa indigna paterentur, clam a Roma auxilium petierunt, missusque Decius Mus libertinos omnes aut in carcere necavit aut dominis in servitutem restituit. *37* Appius Claudius victis Vulsiniensibus cogno-

[52] Publ. Syr. *Sent.* 203. Coarelli–Kajanto–Nyberg–Steinby (1981) 12–15 (paving levels and altar), 34–42 (identification of *porticus* and temple), 91–96 (date of altar inscription). Sall. *BJ* 35–42, esp. 38.7 and 43.1 ('foeda fuga'), 39.1 ('Aulo omnes infesti'). It is possible, but not certain, that the A. Albinus of the altar inscription was the same man as the unfortunate general (later *cos.* 99), serving as *duumvir lege Plaetoria* at an early stage in his career.

[53] Sulla: Vell. 2.43.4, Suet. *DJ* 11, Plut. *Caes.* 6, Val. Max. 6.9.14. Clodius: Cic. *de dom.* 112, 137, *de har. resp.* 33 (*ad Att.* 4.2.5, 3.2 for the restoration of the portico in 57). A.D. 41: Suet. *Gaius* 60.

[54] Livy 26.15.1–16.4; on Appius' wound see also Zon. 9.6.

[55] Sil. 13.445–68, Livy 26.6.5 'cui suos ante prima signa adhortanti [...] ictum est'.

mento Caudex dictus frater Caeci fuit. Consul ad Mamertinos liberandos missus [...etc.]

I think the modern section numbers are misleading in treating the first three sentences as a separate item on Decius Mus, presumably the consul of 279. He is given no *praenomen*, his command against Pyrrhus at the battle of Ausculum is not mentioned, and no cross-reference is made, as would be expected, to his father and grandfather, already dealt with in sections 26 and 27.[56] On the other hand, several items in the collection begin not with the name of the protagonist, but with an introductory passage setting the scene for his exploits.[57] In the case of Ap. Claudius Caudex, the explanation of his *cognomen* – one of the author's favourite themes[58] – requires just such a preliminary account of the punishment of the Volsinienses. For a *caudex* was the log of wood to which imprisoned slaves were shackled.[59]

The word also meant 'blockhead',[60] which is perhaps more in character with Roman habits of bestowing *cognomina*. It may be that the association of Appius with the capture of Volsinii – and the consequent misdating of that event to before his consulship – was the work of a historian anxious to find a more honorific explanation of the name.[61] Certainly the *res gestae* of both Ap. Caudex and Decius Mus were narrated and interpreted in widely differing terms by different annalists. Was it Caudex or M'. Valerius Maximus (*cos.* 263) who defeated King Hiero of Syracuse and celebrated a triumph for it?[62] Did Decius Mus imitate the example of his father and grandfather by sacrificing himself on the field of Ausculum, or at least announce that he would, in order to damage the morale of Pyrrhus' troops?[63] Such questions, and the answers that could be offered to them, clearly

[56] See esp. [Aurelius Victor] *de vir. ill.* 27.1 'Publius Decius Decii filius [...]'. Ausculum: Cic. *de fin.* 2.61, *Tusc.* 1.89, Eutrop. 2.13.4, Zon. 8.5, Dio 10 fr. 43.

[57] E.g. [Aurelius Victor] *de vir. ill.* 11.1, 16.1, 21.1, 25.1, 46.1, 48.1.

[58] E.g. [Aurelius Victor] *de vir. ill.* 11.1 (Cocles), 19.1 (Coriolanus), 24.1 (Capitolinus), 31.1 (Cursor), 49.1 (Africanus), 60.1 (Achaicus), 61.1 (Macedonicus), 75.1 (Felix).

[59] Plaut. *Poen.* 1153, cf. 1365 'lignea in custodia', Prop. 4.7.44, Juv. 2.57.

[60] Ter. *HT* 877, cf. Petr. *Sat.* 74.13. On pejorative *cognomina* see Kajanto (1965) 68f., 264f.

[61] For another suggestion, even more far-fetched, see Sen. *de brev. vit.* 13.4.

[62] Narrative sources: Plb. 1.11–17, Diod. 23.1–4, Zon. 8.8. Caudex is credited with the victory in [Aurelius Victor] *de vir. ill.* 37.5, and with a triumph in Eutrop. 2.18.3 and Sil. 6.662 (implied also by Suet. *Tib.* 1.2?), but the Augustan *fasti* list Valerius' triumph only (Degrassi (1947) 74f.). No doubt Valerius' version prevailed with the help of the famous picture he put up on the wall of the Curia (Plin. *NH* 35.22). See now Eckstein (1980) 181–84.

[63] Narrative sources: Dion. Hal. *AR* 20.1–3, Plut. *Pyrrh.* 21.5–10, Front. *Strat.* 2.3.21, Oros. 4.1.19–22. *Devotio*: Cic. *de fin.* 2.61, *Tusc.* 1.89 (both 45 B.C.), though in 56 B.C. Cicero mentions only the two elder Mures (*Sest.* 48); Ennius *Ann.* 208–10V with Skutsch (1968) 54–59. Intention only: Dio 10 fr. 43, Zon. 8.5. In Flor. 1.13.9 Decius is not even at the battle, which is fought 'Curio Fabricioque consulibus': M'. Curius Dentatus was consul in 290, 275 and 274, C. Fabricius Luscinus in 282 and 278.

mattered to the historians of the second and first centuries B.C., and to their readers, who included the descendants of the great men themselves.

What matters here is that Decius Mus and Ap. Caudex get the credit for what was really M. Fulvius Flaccus' achievement. The Fulvii certainly had some dramatic ups and downs: Cn. Flaccus' defeat in 212 B.C., M. Nobilior's triumph from Aetolia in 189 and his censorship ten years later, the execution of M. Flaccus and his son after the Gracchan *seditio* of 121, and the power and influence of Fulvia in the late forties as the wife of Antony. There is no difficulty in imagining a context in which a historian might wish to take M. Flaccus' *res gesta* away from him and give it to someone else. The point that concerns us here, however, is that the destruction of the *monumentum* itself must have made it much easier for the false version to gain currency, and much more difficult for the Fulvii to nail the lie.[64]

And yet – we must remember the *virgo regia* and the diademed statue. It is possible that even if M. Flaccus' *monumentum* had survived, the malicious ingenuity of a hostile historian might have found a way to misinterpret it as meaning something quite different.

IV

Malice is not at all an inappropriate concept to invoke when considering the motivation of first-century historians. The circumstantial evidence for it is abundant, and there is one example that happens to be explicitly attested: the allegation in Theophanes of treasonable correspondence between P. Rutilius Rufus and Mithridates.[65] We can be sure that some at least of Theophanes' Roman contemporaries, who were quite familiar with the standards of Hellenistic historiography,[66] were capable of equally unscrupulous invention if it suited their purpose.

As we saw at the beginning, works of historiography were *monumenta litterarum*, designed like other *monumenta* to preserve the glory of great deeds. But the corollary of glory is rivalry and *invidia*. When a historian attacked the record of such deeds, by attributing them to

[64] They eventually succeeded, as the Augustan *fasti* show (n. 45 above). But they failed to reverse the usurpation by the Aemilii Lepidi of two of the *monumenta* of M. Fulvius Nobilior, *cens.* 179: Livy 40.51.5, Plut. *Caes.* 29.3 ('Basilica Fulvia'), Varro *LL* 6.4 ('Basilica Aemilia et Fulvia'), claimed by the Lepidi in 78 B.C. (Plin. *NH* 35.13; *RRC* 443f.) and thereafter 'Aemilia monumenta' (Tac. *Ann.* 3.72.1); Livy 40.51.4 (bridge), Plut. *Numa* 9.6 (attributed to an Aemilius).

[65] Theophanes in *FGrHist* 188 F 1 (Plut. *Pomp.* 37.4); even Plutarch, usually an ingenuous acceptor of historical fabrications, recognized Theophanes' κακοήθευμα here.

[66] See for instance Wiseman (1979) 29f. and (1981) 380f.

others or turning them into criminal acts (like the occupation of Italy *per clientelas*), that was simply the equivalent of defacing or destroying the physical monument of a rival *triumphator*. Glory could be preserved in words as well as in stone or bronze, and attacked as effectively by the pen as by the pickaxe.

Cassius and Brutus: the memory of the Liberators

ELIZABETH RAWSON

When the historian Cremutius Cordus was accused of *maiestas* in A.D. 25 the, or a, main charge against him was that he had praised Marcus Brutus and called Gaius Cassius 'the last of the Romans'[1] (probably in fact he quoted approvingly Brutus' supposed salutation of Cassius as such on learning of his death).[2] Cremutius, according to the speech that Tacitus gives him, claimed that a great many authors had recounted the deeds of Cassius and Brutus, and 'nemo sine honore nominavit'; Livy had written of them as 'insignes viros', Asinius Pollio's history had passed on 'egregiam eorundem memoriam', Messalla Corvinus had been wont to call Cassius '(imperatorem suum'.[3]

The prosecution in Cremutius' trial, however, had described the two men as 'latrones' and 'parricidas', as plunderers and as murderers of the most impious kind.[4] In spite of Cremutius' plea, a tradition opposed to the Liberators is visible, centring on these two charges and on the way divine and human justice overtook the conspirators. But it is also interesting to examine the dominant tradition, favourable in varying degrees, and see the different nuances therein, and in particular the relative judgements on Brutus and Cassius, and the comparisons and contrasts drawn between them. (It is less fruitful to try and find names for the sources used by extant writers, and I shall not discuss this question fully.) Clarke (1981) in his recent book on Brutus and his posthumous reputation has been far too brief on this subject, though much work has been done on some of the authors at whom we shall be looking. It may then be worthwhile to draw the threads together – and Cassius, possibly a more interesting, because a more ambiguous, figure than the virtuous Brutus, has

[1] Tac. *Ann.* 4.34.

[2] Appian *BC* 4.114, Plut. *Brut.* 44.2.

[3] Tac. *Ann.* 4.34–35; Suerbaum (1971).

[4] Parricide usually connotes murder of a parent, and Caesar had of course been given the formal title of *pater patriae*; Cic. *ad fam.* 12.3 describes Antony setting up a statue to Caesar in autumn 44: '"parenti optime merito" – ut non modo sicarii sed iam etiam parricidae iudicemini', he says (to Cassius). But Cicero does use the word 'parricida' vaguely, perhaps with an indication of 'murdering the *patria*', of for example Antony's followers, *Phil.* 12.7. No one knew (or knows) what the word really meant.

been extraordinarily neglected, though he will emerge as a figure of fully equal importance.[5]

Brutus owes his predominance over Cassius in part of the ancient tradition largely to his literary and philosophical interests. Cremutius Cordus noted that his speeches were still read, and later the court poet Statius deplored 'Bruti senis oscitationes', perhaps the speeches rather than the philosophic dialogues; but these latter were known to Seneca and Quintilian at least.[6] It is important, I think, that Cicero shared intellectual interests with Brutus, and was much closer to him than he was to Cassius (antiquity could read more of their correspondence than we can); perhaps partly as a result he almost always joins the two men in the order 'Brutus and Cassius', which practically all modern writers echo without thinking about it, even reversing the opposite order, which as we shall see was common, when translating the ancient sources. (It is of course true that Brutus, though the younger man, took official precedence in 44 as urban praetor, and this is reflected in the official documents emanating from the two.)[7]

Brutus' philosophic interests and close blood-relationship to Cato, the Stoic sage and martyr *par excellence*, also made him far more attractive than Cassius to the so-called philosophic opposition of Neronian and later times; Cassius' Epicurean leanings were largely forgotten, and would anyway not, for most writers, have been thought to his credit. The younger Seneca, for instance, never mentions Cassius. In the *de beneficiis* he argues that while Brutus was not wrong, as some held, to have accepted his life from Caesar, he was wrong to kill him – but only, it seems, because Brutus' political views were misguided; as a Stoic he should have realized that 'optimus status civitatis sub rege iusto' (we may retort that Brutus was an Academic, if admittedly a Stoicizing one, and anyway plenty of Stoics had opted for the mixed constitution); and he should have seen that freedom could not be restored once morality had decayed. But he was a 'vir magnus', and, as Seneca says elsewhere, one whom even Cato must have admired.[8] Similarly Lucan, who gives Brutus several dramatic scenes in the *Pharsalia*, has no role for Cassius at all. In the same tradition, Marcus Aurelius looked to Cato and Brutus among others,

[5] No special study has been devoted to Cassius since Fröhlich (1899) wrote the article in *RE*. There are a number on various aspects of Brutus' career.

[6] Tac. *Ann.* 4.34, Statius *Silv.* 4.9.20; Sen. *Consol. ad Helv.* 9.4ff., *Ep. Mor.* 95.45, Quint. *Inst.* 10.1.123. Even his poems seem to have been known.

[7] Cic. *Phil.* 1.8, 2.31, 8.27, 11.26, 27, 28, 36, *ad Att.* 14.17.4, 20.4, 15.5.2, 6.1, 9.1, 19.2, 22.1, 29.2, etc., etc. Official letters of the two are quoted in *ad fam.* 11.2, 11.3; cf. 11.1.

[8] Sen. *de benef.* 2.20, *Consol. ad Helv.* 9.5.

but not Cassius, for his ideal of a free state.[9] And Plutarch, in a rather different philosophic tradition, is also drawn primarily to Brutus.

Tacitus however notes that Cassius' name was not forgotten in the East when, in A.D. 49, another C. Cassius governed Syria – the famous lawyer, who was inspired to energetic action by the example of his ancestor; he probably thought as much of the earlier man's defence of Syria after the disaster at Carrhae in 53 B.C. as of his activities there ten years later.[10] In A.D. 65, indeed, Nero accused the lawyer of having a portrait of the tyrannicide 'inter imagines maiorum', inscribed 'duci partium' – to the, rather than a, leader, or possibly general, of the cause?[11] Tacitus himself generally uses the order 'Cassius and Brutus', as Syme notes, suggesting that he was silently correcting a modern myth.[12] Conceivably he was following Cremutius, whom he makes use the same formula; but, as we shall see, there seems to have been much authority among the historians for preferring this version, though possibly it was sometimes employed chiefly for literary variation.

Let us look, first, at the anti-Liberator tradition. Hostility focused, of course, in the first place on the murder of Caesar, no tyrant, according to his partisans, and the personal benefactor of both Brutus and Cassius. Stories emerged to make the ingratitude of Brutus at least more heinous than ever: Caesar had given special orders at Pharsalus that he should be spared, nay more, he was Caesar's own son by the amour with Servilia. There was an even more implausible tale that Caesar intended to make him his successor. Λέγεται, says Plutarch cautiously of the first two of these stories, and λέγεται again of the assertion, attributed to an enemy of Brutus' deeds, but historically plausible, that Brutus was not after all descended from L. Brutus the founder of the Republic, but from a plebeian family of only recent note.[13] Where Plutarch, who had read widely in the historical and quasi-historical literature of the triumviral and Augustan periods, got these items we do not know. The *de viris illustribus*, a late authority but with interesting material on various republican

[9] M. Aurel. *Medit.* 1.14. Cassius is linked with Brutus as objects of the veneration of Thrasea Paetus and Helvidius Priscus in Juv. 5.36–37 (but Tac. *Hist.* 4.8 omits him) and also of Titinius Capito, Pliny *Ep.* 1.17 (which places Brutus first, as does, much later, Julian *Caesares* 326A and 332B).

[10] Tac. *Ann.* 12.12.

[11] Tac. *Ann.* 16.7. Knierim (1939) does not discuss the expression 'dux partium'; Tac. *Ann.* 1.2, Vell. 2.72.3, and in the plural Tac. *Hist.* 1.66, 3.1, are all in a primarily military context.

[12] Syme (1958) 557 n. 7; Tacitus' Cremutius uses it three times, compared with one of the reverse order; and Dio 57.24.3 says Cremutius was condemned for praising Cassius and Brutus.

[13] Plut. *Brut.* 1.4, 5.2, 8.2. D. Brutus, who was one of Caesar's heirs, is often singled out for his ingratitude, but he cannot be discussed here.

figures, notes Brutus' liaison with the notorious Cytheris (recently doubted, in fact) and his service under the deplorable Ap. Claudius Pulcher in Cilicia in 53/52; but it does not pick up the episode, so well known to us from Cicero's letters, of Brutus' loan on extortionate terms to Cyprian Salamis, from which we tend to think he comes out very badly; and indeed the *de viris* tells us that Brutus was not accused by anyone of complicity in Appius' misdemeanours, so that there does not seem to be a source really unfriendly to Brutus here.[14]

On the other hand there probably is a source hostile to Cassius behind the agreeable notice, in the same work, that Cassius, when he had repulsed the Parthians from Syria after Carrhae, basely trafficked in dates and other local merchandise, to such an extent that he was known as Caryota, the Date.[15] And the biography of Cassius written by Caesar's friend Oppius was surely hostile.[16] It is interesting that the only signs of real personal invective, if that is what we have here, concern Cassius, not Brutus. One wonders who it was who, according to Plutarch, even deprived him of a courageous suicide by saying that Pindarus slew him unbidden.[17]

More generally, Augustus' autobiography is likely to have been hostile to all the Liberators; one notes that Cremutius Cordus is *not* made to say that Augustus too treated Brutus and Cassius leniently. The version that Augustus left to posterity in *Res Gestae* 2 of the events of 44–42 was that he drove those who killed his father into exile, having avenged their crime by the due operation of the courts, and then defeated them twice after they had attacked the *res publica* ('postea bellum inferentes rei publicae vici bis acie' – one way of describing the battles of Philippi). The autobiography is likely to have painted a similar picture. It is true that Nicolaus of Damascus, to whose account we shall come, praises Brutus, and he certainly used Augustus' autobiography; but he is usually thought to have had another source as well.[18]

One of Augustus' strongest charges was that the Liberators were

[14] [Aurelius Victor] *de vir. ill.* 82; for Cytheris, Anderson–Parsons–Nisbet (1979). For Brutus' loan: Cic. *ad Att.* 5.21.10–13. Porcius Latro did condemn Brutus for his early attacks on Pompey, Sen. Rhet. *Controv.* 10.1.8.

[15] [Aurelius Victor] *de vir. ill.* 83. The story that in the mêlée on the Ides he cried 'vel per me feri' illustrates his passionate or bitter nature.

[16] Peter *HRR* II 48.

[17] Plut. *Brut.* 43.6. (Pindarus could not be found after Brutus' death and was presumed to have run away.)

[18] Most recently Dobesch (1978); Scardigli (1983) tries to strengthen the case for the second source being Asinius Pollio. Plut. *Comp. of Dion and Brutus* 5 shows Augustus allowing Mediolanum to keep its statue of Brutus, but makes it clear that he regards Brutus as his own *hostis*. Suet. *Rhet.* 30.6 shows the pleader Albucius Silus getting into trouble with a Roman magistrate at Milan for invoking Brutus as 'legum ac libertatis auctor'.

guilty of renewing the civil wars. This surfaces again in Sentius Saturninus' speech after the murder of Caligula, as reported by Josephus, and again in 69, that year of turmoil: Suetonius was told by his father that the emperor Otho so hated the idea of civil war 'ut memorante quodam inter epulas de Cassi Brutique exitu cohorruerit'.[19] (Note the order of names; Otho of course had no ties with the philosophic opposition.) It was even possible to point out, as the triumviral edict introducing and justifying the proscriptions did, according to Appian, that the assassins of Caesar were proposing to use Parthian troops against Roman citizens; and they had indeed asked for these.[20]

Their conduct of the war could also be impugned, especially that of Cassius, as cruel and extortionate. Hence the name 'latrones'; they needed money desperately to pay their troops and secure their dubious loyalty by generous gifts. They were also charged, as in the proscription edict, with seizing state moneys. Cassius' siege of Rhodes, that famous city so long friendly to Rome, with his subsequent extraction of all its public and private wealth, was central here. Valerius Maximus, more bitter against the Liberators than any other extant source, denounces the 'rapacissimi victoris insolentiam' – he took all the statues of the gods, with one exception: 'I leave them the Sun', he said. The Sun was of course the protecting deity of Rhodes. Valerius sees Fortune avenging these acts by making Cassius leave the light of the real sun in Macedonia – a notably feeble antithesis. But Brutus' activities in Lycia, especially the destruction by fire of Xanthus, could also provide a handle against him; the proscription edict talks of the conspirators burning and destroying cities. Appian calls the fates of Laodicea, Tarsus, Rhodes, Patara and Xanthus περιφανέστατα, implying that there had been much discussion of them.[21]

For the rest, portents and visions were thought to show the wrath of heaven against those who had murdered the Father of his Country, nay a very god (and in the sacred Curia, before the eyes of the gods, as the proscription edict points out).[22] The famous story of Brutus seeing his own evil genius before Philippi is often thought not to be very early (it was not in the account given by Brutus' friend Volumnius, says Plutarch) and to derive from that told by Valerius about Cassius of Parma, the last of all the Liberators to perish, who was put to death at Athens after Actium by Octavian.[23] Less

19 Jos. *AJ* 19.184, Suet. *Otho* 10.1.
20 App. *BC* 4.8; cf. 4.63, Vell. 2.78.1, Just. 42.4.7, etc.
21 Val. Max. 1.5.8; App. *BC* 4.52.
22 Note the pointed way in which Cic. *Phil.* 13.25 says that it is Octavian who is really the father of his country.
23 Plut. *Brut.* 36, 48, Val. Max. 1.7.7.

well known but even more significant is Valerius' account of the famous Cassius ('nunquam sine praefatione publici parricidii nominandus'):[24] at Philippi itself Divus Julius appeared to him, spurring his horse against him. Terrified, Cassius fled, crying 'what more can I do, if to kill him was not enough?' Omens also foreshadowed Brutus' end, 'dignus admisso parricidio eventus'. But even Valerius has to make some admission of Brutus' virtues: he was the murderer of these as well as of the Father of his Country, a single deed plunged them in oblivion and covered the whole memory of his name with eternal execration. And Valerius admired the courage of Porcia and the loyalty of some of the Liberators' followers.[25]

Also basically hostile, as one would expect, is Velleius Paterculus, that loyal client of the emperor Tiberius. The nobly clement Caesar was killed 'incautus ab ingratis' – of course it was to their advantage to claim that he was a tyrant. But Cassius had also wanted to kill Antony and annul Caesar's will. Brutus and Cassius then seized provinces without senatorial authority (Brutus 'extorserat' the forces in the Balkans from Hortensius and C. Antonius) after saying that they would live in exile for the sake of peace; though at one time genuinely afraid of Antony, they now pretended such fear in order to make him unpopular (not that Velleius holds any brief for Antony). It was 'repugnans naturae suae' that Cassius showed clemency in Macedonia. But he prosecuted the siege of Rhodes with energy and died bravely. If one would prefer Brutus as a friend, one would fear the more energetic Cassius more as an enemy; he was a better *dux* than Brutus, who would have been a better man, had not the Ides destroyed all his virtues at a stroke (cf. Valerius Maximus, above). But if the Liberators had proved victorious, Brutus would have been as much better than Cassius as a *princeps* for the *res publica*, as Octavian proved superior to Antony.[26] Velleius in short sees no constitutional issues at stake; contrast Tacitus at the start of the *Annals*, for whom 'Bruto et Cassio caesis nulla iam publica arma': those of Sex. Pompey, Octavian and Antony are all, it is implied, *privata arma*.[27]

[24] Val. Max. 1.8.8. Valerius associates the idea of parricide with him in two other places as well: cf. 3.1.3, 6.8.4; in the latter passage Cassius' death is the revenge of Divus Julius, and the mortal victors are played down. Valerius' level of accuracy is shown by the fact that he made Philippi a night battle, to explain the mix-up that led to Cassius' death.

[25] Val. Max. 6.4.5, 1.4.6, 1.5.7; 3.2.15, 4.6.5, 4.7.4, 6.8.4, 9.9.2. He uses the order Brutus and Cassius consistently.

[26] Vell. 2.57.1, 62.2–3, 69.3, 69.6, 70.2, 72.1–2: see Woodman (1983a) ad locc. At 69.5 Velleius proudly notes that his uncle Velleius Capito joined Agrippa in laying formal charges against Cassius, whom earlier (2.46.4–5), while noting his achievements after Carrhae, he had called 'atrocissimi auctor facinoris'. At 69.3 Velleius is curiously favourable to Brutus, who seemed to the troops, on account of their animus against Vatinius, 'cuilibet ducum praeferendus'.

[27] Tac. *Ann.* 1.2.

The memory that the Liberators left among the provincials was also predominantly adverse. True, Athens, which had been held by Pompey in the last war, welcomed the philosophic Brutus, called him Εὐεργέτης of the city, and set up statues of both Brutus and Cassius next to those of her own tyrannicides.[28] But Athens was hardly typical; and in the event she was to succumb to Antony's favourable treatment of her.[29]

Where Brutus is concerned, it seems to me obvious that the Greek letters handed down under his name are not genuine. One needs only to look at the various epistles that survive on stone from Roman generals to Greek cities, including those from Octavian and Antony which are from just the right period for useful comparison, to see how implausible the exaggeratedly brief, unremittingly gnomic and antithetic notes attributed to Brutus are;[30] they are almost empty of precise historical content, but there are probably chronological and political errors, exposed by Smith (1936). Though Plutarch knew and accepted them, or some of them,[31] I can see no reason to argue even for a genuine nucleus, and Gelzer's idea that they are mere postscripts, added in Brutus' own hand to official missives, seems an equally desperate recourse.[32] Why should Brutus as opposed to all other Roman generals write so many (brief notes on petitions or on copies of letters to others are a different matter)? It would be odd to collect postscripts, and the ancient sources, noting the letters' extreme brevity, clearly regard them as complete. They also regard them as models of epistolography from generals, and they were surely produced as such.[33]

They are not, it seems, meant to discredit Brutus; their editor rather approves of their δεινότης and μεγαλοψυχία, and even of the ὑπεροψία suitable to a ἡγεμών.[34] But one cannot help suspecting that the picture of Brutus continually ordering towns to provide money, arms and men as rapidly as possible,[35] and accompanying his orders with undisguised threats, is indeed the picture most provincials retained of him. The Coans are told bluntly to choose whether to be

28 Dio 47.20.4; Raubitschek (1957, 1959).

29 App. *BC* 5.7. Plut. *Ant.* 23 and 57 show Antony, who was worshipped as a god in Athens, accepting its citizenship.

30 Sherk (1969) esp. nos. 57, 58, 60; Reynolds (1982) c. 3 nos. 6, 10, 12; nos. 13 and 14 are brief but straightforward and concrete *subscriptiones*.

31 Plut. *Brut.* 2.3–5.

32 Smith (1936), Meucci (1942), Torraca (1959); Gelzer (1917). But Magie (1950) 422, 1275, 1289 notes that Menodorus of Tralles (letter 55) is probably a real person: Strabo 14 C649.

33 *Letters*, preface; Philostratus, *Epistles* 364K (= Hercher (1873), *Epistolographi Graeci* 14).

34 *Letters*, preface (the editor, Mithridates, confesses to writing the answers, but perhaps really believed in the authenticity of Brutus' own missives).

35 Almost always in quite unspecified amounts.

δοῦλοι or φίλοι; the Pergamenes to pay up as good subjects or lose their παρρησία. And one wonders whether the epistolary version of Brutus' capture of Xanthus in Lycia may not be closer to the truth than more apologetic ones. He has punished the Xanthians harshly for refusing to capitulate and now rejects their pleas for mercy; their town has been burnt (apparently of set purpose by the Romans) and their young men slaughtered. Others will suffer the same fate if they do not submit. Brutus also says flatly that Rhodes has already been 'enslaved' by Cassius, language that a Roman general would surely not use in this vague but invidious sense of the act of a trusted colleague.[36]

As for Cassius, he seems to have left a perfectly horrific memory in Judaea, if we may trust Josephus.[37] He had ravaged the country after Carrhae (it was admittedly restless), taking Taricheae and enslaving 30,000 Jews; returning in 44/43 he collected arms and men and demanded the huge sum of 700 talents, which the country could not pay (Crassus had already annexed the treasures of the Temple). Its ruler Antipater, fearing Cassius' threats, set his sons and others to collect the money from the different districts. Herod, then a young man, raised his portion from Galilee quickly and became a favourite of Cassius, but the others were less successful. So Cassius sold all the officials involved, and four whole towns, into slavery, and would have sold more (and executed a prominent Jew) had it not been for a timely bribe of 100 talents by Antipater that quenched his ὀργή. We also hear that he controlled Syria by means of tyrannies – Marion of Tyre is named – and, though Josephus does not make the point, this could be seen surely as highly unbecoming in one claiming the name of Liberator. (One assumes that the tyrants displaced the usual oligarchies favoured by the Romans.)

For the narrative of the first part of his works Josephus seems to have been mainly dependent on the histories of Nicolaus of Damascus, and also probably of Strabo;[38] though the former in particular was, as his patron Herod later became, fulsomely loyal to Augustus, both probably disposed of excellent information. And Josephus subjoins a letter from Antony, in which he, in response to Jewish appeals, orders the restitution of all Jews sold in contravention of the laws of war and the return of Jewish territory given to Tyre.[39] Josephus'

[36] *Letters* 13, 3, 11b, 43. The usual version of the fire at Xanthus was that it started accidentally and was encouraged by the Xanthians; App. *BC* 4.80 says that this was the third time that the Xanthians had so destroyed themselves.

[37] Jos. *AJ* 14.119–22; 271–76; 297; *BJ* 1.180, 218–22; 238.

[38] Schürer (1973) 25, 28.

[39] Jos. *AJ* 14.306; cf. Antony's letter to Tyre, 314: the conspirators' ingratitude and perjury, their seizing of the provinces of others and turning over of them to their

documents are basically reliable. This one is a good example of Antony's notorious Asianic rhetoric: the murderers of Caesar are enemies of the Roman people, who have overrun Asia sparing neither cities nor temples, perjurors who have broken the laws of gods and men, from whose deeds the very Sun turned away; they were supported by a mob of half-mad villains. Asia needs peace to recover from a terrible disease.

Later Josephus notes that Rhodes still bore the scars inflicted by Cassius, and he calls Philippi the defeat of Cassius. He also writes of Caesar's murder by τοῖς περὶ Κάσσιον καὶ Βροῦτον, an order unsurprising in one who viewed Roman history from the East; the same order is equally understandably used by Justin's epitome of Trogus in its treatment of Parthian history.[40]

So much for the hostile tradition. Let us look now at the several more extensive accounts that we have of the plot against Caesar and its aftermath, which all happen to be in Greek, though based primarily on Roman sources, and which are all more or less favourable to the Liberators. The earliest in date is from the biography of Augustus by Nicolaus of Damascus, who served Antony and Cleopatra, and then King Herod of Judaea. We have his version only of the assassination itself.[41] Not surprisingly, it praises Caesar, who is described simply as ἡγεμών; his deeds were immense, he was ἁπλοῦς τὸ ἦθος, and his long absence from Rome had made him unused to intrigues. The conspirators' motives are dubious, though it is the ingratitude of D. Brutus that is singled out. But Nicolaus recognizes M. Brutus' high reputation, and his refusal to let anyone else be killed, on the grounds that the innocent must not suffer. M. Brutus was honoured for his consistent σωφροσύνη, ancestral εὔκλεια and the impression that he gave of personal ἐπιείκεια. Cassius is noted as one of the leaders of the plot (with D. Brutus and Casca), but his role is not specially brought out, except that he is said to have been one of those offering Caesar the diadem at the Lupercalia, in order to arouse envy of him,[42] and on the Ides he twice strikes Caesar, the second time in his haste wounding M. Brutus. Nicolaus went into great detail as to who struck where – but does not mention the wound inflicted

adherents. App. *BC* 5.7 shows that Cassius also sold Tarsians; and says that Antony urged the rebuilding of Xanthus and freed the Lycians from taxes.

40 Jos. *AJ* 14.270 (*BJ* 1.218), 301 (*BJ* 1.225, 242). *AJ* 19.184 Sentius' speech – doubtless from a senatorial author's account of Caligula's death, but perhaps rewritten by Josephus – uses the order 'Cassius and Brutus', perhaps natural in the account of a conspiracy led by Cassius Chaerea. Justin, *Epitoma* 42.4.7.

41 Jacoby *FGrHist* 90, frs. 125–30.

42 Probably fictitious; Dio 44.8.1 says Cassius was one of very few senators to vote against honours to Caesar.

by Brutus, let alone regard it as the culminating betrayal. The assassins flee to the Capitol in undignified fashion (Plutarch's account is in notable contrast). Nicolaus' version of Brutus' speech to the people has not come down to us, and unfortunately we have nothing of his version of later events involving the Liberators, unless Josephus' account of Cassius in Judaea comes from him. Nicolaus seems to have been a great exponent of 'tragic history' on the best Hellenistic model; a certain concentration on the figure of M. Brutus may be due to a desire for vividness and dramatic unity. Cassius is perhaps sketched as an intriguer, and passionate; and in fact Nicolaus says 'Cassius and Brutus' as often as 'Brutus and Cassius'. His outlook would appear to be that of Augustus' autobiography, tempered by a historical source more hostile to Caesar and favourable to Brutus.

Our next authors, Appian and Plutarch, date from the early second century. Appian is particularly interesting for the strong favour that he shows to Cassius, which has been several times noted in general terms. In Book 2, in the quarrel between Brutus and Cassius as to which was to have the urban praetorship, it is said that Caesar favoured Brutus, but admitted that Cassius' claim was the better one.[43] There was no real ill-feeling between the two rivals. Brutus is prominent in the actual plot, on account of his family traditions that mark him out as the leader; there is no special praise of him, but it is on receiving his blow that Caesar despairs. Cassius urges Brutus on, and in fact the conspirators are twice οἱ ἀμφὶ τὸν Κάσσιον and only once οἱ ἀμφὶ τὸν Βροῦτον.[44] In Book 3 the former locution is again used rather more often than the latter, but it is noted at the end of the book that Brutus had a reputation for σοφίᾳ τε καὶ πραότητι.[45] Book 4 recounts the events leading up to Philippi entirely from the Liberators' side[46] and is clearly anxious to counter triumviral propaganda: the statement that Caesar had promised Brutus Macedonia and Cassius Syria is perhaps meant to legitimate to some degree their seizure of these provinces (it is probably not true).[47] Noting that Cassius had some Parthian horse-archers, Appian says simply that he got them because of the reputation he gained when, as Crassus' quaestor (really proquaestor), he had seemed to be wiser than his general.[48] This sends our minds back to the account of

[43] App. *BC* 2.112. (In 2.88 he confuses Cassii, but thinks he is talking of the tyrannicide, and calls him πολεμικώτατος.)

[44] *BC* 3.36, 64 against 96; in Books 3 and 4 I count 15 references to 'Cassius and Brutus' to 9 'Brutus and Cassius', but 5 ἀμφὶ τὸν Κ. to 6 ἀμφὶ τὸν Β.

[45] *BC* 3.79.

[46] It is remarkable that all surviving accounts in fact do this.

[47] Kniely (1974) 37–71.

[48] *BC* 4.59.

Crassus' campaigns in Plutarch's Life of Crassus, where (except for the actual battle of Carrhae) Cassius is exceedingly prominent, and repeatedly plays Cassandra to the expedition.[49]

Appian gives a full account of Cassius' operations against Dolabella in 44/43, with his admittedly severe treatment of Dolabella's refuge, Laodicea, and his excellent hopes of taking Egypt, frustrated by Brutus' summons. Cassius imposed heavy contributions on Tyre, but it was the magistrates, not he, who sold into slavery free persons who could not pay, and when he arrives Cassius pities them and remits the rest of the money. At Sardis Brutus and Cassius confer, and Cassius' plans, to deal with Rhodes and Lycia, are accepted.[50] Gabba well analyses Appian's lengthy version of the siege of Rhodes:[51] Cassius is sympathetic to the city where he has studied, and, in the dialogue with his old teacher Archelaus, argues that the freedom-loving Rhodians should not stand by those who would destroy freedom at Rome. It is only the lower class that opposes him; on entry he strictly prohibits plundering, though a few persons are put to death. Equally, Brutus (said to have treated C. Antonius with notable generosity in Macedonia and had him executed only after Antonius had repeatedly tried to corrupt the army) is now gentle with Xanthus: the fire is much played down, and the few free men enslaved were quickly liberated. Brutus much admired the Xanthian love of freedom and tried to prevent the inhabitants' mass suicide by offering terms. On Patara he imposed the same fines and punishments as Cassius did on Rhodes; this is perhaps meant to show that Cassius was no harsher than Brutus.[52]

At the second meeting at Sardis, there is no quarrel. Finally, Philippi: it is Cassius, older than Brutus and having one more legion at his back, who is made to address the troops – twice, at some length. The Liberators, he argues, are fighting for freedom and the rule of law, against monarchy, where one man usurps all the rights of the *dēmos*. The deplorable actions of the *IIIviri* are evoked. It is only before the second battle that Brutus (Cassius is now dead) and Antony are given speeches, and then it is much shorter ones.[53] Appian, who must be working, directly or indirectly, from a number of sources in this part of his work, including Augustus' memoirs, has much about

[49] Plut. *Crassus* 18.4, 20.2, 22.4, 23.3; and cf. 27.5, 28.3–5, 29.1 and 4. For the battle itself, where young P. Crassus is the doomed hero, see Lintott (1976) and Rawson (1982): the source is probably his freedman Apollonius. For the origins of the account as a whole the most various suggestions have been made.

[50] App. *BC* 4.65. Cassius is afraid of a hostile fleet at his back: not unlikely, given his experience in Pompey's navy in the last civil war, Caes. *BC* 3.101. But Bengtson (1970) 36 thinks the decision a gross error.

[51] Gabba (1956) 182.

[52] App. *BC* 4.66–74, 75–81.

[53] App. *BC* 4.90–101, 117–20.

Brutus here, but he gives two versions of Cassius' death, and has Brutus mourn him as the last of the Romans.

At length, Appian sums up:[54] Brutus was gentle and kindly and had trouble with discipline, Cassius αὐστηρὸς καὶ ὀργικός and was promptly obeyed[55] (in fact these characteristics have not been clearly brought out in the narrative); but they both were ἄνδρε Ῥωμαίων εὐγενεστάτω τε καὶ περιφανεστάτω καὶ ἐς ἀρετὴν ἀδηρίτω. Both the allies and the Caesarian veterans were faithful to them; this answers the charge, already voiced by Cicero soon after the Ides, that no one, let alone the veterans, would follow Brutus at least in a war.[56] Cassius, Appian goes on, was entirely devoted to war, Brutus was φιλοθεάμων καὶ φιλήκοος, anxious to go sightseeing and to listen to lectures. The impression left is that Brutus was somewhat ineffectual in comparison with Cassius, who is further the mouthpiece of constitutional ideology and is not charged with real cruelty, or with corruption. It may be added that in Appian's Book 5 references back to recent events involve eight cases of the order 'Cassius and Brutus' to two of 'Brutus and Cassius'.[57]

Gabba, in his now classic account of Appian's *Civil Wars*, does not bring out all this, nor do other analyses of the work.[58] One reason, I think, is that most of them believe that Appian is directly using Asinius Pollio, and feel a secret unease at attributing to him this account, in spite of Cremutius Cordus' assurance that Pollio spoke highly of the Liberators. For Pollio did serve Antony, and then Octavian; could he be so hostile to the triumvirs and pay so little attention to their side of the campaign? True, he was himself in Italy during the war, and could not write from autopsy; one could suppose, as Gabba does, that he turned to a literary source favourable to the Liberators, and perhaps see Appian as touching it up further (though we are repeatedly reminded that the Liberators are paying the penalty for their deeds). But I prefer, I think, to remain agnostic about Appian's basic source, at least for this part of his work; it may be that Pollio was brief, and had to be supplemented.[59]

[54] App. *BC* 4.132–34.

[55] Frontinus *Strat.* 4.2.1 has an anecdote about the superior discipline of Cassius' troops.

[56] Cic. *ad Att.* 14.20.3.

[57] It is perhaps worth noting that App. *BC* 2.90 makes Cassius avenge Pompey by putting to death the rhetorician Theodotus who advised the Egyptian court to kill him; Plut. *Brut.* 33.4 and *Pomp.* 80.6 make Brutus do this.

[58] E.g., Fröhlich (1899), André (1949), Haller (1967). Gabba argues, for Pollio's authorship, that Antony is favoured above Octavian. But, since Bosworth (1972), one should hesitate to suppose Pollio hostile to Augustus.

[59] Gelzer (1958) and Badian (1958b), in reviews of Gabba, remain uncertain about his basic hypothesis.

Plutarch's *Brutus* is well known;[60] I shall be brief and unoriginal. It has rightly been seen as almost a double life, for Plutarch is fascinated by the contrast between Brutus and Cassius. Like Appian, Plutarch ascribes the instigation of the conspiracy to the latter; but he notes that those who deplored this ascribed the good in it to Brutus and the bad to Cassius, less ἁπλοῦς τῷ τρόπῳ and καθαρός, a less straightforward and innocent man. But it is not true that the latter was simply an ἀνὴρ θυμοειδής with private grievances against Caesar, though for Plutarch he does stand for passion, θυμός, against Brutus, the man of λόγος, reason; no, he really did hate tyranny, as his boyish attack on Faustus Sulla showed. It is significant for the characters of the two men that Brutus administered justice in court with care and concentration on the morning of the Ides; and that when, in the senate that afternoon, Popillius Laenas was seen talking to Caesar, Cassius and others panicked and nearly decided to kill themselves, but Brutus saw the conversation was innocent and reassured them by his bearing.[61]

During the campaigns the contrast is very clear. Cassius is an able soldier (his early exploits against the Parthians are planted near the start of the work), but harsh in anger and ruling through fear, though inclined to laughter and sarcasm with his friends.[62] Brutus was loved by the people and nobility alike, and not hated even by his enemies; he was gentle, magnanimous, firm in defence of honour and justice. Plutarch stresses his clemency, πραότης, his steadiness, ἐμβρίθεια, his financial probity (and generosity) and his philhellenism. But Cassius is shrewder; he opposed both sparing Antony and allowing Caesar a public funeral.[63]

Cassius, Plutarch says, was suspected of aiming at power for himself; he was fond of gain, and behaved unjustly at Rhodes – though, when hailed as king and lord, he said he was neither, but the avenger of one who had called himself by these names. Brutus by contrast was kind to all the Lycians, and took little money from them, at first dismissing all captives without ransom; but the Lycians despised his generosity. At Xanthus he tried to put out the fire, which started accidentally, but madness seized the citizens and they encouraged its ravages. Brutus rode round anxious to bring help, and stretching out his hands begged them to save the city, but they destroyed themselves.

[60] But not much studied: Scardigli (1979) 141; add however Moles (1974), Pelling (1979, 1980); little help in the Budé ed. of R. Flacelière and E. Chambry (1978).

[61] Plut. *Brut.* 1.2, 8.3–9.2, 16.2–3.

[62] Plut. *Brut.* 29.1 (the jollity perhaps derived from a knowledge of Cicero's letters?).

[63] Plut. *Brut.* 18.2, 20.1–2.

He could not bear to see, and wept to hear, their fate. He offered rewards to every soldier saving a Xanthian, but very few survived. Brutus then feared to besiege Patara, lest its people behave in the same way, but he released some of its leading women, whom he held, and these by representing him as σωφρονέστατος καὶ δικαιότατος persuaded their menfolk to surrender. The other Lycians did so too. Brutus exacted only 150 talents from the whole country, though Cassius took all the private wealth of Rhodes, 800 talents, as well as 500 from the city as such.[64] This is very unlike Appian's account, where the two act identically at this point.

Plutarch blames neither man specifically for the quarrel at Sardis, but where Cassius holds that his own friends are being too harshly punished by Brutus for corruption, Brutus reminds his friend of the principles inspiring the Ides. As for Philippi, it is perhaps implied that Cassius, who had more military experience, was right in not wanting to fight; thus Brutus perhaps again commits an error. After the first battle he is merciful to the free prisoners (in general, we are told, Cassius was blamed for leading him into ἔνια τῶν βιαιοτέρων), though Plutarch regards his promise at this point to hand over two Greek cities to the soldiers as the one indefensible act of his life – however, he reminds us, Antony and Octavian behaved far worse. Brutus' courage in battle is praised, but it is noted that after Cassius' death he has no really good general and has to do what those with him want.[65] Plutarch's sympathy for his hero is great; but of course, he holds, Providence was working to give Rome a monarchy.

Lastly Dio, writing in the early third century. As one committed at least to the necessity of monarchy, he starts with a strong condemnation of Caesar's murder by jealous and envious men who caused new civil wars (familiar theme) and stresses the ingratitude especially of Trebonius and D. Brutus.[66] But he is at this point not much interested in either M. Brutus or Cassius (though he makes M. Brutus the instigator of the plot, who ropes Cassius in – probably not true – and has the καὶ σύ, τέκνον story). Most of what happens is attributed to 'the conspirators'; it is even οἱ σφαγεῖς who address the people.[67] Dio then turns to a very full account of the relations between Antony and Octavian, postponing any account of the movements of Brutus and Cassius till after the formation of the Triumvirate and start of the proscriptions in summer 43. When the flashback comes, in 47.20ff., there is some confusion – Cassius, not Brutus, is described as urban praetor, and the two have left Italy in fear of Octavian, not Antony (this last however may be from Augustus' autobiography, as it is in Nicolaus).

64 Plut. *Brut.* 29.4, 30.3–32.2.

65 Plut. *Brut.* 34, 39, 45.4, 46.1–4.

66 Dio 44.14.

67 Dio 44.14–21, 34.

But then Dio turns out to be surprisingly favourable to the Liberators, making much of their leniency as a foil to the horror of the triumviral proscriptions. Brutus spared Antony's brother Gaius on taking over his troops (and when Gaius is finally executed, on news of the proscriptions, it is not clear that it was Brutus who gave the order).[68] Cassius sent safely away from Syria the officers who would not join him, allowed Dolabella and his legate decent burial, and again sent away the rest of Dolabella's suite. He took money from Laodicea and hostile Tarsus, but harmed neither city. All this must seem particularly significant after the long account of the proscriptions. Neither Brutus nor Cassius punished L. Gellius Publicola for his plotting against them. Both alike wanted to defend the liberty of the people and overthrow the *IIIviri* καὶ τοιαῦτα δρῶντας – surely a scandalized reference to the proscriptions.[69] And so we go on. Cassius meets no resistance in Rhodes once its fleet is defeated; he was popular there owing to his studies in the town; he does no harm to it apart from taking its ships and treasures (but not the famous chariot of the Sun). Brutus gets a reputation for justice in Lycia, though he sold a few Xanthians before he saw that this did not persuade the people of Patara to come over; when they do give in, they are only fined.[70] The people of Myra are reconciled to him when he frees their generals.[71]

The quarrel of Brutus and Cassius is barely such, being entirely due to the διαβολαί of others.[72] As for the final campaign both, being supremely δημερασταί, would rather have won without a battle, but were forced to fight by their mainly foreign troops. The struggle was for ἐλευθερία and δημοκρατία (republicanism rather than real democracy, no doubt), between the prospect of αὐτονομία and that of δυναστεία. (Here Dio, recollecting himself, slips in that of course it was beneficial for Rome to lose her freedom as she was no longer capable of harmony under a δημοκρατία.) Οἱ περὶ τὸν Βροῦτον address the soldiers on the subject of δημοκρατία, and the opposition of liberty and tyranny, while the other side appeals quite openly to the men's greed and to the desire to lord it over their own countrymen; and what was most effective, promises 20,000 HS apiece. The password of Brutus and Cassius on the day of the battle is noted: it was 'Libertas'.[73]

However, Cassius was not Antony's equal in war. And after Cassius' death Brutus does, in vain, give his friends and soldiers money to ensure their loyalty and is forced 'by necessity and against his will' to put captives to death – which his opponents had been

[68] Dio 47.21, 23, 24.
[69] Dio 47.32.
[70] Dio 47.33–34.
[71] Dio 47.34.
[72] Dio 47.35.
[73] Dio 47.38, 43.

doing all along. Brutus' last words are the famous lines on the vanity of virtue – a moving if probably fictional epilogue. His surviving followers surrendered and were killed, or fled to Sextus Pompey.[74] This is not entirely true; Messalla and some others were forgiven.[75]

Here is a very interesting account, with its unexpected sympathies and the almost equal favour, and importance, given to Brutus and Cassius. (Dio says 'Brutus and Cassius' and 'Cassius and Brutus', evenhandedly.) Dio has often been thought to be using Livy, but Manuwald has shown that there are considerable differences between Dio and the Livian tradition, which in particular stresses much more the ravages and exactions of both Brutus and Cassius, especially in Greece.[76] The suggestion, which has been made more than once,[77] that Dio may conceivably have been using Cremutius Cordus, may receive a little support from our demonstration that his account is partly inspired by hatred of the proscriptions; for one of the few things we know about Cordus' work is that 'proscribentes in aeternum ipse proscripsit'.[78]

It is also worth looking back at an earlier book of Dio, to note that he is our fullest source for Cassius' earlier exploits in Syria after Carrhae. There is no sign of Cassius 'the Warner', so prominent in Plutarch's *Crassus*, though Dio's account is admittedly very compressed for the period before the fatal battle. But after it, we are told, the soldiers μίσει τοῦ Κράσσου offered Cassius supreme command, and Crassus himself acquiesced, but Cassius refused it, till later he was forced to take command in Syria. (Such a refusal was of course proper, though Dio does not say so explicitly.) Subsequently Cassius drove out of the province a small Parthian force, and then a bigger one that reached Antioch and was under the nominal leadership of Pacorus, the king's son, though actually under that of Osaces. Repulsed from Antioch, the Parthians wasted time trying to clear the wooded environs of Antigonea, while being harassed by Cassius, who ambushed them on their retreat, killing Osaces. Pacorus abandoned Syria and there was no new invasion.[79]

We need not, as Regling did,[80] see here Livy building up Cassius' victories as revenge for Carrhae (though it would be nice to imagine Cremutius Cordus claiming for Cassius the role that Antony and then

[74] Dio 47. 47–49.
[75] But see Suet. *Aug.* 13 for Octavian's harshness after Philippi.
[76] Manuwald (1979) 168ff.: note Oros. 6.18.13 and Obs. 70. Cf. Dobesch (1979) 100, 126–27.
[77] See Millar (1964) 85, Manuwald (1979) 254.
[78] Sen. *Consol. ad Marc.* 26.1.
[79] Dio 40.12ff., 16ff., 28.2–3, 29. Appian's account was in his lost *Parthica*.
[80] Regling (1899) 22.

Augustus arrogated to themselves). But it is true that Livy likes Rome to take fairly immediate revenge for defeats, and the Livian tradition does suggest that he made a good deal of Cassius' achievements at this point. Eutropius says 'singulari animo perditas res tanta virtute restituit ut Persas rediens trans Euphratem crebris proeliis vinceret' (that he crossed the Euphrates must be a misunderstanding).[81] Festus is more precise: a 'vir strenuus', he defeated the invading Parthians in three battles 'summa cum admiratione'.[82] Orosius says that on the news of Carrhae many eastern provinces would have revolted if Cassius had not collected the few surviving troops and 'intumescentem Syriam egregia animi virtute ac moderatione pressisset'.[83] (*Moderatio* was not what struck Josephus' source.) Orosius goes on to say that Cassius defeated the huge forces of Antiochus and killed the king himself, before repulsing the Parthians who had actually entered Antioch, and killing Osages. The first part of this statement is certainly wrong: Antiochus must be the king of Commagene who in 51, when Cicero was in Cilicia, was loyally sending information about Parthian movements. But some in Cicero's entourage did not trust him, and Cassius may have had to make threatening gestures.[84] These notices do suggest that Livy had a detailed, and perhaps over-favourable, account of Cassius' achievements.[85] And for the later period too he may have brought out his importance. The famous fragment on Cicero's death uses the order 'Cassius and Brutus'.[86] So does Obsequens (twice) and Florus on several occasions, the title of one chapter being 'Bellum Cassi et Bruti'; while a confused passage in the *periocha* of Livy calls someone (it should clearly be Q. Cornificius, the governor of Africa Vetus) 'Cassianarum partium dux'.[87]

For once, we have some check on the ancient historiographic tradition. A number of letters to and from – and also a number mentioning – Brutus and Cassius survive in the correspondence of Cicero. We have the coins they issued, and some other contemporary

[81] Eutrop. 6.18.2.

[82] Rufius Festus *Breviarium* 17. Eadie (1967) 85 suggests the three victories rest on a confusion with Ventidius' campaigns in Eutrop. 7.5; but Dio's narrative suggests that one could count three battles.

[83] Oros. 6.13.5.

[84] Cic. *ad fam.* 15.1.2. And Antony later had to chastise him for pro-Parthian activities, Plut. *Ant.* 34.

[85] Though Livy *per.* 108 is bald: 'C. Cassius, quaestor M. Crassi, Parthos qui in Syriam transcenderant, cecidit.' Front. *Strat.* 2.5.35 gives a fuller account of Cassius' stratagem against Osaces.

[86] *Apud* Sen. Rhet. *Suas.* 6.17.

[87] Obs. 70 (twice, once B. and C.), Florus 2.16, 17, 19 (but twice B. and C.), Livy *per.* 123.

evidence about them. There is not much support here for the fashionable notion that ancient historiography is a branch of ancient fiction. The historians may be hostile or favourable, they may oversimplify, they may be selective or inaccurate over details, but they do not lose touch with reality – and certainly not with ideas first formulated in the years 44–42. We can see for example that Brutus did have a reputation for *clementia*, based particularly on his treatment of C. Antonius, though Cicero thought it wrong-headed.[88] But Plutarch has clearly exaggerated the πραότης and φιλανθρωπία of a man whom Cicero often found arrogant and difficult,[89] while most of the tradition was so determined to regard him as un-extortionate that even Plutarch, who knew Cicero's letters, averted his eyes from the Salamis episode. The arrogance does once emerge – in a *suasoria* of Varius Geminus, quoted by the elder Seneca; arguing that Cicero should ask pardon from Antony, Varius claims that if Cicero chooses rather to flee he will have to become a slave: 'ferendam esse aut Cassii violentiam aut Bruti superbiam aut Pompei stultitiam'.[90] The nouns are carefully chosen.

But the whole history of Cicero's relations with Brutus does show that he was to some extent under the thrall of the abilities and character, as well as the family position and political importance, of this man who was many years his junior, and makes Brutus' position in his own time, as well as with later intellectuals, entirely understandable. For his devotion to family tradition, the family history produced for him by Atticus, and the coins he issued years before the civil war, are eloquent evidence.[91]

Cassius' complexities were also lost; his Epicureanism was normally expunged – it will have seemed incompatible with the warlike and passionate, if not also corrupt and grasping, figure usually portrayed.[92] Oddly perhaps, the fact that he was Brutus' brother-in-law is often forgotten. And no later source, not even Plutarch, has anything about the family tradition of the Cassii, less ancient and august than that of the Iunii Bruti, but perhaps providing almost equal pressure towards tyrannicide; he came from a house that, as Cicero said, 'non modo dominatum sed ne potentiam quidem cuiusdam ferre potuit'.[93] Family coins show that devotion to Libertas was proclaimed by its

88 Cic. *ad M. Brut.* 1.2a.2.

89 Note esp. Cic. *ad Att.* 6.1.7.

90 Sen. Rhet. *Suas.* 6.14.

91 Nepos *Atticus* 18.3; Crawford *RRC* 455, dating the issue to 54 B.C.

92 Plut. *Brut.* 37, cf. 39, and *Caes.* 66 are the only later references; and Russell (1972) 78 notes that Cassius' speech in the first passage is, though sceptical, quite un-Epicurean.

93 Cic. *Phil.* 2.26. Cf. *I Verr.* 30: 'ex familia cum ad ceteras res tum ad iudicandum severissima' (the reference is primarily to Cassius Ravilla, *cos.* 127). Coins of Q. Cassius with head of Libertas, Crawford *RRC* 452; the tyrannicide's coins, 513ff. But he professed horror of 'crudelitas', Cic. *ad. fam.* 15.19.2.

members. Cassius' own, after the Ides, which like those of Brutus also proclaim 'LEIBERTAS', but unlike his, do not show the portrait of the issuer, might suggest that his devotion to the ideal was at least as genuine.

Contemporary sources do give evidence for the characteristics that were later attributed to Cassius. He may have been in some danger of prosecution for extortion on his return from his proquaestorship in Syria.[94] Certainly Caelius said that there were some who claimed that he had invented the Parthian attacks to cover up his own ravages.[95] For his energy and enterprise in war Caesar, writing of a foe, is our authority: commanding Syrian and Cilician contingents of the navy for Pompey, Cassius surprised the Caesarian fleet at Messana and Vibo, and destroyed it by means of fireships, nearly taking Messana in the process. He retired only on hearing of the result of Pharsalus.[96] (It is curious that this episode is not picked up by later sources.) For a more passionate spirit than Brutus had we may appeal to the famous letter of Cicero describing a family conference in summer 44, at which Cassius with flashing eyes was 'breathing battle'.[97] And for an importance at least equal to that of Brutus, based on superior energy, shrewdness and military experience, which we have seen some sources ascribed to him, what better witness than Antony himself? It is true that he is said to have regarded Brutus' motives alone as pure; but after the amnesty that followed the Ides, Brutus dined with Lepidus, and Cassius with Antony (though, as Dio says, the fact that Brutus and Lepidus were close connexions may be relevant here). If Cicero was prone to write 'Brutus and Cassius', Antony, to judge by the letter dissected in *Philippic* 13, wrote 'Cassius and Brutus'. And when Antony heard of Cassius' death at Philippi, he is said to have exclaimed 'vici!'[98]

[94] It has been argued that *ad fam.* 15.14.4 hints at the threat of prosecution; though Shackleton Bailey refers it to Q. Cassius, perhaps a cousin. But there is a contrast between 'ea quae reliqui tranquilla de te erant' and 'onera tuorum'.

[95] *Ad fam.* 8.10.2 (shown to be a libel by Deiotarus' letters). Cf. *ad fam.* 15.14.3.

[96] Caesar *BC* 3.101. Cic. *ad Att.* 11.13.1 shows him thereafter at Rhodes, thinking of going to Caesar at Alexandria to beg for mercy. *Ad fam.* 6.6.10 suggests that Caesar only made him a legate in 46, so the suggestion that he used him in the war against Pharnaces is dubious.

[97] *Ad Att.* 15.11.1; Cassius himself is inclined to vigorous language in *ad fam.* 12.12.

[98] Plut. *Brut.* 29.5, Dio 44.34, cf. Plut. *Brut.* 19.1, Cic. *Phil.* 13.25, [Aurelius Victor] *de vir. ill.* 83. I append some miscellaneous cases of the order 'Cassius and Brutus': Nepos *Atticus* 11 (perhaps in chronological order of death), Sen. Rhet. *Suas.* 6.11, Front. *Strat.* 4.2.1, Suet. *DJ* 80.4, *Nero* 3.1, *Galba* 3.2.

Dionysius of Halicarnassus and his audience

CLEMENCE SCHULTZE

'He was cotemporary, and, probably, acquainted with Livy, Virgil, Horace, Ovid, and many other learned, and polite authors, with whom that remarkable age was adorned, and was himself a conspicuous star in that bright constellation.'[1] That is Edward Spelman's judgement on Dionysius; many – indeed most – later scholars have been much less generous to him.[2] Considered as a historian, on any unprejudiced assessment he cannot be counted among the greatest, or even among writers of the second rank. The *Antiquitates Romanae* is not read for the insight and originality of its thought; it is not a book of outstanding literary merit; it is of limited use for the actual political and military history of early Rome. But it should not be too readily dismissed as mere rhetorical hackwork – and even a middling work may still be of value for what it reveals about the interests and modes of thought of its author and his intended audience. While he is by no means a great writer or an intellectual pioneer, Dionysius can stand as representative of the educated man of his period – one, moreover, who has given some consideration to the theory and practice of historical writing; he is, as I hope to show, addressing a relatively mixed readership. Much of the interest of studying the *Antiquitates* nowadays comes from the indications it gives of the tastes and assumptions of its target audience. And though its subject lies in the remote past, themes developed in the *Antiquitates* have some relevance to the lives and attitudes of Dionysius' contemporaries in 'that remarkable age'.

The Rome that Dionysius knew was the city of Augustus: he was probably in his mid-twenties when he arrived 'at the time when Augustus Caesar put an end to the civil war' (1.7.2),[3] and he lived

I should like to thank colleagues at the Queen's University of Belfast, and those present at a meeting of the Hibernian Hellenists in 1981, for their comments on an earlier version of this paper; I am also grateful to the participants at Leeds in April 1983 for various points raised in the discussion.

[1] Spelman (1758) vol. 1.iv. The suggestion of acquaintanceship is pure conjecture.

[2] Gabba (1982) now offers a general assessment with a good bibliography.

[3] References in this form are to the *Antiquitates Romanae*; the rhetorical works are cited by title and chapter number, followed by the Teubner volume, page, and line numbering (Usener–Radermacher 1899–1905).

there for at least twenty-two years, until the publication of the first book of the *Antiquitates Romanae* in 7 B.C. (1.3.4).[4] How much longer he remained, before eventually retiring to Halicarnassus, is quite unknown. At any rate, it would seem that his adult working life was spent in a circle of Greeks and cultured philhellene Romans.[5] While some of these friends and patrons are mere names, others are better known; possible further connexions may be deduced or suggested.

Among Dionysius' Greek acquaintances was Pompeius Geminus, quite possibly a client of Pompey.[6] Evidently a man of literary taste – addressee of Dionysius' letter on historians – he was perhaps also the Geminus who wrote on mathematics and astronomy.[7] Another Greek associate, Caecilius of Caleacte, had much in common with Dionysius: both were concerned with literary technique and with Atticism, interested in problems of authenticity and attribution, and in using stylistic and historical methods to resolve them. In addition, they both wrote on historiography as well as composing actual works of history.[8] Strabo – a historian too – mentions Dionysius, and almost certainly knew him.[9]

Romans with whom Dionysius seems to have been on terms balanced between friendship and patronage include the Metilii (counted by Dionysius alone in the list of *gentes Albanae*).[10] The work *de compositione verborum* is dedicated to the younger Metilius, who – if he was, as is likely, the later governor of Achaea and Galatia – was connected by marriage with the historian Cremutius Cordus.[11] However, Dionysius' most important Roman patron was undoubtedly Q. Aelius Tubero, a scholar in several fields, jurist and historian, a friend of Varro and a connexion of Cicero.[12] In addition, he was an

[4] Book 1 was published separately (1.90.2, 2.1–2, 7.70.2); the appearance of the rest of the *AR* may not have taken long, as Book 4 was probably out before 2 B.C. (Gabba (1961) 113–14). There are indications in Book 1 that the rest of the work was already planned out, and at least part of it was perhaps completed. Dionysius' return to Halicarnassus is inferred from the existence of a descendant there (see n. 111 below).

[5] Rhys Roberts (1900), Goold (1961) 189–92, Bowersock (1965) 123–39.

[6] Anderson (1963) for Pompey as intellectual patron. Richards (1938) suggests that Dionysius' addressee was the author of *de sublimitate*; however, so early a date for that work is not very convincing; see also Bowersock (1979) 71.

[7] Aujac (1975) xxii–xxiv.

[8] *FGrHist* 183, Rhys Roberts (1897), Kennedy (1972) 364–69, Russell (1964) 58–59, Bowersock (1979) 65–67. Hurst (1982) 848 suggests that Caecilius forms a possible link with Timagenes and hence with the circle of Asinius Pollio; other likely contacts are with Apollodorus of Pergamum and Theodorus of Gadara (Kennedy (1972) 364).

[9] Str. 14.2.16, C 656, Bowersock (1965) 128–29, Sumner (1967) 133, Syme (1978) 101–2.

[10] 3.29.7 (contrast Livy 1.30.2); Bowersock (1965) 132 n. 2, Wiseman (1971) 206 nn. 3–4.

[11] *PIR*[2] M 185, 382, 395, 396; Groag (1939) 14–15 n. 60, Sumner (1967) 133.

[12] Cicero *Lig.* 1, 10, 21; Cichorius (1922) 227–28, Bowersock (1965) 129–30, Wiseman (1979) 136–39.

admirer of Thucydides and imitated him in his own *Historiae*.[13] It was for this Q. Tubero that Dionysius produced his work *de Thucydide*.[14] Dionysius was evidently a close associate of this family:[15] he may have had its members particularly in mind when speaking of the 'very learned men' (*logiōtatoi*) (1.7.3) who gave him information. His most substantial discussion of a contemporary Roman issue concerns manumission (4.24): the remedies he suggests for the degenerate current practice have something in common with the Lex Aelia Sentia of A.D. 4 – that consul Aelius being Sex. Catus, Q. Tubero's younger son.[16] Close ties linked the Aelii with the Seii and hence with Sejanus;[17] further connexions with the circle of Tiberius are not impossible, given the future emperor's legal interests and Hellenic tastes.[18] In a tribute to the rulers of Rome (*dunasteuontes*), Dionysius praises their culture and discernment, and attributes to their good influence not only the decline of Asianism and the victory of Atticism, but also the generally flourishing state of literature, with the publication of many excellent works, dealing with history, political matters, and philosophy.[19]

For such men, and their sons, Dionysius produced his works on Greek literature, covering various aspects of criticism: style, technique, authenticity.[20] His teaching was at a fairly high level and as a favour: he was not a poor hireling tutor, at any rate not by the period from which his works survive, and he appears anxious to stress that his writings are not *scholikos* and to dissociate himself from the hacks producing handbooks to teach rhetoric by rote.[21] Instead he presents himself as a man of learning, addressing cultured equals and fellow-scholars.[22] All his works, even those of a more didactic character, the addressees of which may fairly be described as pupils,

13 For Q. Tubero rather than his father L. Tubero as author of the surviving fragments (Peter (1914)) see especially Ogilvie (1965) 571, Wiseman (1979) 136–37. *Contra*, Badian (1966) 22.

14 *Thuc.* 1, 55 (UR 1.325.5–6, 326.7–12, 418.19–21); Bowersock (1965) 130 n. 2.

15 A *clientela* link formed when L. Tubero was Q. Cicero's *legatus* in Asia (Cic. *ad Q.f.* 1.1.10) is an attractive but unproved conjecture.

16 Gabba (1961) 112–14, De Dominicis (1966), Sherwin-White (1973) 327.

17 The precise relationship has been much discussed: Hennig (1975) 5–18 offers a summary of earlier views; Levick (1976) 158–59, 311 provides the most economical solution.

18 Suet. *Tib.* 70; Levick (1976) 16–18, 85, 89, 253 n. 33, Bowersock (1965) 77, 133–34, Syme (1978) 107–8, Stewart (1977).

19 *Or. Ant.* 3 (UR 1.5.21–6.12); Bowersock (1979) 65–67.

20 The most recent general discussion is that of Hurst (1982), with bibliography; on individual works see especially Bonner (1939) and Untersteiner (1959).

21 *Dem.* 46 (UR 1.231.19–21), *CV* 22 (UR 2.98.15–17), *2 Amm.* 1 (UR 1.422.3–4).

22 *1 Amm.* 1 (UR 1.257–58), *Pomp.* 1 (UR 2.221.3–18), *Thuc.* 1–2 (UR 1.325–27), 25 (UR 1.364.10–16), *Dem.* 42 (UR 1.223.19–224.12), 49 (UR 1.236.9–10).

assume acquaintance with a variety of Greek authors: poets (epic, lyric and dramatic) as well as prose writers (historians, orators and philosophers). In addition, quite thorough knowledge of some of these writers is taken for granted.[23]

Extensive reading, the investigation of literary technique, and the study of models were of course important parts of Dionysius' activity; it is nevertheless unfair to suggest that as a result he assimilated history to rhetoric, that he had no appreciation of the principles according to which history should be written, or that he was concerned only to elaborate and adorn his subject – criticisms typical of those which have been levelled at Dionysius as a historian.[24] Again, it is obviously unreasonable to demand too much of Dionysius – or of any Greek or Roman historian – in terms of techniques of investigation, methods of assessing evidence, attitude to the subject and scope of history, and so on.[25] As with Cicero, 'we have to ask not whether he had any notion of historical investigation that would satisfy a scholar today, but only whether his standards would have been the best accepted in antiquity'.[26]

Dionysius indicates his historiographical principles in the main preface to the *Antiquitates* (1.1–8), in a second preface midway through the work (11.1), and at a few incidental points; general discussion as well as detailed criticism of individual historians are to be found in the literary-critical works, especially *de imitatione*, the *Epistula ad Pompeium*, *de Thucydide* (to which the second letter to Ammaeus forms an explanatory appendix), and *de compositione verborum*.[27] His remarks suggest that he had high standards for the historian and a clear conception of his task. Truth, the source of *phronēsis* and *sophia*, is enshrined in history; the historian's function is thus of the utmost significance. Historical works reveal the soul and outlast the body; the historian must therefore be fitted both by moral character and by diligent application to treat suitable subjects. An

[23] Dionysius' own knowledge was extensive: Bonner (1939) 14–15, Pritchett (1975) xxii. For the assumptions he makes in the case of his pupils and addressees, note *Is.* 15 (UR 1.114.3–6), *CV* 16 (UR 2.68.1–2), *Dem.* 13, 14, 32, 42, 46 (UR 1.156.21–22, 158.11–12, 159.1–5, 201.16–18, 223.8–11, 231.21–24).

[24] The works of Liers (1886), Schwartz (1903), Halbfas (1910) set the trend for a critical attitude towards Dionysius; cf. Cary (1937) vol. 1.xv: 'an outstanding example of the mischievous results of that unnatural alliance between rhetoric and history which was the vogue after the time of Thucydides'.

[25] On historiographical theory generally see Scheller (1911), Avenarius (1956), Herkommer (1968), Brunt (1979).

[26] Brunt (1979) 316. As he notes (335), Dionysius' views on historians and historical theory are similar to those of Cicero.

[27] Only a brief outline of Dionysius' theory can be given here. For more detail on individual works and on the development of his thought see Halbfas (1910), Bonner (1939), Martin (1969), and Sacks (1983).

unworthy topic betrays a low mind; careless treatment demeans a noble subject. The praise of Theopompus in the letter to Pompeius is particularly revealing: his care and industry (*epimeleia* and *philoponia*) are stressed; he prepared himself carefully, spared no expense in collecting material, consorted with the great men of his day, and made his history the main object of his life.[28] This is like the Thucydidean and Polybian practice,[29] and Dionysius claims to be in the same tradition. His own studies and sources are mentioned in the preface to show that for him too history was no *parergon* but a life's work,[30] while it is noteworthy that Strabo refers to him not as *rhētōr* but as *sungrapheus* – perhaps not merely the way Dionysius preferred to be known, but actually the description Strabo expected his readers to associate with the name.[31] As well as his learning and diligence, Theopompus is equally well endowed with the moral qualities a historian needs. Dionysius praises his philosophical rhetoric, and regards his judgements of character and motive, made with frankness and even acerbity, as very proper. He defends Theopompus from the charge of malice, considering his practice as beneficial, like a surgeon's,[32] though he also admires (and himself follows) the *ethos* of Herodotus and Xenophon, showing pleasure in the good and grief at the bad.[33] In his own work he promises 'goodwill to all good men and to all those who enjoy contemplating fine and noble deeds' (1.6.5).

Great deeds are in Dionysius' view the proper content of a historical work:[34] greatness, novelty, and utility are required in a subject. Thus, in praise of Herodotus, the great deeds of the Persian Wars form a fine subject, and one pleasing to readers (better than that of Thucydides, for the misfortunes of Greece are a distasteful topic).[35] Novelty is a factor which may influence the historian, but which is not absolutely essential: Herototus is praised for excelling his

28 *Pomp.* 6 (UR 2.244.21–245.9).

29 Walbank (1972) 6ff., 40ff., 51ff.; on Polybius, Theopompus and Dionysius see Gozzoli (1976).

30 1.7; there is no need to believe, with Halbfas (1910) 20–21, that most of the twenty-two years was devoted to style alone: τὰ συντείνοντα πρὸς τὴν ὑπόθεσιν suggests a wider scope (1.7.2). On Dionysius' style see Usher (1982).

31 Str. 14.2.16, C 656. This would also bear out the idea that Dionysius' teaching was more or less casual and incidental to his main pursuits.

32 *Pomp.* 6 (UR 2.246.2–247.4).

33 *Pomp.* 3 (UR 2.238.15–17), 4 (UR 2.241.19–21). Thucydides and Philistus by contrast are grudging and condemnatory: 3 (UR 2.238.15–22), 5 (UR 2.243.4–5). On the historian's attitude see Scheller (1911) 34, cf. 48, Halbfas (1910) 46, 62ff.

34 1.1.2–3, 1.2.1. Three aspects of the subject's greatness (μέγεθος, κάλλος, μῆκος) are developed in 1.2.1–3.6. On the *topos* see Herkommer (1968) 39 n. 7, 165–67.

35 *Pomp.* 3 (UR 2.232.19–234.4). Xenophon and Theopompus chose good subjects (UR 2.241.5ff., 244.12ff.), Philistus a bad one (UR 2.242.16ff.). See Avenarius (1956) 82–84.

predecessors on the same theme.[36] Novel or not, however, the most important requirement is that history should be *ōphelimon*,[37] and for this it must be true. Discussing Thucydides' aims, Dionysius remarks that he wrote 'with a view to [his readers'] benefit, as he himself has made clear'. To prove this he quotes Thucydides 1.22.4, and continues: 'All, or at any rate most, philosophers and rhetoricians bear witness on behalf of Thucydides, that he had the greatest concern for the truth, whose high-priestess we wish history to be' (*Thuc.* 7–8, UR 1.334.4–16).[38] The connexion between usefulness and truth in history thus appears not only as necessary, but as widely accepted. Dionysius naturally offers no definition of *alētheia*, but two aspects are apparent in his usage. 'The true' is often the rationalized residue of a traditional story after it has been purged of mythical elements,[39] or tested by the application of commonsense criteria of reasonability. Such testing is one of the historian's duties.[40] Secondly, *alētheia* is closely associated with *akribeia*[41] – and *akribeia* often seems to relate to fullness rather than to precision or discrimination. *Akribeia* and completeness go together, while in contrast are lack of care and a summary treatment.[42] Dionysius promises to be *akribēs* rather than brief,[43] and to 'go through' (*dielthein* or *diexelthein*) all the factors;[44] he is very conscious of the fullness of material available:

[36] *Pomp.* 3 (UR 2.234.10–15). A historian may have to adopt a subject δι' ἀνάγκην (ibid., line 5). Dionysius however claims to offer genuine novelty with his treatment of Rome from the earliest times to the First Punic War (1.2.1; 1.6.1–2). See also n. 104 below.

[37] As Dionysius' is to be: 1.1.2; 1.2.1; 1.6.3–5. Three groups will benefit: the Romans of the past, their descendants (present and future), and the historian himself. Strictly speaking, it is only the second group who will derive the advantage of being inspired to emulate their ancestors and choose noble lives. The good result relating to the other two parties lies rather in seeing justice done: the heroes of the past will gain fitting praise and glory, and Dionysius himself will pay his due tribute of gratitude to Rome and goodwill to lovers of the good. Dionysius thus neatly links the ideas of the historian as the recorder and immortalizer of great deeds and the historian as teacher with a modest presentation of himself as the friend of mankind in general – good men transcend national boundaries – and of Rome in particular. For the theme of usefulness in history see Scheller (1911) 72–78, Avenarius (1956) 22–26.

[38] Brunt (1979) 338.

[39] 1.39.1, 1.40.6–41.1, 1.79.1; Avenarius (1956) 19–20, Wiseman (1979) 49.

[40] 9.22.5, 4.30.3; Avenarius (1956) 72 n. 4.

[41] As by Thucydides 1.22.1–2; see also 5.26.5, 6.55.1, Plb. 12.4d.2, *Din.* 2 (UR 1.299.9–10) with Marenghi (1970) 18–19. Avenarius (1956) 42 n. 12 considers the two ideas as 'almost synonymous' in Dionysius, Diodorus, and Josephus.

[42] Dionysius' predecessors offered ὀλίγα καὶ οὐδὲ ἀκριβῶς (1.6.1, cf. 1.5.4) but his own accurate narrative will have beneficial results (1.6.3).

[43] 7.66.5, 3.18.1. κεφάλαιος and βραχύς are contrasted with ἀκριβής: 1.5.4, 1.6.2, 5.56.1, 11.1.3. See also 7.66.2.

[44] 11.1.1, 11.1.5, 7.66.3. See also Wiseman (1979) 52 and n. 57. But note 4.63.3: δι' ὀλίγων πειράσομαι διελθεῖν.

a plethora of facts and arguments[45] which the historian has to deploy to best advantage.

Exposition is therefore an important aspect of the historian's task: his aim is clarity (*saphēneia*).[46] His work must be well conceived both as regards starting and stopping points, and as regards internal organization, with particular attention to the system of chronological, local or thematic arrangement used.[47] A further requirement is to determine which events demand lengthy treatment, and which shall be summarized. Thucydides receives some criticism here, which does not show Dionysius at his most perceptive;[48] equally, some of Dionysius' detractors have gone too far in condemning him, for he is not in fact merely demanding that similar happenings be treated at similar length. He is offering some criteria for selecting which of two or more similar but chronologically separate episodes to elaborate; he recommends, chiefly, either the fact of priority (i.e. that the earliest example of similar episodes be expanded rather than any of the subsequent ones) or the greater importance of a particular one among similar episodes as measured by its effect on the subsequent course of events, criteria which are in general reasonable enough.

The demonstration (*dēlōsis*) of a particular event, fact or argument is one of the historian's duties;[49] the reciprocal aspect of this is that the reader, instead of hearing, is said to see or to enjoy the contemplation (*theōria*) of some event.[50] This aspect perhaps brings the historian as close as he can come to the orator: the reader who contemplates the attendant circumstances (*ta parakolouthounta*) presented by the historian (11.1.4) is very like the one impressed by Lysias' *enargeia*:[51] Lysias' power of conveying the things he describes to the senses of his audience results from his grasp of *ta parakolouthounta* (*Lys*. 7, UR 1.14.22–15.1). Dionysius clearly considers that for the historian, too, speeches are the best means of expounding the contributory factors and circumstances, and indeed speeches are so important in explaining action that they virtually rank among *aitiai* (7.66.1–3). The arguments contained in the speeches are a matter for

45 This can be mere circumstantial trivia, the sort of thing that Plutarch (*Thes*. 27.3) found in Cleidemus, and Polybius condemned as often invented (3.33.17); Wiseman (1979) 150ff. Often for Dionysius it is the circumstances and causes of great events: Liers (1886) 13, Verdin (1974) 303 with n. 66.

46 See *Thuc*. 9 (UR 1.338.2–3) with Pritchett's (1975) comments ad loc.

47 *Pomp*. 3 (UR 2.234–38), and *Thuc*. 9–21 *passim* for discussion of the various aspects involved.

48 *Thuc*. 15, 16, 18 (UR 1.347–48, 349.13–20, 350.12ff.).

49 1.5.1, 1.8.2.

50 11.1.3: ὁρῶσα; 11.1.4: τῇ παντελεῖ θεωρίᾳ.

51 *Enargeia* is important for the historian too: *Pomp*. 3 (UR 2.239.14–16).

heuresis – in theory a high intellectual gift granted by nature (as, for instance, to Thucydides) and backed up by the technical skill and practice in the use (*chrēsis*) of the figures and concepts (*enthumēmata* and *noēmata*) which are suggested by *heuresis*.[52] The ideas once found, the historian must deploy them in an unstrained, natural, and appropriate manner;[53] style and content should complement each other, for obscurity, whether of thought or style, is no virtue (not even in Thucydides), and, whether due to wilfulness or ineptitude, it must not be allowed to interfere with communication between the historian and his audience.

This, then, is the theory; what about the practice? It is very easy to disparage Dionysius for his sometimes inept or misguided criticisms of historians better than himself, though as he truly remarks 'it does not follow that if we are inferior in ability to Thucydides and other men, we therefore forfeit the right to form an estimate of them' (*Thuc.* 4, UR 1.329.17–19, Pritchett's translation), and it is tempting to use the faults of the *Antiquitates Romanae* as a decisive condemnation of Dionysius for failing as a historian even to live up to his own inadequate precepts as critic. While the various shortcomings of his history – its *longueurs*, its often tiresome repetitiveness of incidents and speeches – are fully admitted, these must be counterbalanced by the real efforts Dionysius makes to achieve his ideals for the historian, given a subject which precluded autoptic investigation.[54] Credit is due for his painstaking collation of sources, for his original and exhaustive efforts at chronological investigation and systematization,[55] and for his serious purpose in offering his readers not just annals in Greek but a *historia* of early Rome – a genuine attempt at historical interpretation.

Three major and interrelated themes can be seen in the *Antiquitates Romanae* – themes which are clearly developed by Dionysius by applying Greek ideas and theories to his largely Roman source material: (1) the Greek origin of the Romans; (2) the development of the Roman constitution, in which the Roman people is seen as a Greek *dēmos*, whose political growth is a progress towards fuller participation within a mixed constitution; (3) the remarkable avoidance of *stasis*, attributed chiefly to the virtues of the constitution and, to an extent, to the Roman character.

The essential Greekness of the Romans is explicitly stated – and demonstrated – in Book 1 of the *Antiquitates Romanae*. The method

[52] *Thuc.* 34 (UR 1.381–82) with Pritchett (1975) ad loc.; Avenarius (1956) 71 n. 2. But *heuresis* can be a merely facile process: *Thuc.* 15 (UR 1.347.6–8); cf. 8.48.4.

[53] *Thuc.* 42 (UR 1.398.6–14).

[54] On autopsy see Nenci (1955) 42, Schepens (1970).

[55] I hope to discuss these aspects elsewhere.

Dionysius adopts there is quite untypical of the rest of the work. With close and detailed arguments he takes all of the incomers to Italy contributing to Roman stock, and proves a Greek origin for each race. The 'proof' consists of testimonia from a wide range of Greek and Roman writers:[56] about fifty authors are named and characterized, with a brief description and setting in context; the item for which they are cited is quoted or paraphrased, and numerous variants are discussed.[57] The method owes something to antiquarian practice, and also something to Dionysius' own familiarity with the use of quotation as illustration in his literary-historical works. At any rate, Dionysius, elsewhere so sensitive to stylistic considerations, here appears quite unconcerned by the resulting divergence of styles: he is far more interested in the clarity of his step-by-step demonstration. He gives his reasons for accepting, rejecting, or occasionally modifying any particular item of testimony: the reader is not tricked, but is shown the stages of the argument, so that he can judge the value of the evidence for himself. However, Dionysius holds that in the end the cumulative effect is bound to prove his contention that the Romans are Greeks (1.13.4, 1.89–90).

This method of explicit comparison and discussion of sources virtually disappears after Book 1, but, although Dionysius scarcely mentions sources or variants in the later books, he is still evidently assessing and selecting from those available.[58] He chooses certain events for extended treatment,[59] he compresses other episodes (including speeches),[60] and he switches sources, particularly in order to attribute cogent and convincing arguments to fit the *personae* and political attitudes of his characters.[61]

[56] Many of them are very obscure; in several cases, Dionysius is the only writer of the first centuries B.C. or A.D. to quote them. It would however be unduly sceptical either to doubt that they were available in libraries in Rome, or to posit another work from which Dionysius derived the references.

[57] 1.48.3, 1.49.1, 1.73.4, 1.80.1 are good examples of his method; see Musti (1970), especially c. 1.

[58] For example 2.24.1, 2.63.1.

[59] Dionysius did not even attempt to allot approximately equal space to the events of every year; instead, major episodes are elaborated at disproportionate length. In the first half of the work, these are the establishment of the Republic, the First Secession and the story of Coriolanus, and the Decemvirate. Books 11 to 20 survive only in part; almost certainly the story of Camillus balanced that of Coriolanus, while other high points may have been the Caudine Forks episode, the passage of the Lex Hortensia (concluding the theme of the plebeian struggle for equal rights), and the Pyrrhic War. Minor episodes are interspersed, while some years are treated very briefly indeed.

[60] 1.84.2–8 (the rationalized version of the Romulus and Remus story) shows the methods by which an episode is 'compressed', in contrast to the full narrative described as that of Fabius, which is given in 1.79.4–83.3. Another example is 2.45–46.1, where both the events and Hersilia's speech are summarized.

[61] It is noteworthy that there are no sharply contrasted 'good' and 'bad' characters; indeed, individual characterization is on the whole avoided by Dionysius, in favour of allowing all speakers to put over fairly reasonable cases for their particular policies or

The second theme is the political development of the 'Roman *dēmos*'. Dionysius presents Rome as a sharply divided *polis*: the *oligoi*, the rich, senators and patricians on the one side, and on the other the *dēmos* or *plēthos*, the poor plebeians (*dēmotikoi*).[62] Distinctions of which Dionysius shows himself well aware in his accounts of institutions often disappear in the course of the narrative. Thus he knows quite well the difference between *assidui* and *proletarii*, *populus* and *plebs*, and has a grasp of the procedural details and membership of the various assemblies, but he is not consistent in the terminology he applies to the voters.[63] When a specific decision is to be taken, it is much more important to him that here is the *dēmos* voting, that it is exercising its threefold function of deciding on laws, war and peace, and election[64] – he does not care whether it is the *populus* or *plebs*, whether the result will be a *lex* or a *plebiscitum*, and whom it will bind. He goes even further in depicting the Roman people in Greek terms: this *dēmos* is shown as taking final and sometimes arbitrary decisions in the spirit of rule by *psēphisma*; magistrates are represented as accountable to the *dēmos* in a sort of *euthuna*; at times of constitutional crisis (for example, the establishment of the Republic, and, probably, the restoration of normality after the Decemvirate) he tends to present the *dēmos* as decisive and, in the last resort, as the ultimate source of authority.[65] The role of the senate is suppressed in favour of the predominance of popular decision, for example at *interregna*; and *vis-à-vis* magistrates, the principle that the *dēmos* has the right to abrogate an office is by implication accepted.[66]

The process of political development is represented broadly as one of gains on the popular side, losses on the senatorial side – viewed with approval by Dionysius, who clearly sees such steps as recognition of the principle of popular trial as progress (7.65–66). However, he does not envisage progress as extending as far as the establishment of actual *dēmokratia*. Democratic elements in a constitution may be appropriate and equitable, *dēmotikos* may figure as a term of praise,[67]

beliefs. See Wiseman (1979) cc. 5 and 6 for illustration of this in the case of Claudii and Valerii; Dionysius' method is similar in his depiction of the various tribunes.

62 Pabst (1969) 70ff., Noè (1979).

63 E.g. δῆμος and δημοτικός do not always indicate plebeians exclusively; Develin (1975) 328 n. 118 is thus relying too heavily on Dionysius' terminology when he tries to show that a plebeian assembly must be meant in such passages as 7.59.9.

64 Aristotle *Pol.* 1298a3–10.

65 E.g. 5.32.2, 9.54.6, 11.52 (overriding the advice of magistrates); 6.40.2, 6.44.3, 9.37.4–38.1, 10.34.2, 10.49.5 (accountability); 4.71.3, 4.74.1–3, 4.84.3–4 (establishment of Republic); 11.5.4, cf. 11.45.1 (overthrow of Decemvirate).

66 2.57.3, with Pabst (1969) 19–23 for the different emphasis in the Livian version of the *interregnum*; 5.10.2 and 7; 5.11.1–2 (abrogation).

67 δημοτικός usually has a favourable application (e.g. 5.2.2, 7.45.4), and is often combined with commendatory terms such as δίκαιος and μέτριος; ὀλιγαρχικός is always unfavourable, and often implies lack of freedom (e.g. 7.20.4, 11.22.1–2).

and yet full democracy is clearly not seen as a desirable goal. Dionysius conceives of the Roman constitution in *miktē* terms from the start,[68] and he shows how it achieved a more appropriate balance of elements in response to changing circumstances.[69] The background to this process of adaptation is one of constant *stasis*, again depicted in Greek terms.

The third theme – eventual compromise and concession promoting political progress and averting *stasis* – recurs throughout the work. Many of the motifs are drawn from Dionysius' reading of Thucydides and Isocrates: bitter divisions, desperate poverty, exile for the plebeians, intransigence on the part of the rich, potential violence.[70] He emphasizes how close Rome came to breakdown of the social order – yet it was always avoided: 'they took no drastic and irrevocable step' is his refrain.[71] By contrast with the irreparable ills – the *anēkesta kaka* – of Greece, the situation in Rome had a different and surprising outcome: *homonoia* or *concordia*. He draws attention to the fact that this *homonoia* (attributable to the Roman constitution) lasted for 630 years – that is, from the city's foundation until the time of Gaius Gracchus, when blood was first shed.[72]

This, Dionysius is aware, will appear *paradoxon* and *apiston* to his Greek readers: in order to convince them, the historian must explain the underlying *aitiai* which brought about a situation so contrary not only to *eikos* but also to the experience of Rome in the post-Gracchan period. Amongst these causes, speeches are an important factor. And it will not be Dionysius' fault if the reader fails to comprehend the *aitiai*, for unlike other historians (whom he condemns) he includes speeches to accompany every stage of the Romans' political progress. With slight variations, three main opinions are expressed: representatives of the *dēmos* state their grievances and beg or demand reforms or concessions; more or less hawkish conservatives advocate standing firm; moderates point out the reasonableness of change. The inclusion of all these speeches is justified in a methodological chapter, apropos of the first *stasis* after the expulsion of the kings.[73] Dionysius

[68] 2.14. The Romulean constitution is discussed by Gabba (1960), and Leavitt (1966) of which latter see especially 77.

[69] At the establishment of the Republic, the ancestral *politeia* is said to be the best (4.73.1) and continuity is stressed (4.75.4), yet in fact the consulship embodies various checks and balances in an entirely new office (4.73.4, 4.74.1–3): thus there both is and is not change. The speech of M'. Valerius (7.54–56) clearly recognizes the need for constitutional change, and combines the ideas of *miktē* and cycle: see especially 7.55.2–4, 7.56.3–4.

[70] For these themes in literature and reality see Fuks (1972) and (1974), Noè (1979), and Lintott (1982).

[71] 7.18.1, 7.26.4.

[72] 2.11.2–3. 630 years is correct by Dionysius' chronological reckoning method, in which the foundation date of Rome is Ol. 7,1 = 752/1 B.C.

[73] See also 6.72.1, 7.17.3. Dionysius does not discuss the inclusion of speeches, still less the authenticity of their content, in his preface: perhaps he felt on shaky ground, or

considers that this *stasis* was concluded not by the establishment of the tribunate after the First Secession, but a little later, when the right of popular trial was achieved in the Coriolanus case. 'I have given a long account of these matters, so that no one will wonder why the patricians agreed to put such great power into the hands of the *dēmos* [...] I considered that my account would have little or no credibility if I said only that the patricians yielded their power to the plebeians, and, when they could have continued to conduct the constitution as an aristocracy, they nevertheless gave the *dēmos* control of the most important matters, and if I left out the *aitiai* for this concession. Therefore I have gone through them all. And since they did not make this change as a result of armed force and compulsion, but because they were persuaded by speeches [*logois peisantes*], I considered it above all imperative to go through the speeches then made by the leading men of each side.' For historians give military matters in great detail, 'yet when they describe civil disturbances and *staseis*, they do not consider it necessary to report the speeches which have brought about these surprising and remarkable events'.[74]

Thus for Dionysius, a situation of *stasis* has here not merely ended without violence, but actually with a positive development along the lines of classic analyses of democracy. There is no dishonourable stalemate or imposed reconciliation, nor the intervention of an individual, whether tyrant or lawgiver. Yet at a very early stage in Roman history, comparable in date to Greek developments, the Romans recognized and accepted the necessity and the responsibility of political participation. This is the political expression of the moral factors which the reader is to admire in the Romans. The promise made in 1.90.2 – that, having demonstrated the Greek *genos* of Rome, Dionysius would add a treatment of its *politeia* – should be seen as being fulfilled in the rest of the work as a whole, rather than in any one section.[75] Dionysius asserts that the Romans have always lived like Greeks ('bion hellēna zōntes' – 1.90.1); this recalls the undertaking in the preface that he will show the whole of the *archaios bios* of the Roman *polis* in his work – all its wars, *staseis*, forms of government, customs, and laws.[76] The close connexion of the *bios* and *politeia* is reminiscent of Isocrates' description of the *politeia* as the

considered the theme too well worn. On the practice in general see Walbank (1965), and on Dionysius in particular, Wiseman (1979) 29, 51–52.

[74] 7.66.1–3.

[75] Thus not, for example, *only* in the accounts of the constitutions of Romulus and Servius Tullius (2.7ff., 4.13ff.), as Pohlenz (1924) 163 n. 2, and Gabba (1960) 181 n. 11 imply.

[76] 1.8.2.

psuchē poleōs (*Areop.* 14).[77] Dionysius similarly regards the *politeia* as more than the mere constitutional bones: rather it shapes the whole attitude and mode of life of the *polis*.

Thus the three aspects are related to one idea: that the Romans are not only Greeks but are better than actual Hellenes, more truly Greek in their customs and behaviour generally, and above all in their *politeia*.[78] For Dionysius, Hellene is as Hellene does, and the prime characteristic is humane behaviour, for which the Romans are outstanding (14.6). Dionysius does not expect this view of the Romans to be readily acceptable. He anticipates readers being sceptical or at least critical. In the first place, then, the historian must convince the reader. This calls into action all those skills and virtues of intellect, technique and character which he should possess. And, in convincing the reader, the historian is also teaching him moral and/or political truths. Thus the reader is meant to realize that the Romans, as presented here, are exemplars, and their behaviour is a model for imitation. Further, the world rule of the Romans is explained, its justification even implied. If, then, the historian is intending to present a lesson from history, it is pertinent to wonder who in actual fact might respond to this offer? Whom did Dionysius envisage as his audience, and what does the composition of a work like the *Antiquitates Romanae* indicate about contemporary expectations and tastes in historical reading matter?

If supply indeed reflects an actual demand, there clearly was a reading public for history in the Augustan age, as in the preceding generation. Cicero's time saw the productions of authors such as Archias, Theophanes of Mytilene, Empylus and Socrates of Rhodes, Diodorus, writing in Greek, as did Romans like Lucullus and of course Cicero himself, while historical composition in Latin seems to have been a minor industry for the leisured class: M. and Q. Cicero, L. Tubero, Varro, Atticus, Caesar, Lucceius, Sallust, Valerius Antias, Tanusius Geminus, Procilius.[79] Then there was Nepos, evidently fulfilling a new need by supplying easy lessons in Greek history, for a public, presumably, of rather less education than Cicero and his friends – one of the indicators that history was moving down-market.[80] Moreover, subject-matter that can be broadly classed as historical was being

[77] Dionysius clearly regards the presentation of the προαίρεσις and ἤθη of the πολιτεία as an important element of the *Areopagiticus* (*Isoc.* 8 (UR 1.65.18–19)).

[78] On the Greek theme in Dionysius see Musti (1970) c. 1, Gabba (1982), Hurst (1982) 851–56.

[79] *FGrHist* 186, 188, 191, 192, 185; Peter (1906, 1914) *sub nominibus*.

[80] Wiseman (1979) 157–66.

treated in quite a diversity of modes, some perhaps more immediately attractive than others: monographs on topics of contemporary history or the recent past, biography and encomium, annals A.U.C., universal history, as well as 'fringe' works of an antiquarian–mythical–genealogical character.[81]

This level and variety of production continued in the Augustan period: among Greeks there were Timagenes, Nicolaus of Damascus, Diodorus of Sardis, Juba of Mauretania, Dionysius' friend Caecilius; and Romans, from the noblest to the obscure, like Messalla Corvinus, Q. Dellius, Asinius Pollio, Cremutius Cordus – these all treating, with varying degrees of sincerity or self-exculpation, the recent past; the Sallustian C. Arruntius who went back to the First Punic War, Clodius Licinus tackling the second century B.C.; Livy, Fenestella, and of course Q. Aelius Tubero, dealing with history A.U.C.; and Pompeius Trogus undertaking universal history.[82]

There were, therefore, plenty of histories available – but did the demand for them come from statesmen and men of affairs (the sort of audience that Polybius envisaged), or was history popular and even widely read?[83] Pliny appears to describe a later public eager for any histories, even poor quality works: 'History always pleases, however it is written. Men are naturally curious and are attracted by information, however badly presented, given that they always enjoy small talk and anecdote' (*Ep.* 5.8.4). Innate curiosity can be counted as a permanent factor; there are, moreover, actual indications that in so far as any type of literature can be described as 'popular' or 'widely read' in the ancient world, history would qualify: it appears to have been regarded as easy reading, and as read for pleasure.

In *de oratore* 2.59 Cicero makes Antonius discuss reading 'delectationis causa': the works he chooses are by Greek authors, and are those 'quae ipsi, qui scripserunt, voluerunt vulgo intellegi'. He avoids works of philosophy, because although they claim to treat well-known subjects like virtue or justice they are so technical that he cannot understand a word, and also poetry, for poets have a language of their own. So what he reads are *res gestae* or speeches, or works written in such a way 'ut videantur voluisse nobis, qui non sumus eruditissimi, esse familiares' (2.61).[84] History is thus included as one of the more accessible forms of literature. Speaking in the

[81] Wiseman (1979) 143ff., esp. 149–51.

[82] Clark (1973) discusses some of these writers individually, and the scope for historians generally in Augustan Rome (184–233).

[83] Plb. 9.1; Walbank (1972) 55ff. Polybius' very insistence on the superiority of his own history and its suitability for an élite indicates the popularity of works of a lower standard.

[84] Brunt (1979) 323.

person of M. Pupius Piso Calpurnianus in *de finibus* 5.51–52,[85] Cicero instances the universal attraction of history. The matter at issue is the pleasure of intellectual curiosity: why do men pursue useless or non-practical knowledge, studying the stars or nature, reading *fictae fabulae* or history (though the latter is admitted to have an element of *utilitas*)? Why are they so interested in learning all sorts of details *minime necessaria* about notable men? The striking point is that these interests are shared by those whose lives and circumstances are utterly remote from public affairs: 'quid quod homines infima fortuna, nulla spe rerum gerendarum, opifices denique delectantur historia? maximeque eos videre possumus res gestas audire et legere velle qui a spe gerendi absunt confecti senectute.' So it seems to be regarded as reasonable and obvious that not only actual (and potential and former) participants in events take pleasure in history, but also the humble and the politically inactive – *opifices denique*.

Dionysius' attitude is similar: his intention is not to appeal only to a narrow literary coterie; on the contrary, he believes that historical works should be accessible to a wide readership. This is clear from the attitude he takes to certain authorities on Thucydides' style:[86] they hold that, while not suitable for political debates or private conversations, it is eminently suited to historical works, which are designed not for traders and artisans[87] but for the highly educated, who have studied philosophy and rhetoric, and to whom 'none of these things will appear strange' (*Thuc.* 50, UR 1.409.8–26). Dionysius' reply is that very few indeed can understand the whole of Thucydides, and even they sometimes require a grammatical commentary: thus he absolutely rejects the pretensions of the educated, and the intellectual snobbery that would claim that Thucydides is easy for the *eupaideutoi*. He goes even further, asserting that such an exclusive attitude obviates the useful purpose of the work: 'By limiting the work to a very few men exactly as in cities of an oligarchic or tyrannical form of government, they remove from the ordinary life of mankind that feature of the work which comprises its indispensability and its universal utility (for nothing could be more indispensable and of more varied use)' (*Thuc.* 51, UR 1.410.8–15).[88] The direct

[85] I thank Professor T. P. Wiseman for discussing this passage with me.

[86] These authorities are unnamed: for Thucydides' *Nachleben* in this period see Strebel (1935) 28–50. They are more likely to be Greeks (Caecilius of Caleacte has been suggested: see Pritchett (1975) ad loc.) than Roman Thucydides-imitators like Tubero. It is striking that Dionysius clearly feels no need either to defer to their judgements or to flatter Tubero by pretending to any excessive admiration of Thucydides.

[87] *Thuc.* 50 (UR 1.409.21–23).

[88] ὅτι τὸ τοῦ πράγματος ἀναγκαῖόν τε καὶ χρήσιμον ἅπασιν (οὐδὲν γὰρ ⟨ἂν⟩ ἀναγκαιότερον γένοιτο οὐδὲ πολυωφελέστερον) ἀναιροῦσιν ἐκ τοῦ κοινοῦ βίου, ὀλίγων παντάπασιν

reference is to the usefulness of Thucydides' own work; however, given that a constant theme of the *de Thucydide* is *mimēsis*, and that mention has just been made of 'those who produce historical works', it can be taken to apply to the whole historical genre.[89] The simile is noteworthy: oligarchy and tyranny stand for all that is narrow, exclusive and unjust; history should be freely available, open, and democratic. The historian must make his work accessible because it is intended above all to be useful.

Dionysius' own work aimed to attract a wide audience. In the preface he says that he hopes to offer satisfaction to three categories of readers: 'to those who occupy themselves with political debates, and to those who are devoted to philosophical speculations, as well as to any who may desire mere undisturbed entertainment in their reading of history' (1.8.3).[90] Polybius had claimed *politikoi* as the historian's proper audience; for Dionysius, the *philosophoi*, though not identical, are closely akin to these, for they are very practical philosophers: 'men who are engaged in the conduct of civil affairs, among whom I for my part include also those philosophers who regard philosophy as consisting in the practice of fine actions rather than of fine words [...]'.[91] In this 'second preface', too, Dionysius does not ignore other readers, for the understanding of *aitiai* is not confined to the *politikoi* and *philosophoi* but appears as a widespread, indeed a universal human desire: 'For the minds of all men take delight in being conducted through words to deeds and not only in hearing what is related but also in beholding what is done.'[92] Moreover, he continues, they want more than just to know the mere outline and result; they demand to understand how, why, and all the circumstances involved. This, then, is a larger group of people, and a higher motive, than that third category in 1.8.3, who wish to be entertained. It seems from 11.1 that all three kinds of readers can, perhaps in varying degrees, derive something useful from history; moreover the *hēdonē* involved has an intellectual aspect which puts it above the 'undisturbed enjoyment' of 1.8.3.

For Dionysius, the opposed aspects of *to terpnon* and *to chrēsimon* in history[93] are by no means of equal importance. The former tends

ἀνθρώπων οὕτω ποιοῦντες, ὥσπερ ἐν ταῖς ὀλιγαρχουμέναις ἢ τυραννουμέναις πόλεσιν. Given in Pritchett's translation; for ἐκ τοῦ κοινοῦ βίου he offers 'the world we live in' as an alternative; Usher (1974) 617 has 'ordinary men's lives'.

[89] τοῖς δὲ τὰς ἱστορικὰς πραγματείας ἐκφέρουσιν (*Thuc.* 50 (UR 1.409.16)). On *mimēsis* see Pritchett (1975) 104 n. 4.

[90] This and the two passages which follow are given in Cary's translation. ἵνα καὶ τοῖς περὶ τοὺς πολιτικοὺς διατρίβουσι λόγους καὶ τοῖς περὶ τὴν φιλόσοφον ἐσπουδακόσι θεωρίαν καὶ εἴ τισιν ἀοχλήτου δεήσει διαγωγῆς ἐν ἱστορικοῖς ἀναγνώσμασιν ἀποχρώντως ἔχουσα φαίνηται.

[91] 11.1.4.

[92] 11.1.3.

[93] Avenarius (1956) 22–29.

to be associated with stylistic beauties, which Dionysius certainly does not condemn – indeed, he considers that numerous historians have paid too little attention to the 'beauty of words' (*CV* 4, UR 2.20.18ff.). However, from the *de Thucydide* it is apparent that Dionysius is interested less in style as an end in itself than as an appropriate means for conveying the historian's thought. Another aspect of the enjoyable element in history is *psuchagōgia*; like Isocrates and Polybius, Dionysius firmly rejects this.[94] For example, digressions are intended as information and explanation, not mere *psuchagōgia*; this is his defence of Theopompus' practice, and his own.[95] Then it is with some deprecation that he mentions the *theatrikos* aspects of a story; in his usage the word has a slightly disparaging sense.[96] An allowable and worthy form of enjoyment is derived from variety (a widespread claim).[97] Polybius asserted that changes of venue give his history a natural and sufficient variety;[98] Dionysius' comes from the inclusion of (relevant) disquisitions on different topics (1.8.2), and from a *schēma* which is not *monoeides* but 'is a combination of every kind, forensic, speculative and narrative' (1.8.3).[99]

Variety thus regarded is close to comprehensiveness; the enjoyable aspect shades into the useful one, for the varied items are not in themselves merely frivolous or exciting. Dionysius frequently mentions that it is 'not inappropriate' to include some particular point; he reminds the reader that the historian is carefully judging and selecting.[100] In this process the useful is a more important criterion than the enjoyable. The *ōpheleia* aspect of history can have two main functions.[101] The first – to help men bear the vicissitudes of *tuchē* – is rare in Dionysius, in contrast to, say, Polybius. The second lies in helping *politikoi* both to formulate their own plans and to convince others to adopt a certain course of action. This does appear, as at 5.56.1, where Dionysius justifies giving precise instructions for exposing conspirators: it is for the benefit of statesmen so that they may have *paradeigmata* in case a similar situation recurs. Convincing

94 Isoc. *ad Nic.* 48–49; Plb. 2.56.11–12. Cf. *Thuc.* 6 (UR 1.333.4ff.); Walbank (1972) 38 n. 29, Gozzoli (1976) 161.

95 *Pomp.* 6 (UR 2.245.15–16), 7.70.1.

96 3.18.1, 9.22.3; Pritchett (1975) 48 n. 5.

97 Scheller (1911) 38.

98 Plb. 38.5–6, with Walbank ad loc.

99 This is Cary's translation of the text, with his own supplement for the lacuna: ἀλλ' ἐξ ἁπάσης ἰδέας μικτὸν ἐναγωνίου τε καὶ θεωρητικῆς ⟨καὶ διηγηματικῆς⟩; Jacoby supplies ⟨καὶ ἡδείας⟩. Cary's suggestion seems preferable: the three categories clearly relate to the three types of reader specified in the passage quoted in n. 90 above, which follows immediately on the present one, and some indication of the content designed to appeal to the third kind of reader is needed.

100 E.g. 2.24.1, 2.63.1, 2.64.5, 7.2.5.

101 Verdin (1974) 298–301.

others occurs at 11.1.5: 'for men most easily recognize the policies which either benefit or injure them when they perceive these illustrated by many examples; and those who advise them to make use of these are credited by them with prudence and great wisdom'.[102]

While this may be part of Dionysius' intention, it has to be admitted that in the context of contemporary Rome or even of the Greek cities of the empire, it is not a wholly realistic aim. The programme stated has similarities with Dionysius' occasional intrusive attributions of 'real' political motivation.[103] There is an element of the conventional in Dionysius' attempt to conform to the model of the historian addressing statesmen. Thus some consideration must be given to his purpose in relation to the wider, non-*politikos* audience. These readers too wish to understand *aitiai*, they too are credited with some appreciation of argument, they too are capable of grasping the explanation which Dionysius provides for Rome's greatness. The exposition and the examples may not have the sole – even the main – purpose of providing the statesman with ammunition; the historian addresses all his readers, in democratic fashion, and, by argument and by demonstration, his aim is to convince them.

The Greek members of Dionysius' audience might be expected to benefit in two ways. Firstly, for them the subject-matter is a novelty or virtually so – Dionysius is very keen to stake his own claim to be giving the first authoritative account of early Roman history – even to the extent of some unfairness to Timaeus.[104] But undoubtedly his treatment must be fuller and more closely based on Roman sources than the latter's, so for the early Republic at least he will be offering Greeks much that is new to them. Explanations of Roman institutions are also mainly aimed at the Greek audience, though possibly in the case of some antiquarian points and the more obscure customs he might have Romans in mind too. Secondly, the Greeks are meant to feel reassured – flattered, even – by the proof that Rome is a *polis Hellēnis*. Rome is firmly and authoritatively set within a Greek mythological–genealogical context; conflicts of tradition are cleared up; the Etruscans are put in their place as autochthonous; and the view that Latin is a Greek dialect is maintained.[105] And it is not a

[102] Cary's translation. In Verdin's view, this aspect is Dionysius' main purpose.

[103] E.g. the attribution of guileful statecraft to Tullus Hostilius (3.3) and Servius Tullius (4.20–21), and the reflections on diversionary wars (8.83.2). In positing such motives, Dionysius reveals a would-be knowing or cynical attitude, as if he suddenly recalls that the historian ought to show experience of the world, scepticism, and penetration.

[104] Dionysius minimizes Timaeus' writings on early Rome (1.6.1), is disparaging about his chronology (1.74.1), and is priggishly dismissive of his researches (1.67.4); denigration of a predecessor is most unlike Dionysius' normal attitude: no doubt he felt Timaeus to be his own most serious rival, and an accepted authority to the Greeks.

[105] Gabba (1963). See also the works cited in n. 78.

matter of mere origins – the cultural superiority of the Greeks is reinforced by the demonstration that all that is good in Roman society, and all its success, is attributable to Greek ideals and Greek culture, and not to *tuchē*;[106] and that the political development of Rome has followed, and in their own age, continues to follow, along the most approved lines of political theory.

Romans, the present descendants of the *isotheoi* men of old Rome to whom Dionysius alludes in his preface (1.6.4), might be expected to appreciate other aspects of the work. Cultured, literary, Greek-speaking Romans such as those whom Dionysius encountered in society will hardly have read his history for the novelty of its actual subject-matter (except for Book 1); the appeal would be in the novelty of interpretation, with the application of political analysis to dignify Rome's early development – and to point a moral for the present and recent past. Dionysius' Roman readers in particular could hardly fail to draw a comparison between the *staseis* of the early Republic and the generation of civil war which ended at Actium – a period during which olden-time *homonoia* had been so conspicuously lacking. Dionysius' reiterated theme of compromise and concession might hold a lesson: that certain rights and powers must be granted to the *dēmos* until the stability of a mixed constitution is achieved; that representatives of all shades of opinion may be sincerely motivated, and may show high principle at one time, and poor judgement at another; and, especially, that a narrow oligarchy cannot expect to retain exclusive power.

A series of political gains, viewed favourably in the narrative, constitutes a process bringing the *dēmos* closer to its proper position in the state. Commenting with approval on the ending of the first great episode of *stasis* in 7.65–66, Dionysius gives an opinion which has a contemporary reference, to Augustus and his constitutional position. The senate has conceded the popular trial principle in an assembly voting by tribes. 'Beginning with this, the *dēmos* rose to great power, and the *aristokratia* lost much of its former prestige', and had to make many concessions (7.65.1). *Iudicia populi* are thus the thin end of the wedge; Dionysius discusses how the institution can be abused, and how this may be checked, mentioning that the Romans have often discussed – but inconclusively – whether it should be repealed. However, *iudicia populi* did not apparently survive into the Principate, nor are there any signs of continued debate on the question.[107] Dionysius has therefore picked up, in reading or discussion, a rather outmoded

[106] The polemic is not specifically against Polybius but is aimed at those detractors of Rome who invoke *tuchē* as the cause of the city's greatness (1.4.2ff.). See Fuchs (1938) 14–15, 40–43 nn. 40, 41; and Gabba (1974) 633, 636.

[107] The last known case was in 43 B.C. (Dio 44.10; see also Dio 56.40.4).

theme. He proceeds, in unusually direct and forceful terms, to give his advice about this supposedly current matter. Everything, he says, depends upon the character of the tribunes: if they are just and moderate, they exercise their power beneficially; if not, the reverse. 'So, instead of reforming the institution as ill-conceived, they ought to look at how *andres kaloi kai agathoi* shall become *prostatai tou dēmou*, so that matters of the greatest importance shall not be entrusted randomly to just anybody.'[108] By Dionysius' day, the tribunate was very much reduced in importance, even becoming hard to fill. The possibility of irresponsible tribunician trials was utterly inconceivable. On the other hand, *tribunicia potestas* in Augustus' hands flourished and was advertised as never before.[109] Dionysius' last words may well be a delicate allusion to the *kalos k'agathos* who was, above all, the one and only *prostatēs tou dēmou* now – not by any means 'just anybody', but one in the highest degree worthy to exercise such a responsible function. This would then allude to the continuance of republican institutions and traditions under the new order – less an advertisement for Augustan policy,[110] than a reminder, or a plea, to the *princeps* for moderation.

The idea of equilibrium between the rights of the *dēmos*, with its champion, on the one hand, and the rights of the *oligoi* on the other, continues the theme of compromise which is so marked throughout the *Antiquitates*. It is, perhaps, essentially the view of an outsider and a theorist, with which Dionysius hoped to gratify his Roman audience. It would have an appeal both to ordinary solid citizens, not actively involved in the upper levels of politics, who regarded the Augustan regime as a haven of peace and stability, bringing far more gain than loss, and to members of the ruling class, who, though gradually becoming aware of the reduced scope for the traditional methods of competition and self-assertion under the new order, still staked their claim to a political role. The theme of political aspiration, *stasis* and *homonoia*, thus has some relevance to Dionysius' own age. While avoiding the tricky subject of more recent disturbances (which he is surely glad to do), he is yet able to offer a model of political development which can be applied to his own times, thus vindicating his claim to be producing a historical work which is not only pleasant but useful – both to ordinary readers and to *politikoi*.

The work is, Dionysius says, a token of gratitude to Rome for the

[108] 7.65.5.

[109] Aug. *RG* 6.2; Yavetz (1969) 55, 89ff.

[110] There is little or no trace in Dionysius of the themes of Augustan propaganda, and attempts to see Augustus portrayed in the guise of one of the heroes or leaders of early Rome are unconvincing: see Clark (1973) 163–71 on the suggestions of Martin (1971, 1972).

paideia and benefits he has enjoyed there (1.6.5); he clearly feels closely associated with Rome and the Romans – and worthy to be so. Relevant here is his only other long and explicit judgement on a current Roman practice: the vehement condemnation of lax manumissions, and the positive interest he shows in reform (4.24.4–8). A Greek scholar like Dionysius might well hope for Roman citizenship. Indignation at the manumission of criminal and unworthy elements would be natural: their admission devalued Dionysius' newly acquired citizenship, if he had acquired it – even more galling to see such men become Roman citizens, if he himself were not one. But it is quite likely, though not provable, that Dionysius indeed achieved the coveted status, through his friends and patrons the Aelii Tuberones, and then left Rome to return to his native city. A *grammaticus* of the Hadrianic period, Aelius Dionysius of Halicarnassus, is said to be a descendant of the Augustan historian.[111] This could of course be a grant from Hadrian, but if it means citizenship inherited in the family, then Dionysius did not address his Roman audience in vain.

[111] Suda p. 110.1174; *PIR*² A 169.

Tacitus' conception of historical change: the problem of discovering the historian's opinions

T. J. LUCE

Reinhard Häussler's book, *Tacitus und das historische Bewusstsein*,[1] is centrally concerned with Tacitus' conception of historical change and might at first seem to leave little scope for further discussion of the topic: it is a long work of over 450 pages. Though it begins with Sartre and moves backward in time in fits and starts until it reaches Homer – and beyond – the latter 250 pages of the whole are devoted to Tacitus himself. The treatment of Häussler, though comprehensive, has not however proved exhaustive. F. R. D. Goodyear has made significant additional contributions to the discussion of an important relevant passage: Tacitus' report in Book 3.55 of the *Annals* of a debate in the senate on luxury, together with the historian's thoughts on the cycle of development through which conspicuous consumption had passed from the days of Augustus to those of Vespasian and himself.[2]

Initially my own intention was to make some further additions and corrections to what Häussler had written. But doubts began to intrude as to the wisdom of some of my conclusions. The chief stumbling-block that developed, bluntly put, was an increasing uncertainty on my part as to how to come to know what Tacitus thought, not merely about historical change, but about a great many other topics as well. For the more I examined the text and compared passages within it, the more uncertain I became as to what could properly be deduced, and whether any deductions I might make could be fitted together to form a tolerably consistent pattern of thinking.[3]

Why is it difficult to know Tacitean opinions? Professor Goodyear cites four chief reasons.[4] First, rhetoric. A man thoroughly imbued with rhetorical precepts, as Tacitus was, could and did argue on all sides of a question both in his own person and in the persons who populate the pages of his histories. Second, the desire to write a literary work that would delight, surprise, and enthral his readers. To

[1] Häussler (1965). [2] Goodyear (1970).

[3] Goodyear seems to have had a similar experience: see his 1976 article entitled 'De inconstantia Cornelii Taciti' and his change of opinion from the first to the second volume of his commentary on *Annals* 1–6 concerning Tacitus' narration of treason trials under Tiberius: Goodyear (1981) 150.

[4] Goodyear (1976) 198–99.

that end he was prepared sometimes to sacrifice carefully weighed judgements, consistency, and verisimilitude. Third, he himself was sometimes filled with doubt about certain questions, and expressed this doubt frankly in his writings: for example, on the role of the gods in human affairs, or whether moral behaviour goes through cycles of change as do the seasons of the year. Finally, his sources. They sometimes conflicted on matters of fact and of interpretation; these discrepancies may appear in Tacitus as he follows one or another.[5]

Professor Goodyear selected the portraits of Seneca and Germanicus for discussion. His aim was to demonstrate that these portraits are in fact inconsistent. My own purpose in the first part of this paper, the product of the above-mentioned scepticism about what can properly be deduced from the text of Tacitus about his opinions, is to explore some general problems connected with the business of extracting Tacitean opinions from ideas embedded in speeches, reported statements, and the like, and, in so doing, to suggest another reason for Tacitus' inconsistency. Having dealt with this prior problem, I want, in the second part, to turn to the much-discussed question of Tacitus' depiction of change in the reign of Tiberius, especially as it touches on the character of the emperor.

The problem of how one can extract Tacitean opinions from speeches, rumours, and views attributed to others is vexing and difficult. Some say it is impossible and should not be attempted. The *Dialogus* was the initial cause of the disquiet that recently came over me, since it is a central document for anyone interested in the problem of historical change in Tacitus. The chief question the interlocutors raise concerns the decline of oratory. Much of the argumentation turns upon the question of how such a change is to be interpreted. There is a long dispute on what can be styled, or deserves to be styled, 'antiquus' (15–27). Even though some of the points brought up in the course of this discussion seem strained or specious, the question at bottom is not frivolous: namely, the relative way time can be viewed from the perspective of the present, and to what extent the mere passing of time can account for the differences between then and now. In the disagreement between Aper and Messalla over the relative merits of the ancients and the moderns, Aper argues for a change for the better: a refining of artistic taste from the backward days of

[5] I am doubtful that in most cases the nature and bias of Tacitus' several sources can be reconstructed from supposed discrepancies in his text. The assumption that the texts of ancient authors are 'transparent overlays' through which their sources can be seen is wrongheaded, especially in an author as idiosyncratic and complex as Tacitus. See my remarks on Livy's use of his sources: Luce (1977) xxii and 139ff.

yester-year. Messalla sees a regression over time: a decline in the standards of education (27–35). The work climaxes with Maternus' speech, in which he pronounces in favour of neither view, substituting instead the notion that the social and political climates of the two periods are the decisive factors in explaining the difference (36–41).

There was a time when I believed that Maternus' speech was the vehicle for expressing Tacitus' beliefs on historical change. After all, it comes last. And Maternus is presented as somewhat of a father figure – a man of courage and authority. And his chief argument – that works of oratorical genius require suitable historical circumstances in which to appear – seems reasonable. Which is to say, it answers to my own prejudices. The argument also seems so right for our budding historian to have held. How remarkable to assert that the potential for greatness exists in every age and that the conditions for realizing that greatness constitute the crucial, indispensable factor! How remarkable not to be attracted into that attitude so beloved by all cultures, but never more than by the Roman, that the past is better because the men who lived then were better!

But fairly early on I realized that Maternus is not Tacitus, if only because of the obvious fact that he is not, and also because of Tacitus' obligation to present Maternus with at least some of the trappings of the man's milieu and temperament. I then began to concede that, of Maternus' arguments both before his last speech and in it, some are less than impressive, while others are at variance with Tacitus' beliefs expressed elsewhere. One example is Maternus' commendation of retirement from public life to the 'groves and glades' of poesy,[6] which is at odds with Tacitus' praise for men such as Agricola and Marcus Lepidus for serving the state actively and well even in the most parlous of times.[7] Further, while Agricola and Lepidus refrained from needlessly provoking their superiors, Maternus seems – lately, at least – to be making something of a career of it: writing a tragedy entitled *Cato* that has offended those in power, and currently engaged on a *Thyestes* that will make plain whatever he has failed to say in the *Cato* (3.2–3, 10.5–8). Yet, seemingly at odds with these activities and with the lament Maternus makes concerning the erosion of free speech in the Empire is his attitude towards the imperial dispensation expressed in the last speech: he praises the security and happiness of the age, the near unanimity of senatorial opinion, the wise rule by a single man, 'sapientissimus et unus' (41.4), the fact that there is little point in taking the initiative to

6 'inter nemora et lucos' (9.6), echoed at 12.1 and by Pliny *Ep.* 9.10.2.

7 *Agr.* 42.3–4, *Ann.* 4.20.

prosecute because there is little wrongdoing, and little need of making impassioned defences when one may fall back upon the clemency of the emperor, which is what I take to be the meaning of 'clementia cognoscentis' at 41.4. None of this fits well with the statements that Tacitus makes in his own person elsewhere in his writings, and some of it contradicts them.[8]

Thus, both Tacitus' obligation to characterize the historical Maternus and the fact that some of Maternus' opinions clash among themselves or with those of the author militate against the simple identification of the interlocutor as Tacitus' spokesman. A third reason is the nature of the argumentation. Maternus, despite his championing the glories of poetry over the powers of rhetoric, uses all the devices of the rhetorical arsenal to buttress his case. Simple exaggeration is one: his argument necessitates giving a dim picture of the last years of the Republic and a favourable one of his own day; that he would heighten the contrast to make a stronger case is to be expected. One should be reluctant to maintain that Maternus' view of the Republic and Empire mirrors Tacitus' belief. Finally, the suggestion by some scholars that Maternus' decision to abandon forensic life for literary pursuits parallels Tacitus' shift from oratory to the writing of history is not to my mind persuasive. Tacitus did not abandon public life after he began to write history, nor do the affinities between poetry and history that some ancient and modern writers cite go very deep.[9]

How may Tacitean opinions be derived from the statements attributed to his historical characters? One approach is to say that, while single persons should not be viewed as Tacitus' spokesmen, his opinions may be embedded here and there in the speeches of various individuals, even at times of those in the same work who oppose one another in the argument.[10] Even if we grant that this may be so, how can we know which elements are Tacitean and which are not? Häussler believes that by excluding sarcasm and irony and by seeking out parallel sentiments expressed directly by Tacitus elsewhere, we can discover his true opinions.[11]

Certainly cataloguing the sentiments Tacitus pronounces *in sua*

[8] Martin (1981) 63–65 and Williams (1978) 26–51 (esp. 33–34) present the evidence against equating the views of Maternus with those of Tacitus.

[9] E.g. Quint. *Inst.* 10.1.31; cf. Martin (1981) 65, Syme (1958) 110, 362–63.

[10] So Häussler (1965) 235: 'Tacitus ist der Historiker Maternus (nicht der verträumte Utopist), Tacitus ist der Moralist Messalla (nicht der ewiggestrige Reaktionär), und Tacitus ist der Ästhetiker Aper (nicht der oberflächliche Utilitarist).'

[11] Häussler (1965) 248 n. 36: 'Was sich nicht als Sarkasmus oder Ironie erweisen lässt und andererseits durch Parallelen wie "*omnem potentiam ad unum conferri pacis interfuit*" gestützt wird, kann inmitten aller Geschichtsdeutung als taciteische Überzeugung angesprochen werden.'

persona would seem promising. I confess to some misgivings, however, if only because of Sir Ronald Syme's misgivings, expressed at the start of his chapter entitled 'Tacitean Opinions': 'What are the true sentiments behind the narrative, the eloquence, and the drama? The first step is to mark down his own declarations. It will not take one very far.'[12] Despite this bleak outlook, collecting and comparing Tacitean opinions – at least on certain subjects – seem to me among the very few ways on the basis of which one can argue that views not expressed in his own person are indeed ones to which he subscribed. Something will be gained if this is successful, but I admit that the gain will not be particularly great – and especially for a reason that I will mention in a moment. Even this possibility of limited success, of course, is predicated on the hope that one will be able to take account of Tacitean inconstancy, caused by factors such as change in opinion, change in mood, striving for rhetorical point or literary effect, adoption for the moment of a particular *persona* (senator, moralist, annalist, advocate, prosecutor, and so forth).

On the other hand, sarcasm and irony are not easily removed; they colour the text as dye permeates a piece of cloth. Galba's speech in adopting young Piso at *Histories* 1.15–16 is an example.[13] However one judges the emperor's constitutional sentiments, he is culpably blind to his past conduct and present predicament, and has made a calamitous choice in Piso. He is the wrong man in the wrong position at the wrong moment: irony necessarily pervades the whole of what he says. Many scholars cite Nerva's recent adoption of Trajan as an important reason for Tacitus' composing Galba's speech. A parallel certainly exists. But what are we to make of it? That Galba's constitutional sentiments are laudable but his translation of them into fact deplorable? If so, what does this say about Nerva? No, whatever its connexion with the contemporary scene, Galba's speech is demolitionary.[14] The sentiments cannot be separated from the man who utters them or the situation in which he finds himself to form a residuum of pure Tacitean 'thought'.

The difficulty in attempting such distillations is well illustrated by the speech given to the *delator* Eprius Marcellus at *Histories* 4.8,

[12] Syme (1958) 520.

[13] Of *Hist.* 1.16.1, Häussler (1965) 248 says: 'Dieser Satz enthält das politische Credo des Tacitus.' In n. 36 on the same page he criticizes the belief of Heubner (1963) 48ff. that Galba's speech is meant to express the particular situation in which the emperor finds himself rather than Tacitus' political credo: 'Doch um den Illusionismus Galbas zu enthüllen, bedurfte es nicht solch grossangelegter und programmatischer Rede.' The implication seems to be that Tacitus does not write long speeches unless they are vehicles for expressing his personal views.

[14] The description is that of Syme (1958) 207. Note his summation on p. 208: 'The quality of rulers matters more than any theory or programme.'

which he delivered in the senate to defend himself from an attack by Helvidius Priscus. Häussler says of Marcellus that he ought not to represent Tacitean belief if only because he is basically 'on the opposite side'.[15] And yet, Häussler continues, the truth can sometimes be expressed by those 'on the other side'. What Marcellus says is identifiable with Tacitean belief if we 'remove it from its wrapping' – the wrapping being 'that of an abased man who leers longingly when those in power come his way'.[16] At the same time, Häussler criticizes Boissier for saying that so effective are Marcellus' words that we stand, at least for the moment, on his side: 'Boissier overlooks the fact that the ability in utramque partem disserendi [...] was a useful device for indirect characterization in Tacitus no less than in Thucydides. Bad and good arguments serve equally to characterize the respective speakers and are not a sign of the laxity, but of the objectivity, of the historian.'[17]

Well said. But the argument plunges us at once into difficulties. First, is it always so clear what the right and wrong sides are? Second, are the wrapping and its contents so separable, so easily disengaged? Third, how can we know how much wrapping to remove? That is, where does the historical character leave off and Tacitean conviction begin? Perhaps Häussler is right to begin by simply laying down the premise that Helvidius is on the right side and Marcellus the wrong. Certainly Tacitus praises Helvidius' devotion to Stoicism 'not in order to conceal a life of inaction under an imposing credo, as many do, but to undertake an active public career steeled against the vagaries of fortune'.[18] Moreover, Marcellus' role as a *delator* cannot have appealed to Tacitus, given his remarks at *Annals* 1.74 on that class of men. And while in the *Dialogus* Aper holds up Marcellus as an example of the successful speaker (5.7, 8.1–3), Maternus will have none of it: Marcellus' abasement before those in power is such that he seems neither servile enough to his masters nor free enough to Maternus and his coterie (13.4). Yet in the context of the clash recorded in *Histories* 4.4–9 Helvidius does not escape censure. Certain unnamed critics said he was too eager for glory, that when danger threatened his resolve deserted him (4.6.1–2). In his eagerness to embarrass Marcellus, he wants to alter the rules of the senate, which that body refuses to countenance. Moreover, when Helvidius proposes that the senate restore the ruined Capitol on its own initiative – without consulting the emperor – 'senators of modera-

[15] Häussler (1965) 249: 'ein Mann, den man in toto von der taciteischen Meinung abziehen darf, nur weil er grundsätzlich auf der "Gegenseite" steht'.
[16] Häussler (1965) 249.
[17] Häussler (1965) 249 n. 39.
[18] *Hist.* 4.5.1. Cf. my discussion: Luce (1981) 1007–9.

tion let the motion pass in silence'.[19] This last observation illustrates well the double-edged sword Tacitus often presents to us. Is Helvidius to be admired for urging the senate to take an independent course, or criticized because the action would be a calculated slight to the emperor?

A nice question. It is one of many nice questions that Tacitus poses. Germanicus the bumbler versus Germanicus the hero. Seneca the time-serving minister versus the persecuted martyr in his last days. Tiberius sitting at one end of the praetor's tribunal to check the improper influence of great men, thereby improving justice but ruining freedom. A long list could be compiled.

Is there some way out of the dilemma of how to ascertain what Tacitus thought? As of this moment I am unsure, but am beginning to wonder whether the questions we are asking are not the wrong ones – or rather are not the ones to pose initially and not the most important ones. In our effort to understand Tacitus, we extrapolate ideas from the concrete events of which a history based on *res gestae* must chiefly consist and from speeches, rumours, and opinions of the dramatis personae. When we come upon remarks that Tacitus makes in his own person, we take them out of context, compare them, and apply the results to other events, speeches, or personal remarks in order to elucidate problems there. All these efforts involve basically the same procedure: divorcing ideas from their contexts, extrapolating with a view to forming a self-contained stockpile of Tacitean opinions from which we can draw for multiple use throughout the text. I want to suggest that this procedure may do more harm than good if it is carried to extremes or is our only procedure, because it runs counter to what Tacitus is trying to do and trying to make us see. After all, if it is so often difficult to know what Tacitus thought – to separate the package from the wrapping – perhaps he doesn't mean us to do so, at least not initially. It may even be that the very difficulty of making such a separation is precisely what he wishes us most to see. He is not trying to present us with a Chinese box-puzzle or a masked costume-party in which we must strip away the deceptive or superfluous in order to find the author underneath. Nor, in philosophic mode, should the accidents be separated out from the essences of individual things in order to ascertain the unchanging common denominator that obtains among groups of things. Quite the reverse. Many of the ideas, opinions, and beliefs we find in Tacitus do indeed form a stockpile, but they are not peculiar to him, but were the common property of his contemporaries who were trained in ancient rhetoric, which is to say nearly the entire educated class.

[19] *Hist.* 4.9.2.

From their early schooling through their official careers and private pursuits to the ends of their lives they were immersed in the technique *in utramque partem disserendi*: the *loci communes*, the division of argumentation into the *honestum* and the *utile* – each with their many subdivisions – the various *colores* to be applied, the different possibilities open to one thoroughly conversant with *inventio* and *dispositio*. In the hands of a man of talent, almost any argument, idea, or attitude might be taken over successfully: the protean uses to which they lend themselves are nearly limitless. So Aper several times in the *Dialogus* is said not to believe what he says; his fondness for speaking on the opposite side gives him away, his opponents say.[20] Compare the passage at *Annals* 2.35, where Cn. Piso and Asinius Gallus disagree in the senate on whether there should be an adjournment of business in the absence of the emperor. Piso argues that the organs of government should carry out their functions as usual, Gallus that all business should be conducted under the eyes of the emperor. Gallus took up this position, says Tacitus, only because Piso had gotten in ahead of him and had taken over the argument based on a specious display of freedom; so Piso adopted the opposite stance by default: 'quia speciem libertatis Piso praeceperat'.

Thus words and actions considered apart and divorced from their contexts are not what our attention should be chiefly directed to. What is crucial in Tacitus is how they are embodied in the situations of actual history: that is, who it is who speaks or acts, what sort of a person he is, what kind of circumstances he finds himself in, what motives he has in speaking or acting as he does. For Tacitus, I would argue, it is the particularity of each event that is more important than any universals that might be abstracted from it. Perhaps this is the reason why we find it so difficult to extract Tacitean opinions from the text: we are not meant to.

Tacitus is suspicious and impatient of generalizations and abstractions. Put crudely, talk is cheap. Ideas are common. When they appear in real life, clothed in flesh or embodied in actions, there is the rub, there is where the trouble begins. Doubts assail us almost at once – or they should – for it is seldom that men and what they do are not compromised by a host of complicated, often conflicting

[20] *Dialogus* 15.2 (Messalla), 16.3 and 24.2 (Maternus). Williams (1978) 43 persuasively argues that these passages are not meant to excuse Aper from his views: they are indeed his own. But his argument that they are meant to undercut these views in the eyes of the reader is unconvincing. Messalla and Maternus are using a familiar rhetorical weapon: putting one's opponent on the defensive by claiming that the motives of the speaker belie his professions. Cicero's treatment of the young Atratinus in the *pro Caelio* is analogous (1–2). The credibility of Aper's views should not be decided or influenced by these allegations of Messalla and Maternus.

circumstances. To discourse about the principles of political power, to cite extenuating circumstances, to derive rules of upright conduct – all such activities are easy, really. In life, as in the study of history, we want the packages to be tidy, we want clear answers. These Tacitus refuses to give because as he looks at history they are not there to give. The opposite is usually the case, and Tacitus takes pains to emphasize anomaly, inconcinnity, and complexity. This applies also, I think, to the stages, moments, and separate events in the life of a single man. The reason is simply that we human beings are, alas, frequently inconsistent. Even in the cases of such consistent heroes as Agricola or Marcus Lepidus, he is at pains to emphasize the necessity for them to walk a precarious tightrope between too much subservience and an excessive display of independence. Note that the question is not *whether* one will comply with the wishes of those in power; one must, one must make compromises, one must flatter a bit. The question is one of degree, not of absolutes: how much to comply, who is complying to whom, and what the circumstances are that affect one's choices on a particular occasion. This is one reason why Tacitus' brand of history is so well suited to an annalistic format: each item needs to be taken up seriatim and dwelt upon separately. Through discrete episodes the milieu peculiar to a particular time is recreated; we can thereby appreciate the complexity of the individual moment, the interplay among events as precedents are established, one man responds to another, experiments of test and challenge are tried.

Throughout his works Tacitus expects us to judge the merits of the individuals who pass before us, however difficult the judging may be. In fact, it is often the difficulty that Tacitus wants us most to realize. In a reflective digression in the fourth book of the *Annals* he explains what benefit his readers will derive from his history: 'Now that the nature of the Roman state has been changed and is nothing but the rule of a single man, it will be useful to record these events, because few men have the good sense to distinguish what is honourable from what is not, or what is useful from what is harmful, while most people learn from what happens to others.'[21] This passage is usually given perfunctory attention by scholars because the claim is a commonplace in Greco-Roman historiography: it seems tame and unexceptional. But when one considers how difficult it sometimes is to make clear distinctions in Tacitus between honourable and dishonourable, useful and harmful, the commonplace takes on an uncommon pertinence, if not irony. A small example concerns parsimony. It was a time-honoured virtue among the Romans, for

[21] *Ann.* 4.33.2.

which Tacitus can and does give praise. Yet it really depends upon persons and circumstance. For Galba it was disastrous: not to bribe the soldiers even a little bit was culpably blind.[22] Acting according to a rigid, outdated, or unseasonable principle, however laudable it is in the abstract, can be downright folly. Galba is judged accordingly.

I want to turn now to consider a much discussed, some might say too much discussed, topic: Tacitus' appraisal of change in Tiberius' reign. It illustrates well the problem of the protean nature of Tacitean judgements. I want to argue, however, that Tacitus' view is not as various and contradictory in at least some of its parts as has been claimed. Much of the change during the reign, of course, seems tied to the changes in Tiberius' character, or what appear to be changes in that character. For three emperors we know that Tacitus traced a course of character development that had significant repercussions: Tiberius and Nero, who changed for the worse, and Vespasian, who changed for the better. Claudius seems not to alter in the portion of the *Annals* that survives to us, although it is possible that in the missing part some sort of progression or turning-point was fixed upon.

Both Tiberius and Nero are depicted similarly in that their true characters – which is to say the things they really wish to do – emerge gradually over time, until they are able to give vent to desires that hitherto had been concealed. The reason for the concealment is the inhibiting presence of other people, which prevents them from acting as they secretly desire: shame and fear before these people are the commonest motives. Consequently, divesting themselves of these annoyances marks the stages in the revelation of the autocrat's true character. As the inhibiting people are eliminated, they are replaced by those who are willing to countenance, encourage, or participate in the activities in which the autocrat wishes to indulge. The end of the reign is marked by increasing frightfulness and by violence.

Having said this, even if we agree with it, we find ourselves facing in the case of Tiberius numerous problems: certain statements and episodes concerning him do not seem to fit well or at all among themselves. Let us begin with the famous obituary at the end, in which five stages are marked out. I give Professor Martin's translation, together with his annotation of the stages:[23]

His character too passed through different phases: (i) excellent both in achievement and reputation, as long as he was a private citizen or held

[22] *Hist.* 1.18.3: 'nocuit antiquus rigor et nimia severitas, cui iam pares non sumus'.
[23] Martin (1981) 105.

commands under Augustus; (ii) given to concealment and an artful simulator of virtue (*occultum ac subdolum fingendis virtutibus*), as long as Germanicus and Drusus survived; (iii) a similar mixture of good and evil during his mother's lifetime; (iv) then a period of loathsome cruelty, but concealed lusts, as long as he had Sejanus to love or fear; (v) then, finally, he threw himself into crimes and vices alike, casting aside all sense of shame and fear, following no inclination but his own. (6.51.3)

Most readers of Tacitus find this appraisal somewhat puzzling. One reason is that the stages as described here have not received particularly strong stress in what precedes. The first under Augustus falls outside the period of our text. The second, whose end is marked by the deaths of Germanicus and Drusus, is a peculiar conflation: three years and a whole book intervene between these two events. In the narrative itself Tacitus does not single out the death of Germanicus as a turning-point, but only the death of Drusus: 'All of which Tiberius kept up – not in a gracious way, but irritating and alarming, until overturned by the death of Drusus. For as long as he was alive, they were in force, because Sejanus was only at the start of his power and wanted to be credited as a man of good counsel.'[24] The words 'quae cuncta' that begin this sentence evidently refer to all the favourable aspects of the first half of Tiberius' reign enumerated in the previous chapter: the relative freedom of the senate, independence of the magistrates, integrity of Tiberius' appointments, fair treatment of the provinces, Tiberius' moderate style of living, and so on.

It is also somewhat puzzling to note that the third stage, which ends with Livia's death, is marked by no real change in Tiberius' character; concealment and artful simulation of virtue remained the same: 'idem inter bona malaque mixtus' (6.51.3). Note the seeming disagreement with what I just quoted in reference to the death of Drusus. The obituary says, in effect, that Tiberius was essentially the same under Germanicus, Drusus, *and* Livia: that is, from the start of the *Annals* to the beginning of the fifth book.

Yet the greatest cause of puzzlement concerning the obituary is the opening of the fourth book of the *Annals*, where a single great turning-point is marked out: at the moment when Drusus dies and Sejanus emerges to full power – which is to say, six years and a book earlier than Livia's death and near the end of the obituary's second stage. On the other hand, Livia's death at the start of the fifth book ushers in a period in which Tiberius' behaviour changes markedly for the worse: 'ceterum ex eo praerupta iam et urgens dominatio' (5.3.1). Tacitus notes that Tiberius' habitual obedience to his mother,

[24] *Ann.* 4.7.1.

as well as Sejanus' reluctance to risk combatting her as long as she was alive, were the factors that ensured her hold over her son.

The role that Sejanus plays in the fourth stage of the obituary is also odd. Although in this stage Tiberius' savagery had free play, his sexual appetites were concealed as long as he loved or feared his minister. This is the only place in the obituary in which Sejanus appears, and he is depicted as much a force for good as for evil: his presence somehow prevented Tiberius' loathsome character from its full emergence, which happened only in the last phase, after Sejanus had gone.

How can the obituary be reconciled with the great division in Tiberius' principate announced at the start of Book 4? One might well suppose, as some have done, that these seemingly conflicting schemata derived from different sources that Tacitus took over either without realizing it or, realizing it, but not caring to attempt a reconciliation among them.[25] Another is to suppose that in the course of writing Tacitus changed his mind about what made Tiberius tick – arriving in the end at a position that conflicts with what went before. I myself do not believe that this is correct. The chief supports for the theory are two passages sixteen chapters apart in the fourth book of the *Annals* (41 and 57). In the first Sejanus urges the ageing emperor to retire from Rome. In the second Tacitus informs us that he took over the first interpretation from his sources, but he now wonders whether the retirement was not more likely to have been the result of Tiberius' own wishes and temperament, seeing that he continued to live on Capri for the six remaining years of his life after Sejanus' death. Tacitus notes in passing (4.57.2) the parallel of Tiberius' earlier retirement to Rhodes under Augustus, where he was able to avoid the common throng and give vent to his suppressed sexual urges. The realization of the import of the Rhodian parallel is taken by some scholars to be what prompted Tacitus to reconsider his statement sixteen chapters earlier; another reference to the retirement to Rhodes at the start of Book 1 (1.4.4) is postulated as an insertion made in the light of this later awareness.[26]

This is possible, but I myself see no strong reason to suppose that these are later insertions into a completed text. Note that Tacitus did not venture to change or reconcile these two passages, which are close together and in the same book. To me, this means that he intended

[25] It is possible that they derive from different sources, but I doubt that Tacitus was unaware of their implications or that, if aware, he was indifferent to reconciling their supposed contradictions.

[26] Sir Ronald Syme is the chief proponent of this hypothesis: Syme (1958) 286, 425 n. 5, 695–96.

that we should read the passages as they stand. Note, too, that the two explanations do not exclude one another, but are, in a way, complementary (although I admit that Tacitus does not present them as such). Moreover, self-correction is a familiar rhetorical device – one that has parallels in other historians.[27] I am therefore not convinced that Tacitus' remark at 4.57 is necessarily proof of a new insight that came to him only then. Even if it is, Tacitus wanted both passages to stand as we see them. They should not be viewed as an inadvertent slip in which we can catch out the historian making rather a mess of things. I believe myself they are as they are because for Tacitus both motives were operative: Sejanus' prompting and Tiberius' inclination. It suited Tacitus to restrict the first passage to Sejanus' alarmed urging, coming as it does after the ominous and peculiar letter from Tiberius rejecting Sejanus' proposed marriage to Livia, Drusus' widow (4.40). The second passage marks Tiberius' actual departure from Rome, in which a number of personal motives are canvassed: not only Tiberius' own inclination, but his desire to retire from public view because of his repulsive physical appearance, as well as to get clear of his domineering mother.

The obituary is based upon the premise that Tiberius' character, his *ingenium*, did not change: that seems inescapable. He was all along an evil man whose motives and passions were perverse and perverted. This view seems to me not to be something realized late or tacked on awkwardly at the end, but to inform Tacitus' portrait of Tiberius throughout. The most obvious sign of this is Tiberius' hypocrisy; during all the stages but the last he had to conceal wholly or in part what he really thought or desired.[28] This trait is present at the outset of the *Annals* and continues to be emphasized throughout. It is especially evident in the first three books, where Tiberius' motives in Tacitus' eyes are at such variance with the actions he feels constrained to perform, given the triply inhibiting presence of Livia, Germanicus, and Drusus for most of the period.

Compare, however, the unchanging nature of Tiberius' evil character with the pronouncement of Tiberius' friend, L. Arruntius, reported at 6.48, three chapters before the obituary. Tiberius, said

[27] I know of two instances in Livy: 29.33.10 and 38.56–57. See Luce (1977) 92ff. and 199 n. 19. The device is analogous to the rhetorical ploy of *reprehensio* or self-correction. In the orators correction usually comes quickly, as in Cicero's notorious confusion between Clodia's *vir* and *frater* in *pro Caelio* 32: 'nisi intercederent mihi inimicitiae cum istius mulieris viro – fratrem volui dicere – semper hic erro'. The historians' use of the device is on a larger scale, but it is no less deliberate.

[28] Yet even at the end he did not wholly abandon his practice of concealment. The anecdote of his response to the doctor Charicles' attempt to take his pulse surreptitiously is a marvellous and characteristic touch (*Ann.* 6.50.2–3).

Arruntius, despite his great experience, had been wholly perverted by holding supreme power: 'Tiberius post tantam rerum experientiam vi dominationis convulsus et mutatus sit.' Many scholars see this as contradicting the obituary and hence as not what Tacitus thought; it is an example of inconstancy, where clashing alternatives are stated but not resolved – the mutability versus the immutability of character.[29] I think this view is unnecessary and mistaken: that is, I believe we do not have here a situation in which either Arruntius or the obituary is right. First, it will not do to say, as has been frequently said, that Tacitus *only* conceived of human character as unchanging and constant. One could argue that the majority of persons in his pages are mixed characters, in whom good and bad qualities intermingle and sometimes fluctuate. Moreover, Tacitus endorses the idea of change in a man. Vespasian is the best example; the same language, 'mutatus', is applied to Vespasian as to Tiberius and describes a change that the principate wrought upon its holder.[30] I therefore reject the argument that Tacitus must have believed in Tiberius' unchanging character because he believed that about all men.

The case of Tiberius should therefore be taken on its own terms. I do not doubt, let me reaffirm, that he viewed the emperor's *ingenium* as perverse and unchanging. But I want to propose that we shift our focus on the question, because it has been bedevilled by almost exclusive concentration on the constancy of character. Of at least equal importance are the *changes* that Tacitus delineates in the obituary. Now, what is changing here, if we agree that it is not character? Clearly, behaviour. And is it not what men do that is of special concern to the historian? This applies with particular force to an annalist such as Tacitus who writes of *res gestae*. What interests him are the circumstances in which men speak and act: the environment, the milieu, the circumstantial web in which they find themselves. For these are what test a man, what contribute to the reasons why he acts and reacts as he does, as much and possibly more than any inborn, genetic inheritance. Certainly this is true for most of Tiberius' life as outlined in the obituary.

In short, the situation is similar to that concerning Tacitean ideas: our attention has been too much fixed on extracting the unchanging – whether ideas or character traits – from the temporal events that Tacitus is chiefly at pains to narrate. Thus, when Arruntius says 'Tiberius vi dominationis convulsus et mutatus sit', I do not see that it contradicts the obituary. On the contrary, it can be taken to support

[29] Cf. Goodyear (1976) 198.

[30] *Hist.* 1.50.4: 'solus omnium ante se principum in melius mutatus est'. *Ann.* 6.48.2: 'Tiberius post tantam rerum experientiam vi dominationis convulsus et mutatus sit.'

and supplement it, which is how I understand it, for I take it to refer to what Tiberius did in his life, to how he behaved. I believe that, for Tacitus, Tiberius' behaviour did change, and for the worse. And when one says of someone that he 'changed', whether in English or in Latin, one can be referring to behaviour as much as to inborn character. Tacitus is admittedly not using precise language; on the other hand, I would not expect him to.

R. G. Collingwood maintained that Tiberius' unchanging character was central for Tacitus: 'Power does not alter a man's character; it only shows what kind of man he already was.'[31] Perhaps to a philosopher a man is corrupt if he has the potential to do evil, yet does not have the opportunity actually to commit evil acts. For the historian the chief emphasis must be on the actual, not the potential. If the historian is perceptive and curious, it is natural that, now and then, he will, like Tacitus, be fascinated by 'might-have-been history'. The question of *capax imperii*, for example: who would have made a good emperor, or a bad one, who would, if given the chance, have grasped for power and who would not. If Tiberius had died before Livia, would we have known the full extent of the evil in his character? Probably not. And think of poor Galba. If only he hadn't become emperor, everyone would have thought he would have made a good one. In short, circumstances may serve as the means or vehicle by which inborn character gradually becomes known; on the other hand, circumstances are what in large part determine behaviour.

I want to end by stressing once again the emphasis I see in Tacitus on the particularity of events: how necessary it is to appreciate the many circumstances that affect and control individual acts and words. As noble, as clear, as convincing as certain ideas, themes, and values may be when considered abstractly, their appearance in real life is all too often compromised by the sad state of the human condition: the 'ludibria rerum mortalium cunctis in negotiis' (*Annals* 3.18.4). A remark of E. R. Dodds in the introduction to his edition of Euripides' *Bacchae* is pertinent: 'It is a mistake to ask what he is trying to "prove": his concern in this as in all his major plays is not to prove anything but to enlarge our sensibility.'[32] This is an illuminating observation which applies with equal force to Tacitus.

[31] Collingwood (1946) 44.

[32] Dodds (1960) xlvii.

Plutarch and Roman politics

C. B. R. PELLING

Is Plutarch really interested in Roman politics? After all, he is writing biography, not history; and there are certainly times when he disclaims any interest in describing historical background. That sort of thing, he says, may be left to the writers of continuous histories;[1] it is often the little things, the words and the jests, which reveal a man's character, not the great battles or the sieges of cities.[2] '*Often*' the little things, we should notice: often, not always. Plutarch's biography is a very flexible genre, and his interest in historical background is one of the things which vary. Sometimes he does write very personal Lives, sketching the historical setting in only the vaguest lines: the *Crassus*, for instance; or the *Antony*, which somehow or other describes the politics of the two years from summer 44 to summer 42 without even mentioning Brutus and Cassius; or the *Cato minor*, where he contrives to describe the formation of the triple alliance of 60 B.C. without naming Crassus. But there are other Lives where his interest in history is very clear indeed, and he is evidently concerned to present the same sort of analysis as those 'writers of continuous history' – though he naturally sets about it in rather different ways. The *Caesar* is a good example. Plutarch is there very concerned to *explain* Caesar's rise to tyranny – the 'absolute power', as he says in the last chapter, 'which he had sought all his life – and he saw only its name, and the perils of its reputation' (*Caes.* 69.1, cf. 57.1). What forces carried him to this power? Plutarch's answer is a clear one. From the beginning, Caesar is the champion and the favourite of the Roman *dēmos*. When they support him, he rises; when he loses their favour, he falls. In the early chapters, the *dēmos* encourage him to become first in the state.[3] When Caesar revives the flagging 'Marian faction', this too is brought into the

Versions of this paper were read at Leeds, to the 1982 meeting of the American Philological Association in Philadelphia, and to the Oxford Philological Society; I am grateful to all three audiences for their patient hearings and many helpful comments. Particular thanks are due to Andrew Lintott, David Stockton, Philip Stadter, Owen Watkins, and Peter Scott for their scrutiny and detailed criticism of the paper as it was nearing its final draft.

[1] *Fab.* 16.6, cf. *Galba* 2.5.

[2] *Alex.* 1.2.

[3] *Caes.* 6.7, cf. 5.1–3, 8.4–5, 14.2–3, 14.6.

same analysis: his opponents denounce the display of Marian *imagines* as 'an attempt to win over the *dēmos*' (6.1–3), while the admirers of the display encourage him to great ambitions: the *dēmos*, they say, will support him as he goes on to conquest and supremacy (6.7).[4] Caesar spends lavishly on the people, and they seek 'new commands and new honours' to repay him (5.9, cf. 4.4–9) – an interesting foreshadowing of the spectacular and odious honours they vote him, and resent voting him, at the end of his life. Plutarch comments that, at the beginning, Caesar's outlays are purchasing the greatest of prizes cheaply (5.8, cf. 4.8); and, at first, the *optimates* are wholly deceived (4.6–9, 5.8). It is only gradually that 'the senate' comes to realize the danger; and it is indeed 'the senate', described like that, which is seen as Caesar's enemy.[5] Caesar is duly victorious, and becomes tyrant – and it is then that he begins to lose his crucial popular support. The Lupercalia outrage, for example, is carefully presented at 60–61 in a way which dwells on the people's reactions, and especially their final dismay; and we can see, I think, that this is a passage where he is *re*writing and *re*interpreting what stood in his source.[6] (Appian, Suetonius, and Plutarch's parallel account in *Antony* all seem to draw on the same source-material as the *Caesar* – probably the account of Asinius Pollio – but none of those versions carries the same popular emphasis.) It is duly οἱ πολλοί who turn to Brutus and Cassius. Caesar is now left vulnerable, and is killed; but the popular fervour then immediately erupts once more, and the victim is the luckless 'Cinna the poet' (68).[7]

So intense an interest in historical explanation is not of course typical; but it is not wholly isolated, either. The Lives of the *Gracchi*, for example, again show Plutarch very eager to relate the brothers' policies and destinies to the attitudes of the urban *dēmos*. The *Marius* and the *Cicero* are both concerned to explain their subjects' rises – what forces and what combinations of support enabled such men to overcome the obstacles which, Plutarch knew, confronted a new man

4 For this 'Marianism' see 5.2–3, 6.1–7; and then note 19.4 (with 18.1) for the continuation of the theme in the military narrative. The stress is an interesting one, and seems individual to Plutarch; neither Suet. *DJ* 11 nor Vell. 2.43.4 give anything like so charged and coloured an account of the Marian display as *Caes.* 6. For the historical importance of Caesar's 'Marian' links see Syme (1939) 65, 89–90, 93–94, Strasburger (1938) 131, 136–37.

5 *Caes.* 7.4, 14.3, 21.7, 60.5, 64.2, cf. 10.6–7. His enemies may also be described as the ἀριστοκρατικοί (13.5, 14.6), or the καλοὶ κἀγαθοί (14.3), or the ἄριστοι (7.4): cf. below, pp. 175–76.

6 See Pelling (1979) 78, where Plutarch's adaptation of his source-material is analysed in more detail.

7 For the historical interests of the *Caesar*, and some further aspects of Plutarch's presentation of his analysis, see Pelling (1980) 136–37.

at Rome.[8] So, in a different way, is the *Cato maior*, though the sort of explanation he there offers is rather more sonorous and less convincing: the Roman people were greater in those days and worthier of great leaders, and so they joyfully chose a man of austerity to be their consul and rejected the demagogues who were his rivals (*C. mai.* 16.8, cf. *Aem.* 11.3–4). Less *our* sort of historical explanation, perhaps – but still a historical generalization intended to make a surprising success more intelligible. But other Lives are naturally less interested in historical themes. The *Sulla* is conspicuously less interested in history than the *Marius*: when historical points are made in the *Sulla*, they are rather inorganic, introducing notions which are simply useful for our *moral* estimate of Sulla's character. Generals by now *had to* spend large sums on bribing their armies, and so it was not surprising that Sulla was harder on Greece than men like Aemilius Paullus or Titus Flamininus – though Sulla himself must equally take some blame for encouraging and accelerating the decline (*Sulla* 12.9–14). Rome was by now so decayed a city that Sulla found it easier to stand out there than Lysander at Sparta (*Sulla* 40(1).2–7). We are some way from the simple interest in making careers historically intelligible which we find in the *Marius* or the *Caesar*.

And, when Plutarch's mind is not primarily focused on history, he is capable of saying some very odd things. The *Crassus*, for example, is a peculiarly lightweight and anecdotal Life. Plutarch evidently decided – wisely enough – that it was simply impossible to write a serious historical biography of Crassus. The weight of that Life falls on the great narrative set-pieces – the exciting escape from Marius and Cinna, the war against Spartacus, then the great Parthian disaster. The political aspects are dismissed very quickly: a notably trivial account of the consulship of 70 B.C., then all the political history of 60–56 – about which Plutarch by now knew a great deal[9] – dismissed in a single woolly chapter (14). The most substantial political analysis is in fact introduced in a digression, placed just before the Spartacus war. It is evidently supposed to provide some guide to the entire twenty years which followed. 'Rome was divided into three powers [δυνάμεις – a very odd phrase], those of Pompey, Caesar, and Crassus: for Cato's reputation was greater than his power, and he was more admired than effective. And the wise and sound part of the state supported Pompey, while the excitable and reckless followed the hopes aroused by Caesar; Crassus stood in the

[8] *Mar.* 6, *Cic.* 11.2–3; and for a new man's difficulties, *C. mai.* 16.4–5.

[9] See Pelling (1979), where I argue that *Crassus* was prepared at the same time as *Caesar*, *Pompey*, *Cato minor*, *Brutus*, and *Antony*. The first three of those Lives all give much more detailed accounts of the politics of the early fifties.

middle, exploiting both sides, continually changing his position in the state, not reliable in his friendships nor irreconcilable in his feuds, readily abandoning both gratitude and hostility when it was expedient for him to do so' (7.7). That is an extraordinary thing to say. It would be hard to find *any* period when this analysis – Pompey as the establishment figure, Caesar the *popularis*, Crassus the inconsistent trimmer – bore much relation to reality; least of all does it fit the part of the Life where we find it, when we are still deep in the seventies. Plutarch knows very well that Caesar only became important ten years later: he makes that clear in both the *Pompey* and the *Caesar*.[10] He knows very well that Pompey never really enjoyed the confidence of this 'wise and sound part of the state' (as he puts it here): indeed, in the *Pompey* he makes it clear that it was only late in the fifties – after Crassus' death, and hence beyond the scope of the *Crassus* itself – that the *optimates* came to any real understanding with Pompey, and that it was the *popular* support for Pompey which was important in the first period of his life, down to 60 B.C.[11] The account in the *Pompey* of the shared consulship of 70 B.C. makes the contrast with the *Crassus* passage very clear. In the *Pompey*, Plutarch *is* concerned to explain the historical background, and he says that 'Crassus had the greater strength in the senate, whereas Pompey enjoyed great power among the people' (*Pomp.* 22.3) – note, incidentally, that characteristic *boulē–dēmos* analysis again. That is evidently quite irreconcilable with the *Crassus* passage, which made Pompey the establishment figure and Crassus the trimmer. In the *Crassus* he is prepared to give the different analysis – much cruder and less satisfactory though it is – simply because it aids the characterization of the Life. Crassus is there the shrewd manipulator, unscrupulously exploiting everyone he can in the interests of his own ambition and (particularly) greed. 'The middle', now supporting one side and now the other, is

[10] Thus, in *Caesar*, his authority 'increased slowly' (4.5), and it was only 'late' (4.7) that his opponents realized the danger; in 61 he flees before his creditors to Crassus, who finds him useful for his own opposition to Pompey (11.1); in 60 Pompey and Crassus are still 'the greatest powers in the state' (13.3). It is the alliance with Pompey in 60 which brings Caesar to real power (28.2–3, cf. *Pomp.* 57.6). (It is true, as Strasburger (1938) 71, 75–76, 85–89 insists, that Plutarch exaggerates the extent and importance of Caesar's early popular *support*; but this does not lead him to exaggerate Caesar's early *power* as greatly as Strasburger's discussion would suggest.) In *Pompey*, Caesar again only comes to prominence with the alliance of 60, which brought him 'gratitude, and power for the future' (47.1); it was Pompey's power which raised Caesar against the city, and finally against Pompey himself (46.3–4, cf. 57.6).

[11] *Optimates* come to an understanding, 54.5–9, 59.1–2, etc.: the accord reached in 57 B.C. (49.6) is very transient. Early popularity: 1.3–4, 2.1, 14.11, 15.1, 21.7–8, 22.3–4, 22.9, 25.7–13, 30.4. This stress disappears in the second half of the Life, for Pompey is then the tool of other, more subtle and degraded demagogues, Clodius and Caesar; it is then *their* popularity which is stressed (46.7, 47.5, 48.3, 48.9, 51.1, 53.6, 58.4). Cf. the firm division of the 'two parts' of Pompey's Life at 46.1–4, and Pelling (1980) 133–35.

evidently the right place for him. That view of Crassus himself is, of course, not without some truth; but it is a far less plausible matter to make *Caesar and Pompey* the two 'powers' between which he oscillated. There, if he thought about it, Plutarch must have realized that he was falsifying and trivializing historical reality.

It is easy enough to find further examples of the same sort of thing. It can be shown, I think, that his view of Clodius varies from one Life to another, depending on the interests and emphases of each Life; in one Life he is an independent figure, bullying the passive Pompey into submission and disgrace; in another, he is relatively meek and subservient, demurely following the triumvirs' will.[12] It can be shown that Plutarch's view of the origins of the Civil War is not always quite the same;[13] and that Pompey's awareness of the menace of Caesar in Gaul is greater in the *Pompey* itself than in the other Lives.[14] All this makes the analysis of his political views and interpretations a rather delicate question. We should not expect him always to be consistent, and we must always be aware that he may be bending his analysis to suit the themes of a particular Life; and we should give more weight to some Lives than to others. It is the Lives where he is most interested in historical analysis – the *Caesar*, perhaps, and the *Marius* and the *Gracchi* – which should provide the kernel of our estimation. We should not be surprised if the views developed in those Lives are muted or trivialized elsewhere.

One further difficulty should be noted. No one, I hope, would now regard Plutarch as a mere excerptor, meekly copying out the analyses of his sources. (Scholars have, in fact, been relatively swift to realize that Plutarch has a mind and a literary hand of his own. That

[12] Pelling (1980) 132–33.

[13] The analysis is set out in its simplest form in *Caesar*, and that Life's treatment is discussed below. In *Cato minor*, affairs are taken further back than the alliance of 60 B.C., to Cato's rejection of the proffered marriage-link with Pompey: *that* was the start of it all (30.9–10), for Pompey was driven to marry Julia instead. The marriage of Julia and Pompey is advanced to the very beginning of the narrative of 59 B.C. in order to emphasize the point (31.6, contrast *Caes.* 14.7–8, *Pomp.* 47.9); and Cato's own insight concerning the 60 B.C. alliance, stressed at *Caes.* 13.6 and *Pomp.* 47.4, is here muted and delayed. The *Cato* explains all in terms of personal factors and personal rebuffs, while the *Caesar* represents the alliance of Pompey and Caesar in purely political terms. That treatment excellently suits the *Cato*, which shows little interest in politics but a considerable concern with the affairs of Cato's womenfolk (24.4–25.13, 30.3–10, 52.5–9). *Pompey* is different again. Pollio's view is retained (47.3–4, cf. 51.1–2, 53.8–10, 54.3); but Plutarch here gives the crucial importance to Pompey's own reactions and attitudes during the fifties (see Pelling (1980) 131–35). In particular, the joyous Italian reaction in 50 B.C., when Pompey recovered from illness, is given extraordinary weight, for this engendered his false confidence: οὐδενὸς μέντοι τοῦτο λέγεται τῶν ἀπεργασαμένων τὸν πόλεμον αἰτίων ἔλαττον γενέσθαι (57.5). No other Life gives such emphasis to this moment.

[14] Pelling (1980) 131–32. Though more aware, he is also more passive: *ibid.*, 133–35.

procedure of scholarly enlightenment is only just beginning with Appian and Cassius Dio.) Yet it is equally clear that Plutarch *sometimes* adopts ideas and interpretations very closely indeed. Take the analysis of the origins of the Civil War, which we find in its simplest form in the *Caesar*. It was not the enmity, but the friendship, of Pompey and Caesar which caused the war: the year 60 was the start of it all. They first combined to destroy the aristocracy, and their final estrangement only sealed the Republic's fate. Cato alone saw the truth. Caesar was always ambitious for tyranny, and purchased his way to power with his Gallic wealth. Pompey was his dupe, first disingenuous, then vacillating, then the prey of conflicting senatorial interests and ambitions. The deaths of Crassus and Julia removed vital obstacles to war; and the parlous state of politics at Rome – its κακοπολιτεία, so acute that many recognized monarchy as the only solution – was the background which made it all possible.[15] It is certainly a powerful analysis; but it is hardly Plutarch's own. Much of it recurs in a tellingly similar form in Appian[16] (and of course elsewhere), and it is surely derived originally from the work of Asinius Pollio. Of course, we are free to criticize it. Pollio, wishing to give his work a powerful beginning, surely exaggerated the importance of the electoral pact of 60 B.C., thus giving rise to that long legend of the 'first triumvirate' (as we used to call it). Horace speaks of 'gravis principum amicitias' as a theme of Pollio's work (*Odes* 2.1.3–4): Pollio perhaps laid too much stress on the personal relationships of the great men, and made them too far-sighted and clear-cut in their ambitions. The treatment of Roman κακοπολιτεία tends to confine itself to violence and bribery in Rome itself – especially the violence and bribery initiated by the great men or their followers; there is no hint that Pollio gave any wider sweep of the empire, armies, and provinces. But, whatever we say, we are really making points about Pollio more than Plutarch: Plutarch simply recognized, and welcomed, the intellectual distinction and power of the analysis.

[15] *Caes.* 28, cf. e.g. 13.4–6, 23.5–7. For the variations in other Lives see n. 13. The analysis is clearest in *Caesar* because Plutarch there brings together so many of the themes in the single powerful survey (28); that analysis, returning the reader decisively to urban politics after the account of the Gallic campaigns, combines many motifs which are exploited earlier in the narratives of the other Lives.

[16] Cf. esp. Gaul as the training-ground for Caesar's army: App. *BC* 2.17.62 with *Caes.* 28.3, *Pomp.* 51.2; κακοπολιτεία: App. 2.19.69–70, with *Caes.* 28.4, *C. min.* 44.3, *Pomp.* 54.3; Pompey's disingenuous behaviour and true ambitions: App. 2.19.71, 2.20.73 with *Caes.* 28.7, *C. min.* 45.7, *Pomp.* 53.9–10, cf. Pelling (1980) 134; monarchy the only remedy: App. 2.20.72 with *Caes.* 28.5–6, *C. min.* 47.2, *Pomp.* 54.7 (and also *Brut.* 55(2).2, an interesting variation of the idea). For Pollio's view, and for other ancient analyses of the Republic's fall, see Pohlenz (1927), Syme (1950), Lintott (1971) 493–98.

Such passages as this certainly help us to see which analyses Plutarch found plausible and welcomed as illuminating and intelligible; and, thus far, they can be used as evidence for his own historical understanding. But, in the end, they will tell us less than those passages where we can see his *individual* judgements and assumptions at work, where we can see him imposing his own views and interpretations on the events he is describing: particularly, where we can see him *re*interpreting what his sources offered – as, for instance, in the *Caesar*'s account of the Lupercalia incident, where (as we saw) he seems to be revising and rewriting Pollio's account to concentrate on the reactions of the *dēmos*; or in the early chapters of that Life, where he goes out of his way to stress the people's encouragement to Caesar to become 'first in the state'.[17] (We can there contrast the early chapters of Suetonius' biography, which are evidently based on very similar source-material, but have no such emphasis on the popular theme.[18]) In those passages we see Plutarch *himself* labouring to make his material intelligible. And in those passages, most insistently, his analysis concentrates on the *dēmos* theme, the popular support which Caesar enjoyed – a theme, incidentally, which is rather lost from sight when Plutarch is reproducing Pollio's analysis of the causes of the war.

In a Life such as the *Caesar*, what Plutarch leaves out can tell us as much about his assumptions as what he puts in. We should not, of course, expect him to say much about Caesar's family relationship to (say) the Aurelii or the Aemilii Lepidi, two highly influential *gentes* at the period of Caesar's early career;[19] however much importance we ourselves may choose to attach to such links (at least in explaining the *first* steps in a young man's career), these are not the sorts of connexion which ancient writers regularly stress. But Plutarch might surely have said more about Caesar's various attempts to conciliate senatorial opinion or foster senatorial connexions – at 5.7, for instance, he does not mention that Caesar's bride Pompeia was Sulla's grand-daughter, though this has clear biographical interest.[20] And it is certainly striking that Plutarch has nothing on Caesar's relations with the great men, Crassus and Pompey: nothing, in this

[17] Above, pp. 159–60.
[18] The uniformity of the tradition for Caesar's early years is demonstrated by Strasburger (1938) 72–73, though the elaborate source-analysis which Strasburger develops is not at all plausible.
[19] For Caesar's connexion with these *gentes* see Suet. *DJ* 1.2; for their power see Münzer (1920) 312f., 324ff. Note Aemilii Lepidi as consuls in 78/7, Aurelii Cottae in 75/4 – precisely the period when Caesar's career was beginning.
[20] He probably knew the item: cf. Suet. *DJ* 6.2, probably from the same source.

Life, on Caesar's support for the *lex Gabinia*, or his pressure for Pompey's recall from the East, or his association with Pompey's lieutenant Metellus Nepos; nothing on Caesar's alleged involvement with Crassus during the Catilinarian affair. All of these are items which Plutarch certainly knew.[21] But, in this Life, Caesar is his own master and agent. He gains his support – that vital popular support – wholly in his own right. Here, as elsewhere, Plutarch gives little indication of the personal attachments, alliances, and deals which most modern scholars would want to stress – however transient, or however firmly based, we might regard them as being; here, as elsewhere, it is the *dēmos* theme which dominates.

Now no one would regard Plutarch's analysis as wholly false. Of course, Caesar *was* a great *popularis*, recognized as such in his own day;[22] and the support of the urban *dēmos* was important to him. What is wrong with the analysis is simply what it leaves out. It is one strand among several important for explaining Caesar's career and success, and it is the exclusiveness of Plutarch's focus on it which is so striking. And it is a type of analysis which recurs time and again. In Life after Life, in much the same way in every period, we have the urban *dēmos* against the senate. There are just these two forces in politics: they can be described as ἀμφότεροι at (for instance) *Marius* 4.7. 'The senate wanted peace, but Marcellus stirred up the people for war' (*Marc.* 6.2); 'Appius Claudius always had the senate and the best men with him – it was his family tradition – while Scipio Africanus was a great man on his own account, but also always enjoyed great support and enthusiasm among the people' (*Aem.* 38.3); Marius 'was a formidable antagonist of the senate, for he was playing the demagogue with the people' (*Mar.* 4.6); in 70 B.C. people criticized Pompey for 'giving himself more to the people than the senate' (*Pomp.* 21.7), and, as we saw, 'Crassus had more strength in the senate, while Pompey was very powerful with the people' (*Pomp.* 22.3); in 66 it was the 'favour of the people and the flattery of the

[21] He mentions Caesar's support for the *lex Gabinia* at *Pomp.* 25.8, but not in *Caesar* (Dio 36.43.2–4, describing Caesar's support for the *lex Manilia* in very similar terms, is probable a doublet: Strasburger (1938) 63, 100–1); Plutarch had already described Caesar's agitation together with Metellus in the earlier *Cicero* (23.1–4), and makes a great deal of it at *C. min.* 27–29, but at *Caes.* 9.1 he blandly states that 'Caesar's praetorship was not at all turbulent'; at *Cic.* 23.5 he had also mentioned Caesar's proposal to recall Pompey from the East, and repeats the story (in a slightly different form) at *C. min.* 26.2, but again does not mention this in *Caes.* He mentions Caesar's involvement with Crassus at *Crass.* 13.4 (with some pride in his learning). In *Caesar*, apart from the casual mention of Pompey at 5.7, the introduction of both Crassus and Pompey is delayed until 11.1.

[22] Cf. esp. Cic. *Cat.* 4.9, *de prov. cons.* 38–39, *Phil.* 2.116, 5.49, Caelius *apud* Cic. *ad fam.* 8.6.5. See Strasburger (1938) esp. 129ff., and C. Meier (1965) *RE* Supplementband 10, cols. 580, 582, 590.

demagogues' which gave Pompey the command against Mithridates, while 'the senate and the best men' felt that Lucullus was being terribly slighted (*Lucull.* 35.9); in 59 Caesar cried out that 'he was driven to court the people against his will, because of the violence and recklessness of the senate' (*Caes.* 14.3); by 50 Cato was making no progress with the people, who 'wanted Caesar to be greatest', but he 'persuaded the senate, who were afraid of the people' (*C. min.* 51.7); in March and April 44 Brutus and Cassius 'had the goodwill of the senate', and turned to courting the people (*Brut.* 21.2–3).[23] These two forces or factors in politics are not quite parties: Plutarch never suggests that there was any organized group of politicians who systematically devoted themselves to promoting the people's interests (though he sometimes talks of 'the demagogues' in terms which have some analogies with this).[24] But, at least, the senate and people almost always act each in their unified and corporate ways, and Plutarch is surprised if the two sides act in concert – if they unite to support Cicero for the consulship, for instance, or if the aristocratically minded Aemilius is as popular as any demagogue (*Cic.* 10–11, *Aem.* 38.6). Other, complicating factors – the *equites*, perhaps, or the Italians, or the veterans – tend to be left out of things, as Plutarch prefers to leave his picture simple and unblurred.

In some ways, Plutarch is hardly alone in this. Nothing could be more natural at Rome than to contrast 'the senate' and 'the people': this mode of analysis is frequent enough in Roman historiography (we shall see that later), and, of course, with its clear analogies to classical Greek stereotypes of the ὀλίγοι and the δῆμος, it was particularly congenial to the *Greek* historians of Rome. The Greek equivalents are clearest in Polybius, who makes the senate and the people two of the three vital factors in his vision of the Roman 'mixed constitution': just as the consuls contribute the elements of monarchy to this, so the senate inject those of aristocracy and the people those of democracy.[25] It is not surprising that this schematism leaves no room for the *equites*, for example: at 6.17, very uneasily, he has to include the equestrian *publicani* among 'the people'.[26] As Clemence Schultze points out elsewhere in this volume, Dionysius of Halicarnassus is

[23] Cf. also e.g. *Marc.* 10.2 (Nola), *C. mai.* 16.4, *Mar.* 9.4, *Pomp.* 25.7, 46.5, 49.3–6, 49.11, 52.2, 59.3, *Lucull.* 38.2, *C. min.* 22.6, 26.1, 28.6, 29.3, 32.1, *Cic.* 33.2, 33.6, 43.4; and the detailed analyses of *Caesar*, *Gracchi*, and *Fabius* elsewhere in this paper. Note the isolated exception at *Mar.* 34.2, where Plutarch is aware that the views of the *dēmos* were divided.

[24] E.g. *Aem.* 38.6, *Ant.* 2.6, *Lucull.* 35.9, *C. min.* 31.2.

[25] Plb. 6.11–18, 43–58.

[26] See e.g. Walbank (1957) ad loc., or Brunt (1965a) 119: 'by the people he of course means the Equites'. Nicolet (1966) 322–23 does not quite bring out the importance of Polybius' schematism.

similarly fond of *boulē–dēmos* antitheses in describing the history of the early and middle Republic.[27] Appian begins his *Civil Wars* with the remark that 'at Rome there was frequent conflict between the senate and people, as they clashed over legislation and debt-cancellations and land-distributions and elections'; and Cassius Dio, too, readily adopts the *boulē–dēmos* antithesis as a favourite device for analysing late-republican history, and equally stresses popular support as the key to Caesar's rise.[28] And yet with these other authors – but not really with Plutarch – there is normally more to it than that. There is often a measure of thoughtfulness in the way these categories are applied, as possibly with Dionysius and certainly with Polybius. The latter has evidently expended an extraordinary amount of intellectual effort in isolating the elements of the Roman constitution which correspond to the Greek stereotypes – and of course concludes that the particular *blend* of monarchic, aristocratic, and democratic factors, though not necessarily any of the factors themselves, is really *unlike* any Greek constitution, and indeed superior to anything the Greeks could offer.[29] It is hard to think that Plutarch's application of the *boulē–dēmos* categories is anything like so reflective. In the other authors, too, there is usually some sense of historical change. Polybius, like Dionysius, stresses that it took considerable time for the distinctive Roman blend of monarchy, aristocracy, and democracy to develop;[30] and Appian, in his introductory survey, tends to regard *boulē–dēmos* strife as the main strand in *earlier* Roman history – before the Gracchi. The Gracchi marked the introduction of violence into politics;[31] afterwards Appian concentrates much more on the theme of the 'returning general', with his discontented army which needed to be settled.[32] The analysis recurs later in Appian's history, and his use of the *boulē–dēmos* antithesis is correspondingly sparing.[33] He, like Cassius Dio, shows much more awareness than Plutarch that the *boulē–dēmos* contrast often breaks down, and other strands of explanation need to be employed. Thus both Appian and Dio have rather more of the veterans, for example, and the *equites*;[34] thus Appian

[27] Above, pp. 130–31, 139–40.

[28] *Boulē–dēmos*: e.g. 36.24.1–2, 36.24.5, 36.37.1, 36.38.3–5, 36.43.2–5, 36.51.3, 37.26.3, 37.29.3, 37.41.3, 37.42.3, 37.43.1, 37.51.3, 37.56.5, 38.1.1, 38.12.4–13.1, 38.15.3, 38.16.3, 38.16.6, and so on. Popular support for Caesar: 36.43.2–4, 37.22.1, 37.37.2–3, 37.56.1–2, 38.11.3–6, 39.25.1–3, 40.50.5, 45.6.1, 45.11.2. Cf. Brutscher (1958) 43–46. But, as Strasburger (1938) 98–106 observes, he does make considerably more than Plutarch of Caesar's associations with Pompey during the sixties.

[29] Plb. 6.43–58.

[30] Plb. 6.10.13–14, 51.5; for Dionysius see Schultze, above pp. 130–32, 139.

[31] App. *BC* 1.2.4, cf. Plut. *Gracch.* 20.1.

[32] App. *BC* 1.1–6, esp. 1.2.4ff.

[33] 'Returning general' theme: cf. 1.55.240, 1.60.269–70; 5.17 brings out the importance of finding a *settlement* for such an army. Sparing use of *boulē–dēmos* antithesis: e.g. 1.21.87–89, 1.38.169, 1.69.316–17, 1.107.502.

[34] Below, pp. 179–81.

knows that Pompey can be both 'a friend of the people', φιλόδημος, and thoroughly responsible in his behaviour towards the senate;[35] thus Dio can introduce the interesting and revealing descriptions of Cato, and then of Brutus and Cassius, as 'lovers of the people' (δημερασταί);[36] and he can talk – admittedly in a rather bewildering way – of the various 'associations' (ἑταιρεῖαι) which Pompey and Crassus respectively brought to the alliance of 60 B.C.[37] What strikes one about Plutarch is how rarely such complicating factors are adduced, and how relentlessly and exclusively he presses the simple *boulē–dēmos* antithesis – indeed, how often he reduces and simplifies other modes of explanation so that he can phrase them in these terms. We are certainly here confronting an *individual* feature of Plutarch's technique.

Particularly striking and illuminating are the Lives of the *Gracchi*. There we find analyses very similar to those given in the *Caesar*, and there, too, elements which complicate the simple picture tend to be cut away. Tiberius is greeted by popular acclaim (*Gracch.* 7.3–4, 8.10, 10.1), and his policies are aimed at the urban *dēmos*.[38] The senate – or, more usually in this Life, 'the rich'[39] – naturally respond with hostility. Led on by the people's enthusiasm, Tiberius manages to depose Octavius – but, at that, his popular support begins to waver (15.1). He finds himself forced into policies which are more extreme (16.1), but the people remain cool: the enraged opponents of the bill seize their chance, and Tiberius is killed. But, by the time of his death, the popular fervour is beginning to erupt once more (21) – exactly, one remembers, as it did when Caesar was killed, and Cinna the poet became the victim. Indeed, the whole sequence is closely similar to the pattern developed in the *Caesar*: popular support brings success, popular cooling drives a man to fatal mistakes, popular fervour reasserts itself at the end. A few years later, and the whole pattern starts again with Gaius: we see the great initial popularity, and Gaius responding to it with a collection of popular measures; then we have

35 App. *BC* 2.20.72.

36 Dio 37.22.3, 43.11.6, 47.38.3 (with Rawson, above p. 115). Dr Lintott notes that Dio's view of Helvidius Priscus is interestingly similar (65.12.2), and suggests that Dio's interpretation of Helvidius' philosophical ideals may have influenced his portrayal of Cato.

37 Dio 37.54.3, 37.57.2; for the use of ἑταιρεία cf. Nic. Dam. *Vit. Aug.* 103, 105.

38 *Gracch.* 8.10, 9.3, 10.1, 12.6, 13.4, 13.6.

39 *Gracch.* 10.9, 11.1, 11.4, 12.6, 18.3, 20.3. These 'rich' dominate the senate (11.4, though cf. 18.3), and indeed seem closely equivalent to the political grouping which Plutarch normally describes simply as 'the senate': cf. 14.3, 16.2, 21.1–4. Plutarch here calls them 'the rich' simply to phrase the conflict in the relevant terms, i.e. economic ones. When political rather than economic divisions come to be more relevant, he naturally reverts to describing Tiberius' opponents as 'the senate' (20–21). Economic considerations were less central to his treatment of Gaius, and his antagonists are again usually 'the senate': 26.1, 27.1–2, 29.3–6, 30.1–2, 30.6–7, 32.5, 33.3, 35.2.

the wavering of popular support, this time caused less by any mistake of Gaius than by the shrewdness of his opponents, who use M. Livius Drusus to outbid Gaius' proposals. Gaius is forced to more extreme tactics; the opponents take their chance, and he dies; the popular fervour returns after his death.[40] Once again, all is focused on the urban *dēmos*, whose support brings success and whose indifference brings failure and death; and the pattern of the *Caesar* comes back in the *Gracchi*, and comes back twice.

What is more, we can see that Plutarch has removed material which does not fit. Consider *Gracch.* 8, where Plutarch is setting out the background of the troubles. That chapter seems clearly to come from the same source as Appian *BC* 1.7,[41] but we can see that Plutarch and Appian have selected rather different strands to stress. Appian, as is well known, makes a great deal of the *Italian* strand. The problem is the εὐανδρία or δυσανδρία of the Italian race, and Tiberius tries to favour the poor – including the allies, it is clear[42] – throughout Italy. One particular concern is that, on the large estates, landowners prefer slave to freeborn labour, because the freeborn are eligible for military service; and this *military* strand is given great stress. Now Plutarch does seem to know of this type of explanation, and it is reasonable to infer that something like this stood in the shared source. Plutarch does mention, for instance, that 'the poor did not enlist enthusiastically for military service', and that they 'did not care to bring up their young, so that shortly *all Italy* would be afflicted by a shortage of free men'; and he records Tiberius' resonant speech, proclaiming the plight of those who 'fight and die for Italy'.[43] But none of this is brought to the centre of the analysis, and the isolated mention of 'all Italy' remains rather opaque. All Plutarch's weight falls on the urban *dēmos*, whom Tiberius is trying to benefit and placate. The public land had been distributed 'to the destitute and

[40] Initial popularity: *Gracch.* 22.7. Demagogic proposals: 24.5, 25.1, and especially 26, the bills which he introduced τῷ δήμῳ χαριζόμενος καὶ καταλύων τὴν σύγκλητον (26.1); 27.5. people rejoice: 25.4, 27.1, 28.1. Γνωριμώτατοι launch Livius Drusus: 29.4, 31.3–4. People waver: 30.7 ('the people became more gently disposed to the senate'), 32.4, 37.7. Gaius more extreme: 33. Death: 36–38. Popular hatred of Opimius: 38.8–9, 39.2; and demonstrations for Gaius after death: 39.2–3.

[41] The sequence and selection of material in the two authors is tellingly similar. The usual view (and surely the right one) is that they share a source (cf. Gabba (1958) on App. *BC* 1.7.26): see esp. Tibiletti (1948) 206–9 (who seems right against Gabba on 1.7.28), Shochat (1970) 34ff., with extensive bibliography at n. 31, Badian (1972) 707. The principal dissenter is Göhler (1939) 74–75, but his strongest argument rests on precisely the difference of interpretation – Appian stressing the Italians, Plutarch the urban poor – which is here explained in terms of Plutarch's individual techniques.

[42] See esp. *BC* 1.7.28, 1.8.32, 1.18.74, 1.21.86–87, with Gabba's notes; Göhler (1939) 76–82.

[43] *Gracch.* 8.4, 9.5. Cf. Gabba (1956) 37 n. 1, Shochat (1970) 36–37, Richardson (1980) 2.

landless *citizens*', and these had now been dispossessed. Tiberius tries to reverse the process.[44] Plutarch is clearly thinking of the citizens *in Rome* as the beneficiaries of his measures: a conventional γῆς ἀναδασμός, in fact, in very Greek terms. (That indeed is the charge of his enemies: he is introducing a γῆς ἀναδασμός and starting a revolution, 9.3.) Later, Appian speaks of 'the countrymen' (1.10.41) coming to Rome to support Tiberius, and then of the country citizens who might come to vote for his re-election (1.14.58): in each case there may be some confusion in Appian's detail, but something like these notices surely stood in the shared source.[45] Plutarch again cuts the details away, reducing everything to the urban *dēmos*. His treatment of Gaius is very similar, again concentrating purely on the popular elements. The laws – including the συμμαχικός law, extending the citizenship to the allies – all have one absolutely straightforward aim, and Plutarch has no doubts about it: Gaius is trying to win the goodwill of the *dēmos* (*Gracch.* 26, esp. 26.2). Once again, too, there are hints that Plutarch is recasting and simplifying his source-material. There is, for instance, his casual mention that the Italians gave Gaius their support, or the notice of the accusations that he and Fulvius Flaccus were stirring up the allies to revolt.[46] Passages like those certainly suggest that Plutarch's source had rather more material on the Italians (as indeed does Appian). But in Plutarch this material again remains tangential and unexplained. The centre of the analysis remains the urban *dēmos*, wooed in a stereotyped way by Gaius, a stereotyped demagogue. That stress on the *dēmos* certainly fits the structure of the Lives – and not merely the structure of the Lives, but of the double pair. The Gracchi are compared with Agis and Cleomenes, and all four are seen as demagogues, even if they are initially idealistic ones: that is the whole point of the comparison (*Agis and Cleomenes* 2.7–11, cf. *Gracch.* 42(2) and 44(4)). But it certainly seems clear that Plutarch is drastically simplifying and recasting in order to produce this clear-cut popular focus.

It is worth spending a moment on the significance of this for the Roman historian. The tendency of *Appian*'s account of the Gracchi is often examined closely, and we are frequently warned to beware of the 'pan-Italic motif' in Appian *BC* 1;[47] and scholars have often

[44] *Gracch.* 8.1, 9.2; for the stress on the *dēmos* see n. 38.

[45] For countrymen coming to Rome in 133, cf. Diod. 34/5.6.1.

[46] *Gracch.* 24.1–2, 33.1 (Italian support); 24.1–2, 31.3 (accusations of stirring revolt).

[47] Particularly by Badian: see Badian (1958a) 172, and Badian (1972) 701 n. 100, 717 and n. 146, 731 n. 183. Gabba (1956) discusses 'il motivo alleato' with great care, but is much more ready than Badian to believe that it may bear some relation to historical reality.

sought to exploit Plutarch against Appian in order to discredit that 'Italian' material. Most influentially, Badian, when arguing that Tiberius' land-grants were to be limited to Roman citizens, has explicitly defended Plutarch's authority: Plutarch's emphasis on the urban *dēmos*, he thinks, represents an earlier and more authentic stage in the tradition than Appian, and all these Italians were sneaked into the tradition by Appian's immediate source (who, he thinks, was a *popularis* historian of the late-republican or Augustan period).[48] More recently, Bernstein has sought to reconcile Plutarch and Appian by suggesting that Tiberius first intended to include the Italian allies in his grants (Appian) – but then changed his plan and confined the distribution to Roman citizens (Plutarch).[49] What is worrying about all this is how little attention is being paid to *Plutarch*'s methods – how often he is the dumb partner in the comparison with Appian. If we can see, as we surely can, that it is absolutely characteristic of Plutarch to reduce complicated descriptions to the simple *boulē–dēmos* categories, then surely it is much more likely that *he* is the one who is sneaking the Italians *out of* his account, not Appian, or Appian's immediate source, who is sneaking them *in*. If it is right to assume a shared source, it is surely likely to be Appian, not Plutarch, who is preserving its spirit.

If this is so, it becomes much harder to discard Appian's evidence for this 'Italian' strand, and harder, in particular, to reject his statement that Tiberius intended the Italian allies to share in the grants of land.[50] 'Italian' needs further definition, of course: who were these people? Not just the rural citizens, it seems, unless Appian has wildly misunderstood his source;[51] but Latins and allies, or just allies? And were they to receive the citizenship as well as their parcel of land, as Richardson suggests?[52] Those are real questions, and

[48] Badian (1958a) 168–74, cf. Badian (1972) 731 and n. 183; he was following and developing some suggestions of Gelzer (see esp. Gelzer (1929) 299–303). See also e.g. Earl (1963) 20–23, and Nagle (1970) 373–76, for similar arguments.

[49] Bernstein (1978) 137–59. Bernstein also argues that reflections of this change of plan can be seen in Appian's own narrative: this is no place for a discussion, but his argument is not at all cogent. Cf. Astin (1979) 111f., Richardson (1980) 2–3.

[50] Naturally, not all the material relevant to this complicated issue can be discussed here: any serious treatment would have to consider the terms of the *lex agraria* of 111 B.C., as well as the various (largely enigmatic) statements made by Cicero. I here limit myself to those arguments drawn from the divergence of the narratives of Plutarch and Appian – arguments, it is true, which most scholars have felt to be of particular importance in discussing this question. For fuller recent discussions see Shochat (1970) and (1980), Richardson (1980) (Italians included in the grants); Brunt (1971a) 76 n. 1, Sherwin-White (1973) 217–18, and Stockton (1979) 40–46 (cautious, but not excluding Italian participation); Nagle (1970), Badian (1972) (Italians excluded); and Bernstein (1978) (discussed above).

[51] Cf. Göhler (1939) 76–82 (showing that by 'Italians' Appian certainly means Italian allies), Cuff (1967).

[52] Richardson (1980).

perhaps there is not sufficient evidence to give firm answers. And it may well be that this whole 'Italian' strand did not figure quite so prominently in Tiberius' propaganda and programme as Appian would suggest. It is certainly very important to Appian's vision of the whole period to stress Italian discontent, for he is already preparing and developing the themes which will return in his treatment of the Social War: all that is traced with great sensitivity by Gabba and by Cuff.[53] Appian might well want to make the most of any Italians he found – and that anyway suits his way of doing history. He is not particularly 'Italophile' (it is not a question of that, as again Cuff has shown); but he *is* unusually sensitive to social factors in his history, and particularly the relevance of the countryside in providing support.[54] But 'making the most of any Italians he found' is one thing, widespread fabrication is another. It is foreign to anything we know about Appian, or anything we can infer about his source-material, to believe that this strand has no foundation at all in historical reality. There is certainly nothing in Appian's account to justify the dismissive attitude shown, for instance, by Badian. When he discards the 'chatter about the opposition between "the rich" and "the poor"' which he finds in both Plutarch and Appian as 'no more than a stereotype of *stasis*, a purely literary device of little use to the historian',[55] Badian obscures the extremely important differences between Plutarch and Appian here. As far as Plutarch is concerned, the historian is right to be sceptical: the rich–poor antithesis is more than *a* stereotype, it is a version of *his* distinctive stereotype, and we can indeed see that he is simplifying a complex reality in order to make it fit. But Appian really is rather different. For him the rich–poor conflict is just one strand in a much more complex reality: town and country, Roman and Italian are in fact much more important to his analysis. The categories are of course rough ones,[56] but that need not in itself arouse suspicions. The most complex political divisions regularly embrace contrasts which can perfectly fairly, if roughly, be described in such terms. The blend of factors may be confusing, but it is certainly not stereotyped: Gabba is indeed right to comment on the *un*stereotyped and *un*conventional nature of Appian's analysis in this part of *BC* 1.[57] It is very hard to believe that the Italian material is simply drawn from the air.

To return to Plutarch: something similar has probably happened

[53] Gabba (1956), Cuff (1967).

[54] This emerges with particular clarity in Book 5 (which, *pace* Gabba, is surely not drawn from the same source as the early parts of Book 1): cf. esp. 5.12–14, 5.23.90, 5.27.106. See also Cuff (1983).

[55] Badian (1972) 707; cf. the criticisms of De Ste Croix (1981) 359.

[56] As Badian (1972) 717f. and n. 149 rightly insists.

[57] Gabba (1956) 62.

in his account of Saturninus and Glaucia, which he gives at *Marius* 28–30. *Marius* is of course another Life in which Plutarch is extremely interested in historical analysis, and he is most concerned at that point to analyse Marius' wavering popular support. Once again, it is likely that he is drawing his material from the same source as Appian, who gives a parallel account at *BC* 1.28–33.[58] But, once again, the emphases of the two authors are very different. Appian is very clear that it was 'the Italians' who supported Saturninus, and were to benefit from his land-bill. The urban *dēmos* (πολιτικὸς ὄχλος, 1.30.133) oppose Saturninus fiercely, and in this they are at one with the senate. When Saturninus tries to drive Metellus into exile, the Italians again support him (1.31.139–40), and again threaten to come to blows with the city-dwellers; and, once Saturninus is overthrown, the *dēmos* and the senate, again at one, gratefully seize their chance to press for Metellus' recall. (I take it that Appian means 'the Italian allies' when he speaks of the 'Italian' or 'rustic' support for Saturninus; even if, as many suppose, he means the 'rural citizens', the fact remains that he is drawing a firm distinction between countrymen and city-dwellers.)[59] All that is much too complicated for Plutarch. He turns Saturninus, like the Gracchi, into a very conventional demagogue. Saturninus aims at the 'destitute and turbulent mob' (πλῆθος ἄπορον καὶ θορυβοποιόν, 28.7, cf. 29.9): it is clearly the urban *dēmos* which supports him (29.7, 29.11, 30.2), and the senate which is opposed. The land-bill seems aimed, once again, at the urban *dēmos*: not a word of those 'countrymen' or 'Italians' of Appian. (Nor indeed, in this context, of Marius' veterans, though he has mentioned them in the preceding chapter (28.7); more of that later.) This leaves the final popular surge *against* Marius (30.5) and the popular pressure for Metellus' recall (31.2) harder to explain – but Plutarch is not too concerned: mobs, after all, are fickle. Appian's version of all this is much more subtle and sophisticated, whatever its relation to historical reality;[60] if he and Plutarch do share a source,

[58] This is likely, though less certain than in the case of the accounts of the Gracchi. The exile of Metellus is certainly described in extremely similar terms by both authors (App. *BC* 1.29, Plut. *Mar.* 29), and must surely come from a common source. It is possible that one or the other has turned to a different source for the political background – but, in view of Plutarch's capacity for recasting material, there is no *need* to resort to that assumption.

[59] See Badian (1958a) 207 n. 2, Göhler (1939) 80f. (Appian means allies); Shochat (1970) 40 and n. 44, Gelzer (1929) 298, Brunt (1965b) 106 (rural citizens); Lintott (1968) 178–81 (Appian confused).

[60] Historians normally accept that Saturninus proposed some distribution to Italians, but argue (or imply) that only Italian *veterans* – particularly those of Marius' army – were to benefit: Göhler (1939) 197–203, Badian (1958a) 203–8, Gabba (1951) 178–79 and (1956) 75–76. I suspect that this needs reconsideration. The veterans were clearly of central importance (cf. *Mar.* 28.7, App. *BC* 1.29.132), and would doubtless be the first

it is surely likely that it is Appian, not Plutarch, who is retaining more of the complexities of the source's analysis. And, once again, we see Plutarch's reductionism, his readiness to simplify the most complex events into simple *dēmos* and *boulē* conflict, and his readiness to cut away material which would complicate and blur that simple stereotype.

I mentioned previously the γῆς ἀναδασμός of Tiberius as described 'in very Greek terms', and it is naturally tempting to take this suggestion further. This whole *boulē–dēmos* analysis does remind one irresistibly of the way Plutarch talks about Greek politics, and the stereotypes of Greek political thought: not, perhaps, the *boulē*, but at least the *oligoi*, who are predictably and violently opposed to the fickle *dēmos*. Before he came to write the *Parallel Lives*, Plutarch evidently had an extremely thorough knowledge of Greek history and literature, whereas his knowledge of detailed Roman history was probably scanty; is Plutarch here imposing Greek concepts on Roman reality, bending Roman history to fit stereotypes which did not wholly match the reality? It is interesting to note that Gomme made the converse suggestion, which is equally attractive – that Plutarch sometimes imposed Roman stereotypes on Greek history: Nicias buying the goodwill of the *dēmos* with expensive shows, for instance, or Cimon as the soldier who is lost when it comes to the tricks of domestic politics.[61] And certainly the similarity of the terms used for the Greek and Roman worlds was sometimes very *useful* to Plutarch, making his parallels all the closer. Just as Dion and Brutus have to kill similar tyrants, so Pericles and Fabius have to confront similar mobs and similar demagogues; and the corruption of good programmes into rank demagogy can link Agis and Cleomenes with the Gracchi.

Certainly, the similarities of Plutarch's language to that in his Greek Lives do seem very close. The opponents of the Roman *dēmos* may be described in various ways, though they can usually be seen to be equivalent to (or at least to dominate) the senate: they are the ἀριστοκρατικοί,[62] or the γνώριμοι,[63] or the καλοὶ κἀγαθοί,[64] or the χαριέντες,[65] or the ὀλιγαρχικοί,[66] or the ἀξιόλογοι,[67] or the

to be settled; but there seems no reason to assume that *only* veterans were to receive benefits.

[61] Gomme *HCT* 1.72–74.

[62] *Caes.* 13.5, 14.6, *Aem.* 38.2, 38.6, *Tit.* 18.2, *Mar.* 28.6, *C.min.* 26.4, *Pomp.* 30.3–4, *Lucull.* 38.2, *Cic.* 10.1, 33.2, cf. 22.2.

[63] *Aem.* 31.2, *C.mai.* 16.4, *Gracch.* 24.2, 29.6, 30.7, *Pomp.* 4.8, *Brut.* 24.4.

[64] *Caes.* 14.3, *Cic.* 11.2, 29.4.

[65] *Gracch.* 40.3, *Pomp.* 4.8, *Brut.* 24.4, *C.min.* 27.8, cf. 49.3.

[66] *Gracch.* 32.4, 35.2, *Cic.* 9.7.

[67] *Mar.* 9.4, cf. *Otho* 3.3.

δοκιμώτατοι,[68] or the δυνατώτατοι,[69] or the κράτιστοι,[70] or simply the πρῶτοι or ἄριστοι.[71] Those, indeed, are precisely the terms in which Plutarch is accustomed to speak of Greek politics.[72] The sort of analysis he gives in *Caesar* or the *Gracchi* – the hero wins popular support, then forfeits it, then it is finally reasserted – has considerable parallels with, say, the *Pericles*. Just as in Greece, an individual tries occasionally to become first man in the state; then, particularly if that individual is hoping to exploit his popularity with the *dēmos*, Plutarch usually assumes that he hoped for or achieved a τυραννίς, a δυναστεία, a μοναρχία. These accusations were of course thrown around in the real world of Roman politics, and it is perhaps natural that Plutarch should say such things of Sulla, Marius, Cinna, Saturninus, Cicero, Caesar, or Pompey; it is more striking that he should casually note that 'C. Gracchus had by now acquired a sort of monarch's strength', or record the suggestion that 'Cassius was seeking to secure a δυναστεία for himself, not freedom for his fellow citizens'.[73] If a man's aim is specified more closely, it is rarely any more informative than 'revolution' – μετάστασις or σύγχυσις τῆς πολιτείας: so, naturally enough, of the Catilinarians and of Caesar; so also, though, of Saturninus; and even, once again casually, of the supporters of Pompey in the late sixties – 'a sizable part of the *dēmos* wanted Pompey's return because they looked for a revolution' (*C. min.* 27.1, cf. *Pomp.* 43.5); and notice the charges laid against the ruling class during the Hannibalic War: 'they were exploiting the war to destroy the *dēmos* and introduce an absolute monarchy' (*Fab.* 8.4).[74] This assumption that political aims and achievements are regularly to be explained in terms of constitutional change is really very Greek. Plutarch has little idea of the characteristic Roman desire to be first within the system, rather than change it. When he writes of Marius or of Pompey, he writes of their φιλαρχία, their quest for offices or

[68] *Marc.* 27.4.

[69] *Fab.* 8.4, *Gracch.* 13.2, 20.1, *Lucull.* 37.3, *Pomp.* 25.7, *Caes.* 10.6; cf. *Mar.* 9.4, 30.5, *Gracch.* 24.3.

[70] *Mar.* 30.2.

[71] *Fab.* 8.4, *Marc.* 27.4, *Aem.* 38.2–3, *C. mai.* 16.4, *Mar.* 14.14, 29.7, 34.6, *Lucull.* 35.9, 37.3, *Pomp.* 16.3, 49.3, 51.6, *Crass.* 4.1, *Caes.* 7.4, *C. min.* 27.8, *Brut.* 27.5, 29.3.

[72] A representative selection of Greek passages: *Arist.* 2.1, 26.2, *Cim.* 10.8, 15.1–2, *Nic.* 2.2, 11.2, *Alc.* 13.5, 21.2, 26.2, *Dion* 28.1; and esp. *Per.* 7.3–4, 9.5, 10.7–8, 11.1–3 (with Meinhardt (1957) 38, and Andrewes (1978) 2), 15.1. In general see Rhodes (1981) on [Arist.] *AP* 2.1.

[73] Sulla: *Sull.* 30.5–6 (etc.), *Pomp.* 9.3, *Brut.* 9.2, *Cic.* 17.5, 27.6. Marius: *Mar.* 46.6, *Sull.* 30.5, cf. *Pomp.* 81(1).2. Cinna: *Mar.* 41.2, *Sull.* 22.1, *Cic.* 17.5, *Caes.* 1.1. Carbo: *Sull.* 22.1. Saturninus: *Mar.* 30.1. Cicero: *Cic.* 23.4. Caesar: *Caes.* 4.8, 57.1, 64.5, 69.1, *C. min.* 55.4, 58.7, 66.2, *Ant.* 12.5, *Brut.* 12.3. Pompey: *Pomp.* 25.3, 30.3–4, 43.1, 54.5, *Caes.* 41.2, *Lucull.* 38.2, *C. min.* 47.2. C. Gracchus: *Gracch.* 27.1. Cassius: *Brut.* 29.5.

[74] Catilinarians: *Cic.* 10.2, 10.5. Caesar: *Caes.* 4.9, 13.4, *Cic.* 20.6. Saturninus: *Mar.* 30.1. On *Fab.* 8.4 see below, p. 184.

commands;[75] he has no notion of an ambition for a position of prestige and respect within an appreciative state. There is certainly little feel for the importance of such ideas as *dignitas* or *auctoritas*. He does, perhaps, have rather more feeling for the Roman passion for *gloria*: he certainly seems clear enough, for instance, that T. Flamininus was eager to avoid handing the war with Philip over to a successor, and was prepared to make peace rather than see this. 'He was fiercely ambitious for honour, and was afraid that he might forfeit his glory if another general were sent to the war' (*Titus* 7.2, cf. 13.2); Plutarch does not find that at all remarkable or perplexing.[76] But, usually, when he speaks of such ambition for glory, he does so with considerable bitterness and hostility: in particular, this was the decisive failing of the Gracchi (*Agis and Cleomenes* 2), and it was an important aspect in which the elder Cato fell short of Aristides (*C. mai.* 32(5).4). Plutarch has certainly not felt his way into the values of Roman public life, and gives no sense of the respect and value Romans accorded to a competitive quest for glory.[77]

Where Greek analogies of Roman institutions exist, Plutarch is quite good: he does, for instance, seem to understand a fair amount about political activity in the lawcourts, and his discussion of political trials at *C.mai.* 15 is sensible enough. Things in Greece were perhaps not so very different – or at least *less* different than they were in many other aspects of political life.[78] When Greek equivalents are absent, he is in trouble. It may be a particular institution which defeats him: the tribunate, for instance, was a very curious thing to a Greek of the Roman empire, and Plutarch several times incorrectly explains the tribunicial veto, speaking as if a tribune could only veto the acts of a fellow tribune.[79] Certain aspects of the early days of January 49 B.C. are therefore beyond him: at *Ant.* 5.10 he can only refer to the infringement by the *optimates* (τῶν ἀπὸ βουλῆς) of the tribunes' freedom of speech, and gives no hint of the overriding of their veto.[80]

[75] Marius: *Mar.* 2.4, 28.1, 31.3, 34.6, 45.4–12. Pompey: *Pomp.* 30.7–8. (There is little on Pompey's wishes – for commands or for anything else – in the second half of that Life: see Pelling (1980) 133 and n. 32.)

[76] This ascription of motive derives from Polybius (18.10.11–12, 18.39.4). Livy, interestingly, finds the charge embarrassing and plays it down: see Livy 32.32.5–8 and 33.13.15, with Briscoe (1973) 22 n. 4, and notes on both passages. For a powerful modern discussion see Badian (1970) 295ff.: note esp. 310ff., with some trenchant remarks on Roman views of *gloria*.

[77] Wardman (1974) 120 brings this out well.

[78] The important political aspect which Plutarch does *not* see concerns the composition of the juries. To understand this he would need to show much more grasp of the *equites* than he does: see below p. 179.

[79] *Ant.* 5.8, *Gracch.* 10.3, *C. min.* 20.8 – though, oddly enough, he gets it right at *QR* 81 (*Mor.* 283c).

[80] *Caes.* 35.6–11, Caesar's clash with the tribune Metellus, is another case where Plutarch does not bring out the importance of the veto.

Or it may be a convention of political life which he finds difficult, or tends to obscure. He certainly knows the importance of the Roman political family, and of family traditions: the Claudii, for instance, and the Metelli are by tradition aristocratically minded (*Aem.* 38.3, *C.min.* 26.4). He sees the importance of kinsmen, too, in persuading Aemilius Paullus to stand for the consulship at a time of national crisis (*Aem.* 10.2). But he does not seem to sense the extent of the authority exercised by the *very* great families, the Scipiones or the Metelli or even (despite *Gracch.* 1) the Sempronii. When he seeks to explain the early electoral successes of Marcellus, it never occurs to him to mention the importance of the *family* (*Marc.* 2): the answer must be found in his military promise. The senate are the ἀριστοκρατικοί; Plutarch has no notion of the importance of *nobilitas*, and makes no attempt to distinguish grades of aristocracy within the senate itself. When the terms εὐγενής or εὐπατρίδης do occur, they often seem rather to refer to the *patriciate*.[81] All that scarcely conveys the flavour of the realities of Roman aristocratic society.

And Greek stereotypes could certainly not accommodate so unfamiliar an institution as *clientela*. Plutarch's definition of *patronus* at *Fab.* 13.6 is feeble and inadequate; and, when he mentions a *cliens–patronus* relationship, it is normally to explain the adhesion or obligation of *one* individual – normally a fairly important individual: Marius to Metellus or to C. Herennius, for example, or Mucius (if that was the man's name) to Ti. Gracchus.[82] He has no feel for the electoral or military significance of a *large body* of clients.[83] Thus the senatorial opponents of Ti. Gracchus can arm only 'their slaves and friends' against him (*Gracch.* 18.3); thus – though he knows Pompey was always welcome in Picenum, that he liked being there 'because people liked him so much', and that his popularity was inherited from his father (*Pomp.* 6.1) – he can still describe Pompey's raising of a private army in the eighties without any explicit mention of *clientela*. Nor is he alert to the importance of *clientelae* which are foreign – though he *is* always very interested in his subjects' achievements in

[81] See esp. *Sull.* 1.1, γένει μὲν ἦν ἐκ πατρικίων, οὓς εὐπατρίδας ἄν τις εἴποι, and *Ant.* 12.3. Most men so described are in fact both *nobiles* – whether on Gelzer's definition or on Mommsen's, revived by Brunt (1982) – and *patricii*: P. Clodius (*Caes.* 9.2, *Cic.* 28.1), Cornelius Lentulus at Cannae (*Fab.* 16.7), Valerius Flaccus (*C. mai.* 3.1), P. Cornelius Dolabella in A.D. 69 (*Otho* 5.1), the house of the Servii (*Galb.* 3.1). But the terms are clearly vague ones: cf. *Popl.* 18.3, *Cam.* 33.4, *Cic.* 40.2. Note *Sert.* 25.2, on Perperna's εὐγένεια (Perperna was not *patricius*, but he was *nobilis*, Gelzer (1969) 51 n. 457); and *C. mai.* 16.4, where the εὐπατρίδαι monopolize the consulship (clearly *nobiles*, for he knows that one plebeian had to be elected, 16.2). Plutarch simply follows any source which refers to high birth, and has no awareness of subtle distinctions.

[82] *Mar.* 4.1, 5.7–9, *Gracch.* 13.2: cf. *Cor.* 21.4, *Pomp.* 4.7, *C. min.* 34.6.

[83] *Cor.* 13.5 is an exception, but relates to a very different political climate.

the provinces, and in particular the justice and humanity of their administration. (A rather distinctive feature, this, and one which marks him out from Greek historians more steeped in Roman life and Roman historiography, Appian and Cassius Dio; and Plutarch, incidentally, has few illusions about the savagery and rapacity which typified most Roman governors.)[84] But, still, he can describe the links of Aemilius Paullus with various foreign nations in extremely wondering terms, and regard his continuing concern for their welfare as a quite remarkable trait (*Aem.* 39.8–9); and, still, he can describe the enthusiasm shown by the Spaniards for Ti. Gracchus as simply 'inherited from his father', with no hint that there was any more formal bond of duty or obligation (*Gracch.* 5.4–5).

Very often, he modifies unfamiliar ideas and forces to ones he can understand: again, usually to the familiar *boulē–dēmos* antithesis, by the same characteristic reductionism. He of course knows that the equestrian order existed, but he rarely brings it into his political analysis: he can, for instance, mention Sulpicius' 'anti-senate' of 600 *equites*, but there is no deeper analysis of Marius' equestrian support.[85] (He has therefore, very uneasily, to represent Marius as a curious sort of incompetent trimmer, spasmodically courting the *dēmos* 'against his true instincts' (28.1), but tending to drift away from them at inexplicable moments (e.g. 30).) When Tiberius or Gaius Gracchus or Pompey proposes to give the knights a share in the juries for the lawcourts, in each case Plutarch knows the political significance: in all three cases, they were trying to win the goodwill – of the *dēmos*![86] His treatment of the *publicani* is similar: resentful *publicani* determine to do down Lucullus in Roman politics – but the only way they can do so is by using 'demagogues' (*Lucull.* 20.5). In all this Plutarch contrasts with Appian and Cassius Dio, who both (especially Appian) have a good deal of the equestrian order – perhaps, indeed, rather too much.[87] But there is no doubt that Plutarch has too little.

[84] For Plutarch's interest see e.g. *Fab.* 20.1, *Marc.* 20, *Tit.* 2.3–5, 5.1–2, 12.6, *C. mai.* 6.2–4, 10.4–6, *Aem.* 6.6–7, 28.6ff., 39.7–9, *Gracch.* 3.1, 23.2, *Lucull.* 20, 29, *C. min.* 34–40, *Pomp.* 10.2, 28, 39, 50, *Caes.* 11–12, *Cic.* 6.1–2, 36, 52(3). As emerges most clearly from *Pompey*, he tends to be more interested in mildness of everyday administration and equity in routine jurisdiction than in the great administrative *settlements*. For his awareness of general rapacity see esp. *C. mai.* 6.2–4, *Cic.* 52(3).3, *C. min.* 12.3–6, *Brut.* 6.10–12, and the other instances collected by Jones (1971) 100.

[85] *Mar.* 35.2; other casual mentions of *equites* at e.g. *Mar.* 30.4, *Cic.* 10.5, 13.2, 31.1, *Pomp.* 14.11 (where again note that Plutarch stresses the enthusiasm of the *people* at Pompey's equestrian demonstration). Brunt (1965a) 130 is therefore right to notice the absence of *equites* from Plutarch's account of Marius, but wrong to find this surprising or significant.

[86] *Gracch.* 16.1, 26.2, *Pomp.* 22.3.

[87] Dio: esp. 38.12.4, 38.13.1, 38.16.2–3, 38.16.6; casual references are also more frequent than in Plutarch, e.g. 40.49.4, 40.60.4, 40.63.3, 41.7.1, 42.51.5, 43.25.1, 44.6.1, 44.9.1. Appian: esp. *BC* 1.22.91–97, 1.35.157–36.162, 1.37.165–68, 1.100.468, 2.13.47–48.

We can certainly see a similar reductionism in Plutarch's treatment of the army, particularly the army in politics. Here he is quite good on some aspects. He knows the perils presented by the returning generals, dangerous men at the head of devoted armies: he digresses on these in the *Sulla* (12), and the theme recurs – though not very insistently – in the *Pompey*.[88] But what do these returning armies *want*? Here he is less good, and he certainly does not understand their imperative need for *land*. He knows that the veterans were in some way connected with the land-bills of 59 B.C.; he even knows that Pompey 'filled the city with soldiers' to pass the measure; but still he does not see the connexion. The bills are aimed 'to win the goodwill of the mob'; they distribute land 'to the poor and destitute'.[89] His treatment of Saturninus' land-bill is exactly similar. There too he knows that Marius introduced his soldiers into the assemblies to help Saturninus (*Mar.* 28.7) – but the land-bill is still, as we saw, aimed at captivating and benefitting the urban *dēmos*. Just as he strips away the Italian allies from his analysis, so also with the veterans: once again, everything is reduced to a simple, conventional γῆς ἀναδασμός, aimed at the urban mob. As he is so blind to the veterans' interest in land, it is hardly surprising that he seems to miss the point of the Marian military reforms. He knows that Marius introduced a new type of recruit into the Roman army, but makes a revealing error when he mentions this: Marius is recruiting 'destitute men and *slaves*' (*Mar.* 9.1). He clearly does not realize that it is a different type of *citizen*, the man without capital or land, who is involved: it is clear that his stereotype of the *dēmos* is too simple to admit of subtle distinctions between *assidui* and *proletarii*. In the *Sulla*, similarly, when he digresses on the theme of the 'returning general' he does not bring out that Sulla's army included these new, landless types of recruit. He does not see that this army was in important ways different from the forces of Flamininus, Acilius, and Aemilius Paullus, with whom he compares it (*Sull.* 12.8–14); and that these differences were central in explaining the new bond between generals and troops, and the violent consequences this produced.

Indeed, he is not really very interested in the soldiers at all. Very often, he simply leaves them out completely when he is describing politics. In the turbulent days of spring and summer 44 B.C., he rarely mentions the veterans; it is again usually the urban *dēmos* for whose

[88] *Sull.* 12.12–14, *Pomp.* 20.1, 21.5–7, 43.1–3.

[89] τὸ στρατιωτικόν somehow involved: *C. min.* 31.2. City filled with soldiers: *Pomp.* 48.1. Mob's goodwill as the aim: *Caes.* 14.2. Land distributed to the poor and destitute: *C. min.* 31.5, 33.1, *Pomp.* 47.5. *Dēmos* enraptured: *Pomp.* 48.2.

favour Brutus, Octavian, and Antony contend.[90] Plutarch certainly has little notion that the veterans might have *genuine* loyalties, worth discussing and analysing: 'the armies', he says in an aside in the *Brutus* (23.1), 'were on sale – it was just like an auction: they gave themselves to the highest bidder [...]'. When he comes in *Antony* to describe the treaty of Brundisium, it is simply the 'friends' of Antony and Octavian who urge them to come to terms, and cement their alliance with the marriage agreement.[91] Appian, again probably drawing on similar material, makes it very clear that it was the veterans who began this pressure on their leaders to agree on peace.[92] Indeed, the entire history of the Triumvirate reads very differently in our other accounts, and especially in their treatment of the soldiery: Appian, in particular, has a great deal more on the impact of their veterans and their loyalties on political life, even though he seems to be using similar source-material. Cassius Dio has his blind spots about the soldiers, but he too knows that their loyalties were not wholly for sale; Nicolaus of Damascus, also, is more in tune with historical reality.[93] Plutarch cuts the theme away, and again it is the urban *dēmos* which matters.

It is perhaps time to return to the question of the *origins* of these assumptions of Plutarch. I have been dwelling on the 'Greekness' of it all, and suggesting that he is imposing his own categories, drawn from classical Greek history and political thought, on Roman realities which do not wholly fit. But, of course, we must not overstate the differences between Greek and Roman political stereotypes. That *boulē–dēmos* analysis, for instance: is it so very different from Sallust's view of the 'duas partis' of the Roman state, the *pauci* (or *nobiles* or *potentes* or just *senatus*) and the *plebs*?[94] Sallust, too, often omits the *equites* from his analysis; and Sallust too dwells on the *plebs*, the

[90] *Brut.* 18.10–14, 20.1, 20.4–11, 21.2–6, 22.3, *Ant.* 14.5, 16.6–8. Scanty references to the soldiers: *Ant.* 16.6–8, *Brut.* 21.4, 22.3, 23.1.

[91] *Ant.* 30.6–31.3.

[92] App. *BC* 5.63–64.

[93] App. *BC* 2.119.501, 2.120.507, 2.125.523, 2.135.565, 3.6.18, 3.11.38–12.41, 3.21.78, and so on, esp. 5.17 (see e.g. n. 52): a glance at the *index locorum* of Botermann (1968) reveals how much of the evidence for the political loyalties and impact of the veterans is drawn from Appian. Dio's blind spots on the veterans: see Botermann (1968) 30, but note e.g. 45.7.2, 45.12–13, bringing out both their genuine loyalties and their capacity to be influenced by largesse. Nic. Dam.: see *Vit. Aug.* 41, 46, 56, 95, 99, 103, 108, 115–19, 121, 130–33, 136–39.

[94] Cf. esp. Sall. *BJ* 41, *BC* 37–38, *Hist.* 1.6–13M, and (if authentic) *ad Caes.* 2.5.1. For Sall.'s usage see Hanell (1945), Syme (1964) 17f., 171ff., Hellegouarc'h (1963) esp. 110ff., 430, 438, 442ff., 512. Sallust is, of course, heavily indebted to Thucydides in his use of these categories, and applies them to Roman politics with little intelligence or insight.

'artisans and rustics', as the decisive force which carried Marius to the consulship.[95] The incautious reader might well assume – just as Plutarch often seems to assume[96] – that the poorest citizens could genuinely dominate the wealth-based *comitia centuriata*. Livy as well sometimes describes events in similar terms, with the senate (or *nobiles*) striving valiantly to resist stereotyped popular fury.[97] Cicero, in his tendentious little account in the *pro Sestio*, feels he can get away with speaking of the two great traditions in the Roman state, the *optimates* and the *populares*; and he then describes the Gracchi in terms very similar to Plutarch, affirming that they introduced laws which were welcome to the people but hateful to the *boni*.[98] Tacitus, too, can refer to 'assidua senatus adversus plebem certamina' as a conspicuous feature of the last phase of the Republic.[99] And all that quest for tyranny and revolution: was this not the stuff of political abuse, and occasionally of reality, in the late Republic – 'uterque regnare vult', and so on?[100] Is there not a real chance that here – just as in the case of Pollio's explanation of the war which we noticed earlier – Plutarch is simply following the analysis of some Latin sources, and the similarity of his language and interpretation to the ways he speaks of Greek politics is just a fortunate coincidence?

There may be something in that objection. It is certainly true that he may not have found any very clear *correctives* to his natural assumptions in the Roman historical tradition, and so it is not surprising that the later Lives are not conspicuously more sophisticated in their historical interpretations than the ones which he had written

[95] See *BJ* 73.6–7 ('[...] plebes sic accensa [...] opifices agrestesque omnes'), 84.1 ('cupientissuma plebe consul factus'). For the general omission of the *equites* (though note 65.4) see Syme (1964) 173: 'a serious omission [...] if nothing worse'.

[96] E.g. *Pomp.* 15.1, 22.2, *C. min.* 21.3.

[97] Though he admittedly tends to confine such analyses to the early books, where such categories are natural enough for the description of the struggle of the Orders (see e.g. Hellegouarc'h (1963) 430 with nn. 1 and 7, 436 with n. 2, 515–16). His use of such categories to describe Roman politics is extremely sparing in the third, fourth, and fifth decades (except in Book 22, esp. 22.34.1–35.3, 22.40.1–4: rather a special case, as I suggest below). Such instances as 21.63.4, 31.6.4, or 43.14.2–3 are in fact fairly isolated. Interestingly, he is far readier to use such terms for non-Roman states, e.g. Capua (23.2.3, 4.2–4, etc.), or 'all the states of Italy' (24.2.8), or Carthage (e.g. 34.62.1), or the states of Greece (35.34.3), or Phocaea (37.9.4).

[98] *Sest.* 103, cf. *de leg. agr.* 2.10, 81 (and *de off.* 2.78–81, where his language very much suggests a γῆς ἀναδασμός). But, once again, this should not be overstated. Hellegouarc'h (1963) 512 could reasonably comment on the *rarity* with which Cicero employs *patres–plebs* or *nobiles–plebs* antitheses, or speaks of the *plebs* as a political group.

[99] *Dial.* 36.3. Cf. his conspectus of all republican history at *Ann.* 4.32–33, especially 'plebis et optimatium certamina' (32.1), '[...] plebe valida vel cum patres pollerent' (33.2).

[100] Cic. *ad Att.* 8.11.2; see passages collected by Hellegouarc'h (1963) 560–65, and Seager (1972) 335 n. 11.

earlier.[101] But it is also true that few Roman writers (and few Greek writers, as we noticed earlier) apply the *boulē–dēmos* analysis quite so relentlessly and quite so exclusively as Plutarch does. Consider, for example, the wide group of people whom Cicero would class as *optimates* in the *pro Sestio*, or the various different classes of supporters who contributed to Marius' *honestissuma suffragatio* in Sallust.[102] And there is some way between abusive *allegations* that individuals are aiming for tyranny, uttered by political opponents with ferocity and passion, and Plutarch's casual *assumption* that such allegations are regularly true. But it anyway seems clear that Plutarch is not simply taking over categories which he finds in his sources; on the contrary, he is regularly reinterpreting his material in order to bring out these favoured categories, and is not at all the slave of the tradition. We saw a certain amount of this earlier, in examining his recastings of Pollio in describing Caesar, and of an unidentifiable source in telling the story of the Gracchi. And the recastings will emerge even more clearly if we go back to an earlier period of Roman history, where we can compare Plutarch with his source-material – or something very like his source-material – rather more closely.

If we had to pick a piece of Roman historiography to remind us of Greek *dēmos* and demagogue stereotypes, we might well choose Livy 22. Minucius and Varro, in turn, are the Cleon-like demagogues, mobilizing the uncontrollable forces of the vulgar mob; on the other side, we have the sober and sensible Fabius and Paullus, and the sober and sensible senate. And this is a place where we can compare Plutarch very closely: for his narrative in *Fabius* is often very similar indeed to Livy – so similar that we should either assume that he is using Livy directly, or an earlier authority to whom Livy, too, kept very close.[103] In either case, Livy can give us a very good idea of the

[101] Not that it is a particularly easy matter to establish the relative chronology of the Lives. Jones (1966) gives the best discussion, but needs to be treated with some caution: see Pelling (1979) 80–82.

[102] *Sest.* 97–98, 132–39, esp. 138; Sall. *BJ* 65.5.

[103] The extreme closeness of much of *Fabius* to Livy is quite clear, but several passages seem to show accurate knowledge of non-Livian detail: e.g. the 15,000 prisoners at Trasimene, 3.3; the deception at Rome when news of the Trebia arrived, 3.4; the 4,000 men of 6.4. Such elements suggest either that Plutarch knew Livy's source rather than Livy himself (so Peter (1865), Soltau (1897), etc., suggesting Coelius Antipater; Klotz (1935), suggesting Valerius Antias); or a systematic, though small-scale, supplementation of Livy from a closely parallel account. (There is larger-scale supplementation at e.g. *Fab.* 15, 20, 26, but those passages are not woven so closely into the Livian material, and can easily represent additions from Plutarch's own memory and general reading.) Some parts of Plutarch show knowledge of those parts of Livy which are most likely to be Livy's own contribution (e.g. the arguments of Herennius Balbus, 22.34 and *Fab.* 8.4; the Camillus echo at 22.3.10 and *Fab.* 3.1; the words of Fabius, 22.18.8 and *Fab.* 8.1); and it is on balance more likely that Plutarch knows Livy himself, not his source. It may well be that a slave or freedman assistant was sent to consult (say)

content of Plutarch's source-material. What is interesting is the way in which Plutarch takes those *dēmos* and demagogue stereotypes even further than Livy:[104] even this very Greek passage of narrative was insufficiently reduced to the *boulē–dēmos* terms which he wanted. In Plutarch, much more than Livy, Fabius is initially created dictator by a mindless surge of popular panic – precisely the sort of mindless surge which he himself will later have to confront; Livy, like Polybius, had simply dwelt on the confusion in Rome at the time, and had not given any such *popular* stress.[105] In Plutarch, Fabius gives a speech to the *dēmos* as soon as he is appointed, reassuring them and quelling their panic; in Livy it was not delivered to the *dēmos*, but to the senate.[106] When Fabius is deceived by the oxen stratagem, and again when Minucius wins his initial delusive successes, it is the popular enthusiasm for Minucius – and the popular fears for his safety, if Fabius got his hands on him – which Plutarch stresses; on both occasions, Livy had concentrated on the attacks on Fabius delivered in the senate.[107] When Fabius is attacked, the demagogue Metilius claims that the senate 'had provoked the whole war to destroy the *dēmos* and impose an absolute monarchy' (8.4). 'To impose a monarchy'? That sounds very odd, and very much like Plutarch himself: and, sure enough, Livy has nothing like this. Plutarch seems in fact to be borrowing from a passage rather later in Livy, when Varro accuses the nobles of 'using the war to gain control of the *comitia*'.[108] 'To gain control of the *comitia*' is rather milder, and much more plausible: Plutarch is again rewriting the Roman original to stress his own favoured theme. This *boulē–dēmos* analysis is indeed very important to *Fabius* – and not just to the Life, but to the whole pair. Stadter[109] has shown that the comparison of Pericles and Fabius is very elaborate, and the two men's reactions to hostile mobs and hostile demagogues are an important element in the pairing. Later in the *Fabius* – and this is a most interesting development – we see related themes coming back when Fabius is in decline, woefully jealous of the successes of the young Scipio. Fabius

Coelius or Polybius, and report back to Plutarch any significant variations from Livy's account, or useful extra details: we too readily ignore the possibility of such 'research assistants' (see Jones (1971) 84–87, and Pelling (1979) 95). At all events, even if it is Livy's source, not Livy himself, who is Plutarch's main authority, Livy's general closeness to Plutarch suggests that he is generally remaining very faithful to the source which, on this hypothesis, he and Plutarch share.

104 Hoffmann (1942) 38–39 brings out this feature of Plutarch's narrative very well, though he is surely wrong in attributing the recasting of the material to Plutarch's source, not Plutarch himself.

105 *Fab.* 3.6–7, cf. Livy 22.8, Plb. 3.86–87.

106 *Fab.* 4.4, cf. Livy 22.9.7.

107 *Fab.* 7.5–7, 9.1, cf. Livy 22.23.5–7, 22.25.12.

108 Livy 22.34.9.

109 Stadter (1975).

may still be urging his distinctive caution, but he is also showing exactly those characteristics which we earlier saw in the demagogues: he is overcome by petty φιλονικία, scoring political points rather than prosecuting the war, 'crying out' (βοῶν) in the assembly, desperate to mobilize popular pressure against a great general.[110] As Pericles in old age gains a stature lacking from his demagogic youth, so Fabius' demagogic decline compromises the dignity which he has won in the years of his greatness: the pair as a whole shows an extremely elegant 'hour-glass structure' (to use the term of E. M. Forster).[111] And once again the neatness of the analysis seems to be Plutarch's own. We would be hard put to it to find any similar thematic links between Fabius' greatness and decline in the treatment of Livy.

In *Fabius*, then, Plutarch certainly does *not* seem to be at the mercy of his sources. Even where they offered an analysis which must have been congenial to him, he was not content to take it over: skilfully, he took it much further. One can trace the same individuality in other passages, and can see how reluctant he was to take over blindly the themes which his Roman sources developed. We might conclude by looking at some passages where he shows his awareness of the characteristic motifs of Roman historians: the importance of *metus hostilis*, for example, in keeping Rome morally upright, or the nature of moral decline from ancestral simplicity, or the disastrous effect of foreign culture. As Jones has stressed,[112] Plutarch often takes over some of these views himself, in a not very original way: in particular, he has some splendid passages of routine nostalgia, reflecting wistfully on the days before ambition and greed overtook the state.[113] But there are also passages where he gives such Roman ideas as *metus hostilis* a rather individual twist; and one can indeed see that some of the most cherished Roman beliefs would have been hateful to him. *Metus hostilis*, vital to keep the state morally healthy? Plutarch found such glorification of war extremely distasteful, surely: on a related theme, he insists with some feeling that triumphs would far more appropriately be given for the arts of *peace* (*Marc.* 22.9–10, cf. *Pomp.* 13.10–11). And the disastrous effect of external, especially Greek,

[110] φιλονικία: *Fab.* 25.3–4 (cf. 22.5). Political point-scoring rather than fighting the war: esp. 25.3–4 (where χρήματα δοθῆναι πρὸς τὸν πόλεμον οὐκ εἴασε, 25.3, closely reverses the story of 7.5–8). Shouting: 26.1, contrast 7.5, 14.2. Even in his distinctive πραότης he is now outdone by Crassus (25.4): that is prepared already at 22.8, when Marcellus emerges as more πρᾶος than Fabius. On the nature of the tradition see Hoffmann (1942) 92–93: the *contrast* of Fabius and Scipio seems well founded in the historical tradition, but the personal pettiness of Fabius seems individual to Plutarch's account.

[111] Forster (1962) 151, discussing Anatole France's *Thais*.

[112] Jones (1971) 99–100.

[113] E.g. *Pomp.* 70, *C. mai.* 4.2, 16.8, 28(1).2–3, *Aem.* 11.3–4, *Sull.* 1.5, 12.8–14, *Phoc.* 3.3.

culture? He clearly knows the idea (cf. *C. mai.* 4.2)[114] – but it was hardly a theme to appeal to him! He feels that Romans should have learnt a lot more from Greece (*Mar.* 2); and he indeed criticizes the elder Cato most forthrightly for his prophecy that Greek influences would be fatal to Rome. 'Time shows that he was wrong; for the time of Rome's greatest achievements was the time when it was most ready to welcome Greek studies and Greek culture' (*C. mai.* 23.3). When Plutarch does echo such Roman *topoi* he is therefore keen to adapt them, and the nature of these adaptations is again extremely suggestive. Marcellus was criticized for bringing back the treasures of Syracuse and corrupting – corrupting whom? Corrupting the Roman *dēmos*, turning them from farming and warfare to luxury and idleness, filling them with laziness and chatter, so that they spend most of the day discussing arts and artists...(*Marc.* 21.6)! It is a very mild form of criticism, and Plutarch is clearly on Marcellus' side.[115] He has just been stressing the great superiority of Greek culture, and bringing out the wretchedly primitive character of Rome at the time: as he makes Marcellus say, he is *educating* these people. So much for that *topos* of Greek influence; even that is fitted into the *dēmos*-emphasis, and given a very individual turning. The same sort of thing emerges with *metus hostilis* in the famous passage at the end of *Cato maior*, when Scipio Nasica is arguing that Carthage should remain standing: 'for Nasica saw that the *dēmos* was going wildly astray through their *hubris*, and were hard for the senate to control [...] he wished the fear of Carthage to remain a bridle on the recklessness of the mob' (*C.mai.* 27.3).[116] Again, quite characteristic: the Roman idea is given a very individual twist, and itself tied into the distinctive *boulē–dēmos* analysis.

[114] When the theme is first introduced at *C. mai.* 4.2, Plutarch simply talks of Rome 'not preserving her purity because of her very size: her control of so many affairs and so many peoples was exposing her to many different customs and examples of many different sorts of life'. Nothing specifically on *Greece* there – probably because Plutarch is so far reluctant to cast any shadow of hesitation or doubt on Cato's moral insight. It is only at 22.4–23.2 that Cato's hostility to Greek culture is specifically stressed and criticized: at that stage of the Life Plutarch is tracing with more subtlety the manner in which Cato's strengths and flaws both spring from the same basic traits. By then we have come to appreciate the man's moral force, and respect his concern for old-fashioned Roman virtue: we now see the excesses which this attitude can bring.

[115] Contrast the much more sombre emphasis of Plb. 9.10 and Livy 25.40.2.

[116] Contrast the parallel passage at Diodorus 34/35.33.4–5, doubtless inspired by the same source (probably Posidonius). Diod. has no such emphasis on the *dēmos*, and speaks more vaguely of external fear as a stimulus to concord: indeed, his Nasica brings in concepts such as 'the need to rule Rome's subjects with equity and good repute', and the threat to Rome from dangerous *allies*. For recent discussions of Nasica's insight see Astin (1967) 276–80, and Lintott (1972) 632–38: Gelzer (1931) 272–73 and others were clearly quite wrong to see the hand of *Polybius* in influencing Plutarch's stress on the *boulē* and *dēmos*.

The emphasis on the *dēmos* is clearly Plutarch's own: the great preconception with which he came to write about the Roman Republic. And, of course, no one would want to suggest that he was wholly wrong. The reduction of so many other forms of analysis to this theme is disquieting, and so is the assumption that the analysis is equally applicable to every period; but few of us would doubt that Plutarch captured something very important about the late Republic by describing it in this way. It was not Plutarch, it was Sir Ronald Syme, who described the end of the Republic as 'the Greek period of Roman history, stamped with the sign of the demagogue, the tyrant, and the class war'.[117]

[117] Syme (1939) 441.

Between men and beasts: barbarians in Ammianus Marcellinus

T. E. J. WIEDEMANN

Dietary practices are among the more obvious ways in which one group of people can differentiate itself from another. What I eat and drink is normal and natural. A person who does not eat or drink what I do is peculiar: in structuralist jargon, I am central and he is marginal. He may be marginal geographically – simply foreign – or morally: a saint/hero (between man and god) or a sinner/heretic/revolutionary (between man and beast).[1] The ultimate dietary rule is the ban on eating the flesh of another human being. A recent study by Arens of accounts of cannibalism predictably aroused considerable discussion.[2] Its thesis might be summarized as follows. To eat human flesh is the mark of an animal. A human who eats human flesh thus shares in his person the characteristics of a man and of an animal: cannibalism symbolizes the mid-point between humanity and bestiality. It follows that any group satisfied that its own behaviour patterns are normal will tend to ascribe the qualities of cannibals to individuals or groups whom they consider to be hostile to their behaviour patterns or values. Thus – according to Arens – the statement, '*x* is a cannibal' should not be taken at its face value as a piece of descriptive ethnography; it is rather a moral evaluation, labelling *x* as being marginal with respect to the speaker's perception of his own values or social position. Arens presses this thesis as far as it will go, and – excepting some cases of anthropophagy in dire emergencies[3] – denies that cannibalism has ever existed as an established social ritual in any human society; he would put reports of cannibalism among sixteenth-century Amerindians, eighteenth-century Polynesians, nineteenth-century Africans, or twentieth-century Papuans, on the same level as the atrocity stories found directed against the early Christians, medieval Jews, or the German army which occupied Belgium in 1914.[4]

We do not have to follow Arens all the way; his views are

[1] Food taboos: Douglas (1966), Bremmer (1980) 33 n. 9.

[2] Arens (1979).

[3] Some ancient instances: Hdt. 3.25.6, Thuc. 2.70.1, Plb. 1.85.1, Diod. 33/34.2.20, Caesar *BG* 7.77.12, Jos. *BJ* 6.3.4; but not Ammianus 25.8.15.

[4] Cf. Sall. *BC* 22 (conspirators drink human blood).

interesting enough if it is the case that, in *some* instances, ascriptions of cannibalism are not descriptive, but evaluative. Ethnographical passages in classical literature contain a series of stereotypes, associated with barbarians in general, to which the Arens thesis may easily be applied. One could take as a classic example Strabo's well-known description of Ireland (4.5.4):

Besides some small islands round about Britain, there is also a large island, Ierne, which stretches parallel to Britain on the north, its breadth being greater than its length. Concerning this island I have nothing certain to tell, except that its inhabitants are more savage than the Britons, since they are man-eaters as well as grass-eaters [or 'great eaters', depending on the reading], and since, further, they count it an honourable thing, when their fathers die, to devour them, and publicly to have intercourse, not only with the other women, but also with their mothers and sisters; but I am saying this only with the understanding that I have no trustworthy witnesses for it; and yet, as for the matter of man-eating, that is said to be a custom of the Scythians also, and in cases of necessity forced by sieges the Celts, the Iberians, and several other peoples are said to have practised it.

Strabo's insistence that he is merely repeating what others say (λεγόνται) is crucial: stories ascribing irregular or peculiar dietary or sexual habits should not, or at least need not always, be believed. The Irish behave marginally in these respects because they are, quite literally, at the edge of the human world. Indeed, they are in a sense already over the edge of the world, since they live on an island in the Ocean. Islands are distinctly marginal: they are, so to speak, both of the sea, and of the land. The seashore is another such locus of marginality, both sea and land. Caves, too, are marginal places, being both under the earth, and yet accessible to those who walk on its surface. It is only to be expected, then, that Sophocles' Philoctetes, on the margin of human society, inhabits an island-cave by the shore.[5]

The limits of the human world separate us both from beasts and from the divine. Islands, caves, and seashores are thus heavily populated by superhuman as well as sub-human beings. One could cite as examples the birthplace of Zeus, the cave of the Eumenides, the Homeric island-caves of the Cyclops and of Calypso, the cave in which Euripides wrote his plays, the caves in which the Druids are said to have done their teaching,[6] or the unscriptural cave under the Church of the Nativity at Bethlehem; and perhaps also the cavemen postulated by nineteenth-century archaeologists who believed in Darwin and were desperate to find a missing link between men and beasts. One difference between the classical and the modern picture

[5] Buxton (1982), Avery (1965).

[6] Pomponius Mela 3.20.

of the savage caveman is that, since the Enlightenment, Europeans have tended to place the savage in an evolutionary sequence; previously, the savage's marginality had been one of distance, rather than time.[7] John Locke's celebrated phrase, 'In the beginning, all the World was America',[8] combines the Enlightenment view that savagery is a social period prior to modern civilization, with an earlier idea that it is something to be found at the geographical margins of the known world.

These margins need not of course point downwards; the edges of the world may also be places where a much better society can be found. Thus utopias in the classical period may be found not just at the time when the world was newly created – chronologically marginal – but also at the edge of the world, typically on islands in the Ocean like Panchaea in the Far East or the Fortunate Islands or Atlantis in the Far West; the Hyperboreans, too, live on an island.

Utopians and savages, both of them marginal to normal societies, thus share certain characteristics like living on islands. They may share social characteristics, too. Freedom from social normality may consist in sexual promiscuity, or the absence of private property. The inversion of normal rules of behaviour is a characteristic of such people. One is reminded of anthropologists' findings about the Temne in Sierra Leone, who believe that white people must normally walk upside down. This is the context of stories about the Thracians mourning a person's birth, not his death, and of a whole series of *topoi* about Egypt. Because Egypt is unlike Greece, it must be the opposite of Greece, and therefore – since Herodotus – they do all sorts of things the wrong way round, like writing: 'suis litteris perverse utuntur'.[9]

One might set up an ideal type of the marginal group in terms of classical literary commonplaces. Such people, living on an island (possibly in the Ocean), would wear no clothes (Britons and Agathyrsi, like Red Indians, are noted for painting their bodies; and the Balearic Islands are 'Gumnēsiai' in Greek because of the nudity of the natives).[10] They would not live in houses, but in caves,[11] wagons (Scythians), or tents (Saracens). They would be nomads rather than sedentary farmers. If not cannibals, they would at least eat curious food and drink something other than the regular Graeco-Roman wine

7 Meek (1976).

8 John Locke *Two Treatises of Government* 2.49 in edition by Laslett (1967) 343.

9 Pomponius Mela 1.75. My informant on the beliefs of the Temne is Dr I. Hamnett (personal communication).

10 Diod. 5.17.

11 Like Diodorus' Balearic islanders. For Trogodytae [*sic*] cf. Pliny *NH* 6.189f., Aelian 6.10.1, 9.55, Virgil *G*.3.376f.

mixed with water.[12] They might practise incest or polygamy, or make love in public;[13] if not, then at least they might reverse the proper relationship between the sexes, and be ruled by women, like the Picts. Silius Italicus, in his list of Carthaginian allies,[14] stresses that in Galicia in Spain the roles of men and women in agriculture are reversed. Otherwise he ignores non-military characteristics, except when he comes to describe the Gaetuli:

> Nulla domus: plaustris habitant; migrare per arva
> mos, atque errantes circumvectare penates.

Such people are not merely savage fighters,[15] but fight in a peculiar way: women may share in the fighting; or the men may use bows,[16] a peculiar weapon in the Graeco-Roman context, as we are reminded by the story of Philoctetes. The ultimate symbol of the barbarian's intermediate position between Greeks and beasts is when he actually turns into that quintessentially marginal animal, the wolf: the Scythian Greeks insisted to Herodotus that every single Neurian practised lycanthropy.[17]

If these *topoi* are seen as illustrations of geographical marginality, rather than objective descriptions, it becomes less surprising that we should find the same peoples variously held up as paradigms of morality, and of bestiality. The Scythians may appear as fierce, cannibalistic and primitive, but equally as sharing some of the features of an ecological paradise: 'Cultores iustissimi, et diutius quam ulli mortalium et beatius vivunt. Quippe festo semper otio laeti non bella novere, non iurgia.'[18] This positive picture of the Scythians appears elsewhere in classical literature: Horace refers to the

> Campestres melius Scythae
> Quorum plaustra vagas rite trahunt domos [...].[19]

[12] Food and drink: Bremmer (1980) lists references to Scythians and Indians as drinkers of either unmixed wine, or water. Cf. also Str. 16.4.17 on the Trōglodutai; Hdt. 4.104 remarks that the nomadic Scythian Boudinoi are φθειροτραγέουσι (eaters of pine-cones, rather than lice, perhaps?). Further fruit-eaters occur near the Caspian Sea (Hdt. 4.203).

[13] Scythians: Hdt. 4.104 (where wife-sharing is said to eliminate jealousy); Trōglodutai: Str. 16.4.17. Unashamedly public sex: Hdt. 1.203 (Caspian Sea), Xen. *Anab.* 5.4.33 and Ap. Rhod. 2.1023ff. (the Mossynoeci). The comment of How and Wells (1912) 1.153 on this 'lowest stage of degradation' is illuminating: 'But among modern savages it is, to say the least, very rare.'

[14] *Punica* 3.349ff.

[15] On savagery: Scyths: Hdt. 4.62 (human sacrifice), 64–66 (scalping, blood-drinking). Violence is of course appropriate to barbarians, as persuasion is to adult male Greeks: Isoc. *Philip* 16; Buxton (1982), esp. on Aeschylus' *Suppliants*.

[16] Cf. Sophocles *Philoctetes*; Scythians, Amazons, Macrobian Aethiopians (Hdt. 3.21 etc.).

[17] Hdt. 4.105.2.

[18] Pomponius Mela 3.5.

[19] Hor *Odes* 3.24.9f.

The Ichthyophagi in Ethiopia are another group of savages noted for their justice.[20]

We would expect to find these same elements in the ethnographical digressions of a classicizing historian like Ammianus Marcellinus. It may be worth noting that Ammianus' digressions are extremely formal. Almost without exception, digressions are divided off from the previous narrative by an explicit introduction, and come to an end with a formal close.[21] Ammianus was all too conscious that he was writing a work of *literature*: we need only recall the many references to and quotations from Cicero, Virgil, and Homer. I suspect that this is not so much a case of a Greek-speaker who is self-conscious about writing in a foreign language, or keen to parade his literary studiousness, as that Ammianus is a soldier and official who wants to be obedient to the clear, straightforward rules of historical writing. Which is why the formal digressions contain exactly that ethnographical material which we would expect. The Saracens[22] are 'seminudi, coloratis sagulis pube tenus amicti'; they do no agricultural work, but instead 'errant sine lare, sine sedibus fixis aut legibus'. Their sex-life is peculiar: 'uxores mercennariae, conductae ad tempus ex pacto [...] et incredibile est, quo ardore apud eos in venerem uterque solvitur sexus.' So is their food: 'victus [...] caro ferina est, lactisque abundans copia [...] et plerosque nos vidimus frumenti usum et vini penitus ignorantes.'[23] 'Hactenus', concludes Ammianus, 'de natione perniciosa.' The digressions about the nations living around the Black Sea, the eastern provinces of the Persian empire, ancient Thrace, and about the Huns[24] contain more of the same. Thus the Scythians 'palantes per solitudines vastas, nec stivam aliquando nec sementem expertas [...] ferarum taetro ritu vescuntur'.[25] Again, we find some uncertainty whether these people are savages who indulge in human sacrifice[26] or 'iusti homines placiditateque cogniti'.[27] In Thrace, the Scordisci used to be 'saevi et truces'; they sacrificed their war-captives and drank their blood

[20] Hdt. 3.20f.

[21] The exception is where the end of a digression corresponds to the end of a book, as with the excursus on the Persian provinces at 23.6: cf. Wiedemann (1979) 13f. On Ammianus' digressions generally, Rosen (1982) 79–86.

[22] 14.4.

[23] Note the 'nos': the claim to autopsy appears in other such accounts, e.g. Cassius Dio 29.36.4, on the Pannonians. But whether in fact the writer had seen what he describes is irrelevant; the point is that he reports what his audience expects him to report.

[24] 22.8, 23.6, 27.4, 31.2.

[25] 22.8.42.

[26] 22.8.34: skulls fixed to the temple of Orsiloche/Diana.

[27] The Aremphaei, 22.8.38.

out of human skulls.[28] The Odrysae went so far as to kill their own people when there was a shortage of enemies to slaughter – 'vagantes sine cultu vel legibus'.[29] Yet Thrace had been part of the Graeco-Roman world for seven centuries when Ammianus wrote this. The Huns[30] do not cook their food, avoid houses and huts 'sed vagi montes peragrantes et silvas'; they dress in clothes made from the skins of field-mice, and wear the same clothes indoors and out until they turn to rags and fall off their backs.[31] And day and night they sit on their horses: 'Inconsultorum animalium ritu, quid honestum inhonestumve sit penitus ignorantes, flexiloqui et obscuri, nullius religionis vel superstitionis reverentia aliquando districti [...].'[32]

These collections of commonplaces going back to Herodotus are exactly what we would expect in literary digressions. Much more interesting is their absence from the digression on Gaul and its people.[33] The Gauls do have a peculiar drink, beer, which Ammianus claims to have tasted himself, and there is a hint of sexual role-reversal in the statement that a Gaul's wife is 'multo fortiore et glauca', with a punch like that of a Roman catapult (Ammianus omits to say whether he had had personal experience of that too). It looks as though Ammianus was quite capable of avoiding *topoi* if he wished; and it might therefore be worth examining how stereotyped his treatment of non-Romans is in the rest of his narrative.

One is immediately struck by the frequency of adjectives like 'efferati'.[34] Isaurian bandits are 'flagrans vesania';[35] they become bolder as a consequence of madness – 'rabie saeviore amplificatis viribus'.[36] The German tribes who invaded Gaul are 'superbae gentes';[37] theirs is a 'barbarica rabies'.[38] The Alamanni may act with even more savagery than usual, 'saevientes ultra solitum',[39] and we are told about their horrible war-cries – 'ululantes [...] lugubre'.[40] At the battle of Strasburg, Julian in his speech to the Romans talks of their 'rabies et immodicus furor'; Ammianus himself uses the terms 'barbara feritate', 'frendentes immania, ultra solitum saevientium comae fluentes horrebant, et elucebat quidam ex oculis furor'; 'violentia iraque incompositi [...] in modum exarsere flammarum'; they attack 'velut quodam furoris afflatu'.[41] And everywhere else too, the qualities repeatedly ascribed to the Germans are 'furor, amentia,

[28] 27.4.4.
[29] 27.4.9f.
[30] 31.2.
[31] Cf. Hippocrates *Airs, Waters, Places* 19.
[32] 31.2.11.
[33] 15.12.
[34] In the digression on ancient Thrace: 27.4.9.
[35] 14.2.15.
[36] 14.2.14.
[37] 15.8.7.
[38] 16.5.16f.
[39] 16.11.3.
[40] 16.11.8.
[41] 16.12.31, 16.12.2, 16.12.36, 16.12.44, 16.12.46.

feritas'.[42] The same qualities appear in connexion with the barbarians who cause havoc in Britain,[43] as well as the Sarmatians.[44] The Moors too suffer from 'barbarica rabies'.[45] The Saxons may be merely 'superbi';[46] the Goths, on their first appearance, are 'saepe fallaces et perfidos'.[47] At one point – after the death of Julian – we have a regular list of what Ammianus considers to be 'gentes saevissimae' endangering the empire: the Alamanni, Sarmatians, Picts, Saxons, Moors, Goths and Persians.[48]

But none of this is sufficiently specific to deserve the status of ethnography. All Ammianus is saying is that the enemies of Rome are undomesticated ('ferae'), violent, insolent, or mad when, and in so far as, they attack the Roman empire; we should not interpret these epithets as evidence that he thought he was describing a peculiarity of the tribe in question. In the case of the Persians, there may be a slight tendency for Ammianus to associate them with a particular characteristic, viz. duplicity; that of course is a traditional element in Roman attitudes to Persia, a state which could not so easily be visualized as hostile to order and good government *per se*. Interestingly, the Persians alone of non-Romans are themselves said to be engaged in fighting 'ferocissimas gentes', or 'ferarum gentium'.[49] But Ammianus does not use this theme often. More usually, it is the Persian king, Sapor, individually who is described as enraged ('effrenata regis cupiditate'), as 'truculentus rex ille Persarum, ardore obtinendae Mesopotamiae flagrans', or as 'turgidus'. At one point, he is 'ultra hominem efferatus'. His 'ira', 'efferata vesania', and 'rabies' are mentioned[50] – but then, so are those of some Roman emperors. The Persian king's 'perfidia' is mentioned only once, when he attacks Armenia 'per artes fallendo diversas' in A.D. 368.[51] As for the Persians as a nation, they are 'fallacissima gens' and called 'gentem asperrimam per sexaginta ferme annos inussisse Orienti caedum et direptionum monumenta saevissima'. Julian refers to their treachery in a set speech: 'nihil enim praeter dolos et insidias hostium vereor, nimium callidorum.'[52]

What is noteworthy about this is not that Ammianus should describe Rome's enemies in these terms – he himself, after all, had personally been involved in the business of fighting most of them – but how infrequently he applies these critical and negative concepts,

42 E.g. in the necrology of Julian, 'regna furentium Germanorum exscindens' (25.4.10).
43 'gentium ferarum excursus': 20.1.1.
44 'latrocinandi peritissimum genus': 16.10.20.
45 27.9.1.
46 28.5.3.
47 22.7.8.
48 26.4.5.
49 14.3.1, 18.4.1.
50 17.5.15, 20.6.1, 27.12.11, 20.7.3–11.
51 27.12.2–4.
52 21.13.4, 22.12.1, 23.5.21.

and how unsystematically. *Furor* or *ira* are qualities of people Ammianus does not like, whether they are Romans or not: they are not national characteristics. This is the common-sense approach of a soldier whose job it is to hurt the enemy without getting hurt himself; and it is striking how many examples of *fallacia* or *saevitia* on the Roman side Ammianus describes, without moral comment – occasionally even with approval. There are at least a dozen such instances: the Romans massacre some Alamanni 'promiscue virile et muliebre secus, sine aetatis ullo discrimine'; Julian's duplicity in attacking the Franks after having pretended to come to an agreement with them is praised; twice peaceful Alamanni are massacred 'sine ulla parsimonia' (in both cases by Roman soldiers under the influence of 'ira' or 'incitante fervore certaminum'). During Julian's campaign against Persia, Ammianus describes without comment how the Romans butcher women and children: 'qua [sc. civitate] incensa, caesisque mulieribus paucis quae repertae sunt'; at Maiozamalcha, the massacre is 'sine sexus discrimine vel aetatis'. On the other hand, a non-Roman chieftain who acts thus is a brigand: 'Malechus Podosax, famosi nominis latro, omni saevitia per nostras limites grassatus.' The Romans may be praised for using 'dolos occultiores' against the Saxons; Ammianus approves of the massacre of a group of Syrian brigands, the Maratocupreni, and shows no concern at the killing of all their young children. Count Theodosius tortures and burns alive Moorish rebels. Valentinian executes a group of Quadi 'iugulata aetate promiscua'.[53] What these examples show is that Ammianus does not intend his readers to understand his ascription of savagery and duplicity to the enemies of Rome as in any sense ethnographic. He is well aware that Roman armies behave no differently.

Instead of looking at straightforward moral characteristics for evidence of how Ammianus saw particular ethnic groups, it might be worth examining one particular group of literary similes, namely comparison with animals, to see how it is applied to barbarians. After all, if what makes barbarians 'efferatae gentes' is the fact that they are at the margins of the human world, not just geographically but also so to speak zoologically, by sharing certain social characteristics with sub-human animals, it is not surprising that, in more or less literary passages, Ammianus should use a series of animal metaphors to depict the behaviour of such groups. To describe Isaurian bandits, he quotes from Cicero's *pro Cluentio*:[54] 'Atque – ut Tullius ait – ut etiam bestiae, fame monitae, plerumque ad eum locum ubi aliquando

[53] 16.11.9, 17.8.4, 17.10.6, 17.13.13, 24.2.3, 24.4.25, 24.2.4, 27.8.9, 28.2.14, 29.5.49f., 30.5.14.

[54] 14.2.2; Cic. *pro Cluentio* 25.67.

pastae sunt revertuntur [...].' The transrhenane Germans continued to attack Gaul even when Julian, as Caesar, had shown that he was prepared to fight them:[55] 'Utque bestiae custodum neglegentia raptu vivere solitae, ne his quidem remotis, appositisque fortioribus abscesserunt, sed tumescentes inedia, sine respectu salutis, armenta vel greges incursant.' In the digression about the lands to the north of the Black Sea he says that the Scythians – or at least most of them – know no agriculture, but 'ferarum taetro ritu vescuntur'.[56] And the Goths, on the day after they had destroyed Valens' army at Adrianople, attack the city itself 'ut bestiae sanguinis irritamento atrocius efferatae'.[57] That Isaurian bandits, Germans, Scythians, and Goths should be described as wild beasts fits into the rhetorical pattern. What is surprising is that Ammianus should use this metaphor for barbarians so rarely. When he describes the Gothic attack on the Romans in A.D. 378, and wants to use epic literary metaphors to stress the scale and importance of that invasion, he likens the Goths to burning fire-darts ('ut incensi malleoli') or to a torrent ('ut amnis immani pulsu undarum obicibus ruptis emissus [...]').[58] The only application of the beast-metaphor to the Persians appears to be at 24.8.1, where Julian – now aware that his army is in grave danger of being cut off and destroyed – parades a number of starving Persian prisoners in order to persuade the Romans that they are not formidable as foes, and calls them 'deformes illuvie capellas et taetras' (ugly she-goats disfigured with filth). This should not lead us to think that Ammianus considered Persians to be animals; it is Julian who says this, and it is rhetoric. Indeed, there is a parallel passage where the Romans are, by implication, compared to wild beasts. It is in the Persian king Sapor's letter to Constantius, advising Roman withdrawal from the disputed provinces of Mesopotamia, and inviting him to reflect that 'hocque bestias factitare: quae cum advertant cur maxime opere capiantur, illud propria sponte amittunt, ut vivere deinde possint impavidae'.[59]

There are two other groups of persons to whom Ammianus applies the beast metaphor. He expresses surprise that Eutherius, although a eunuch, was a good man (eunuchs being, of course, the marginal group *par excellence*): 'sed inter vepres rosae nascuntur, et inter feras non nullae mitescunt.'[60] And there is the notorious reference to the violent enmity among Christians: 'nullas infestas hominibus bestias, ut sunt sibi ferales plerique Christianorum'.[61]

Much more frequently, however, Ammianus uses animal metaphors

[55] 16.5.17.
[56] 22.8.42.
[57] 31.15.2.
[58] 31.7.7, 31.8.5.
[59] 17.5.7.
[60] 16.7.4; Patterson (1982).
[61] 22.5.4.

to illustrate specific behaviour, or the behaviour of specific individuals, rather than to typify groups. People in an extreme state of degradation or passivity are said to be, or to be treated like, animals: the supporters of Magnentius, when imprisoned by Constantius, are dragged about like beasts ('in modum beluae trahebatur'). During Julian's campaigns against the Germans, innocent women and children are massacred 'ut pecudes'. When some Roman soldiers lay an unsuccessful ambush for the Armenian king Papas, they are said to expect him to behave like a hunted beast running into a trap: 'quasi venaticiam praedam'.[62]

Usually it is some aspect of ferocity that Ammianus wants to stress. The parallel is frequently taken from the Roman arena.[63] Ammianus himself, sent to Cologne in the entourage of Ursicinus to deal with Silvanus' revolt, feels himself 'ut bestiarii, obiceremur intractabilibus feris'. At the siege of Amida in A.D. 359 Ammianus noted that some Gallic soldiers threatened their tribunes for not allowing them to sally forth against the Persians: 'utque dentatae in caveis bestiae, taetro †paedore acerbius efferatae, evadendi spe repagulis versabilibus illiduntur [...].' Presumably Ammianus himself was one of these tribunes, and the wild-beast metaphor represents his feelings at the time. Before the battle of Adrianople, the Goths are described as ransacking Thrace 'velut diffractis caveis bestiae'. And in two places an individual is compared to the animals in the amphitheatre: Maximinus, as prefect of Rome, 'effudit genuinam ferociam, pectori crudo affixam, ut saepe faciunt amphitheatrales ferae, diffractis tandem solutae posticis'. And there is the emperor Valens, anxious that all who might be involved in Theodorus' treason be punished: 'totus enim devius ab aequitate dilapsus, iamque eruditior ad laedendum, in modum harenariae ferae, si admotus quisquam fabricae diffugisset, ad ultimam rabiem saeviebat.'[64] Some other individuals appear as unspecified beasts. These comparisons are usually decidedly negative; an apparent exception is that of the circumstances of Procopius, hiding out of fear of Jovian, to the life-style of a wild beast, 'ferinae vitae'; he lived 'in locis squalentibus, stringebatur, hominumque egebat colloquiis'. Later it becomes apparent that, far from evoking our sympathy, the animal metaphor shows how Ammianus dislikes Procopius: at c. 10 he likens Procopius in hiding ('latenter') to a beast of prey in its lair:

[62] 14.5.3, 16.11.9, 30.1.15.

[63] It is interesting that Ammianus chooses parallels taken from his own experience as an official from an urban, curial background, rather than metaphors involving agricultural beasts as was usual in classical literature.

[64] 15.5.23, 19.6.4, 31.8.9, 28.1.10, 29.1.27.

'subsidebat ut praedatrix bestia: viso, quod capi potuerit, protinus eruptura'. Elsewhere the criticism is obvious. Rusticus Julianus, a potential candidate for the imperial office in A.D. 367, is described as 'quasi afflatu quodam furoris [sc. smitten by] bestiarum more humani sanguinis avidus'. Valentinus, an opponent of Count Theodosius, is irked at being exiled to Britain, 'quietis impatiens ut malefica bestia'.[65]

So much for beasts in general. Of particular beasts, there are seven comparisons of people to vipers. These include groups of people: the Isaurians again, five years after the police actions against them in A.D. 354 (recorded at 14.2.2), are described as 'paulatim reviviscentes, ut solent verno tempore foveis exsilire serpentes [...]'. The Roman mob, demonstrating against the urban prefect Leontius in A.D. 355, is likened by Ammianus to serpents: 'Insidens itaque vehiculo, cum speciosa fiducia contuebatur acribus oculis tumultuantium undique cuneorum, veluti serpentium, vultus [...].' Among individuals, there is the notary Paulus, responsible for various administrative disorders, 'ortus in Hispania coluber quidam' (according to Bentley's restoration of the text). The Caesar, Gallus, aware that Constantius plans to remove him, behaves 'ut serpens appetitus telo vel saxo'; this refers to a fit of anger leading to the murder of various officials loyal to Constantius. During the treason trials which followed Gallus' downfall, Arbitio's attack on Ammianus' commander Ursicinus is described as follows: 'ut enim subterraneus serpens, foramen subsidens occultum, adsultu subito singulas transitores observans incessit: ita ille odio alienae sortis [...]'. After describing the judicial crimes of Maximinus, vice-prefect of Rome, Ammianus says that, when appointed praetorian prefect, he continued to be dangerous at a distance, 'ut basilisci serpentes'.[66] It may be worth noting in this context that Ammianus did have alternatives to animal- or snake-metaphors which he chose to use when it came to describing brutal administrators: Simplicius of Emona is compared, not to a beast, but to the literary tyrant-king Busiris.[67] In A.D. 373, Valens sent two officials to re-arrest the Armenian king Papas, who had escaped from imprisonment by the Romans at Tarsus. The two officials Danielus and Barzimerus failed in the attempt – and 'probrosis lacerati conviciis, ac si inertes et desidentes, ut hebetatae primo appetitu venenatae serpentes, ora exacuere letalia, cum primum potuissent, lapso, pro virium copia nocituri'. In fact they accused Papas of practising the magic arts, thus persuading Valens

[65] 26.6.4, 26.6.10, 27.6.1, 28.3.4.

[66] Vipers: 19.13.1, 15.7.4, 14.5.6, 14.7.13, 15.2.4, 28.1.41.

[67] 28.1.46.

to have him assassinated by the general Trajanus, an act which Ammianus deplores as totally contrary to the rules of war.[68]

There are some other straightforwardly negative animal similes. Picking up a Ciceronian comparison of two associates of Verres to hunting-dogs, he says that the informers who took advantage of the overthrow of Gallus are 'honorum vertices ipsos ferinis morsibus appetentes [...] non ut Cibyratae illi Verrini, tribunal unius legati lambentes, sed rei publicae membra totius per incidentia mala vexantes'. He goes on to describe their leader Mercurius 'ut clam mordax canis interna saevitia, summissius agitans caudam'. The comparison with hunting-dogs appears in another much later reference to informers, in Ammianus' celebrated digression on lawyers and lawsuits; it is possible, he says, to see powerful and rapacious men 'ut Spartanos canes aut Cretas, vestigia sagacius colligendo, ad ipsa cubilia pervenire causarum'.[69] There are two comparisons to birds of prey. One refers to the Saracens, 'milvorum rapacium similes', the other to a North African tribe which attacked the cities of Tripolis, Lepcis and Oea, the Austoriani: 'Austoriani successu gemino insolentes, ut rapaces alites, advolarunt, irritamento sanguinis atrocius efferatae.' But if a tribe of barbarians can be likened to vultures, an equally unflattering comparison can be applied to the senators of Rome in a famous passage of satire: 'ex his quidam cum salutari pectoribus oppositis coeperint, osculanda capita, in modum taurorum minacium, obliquantes, adulatoribus offerunt genua savianda vel manus [...]'. Indeed there appears to be only one instance of an animal comparison which is at all positive, and that is of Ammianus' general Ursicinus to a lion; but in fact Ursicinus is compared to a *disabled* lion, to explain why he was unable to assist the beleaguered Amida: 'ut leo magnitudine corporis et torvitate terribilis, inclusos intra retia catulos periculo ereptum ire non audens, unguibus ademptis et dentibus'. Of course, Ammianus is here exploiting the association between lions and kingliness, which goes back to Aesop and beyond, in order to flatter his hero. Ammianus is well aware that lions are traditionally royal, and positive: this is clear from the account of the omen of the dead lion found by Julian shortly before his own death. There are of course old and powerless lions in Aesopian fable. But it is interesting that Ammianus should choose to use the figure of a lion to illustrate Ursicinus' weakness, not his strength. And there is another negative comparison of someone to a lion. Gallus indulged in a string of judicial executions; 'post quorum necem, nihilo lenius ferociens, Gallus, ut leo cadaveribus

[68] 30.1.16.

[69] 15.3.3, cf. Cic. *II Verrines* 4.21.47 and 4.13.30; 15.3.5, 30.4.8.

pastus, multa huius modi scrutabatur.' So in the last analysis *all* animals illustrate negative qualities for Ammianus – ferocious like the beasts in the arena, keen on human blood, insidious like snakes, or insufferably proud like bulls.[70]

On the other hand, Ammianus does not particularly associate animal qualities with marginal groups. There are occasions where he does that, but he also has a wide range of alternative literary metaphors to choose from, and is as happy (for instance) to liken the Goths in Book 31 – where the description of the battle of Adrianople allows him to wallow in epic similes – to rivers, firebrands, collapsing walls, warships, or forest fires. Animal metaphors are applied to any person or group he disapproves of as falling short of the standards of civilized human behaviour, whether emperors or usurpers, officials or informers, Roman Christians, the Roman mob, or Roman senators. The last of these at least can scarcely be labelled marginal. Bestiality is not a special mark of non-Roman barbarians.

I would conclude not only that we should be wary of believing that the material contained in Ammianus' ethnographic digressions is descriptive, but also that Ammianus himself did not intend these statements about barbarian tribes as descriptive ethnography. Some barbarians, like some Romans, threatened imperial order and stability; Ammianus, as a soldier and official, described such persons in negative terms. But as a historian, he felt that the rules of his genre of literary writing required regular digressions, some of them ethnographic; and he knew that his audience required such digressions to contain the centuries-old stereotypes about marginal groups. A historian writing in the classical tradition could not disappoint his audience. Perhaps his audience was rather disappointed since there is only one reference to cannibalism in the surviving books.[71]

[70] 14.4.1, 28.6.13, 28.4.10, 19.3.3, 23.5.8, 14.9.9.

[71] 31.2.15.

Epilogue

Why did Herodotus and Thucydides choose to write about war? With this question, raised by Cobet, we immediately confront an issue which has come to dominate recent study of the ancient historians and to which members of our conference repeatedly returned.

Dissatisfied with Momigliano's contention that war was simply a fact of life in the Greek world, Cobet himself suggests that Herodotus and Thucydides reveal in their narratives evidence of theoretical reflection on the general nature of war. For them war represents historical change in its most spectacular and intensive form, affecting groups, societies and whole states; both historians see war as a struggle for power, success and fortune; they stress the positive rather than the negative side of war, and express no elaborate concern for the personal grief and pain which war inevitably provokes.

Yet this view invites some qualifications in its turn. Schultze's remarks on Dionysius of Halicarnassus and his audience illustrate that modern and ancient readers do not necessarily see ancient historians in the same terms. Dionysius himself described Herodotus as Ὁμήρου ζηλωτής (*Pomp.* 3), while the author of the *de sublimitate* famously called him Ὁμηρικώτατος (13.3). It is thus a reasonable assumption that, in choosing to write about the war to which, as Cobet says, the earlier parts of his work form the prelude, Herodotus' motives were at least partly literary. Homer had written about war, and the classic nature of his work constituted a challenge to the inspiration and emulation of later writers. In Homer's poetry war itself is usually described in negative terms, as Cobet notes; yet its very existence provides individuals with the opportunity for glory (κλέος). Herodotus, though he mentions the κακά which the Persian Wars entailed (6.98), nevertheless chose to present his account in positive terms. The wars are an ἔργον μέγα τε καὶ θωμαστόν (1.1.1), and Athens, being the saviour of Greece (7.139.5) against an army which was larger even than that sent to Troy (7.20), is therefore the deserving recipient of unprecedented glory.[1]

Thucydides also ἐζήλωσεν Ὅμηρον, according to his biographer Marcellinus (37), yet his perspective of war is significantly different

[1] For discussion of Herodotus' view of Athens on the basis of 7.139.5 see Evans (1979b).

from that of Herodotus. By far the largest part of his preface is devoted to emphasizing the magnitude of the Peloponnesian War; and the space he devotes to depreciating the scale of the Trojan War (1.9–11) suggests that he, no less than Herodotus, sees his own subject in terms of that of his epic predecessor. Yet, as Immerwahr has rightly observed, Thucydides measures greatness 'by the power of the contestants rather than by their splendour or virtue'.[2] The programme at 1.23.1–3, which lists the sufferings concomitant with the war, need not be regarded, as it is by Cobet and others, as representing a change of perspective on Thucydides' part. It may rather be seen as introducing for the first time the way in which Thucydides views the war. To quote Immerwahr again, Thucydides 'differs from Herodotus [...] in emphasising suffering rather than glory. His manner of writing history, so far as it can be understood from the proem alone, does not stress achievement, and neither praise nor fame are mentioned as his themes at the beginning of his work.'[3] From the presentation of war as offered by Homeric epic Thucydides has thus chosen to stress the converse of that stressed by Herodotus.

It is of course true that Thucydides' personal comments on the war, though numerous in themselves and especially when compared with similar statements in Herodotus, are relatively few in comparison with the volume of his work as a whole. Cobet underlines this point and concludes that Thucydides' responses to the horrors of war are routine and stereotyped, given with no particular concern for the conquered. Such a view, however, takes no account of the way in which Thucydides' work is structured. It can be argued that his history is composed around a series of reversals, the tragic nature of which speaks for itself and makes any authorial comment superfluous and counter-productive. Indeed such περιπέτειαι, in which arrogant and/or ignorant protagonists move through error to disaster, are also a feature of Herodotus' work, no less than of Thucydides': the narratives of both historians resemble the epic and dramatic treatment of Homer and the Attic tragedians, with whom they also share the devices of irony and recognition. Homer's Patroclus (*Iliad* 16.744–50), Herodotus' Harpagus (1.119) and Thucydides' Athenians (6.32) rejoice like Sophocles' Theban elders (*OT* 1086–1109) as they move in ignorance towards disaster, and, when disaster comes, similar recognition joins together Hector (*Iliad* 22.296–305), Cambyses (Hdt. 3.64–65), the Athenians (Thuc. 7.75) and Oedipus (Sophocles *OT* 1307–66). Since creative literature is concerned to imitate real life, it is not surprising that the narration of real life should resemble creative literature in structure and detail. Both

[2] Immerwahr (1960) 277.

[3] Immerwahr (1960) 279.

reflect at different levels a society's apprehension of what is real in human experience.

Yet, though considerable attention has recently been paid to the resemblances mentioned here,[4] the effect has perhaps been to reduce historiography to a literary genre intermediate between epic and tragedy: by emphasizing the affinities of ancient historiography with creative literature we may be in danger of obscuring its very essence. What gave birth to the earliest historiography was precisely a replacement of the creative imagination of the epic tradition by a rational concern for truth. Hecataeus rationalized the orally transmitted stories of the past and stripped them of their poetry;[5] Herodotus employed methods of argument developed within the Ionian pre-Socratic tradition to establish past and present truths;[6] and Thucydides was deeply influenced by contemporary sophistic concern with *phusis*, as Smart has undertaken to demonstrate by an examination of his chronological scheme, and shared the scientific faith of contemporary Hippocratic medical inquiry. Although such a view of the origins of historiography in the growth of rationality has come under strong attack in recent years,[7] what originally differentiated historiography from creative literature, and continued to differentiate it from historical fiction, was the effort, through the application of a rational methodology (Hdt. 1.5, Thuc. 1.21–22), to describe what actually happened.

Xenophon's *Hellenica* contains references to, or accounts of, numerous battles, some of which have been impugned by scholars for various reasons. Tuplin argues that there are good reasons for accepting the reliability of Xenophon's accounts and that where there are cases of conflict these are to be imputed to the 'creative writing' of the Oxyrhynchus historian or his successors. Those scholars who have believed the latter instead of Xenophon himself have been misled by the seemingly authentic nature of circumstantial details. While this argument, if accepted, certainly vindicates Xenophon, it does not do away with the problem under discussion but merely transfers it to the Oxyrhynchus historian, for whose alleged invention Tuplin does not venture to offer an explanation.

Yet the explanation may be nothing more sophisticated than an author's natural desire to accommodate his writing to the interests

4 For Thucydides in particular see Macleod (1983) 140–58.

5 See Jacoby (1912) 2733–42.

6 E.g. 2.19–27, with Lloyd (1976) 91–107, on the causes of the inundation of the Nile, and 2.116–20, with Hunter (1982) 52–61, on the 'truth' of Helen's presence at Troy. See further and in general Lloyd (1975) 156–70.

7 A good summary of the origins of the attack can be found in Connor (1977). For the use of the term 'rationality' see Hunter (1982) 107–15.

and enthusiasms of his readers. Schultze points out correctly that historiography was regarded as being one of the more popular genres of literature and that one of its principal aims was the entertainment of readers. It is self-evident that ancient readers relished the detailed description of battle-scenes, so it is hardly surprising if historians sought to provide them. Yet Schultze also observes that in Dionysius' opinion ἀλήθεια is closely associated with ἀκρίβεια, and that the latter seems to refer to fullness and completeness rather than to precision or discrimination. If we assume that Dionysius was reflecting the common view, we can also assume that ancient readers would have preferred the Oxyrhynchus historian to Xenophon, not only because he provides more of what they wanted to read but also because his account is more 'true'. This raises once again the central question of what truth is.

What are we to make of historians' claims to tell the truth? A purely literary approach to ancient historiography would wish to conclude from Hellenistic and subsequent practice that ancient historical writing from its very beginnings constituted a form of conventional composition with only a limited reference either to the real events it claimed to describe or to the real circumstances within which it was composed. In complete isolation from past and present realities it operated within the closed confines of its own conventions and was concerned with the pleasure, rather than the benefit, of its readers. In the cases of Herodotus and Thucydides, Cobet on the contrary emphasizes the importance of their experience of contemporary reality in determining their choice of war as their subject and their conception of its true description. Herodotus deals with, and explains, the failure of expansionism both barbarian (1.73–91, Croesus; 1.201–14, Cyrus; 3.17–26, Cambyses; 4.83–142, Darius; 7.5–9.122, Xerxes) and Greek (3.39–43, 122–25, Polycrates), and is in particular concerned with the causes of the conflict between Greeks and barbarians and the problem of the Greeks in Asia.[8] Thucydides similarly deals with, and explains, the failure of the Athenian empire; he places especial emphasis on the Sicilian expedition and its effect upon the Syracusans, analogous to the earlier effect of Persian expansionism upon the Athenians themselves, in stimulating their own imperial development.[9] Which factors influenced the historians more in their choice of subject and view of its true representation? The existence of the epic tradition of the Trojan War? Or, if one

[8] The Asiatic Greeks stand at the beginning (1.6–27, 1.141–70), middle (5.28–6.32) and end (9.90–106) of the *Histories*, and Herodotus is throughout concerned with mainland Greek intervention in their defence (1.141, 1.152–53, 5.38–97, 9.106). He would appear not to recommend it.

[9] See Hunter (1982) 45–46, 266–70.

accepts a late date for Herodotus, their shared experience of the fall of Athens and the emergence in Sicily of a new Syracusan empire under Dionysius I and in Asia of conflict between Greeks and Persians for possession of Ionia? Gabba has rightly insisted that 'the relationship between history and poetry goes back to the earliest times and the origin of historical narrative is in a sense unintelligible without it';[10] but any attempt at seeing Herodotus and Thucydides as literary artists who intentionally followed the Homeric tradition should not deny them their role as historians or discount whatever other factors motivated them to write their histories.[11]

The Roman successors of Herodotus and Thucydides, according to Quintilian (10.1.101), were Livy and Sallust respectively; and although they wrote four centuries after their great predecessors, their works invite similar questions. According to Livy, there are always new historians coming along 'who think either that they have some more exact knowledge to impart or that their literary skill will improve on the inferior standards of their predecessors' ('in rebus certius aliquid allaturos se aut scribendi arte rudem vetustatem superaturos credunt': *praef.* 2). Such aspirations constitute an important element of an historian's motivation in turning to historiography: they are a means of claiming originality. But to what extent can Livy's dichotomy between research and style be maintained – or, putting the question another way, to what extent can literary analysis illuminate what is traditional in an author's work and distinguish it from what is original?

The problem is found in perhaps its most acute form in the earlier Roman annalists. One can compare Livy's accounts of the exploits of Manlius Torquatus and Valerius Corvinus with those of Claudius Quadrigarius and conclude that Livy's contribution is merely one of *ars scribendi*: the 'facts' of the episode are the same in each case. But are these 'facts' themselves factual? Wiseman (1979) has already argued that much of what was written by the annalists was creative reconstruction based on some form of traditional chronological framework, and in the present work he demonstrates how some false traditions can arise. Cornell, on the other hand, argues that the annalists preserved and handed down a sound body of authentic historical information, a record of events set against a background of political, military and social institutions. He sees a living tradition that formed part of the consciousness of the entire community of Roman citizens, an ideological construct designed to control, to

[10] Gabba (1981) 52–53.

[11] On this whole question apropos of Thucydides see the interesting remarks of Dover (1983).

justify and to inspire. Yet is this interpretation as far from Wiseman's as it may appear at first sight? Though the two scholars may differ as to the manner in which the tales of early Rome assumed the stature which they have in Livy, the existence of a living tradition in the consciousness of the citizens is no guarantee of the genuineness of that tradition. The items of information for which it is responsible are presumably no more reliable than those which Herodotus recorded on the basis of oral tradition.

It nevertheless remains true that, if we are to investigate the history of the ancient world, we must attempt to identify and evaluate the preconceptions and ideologies which the ancient writers, upon whose statements a modern narrative must too often depend, bring to bear upon their subject-matter. Can such assumptions be isolated? What is their frequency and extent? And how far do they colour the content of history? Explicit acknowledgement of their existence and nature by a particular author – whether it be Sallust, Livy or Tacitus – may be initially disarming but does not deter the intrepid critic from pursuit of what is ἀφανέστατον.

Luce devotes the first part of his paper on Tacitus to a discussion of the methodological questions whether, by what means, and to what extent it is possible to identify Tacitus' own views on his material. Criticizing as over-schematized any approach which divorces the writer's thoughts from the contexts in which they are vouchsafed, Luce suggests that it may be wrong in principle to assume that Tacitus himself had a predisposition for inductive generalization: he does not often proceed far beyond the particular in his writing. His reactions to the events he describes, and his evaluations of the persons he mentions, are simply not predictable – either because his preconceptions are minimal or because he makes very little use of them. He assesses each episode on its own terms. Luce illustrates this general point by detailed consideration of Tacitus' treatment of Tiberius' character and record as emperor. Tacitus' handling of this subject has been thought to be inconsistent or even contradictory because critics have often failed to acknowledge that he independently assesses Tiberius' behaviour at different stages of his career in the light of changing circumstances. Just as there is no inconsistency between the estimates of Tiberius before he became emperor which are given at *Annals* 1.4.3–4 and 6.51.3, since the latter is spoken *in propria persona* but the former is in *oratio obliqua*, so Tacitus can without inconsistency suggest that Tiberius was evil and hypocritical at the beginning of his reign and yet appear to agree with Arruntius' proposition that, by the end, he was corrupted by supreme power. It is simply a mistake to suppose that Tacitus must have held one view rather than the other, but should not have held both. Tacitus is well known for his habit of suggesting alternative motives for individual actions; Luce has interpreted the larger subject of Tiberius' character in analogous terms and in so doing has placed in a different light an author who has always been noted for the strength of his preconceptions.[12]

By contrast, Plutarch was traditionally considered to have been incapable of thinking for himself at all. More recently, it is true, scholars have come to appreciate his independence of his sources in terms both of content and style; and in the present work Pelling carries a stage further his systematic attempt to define the extent of Plutarch's interest in history as opposed to biography, and the kind of model he brought to bear on the presentation of Roman history.[13] The *Gracchi*, the *Marius* and the *Caesar* contain more information which is not simply personal than many of the other Lives. Within these the most informative passages are those in which we can be reasonably certain that Plutarch is not adopting ready-made the interpretation of his source. In each of these Lives there is prominent emphasis given to a rather simplistic version of the *boulē–dēmos* confrontation as an explanation of the political realities of the late Republic. Though such an analysis of Roman history is not unique to Plutarch (cf. e.g. Dionysius of Halicarnassus *AR* 2.11.1–3, with Schultze's discussion),[14] his commitment to it as an interpretative model is more single-minded and more thoroughgoing than that of others. He also tends to present Roman history in terms of a struggle to modify the constitution. Applicable as this may be to the conflicts of the early Republic, it is in general a mode of analysis more appropriate to Greek than to Roman history and is hardly suitable to the first century B.C. when the struggle is rather between individuals in the race for *dignitas*, *auctoritas* and *potentia*. His choice of model is in fact paradoxical, in this case, for an author whose stated genre is biography. On occasion too there are omissions, or oversimplifications of other kinds, in his presentation of Roman history. So far as he can, he assimilates Roman reality to a Greek prototype; where this latter does not exist, he tends to underplay or misunderstand. Of course the interpretations by some Romans of their own past often involve reductionism and stereotyping, especially in the revolutionary period; but Plutarch is more consistent and determined than any individual one of his sources in the application of the *boulē–dēmos* analysis to Roman history. It can be shown from different periods

[12] On Tacitus' treatment of Tiberius' character see also Gill (1983).
[13] Cf. Pelling (1979, 1980).
[14] See above pp. 128–33 with notes.

where comparison with other sources is possible that Plutarch does impose his own interpretation on material which he shares in common with them. The strong likelihood is, therefore, that Plutarch's vision of the political clashes of the late Republic as a conflict between *boulē* and *dēmos* is personal and not merely derivative.

Modern students of the ancient world should be delighted on the few occasions when they can identify, with at least strong probability, a writer's original thoughts on a period. If all writers resembled Diodorus, life might be easier, and would certainly be much less interesting. But when we are confronted with the probability of such original treatment, we are less content than concerned with its ineptness. Such a paradoxical reaction in the face of independence and originality is presumably to be traced to unease at the incomplete state of our evidence. Though certainly we want to be aware of the independent ideas and personal preconceptions of our literary sources before attempting our own reconstructions, such knowledge does not make us comfortable, and instinctively we are concerned to discover whether a secondary tradition accurately reflects the realities of an earlier time. Generally there is no opportunity for a definitive demonstration: hence, for example, the continuing disagreements over the divergences between Plutarch and Appian on the question whether Romans only or all Italians were to benefit from land distributions, alluded to by Pelling and illuminated by his discussion. But, as Rawson shows, the tradition about the Liberators is different, since letters, coins and other contemporary evidence enable the secondary sources to be checked. The tradition itself is not monolithic: Velleius Paterculus, Valerius Maximus, the sporadically attested attitudes of the provincials, and the autobiography of Augustus and its derivatives are all essentially hostile to Brutus and Cassius, though each in differing degrees, while Plutarch, Appian and Dio, though they all happen to write in Greek, represent a different side of the Roman tradition which is favourable to them. Nicolaus of Damascus, Augustus' biographer, belongs essentially to this latter group, though elements of the hostile tradition deriving from Augustus' autobiography are also discernible in his work. There are notable differences too in the secondary tradition, reflected often in the order in which the principal Liberators are named, about the relative importance of Brutus and Cassius. There is of course a prima facie likelihood that the tradition is correct to preserve evidence of divergence of view on an act and its agents which were inevitably controversial. But on this issue we are fortunate to be able to confirm this probability by reference to the primary documentation: though the subsequent tradition has a tendency to polarize, to simplify, or to rationalize the complexities and contradictions which are evident in the contemporary assessments, the content of that later tradition is seen to be well grounded upon the actualities of the years 44–42 B.C. Neither the exigencies of working within the confines of a demanding literary genre nor the limitations, preconceptions or prejudices of individual writers have erased the independently attested reality.

With Wiedemann's investigation of Ammianus, however, we are at the opposite end of the spectrum. He sees the historian's descriptions of 'marginal' places and peoples, such as islands and barbarians, entirely in terms of anthropological and literary convention.[15] Ammianus' descriptions do not constitute the communication of genuine information but are a collection of *topoi* which the author knew would be expected by his readers. Moreover, several of his *topoi* make their first appearance in Herodotus, for whom, it is assumed, they were not *topoi* but genuine items of information. Yet Herodotus, though *pater historiae*, was dependent upon oral traditions which themselves stretched back into the mists of antiquity and were in many cases no more reliable than the digressions in Ammianus.[16] In this respect Herodotus himself, no less than Ammianus, may have been heir to a tradition of conventional composition.

It will be evident that with these remarks we are back to the problem with which we started and which remains, not surprisingly, unresolved. In the nature of the case the problem is, on most occasions, insoluble. We can do no more than express the belief that historical problems are usually inseparable from the historiographical, and that historians who wish to understand the ancient world should show themselves alert to the nature of the literary sources on which their evidence depends.

[15] On islands in particular see also Gabba (1981) 55–60.
[16] For a sceptical view of Herodotus see Armayor (1980).

Abbreviations and bibliography

Note. List A is the key to the abbreviations of standard works adopted in the book. List B, which is a cumulation of all works cited by author and date in the text and notes, provides the essential bibliographical information. Only abbreviations of periodical titles attested from *L'Année philologique* have been employed.

A. Abbreviations

ANRW	*Aufstieg und Niedergang der römischen Welt*, ed. Temporini, H.–Haase, W. Part I. 1–4 (1972–73), Part II. 1– (1974–84). Berlin/New York
FGrHist	Jacoby, F. *Die Fragmente der griechischen Historiker*, 3 parts in 15 vols. Berlin/Leyden, 1923–58
HCT	Gomme, A. W.–Andrewes, A.–Dover, K. J. *A Historical Commentary on Thucydides*, 5 vols. Oxford, 1945–81
ILLRP	Degrassi, A. *Inscriptiones Latinae Liberae Rei Publicae*, vol. 1 (2nd edition, 1965), vol. 2 (1963). Florence
LSJ	Liddell, H. G.–Scott, R.–Stuart Jones, H.–McKenzie, R. *A Greek–English Lexicon*, 9th edition. Oxford, 1940
ML	Meiggs, R.–Lewis, D. *A Selection of Greek Historical Inscriptions to the End of the Fifth Century* B.C. Oxford, 1969
*PIR*²	*Prosopographia Imperii Romani saec. I. II. III*, Parts 1–3 (2nd edition, 1933), ed. E. Groag and A. Stein; Part 4 (2nd edition, 1952–66), ed. A. Stein and L. Petersen. Berlin/Leipzig
RE	*Paulys Real-Encyclopädie der classischen Altertumswissenschaft*, ed. G. Wissowa *et al.* Stuttgart, 1893–
RRC	Crawford, M. H. *Roman Republican Coinage*. Cambridge, 1974

B. Bibliography

Adcock, F. E. (1951). 'Thucydides in Book I', *JHS* 71.2–12

Adcock, F. E. (1963). *Thucydides and his History*. Cambridge

Alföldi, A. (1935). 'Insignien und Tracht der römischen Kaiser', *MDAI(R)* 50.1–171

Alföldi, A. (1965). *Early Rome and the Latins*. Ann Arbor

Anderson, J. K. (1970). *Military Theory and Practice in the Age of Xenophon*. Berkeley/Los Angeles

Anderson, J. K. (1974). 'The battle of Sardis', *CSCA* 7.27–53

Anderson, R. D.–Parsons, P. J.–Nisbet, R. G. M. (1979). 'Elegiacs by Gallus from Qaṣr Ibrîm', *JRS* 69.125–55

Anderson, W. S. (1963). *Pompey, his Friends, and the Literature of the First Century B.C.* University of California Publications in Classical Philology 19.1. Berkeley

André, J. (1949). *La Vie et l'oeuvre d'Asinius Pollion.* Paris

Andrewes, A. (1978). 'The opposition to Pericles', *JHS* 98.1–8

Andrewes, A. (1982). 'Notion and Kyzikos: the sources compared', *JHS* 102.15–27

Arens, W. (1979). *The Man-Eating Myth.* Chicago

Armayor, O. K. (1980). 'Sesostris and Herodotus' autopsy of Thrace, Colchis, inland Asia Minor, and the Levant', *HSPh* 84.51–73

Astin, A. E. (1967). *Scipio Aemilianus.* Oxford

Astin, A. E. (1978). *Cato the Censor.* Oxford

Astin, A. E. (1979). Review of Bernstein (1978) in *CR* 29.111–12

Aujac, G. (1975). *Géminos. Introduction aux Phénomènes.* Paris.

Avenarius, G. (1956). *Lukians Schrift zur Geschichtsschreibung.* Meisenheim

Avery, H. C. (1965). 'Heracles, Philoctetes, Neoptolemus', *Hermes* 93.279–97

Badian, E. (1958a). *Foreign Clientelae.* Oxford

Badian, E. (1958b). Review of Gabba (1956) in *CR* 8.159–62

Badian, E. (1966). 'The early historians' in *Latin Historians* (London), ed. T. A. Dorey, 1–38

Badian, E. (1970). *Titus Quinctius Flamininus, Philhellenism and Realpolitik.* Semple Memorial Lecture. Cincinnati, Ohio

Badian, E. (1972). 'Tiberius Gracchus and the beginning of the Roman Revolution' in *ANRW* 1.1.668–731

Balsdon, J. P. V. D. (1953). 'Some questions about historical writing in the second century B.C.', *CQ* 3.158–64

Barbagallo, C. (1926). *Il problema delle origini di Roma.* Milan

Barbieri, G. (1955). *Conone.* Rome

Barbu, N. (1933). *Les Sources et l'originalité d'Appien dans le deuxième livre des Guerres Civiles.* Paris

Beloch, K. J. (1926). *Römische Geschichte bis zum Beginn der punischen Kriege.* Berlin/Leipzig

Bengtson, H. (1970). *Zur Geschichte des Brutus.* SBAW, Philosophisch-Historische Klasse, vol. 1. Munich

Béquignon, Y. (1937). *La Vallée du Spercheios.* Paris

Bernstein, A. H. (1978). *Ti. Sempronius Gracchus, Tradition and Apostasy.* Ithaca, N.Y.

Bloedow, E. F. (1973). *Alcibiades Re-examined.* Wiesbaden

Bömer, F. (1953). 'Thematik und Krise der römischen Geschichtsschreibung im 2. Jahrhundert v. Chr.', *Historia* 2.189–209

Bommelaer, J. (1981). *Lysandre de Sparte.* Athens/Paris

Bonfante, L. (1978). 'Historical art: Etruscan and early Roman', *AJAH* 3.136–62

Bonner, S. F. (1939). *The Literary Treatises of Dionysius of Halicarnassus*. Cambridge

Bosworth, A. B. (1972). 'Asinius Pollio and Augustus', *Historia* 21.441–73

Botermann, H. (1968). *Die Soldaten und die römische Politik in der Zeit von Caesars Tod bis zur Begründung des Zweiten Triumvirats*. Zetemata 46. Munich

Bowersock, G. W. (1965). *Augustus and the Greek World*. Oxford

Bowersock, G. W. (1979). 'Historical problems in late republican and Augustan classicism' in *Le Classicisme à Rome* (Entretiens sur l'antiquité classique 25) (Vandoeuvres–Geneva), 57–78

Breitenbach, H. (1873–76). *Xenophons Hellenika*, vols. 1 (1873), 2 (1874), 3 (1876). Berlin

Breitenbach, H. R. (1971). 'Die Seeschlacht bei Notion, 407/06', *Historia* 20.152–71

Bremmer, J. (1980). 'Marginalia Manichaica', *ZPE* 39.29–34

Briscoe, J. (1973). *A Commentary on Livy* XXXI–XXXIII. Oxford

Briscoe, J. (1981). Review of Wiseman (1979) in *CR* 31.49–51

Bruce, I. A. F. (1967). *An Historical Commentary on the Hellenica Oxyrhynchia*. Cambridge

Brunt, P. A. (1965a). 'The equites in the late Republic', *Second International Conference on Economic History 1962* (Aix-en-Provence), 117–49. (Reprinted in *The Crisis of the Roman Republic* (Cambridge, 1969), ed. R. Seager, 83–117)

Brunt, P. A. (1965b). 'Italian aims at the time of the Social War', *JRS* 55.90–109

Brunt, P. A. (1971a). *Italian Manpower*. Oxford

Brunt, P. A. (1971b). *Social Conflicts in the Roman Republic*. London

Brunt, P. A. (1979). 'Cicero and historiography' in *Miscellanea di studi classici in onore di Eugenio Manni* (Rome), ed. M. J. Fontana *et al.*, 1.311–40

Brunt, P. A. (1982). 'Nobilitas and novitas', *JRS* 72.1–17

Brutscher, C. (1958). *Analysen zu Suetons Divus Julius und der Parallelüberlieferung*. Berne

Buckler, J. (1979). 'The re-establishment of the Boiotarkhia', *AJAH* 4.50–64

Buckler, J. (1980a). *The Theban Hegemony*. Cambridge, Mass./London

Buckler, J. (1980b). 'Plutarch on Leuctra', *SO* 55.75–94

Busolt, G. (1893–1904). *Griechische Geschichte*, vols. 1 (1893), 2 (1895), 3.1 (1897) and 3.2 (1904). Gotha

Bux, E. (1915). *Das* προβούλευμα *bei Dionys von Halikarnass*. Dissertation. Leipzig

Buxton, R. G. A. (1982). *Peitho*. Cambridge

Carpenter, R.–Bon, Antoine (1936). *The Defenses of Acrocorinth and the Lower Town*. Corinth: Results of excavations conducted by the American School of Classical Studies at Athens, vol. III.2. Cambridge, Mass.

Cary, E. (1937–1950). *The Roman Antiquities of Dionysius of Halicarnassus*, 7 vols. London/Cambridge, Mass.

Cavaignac, E. (1925). 'À propos de la bataille du torrent de Nemée', *REA* 27.273–78

Cawkwell, G. L. (1972). 'Epaminondas and Thebes', *CQ* 22.254–78

Cichorius, C. (1922). *Römische Studien*. Leipzig/Berlin

Clark, E. G. (1973). 'Augustus and the historians'. Unpublished D.Phil. thesis. University of Oxford

Clarke, M. L. (1981). *The Noblest Roman: Marcus Brutus and his reputation*. London

Classen, J.–Steup, J. (1892–1922). *Thukydides*. With commentary by Johannes Classen; revised by Julius Steup. 8 vols.: 1 (1919), 2 (1914), 3 (1892), 4 (1900), 5 (1912), 6 (1905), 7 (1908), 8 (1922). Berlin. (Reprinted 1963)

Coarelli, F. (1972). 'Il sepolcro degli Scipioni', *DArch* 6.36–106

Coarelli, F. (1974). *Guida archeologica di Roma*. Verona

Coarelli, F. (1977). 'Il comizio dalle origini alla fine della repubblica', *PP* 32.166–238

Coarelli, F. (1980). *Roma*. Guide archeologiche Laterza. Bari

Coarelli, F.–Kajanto, I.–Nyberg, U.–Steinby, M. (1981). *L'area sacra di Largo Argentina*, vol. 1. Rome

Cobet, J. (1971). *Herodots Exkurse und die Frage der Einheit seines Werkes*. Historia Einzelschrift 17. Wiesbaden

Cobet, J. (1977). 'Wann wurde Herodots Darstellung der Perserkriege publiziert?', *Hermes* 105.2–27

Collingwood, R. G. (1946). *The Idea of History*. Oxford

Connor, W. R. (1977). 'A post-modernist Thucydides?', *CJ* 72. 289–98

Cook, J. M. (1972). *The Troad*. Oxford

Cornell, T. J. (1975). 'Aeneas and the Twins: the development of the Roman foundation legend', *PCPhS* 21.1–32

Cornell, T. J. (1980). 'Alcune riflessioni sulla formazione della tradizione storiografica su Roma arcaica' in *Roma arcaica e le recenti scoperte archeologiche: Giornate di studio in onore di U. Coli, Florence 1979* (Milan), 19–34

Cornell, T. J. (1982). Review of Wiseman (1979) in *JRS* 72.203–6

Cornell, T. J.–Matthews, J. F. (1982). *Atlas of the Roman World*. London

Crawford, M. H. (1976). 'The early Roman economy' in *L'Italie préromaine et la Rome républicaine. Mélanges offerts à Jacques Heurgon* (Paris), 2 vols., 1.197–207

Crawford, M. H. (1978). *The Roman Republic*. London

Cuff, P. J. (1967). 'Prolegomena to a critical edition of Appian, *BC* 1', *Historia* 16.177–88

Cuff, P. J. (1983). 'Appian's *Romaica*: a note', *Athenaeum* 61.148–64

Davis, N.–Kraay, C. M. (1973). *The Hellenistic Kingdoms: portrait coins and history*. London

De Dominicis, M. A. (1966). 'La Latinitas Iuniana e la legge Elia Senzia' in *Mélanges d'archéologie et d'histoire offerts à A. Piganiol* (Paris), ed. R. Chevallier, 3.1419–31

Degrassi, A. (1947). *Inscriptiones Italiae*, vol. 13. 1. Rome
De Ste Croix, G. E. M. (1972). *The Origins of the Peloponnesian War*. London
De Ste Croix, G. E. M. (1981). *The Class Struggle in the Ancient World*. London
De Sanctis, G. (1907). *Storia dei Romani*, vol. 1. Turin
De Sanctis, G. (1931). 'La battaglia di Notion', *RFIC* 59.222–29
Develin, R. (1975). 'Comitia tributa plebis', *Athenaeum* 53.302–37
Dobesch, G. (1978). 'Nikolaos von Damaskus und die Selbstbiographie des Augustus', *GB* 7.91–174
Dodds, E. R. (1960). *Euripides' Bacchae*, 2nd edition. Oxford
Dontas, G. S. (1967). 'Τοπογραφικὰ θέματα τῆς πολιορκίας τῆς Κερκύρας τοῦ ἔτους 373 π. Χ.', *AE* for 1965. 139–44
Douglas, M. (1966). *Purity and Danger: an analysis of concepts of pollution and taboo*. London
Dover, K. J. (1953). 'La colonizzazione della Sicilia in Tucidide', *Maia* 6.1–20. (Reprinted as 'Die Kolonisierung Siziliens bei Thukydides' in *Thukydides. Wege der Forschung* 98 (Darmstadt, 1968), ed. H. Herter, 344–68)
Dover, K. J. (1972). *Aristophanic Comedy*. London
Dover, K. J. (1983). 'Thucydides "as history" and "as literature"', *History and Theory* 22.54–63
Drews, R. (1973). *The Greek Accounts of Eastern History*. Cambridge, Mass.
Dušanić, S. (1970). *Arkadski Savez IV veka* [*The Arcadian League in the 4th c.*]. Belgrade
Eadie, J. W. (1967). *The Breviarium of Festus*. London
Earl, D. C. (1963). *Tiberius Gracchus: a study in politics*. Collection Latomus 66. Brussels
Eckstein, A. H. (1980). 'Perils of poetry: the Roman "poetic tradition" on the outbreak of the First Punic War', *AJAH* 5.174–92
Ehrhardt, C. (1970). 'Xenophon and Diodorus on Aegospotami', *Phoenix* 24.225–28
Evans, J. A. S. (1979a). 'Herodotus' publication date', *Athenaeum* 57.145–49
Evans, J. A. S. (1979b). 'Herodotus and Athens: the evidence of the *encomium*', *AC* 48.112–18
Finley, M. I. (1981). *Economy and Society in Ancient Greece*. London
Flacelière, R.–Chambry, E. (1978). *Plutarque: Vies*, vol. XIV: Dion–Brutus. Paris
Flach, D. (1973). *Tacitus in der Tradition der antiken Geschichtsschreibung*. Göttingen
Flory, S. (1980). 'Who read Herodotus' Histories?', *AJPh* 101.12–28
Fornara, C. W. (1971a). 'Evidence for the date of Herodotus' publication', *JHS* 91.25–34
Fornara, C. W. (1971b). *Herodotus. An interpretative essay*. Oxford
Fornara, C. W. (1981). 'Herodotus' knowledge of the Archidamian War', *Hermes* 109.149–56

Forster, E. M. (1962). *Aspects of the Novel*. Harmondsworth

Fraccaro, P. (1952). 'La storia romana arcaica', *RIL* 85.85–118. (Reprinted in Fraccaro (1956) 1–23)

Fraccaro, P. (1956). *Opuscula*, vol. 1. Pavia

Fraccaro, P. (1957). 'The history of Rome in the regal period', *JRS* 47.59–65

Fraser, P. M. (1972). *Ptolemaic Alexandria*. 3 vols. Oxford

Fraser, P. M.–Bean, G. E. (1954). *The Rhodian Peraea*. Oxford

Frier, B. W. (1979). *Libri Annales Pontificum Maximorum*. Rome

Fröhlich, F. (1899). 'C. Cassius Longinus' (59) in *RE* 3, cols. 1727–36

Fruin, R. T. A. (1894). 'Beiträge zur Fastenkritik', *Jahrbücher für classische Philologie = Neue Jahrbücher für Philologie und Paedagogik* 149.103–18

Fuchs, H. (1938). *Der geistige Widerstand gegen Rom in der antiken Welt*. Berlin

Fuks, A. (1972). 'Isokrates and the social–economic situation in Greece', *AncSoc* 3.17–44

Fuks, A. (1974). 'Patterns and types of social–economic revolution in Greece from the fourth to the second century B.C.', *AncSoc* 5.51–81

Gabba, E. (1951). 'Ricerche sull' esercito professionale romano da Mario ad Augusto', *Athenaeum* 29.171–272

Gabba, E. (1955). 'Sulla "Storia Romana" di Cassio Dione', *RSI* 67.289–333

Gabba, E. (1956). *Appiano e la Storia delle Guerre Civili*. Florence

Gabba, E. (1958). *Appiani Bellorum Civilium Liber Primus*. Edition and commentary. Florence

Gabba, E. (1960). 'Studi su Dionigi da Alicarnasso I. La costituzione di Romolo', *Athenaeum* 38.175–225

Gabba, E. (1961). 'Studi su Dionigi da Alicarnasso II. Il regno di Servio Tullio', *Athenaeum* 39.98–121

Gabba, E. (1963). 'Il latino come dialetto greco' in *Miscellanea di studi alessandrini in memoria di A. Rostagni* (Turin), 188–94

Gabba, E. (1967). 'Considerazioni sulla tradizione letteraria sulle origini della repubblica' in *Les Origines de la république romaine* (Entretiens sur l'antiquité classique 13) (Vandoeuvres-Geneva), 133–74

Gabba, E. (1974). 'Storiografia greca e imperialismo romano (III–I sec. a.C.)', *RSI* 86.625–42

Gabba, E. (1981). 'True history and false history in classical antiquity', *JRS* 71.50–62

Gabba, E. (1982). 'La "Storia di Roma arcaica" di Dionigi d'Alicarnasso' in *ANRW* II.30.1.799–816

Garlan, Y. (1972). *La Guerre dans l'antiquité*. Paris

Geiger, F. (1922). 'Kopais' in *RE* 11.2, cols. 1346–60

Gelzer, M. (1917). 'M. Iunius Brutus' (53) in *RE* 10.1, cols. 973–1020

Gelzer, M. (1929). Review of F. Taeger, *Tiberius Gracchus* in *Gnomon* 5.296–303. (Reprinted in his *Kleine Schriften* 2 (1963) 73–80)

Gelzer, M. (1931). 'Nasicas Widerspruch gegen die Zerstörung Karthagos', *Philologus* 86. 261–99. (Reprinted in his *Kleine Schriften* 2 (1963) 39–72)

Gelzer, M. (1934). 'Der Anfang römischer Geschichtsschreibung', *Hermes* 69.46–55. (Reprinted in Gelzer (1964) 92–103)

Gelzer, M. (1954). 'Nochmals über den Anfang der römischen Geschichtsschreibung', *Hermes* 82.342–48. (Reprinted in Gelzer (1964) 104–10)

Gelzer, M. (1958). Review of Gabba (1956) in *Gnomon* 30.216–18. (Reprinted in Gelzer (1964) 286–89)

Gelzer, M. (1964). *Kleine Schriften*, vol. 3. Wiesbaden

Gelzer, M. (1969). *The Roman Nobility*. Translated by R. Seager. Oxford

Gill, C. (1983). 'The question of character-development: Plutarch and Tacitus', *CQ* 33.469–87

Gjerstad, E. (1960). *Early Rome*, vol. 3. Lund

Göhler, J. (1939). *Rom und Italien*. Breslau

Goodall, B. (1976). 'The reflexive pronoun in Xenophon's *Anabasis* and *Hellenica*', *CSCA* 9.41–59

Goodyear, F. R. D. (1970). 'Cyclic development in history: a note on Tac. *Ann.* 3.55.5', *BICS* 17.101–6

Goodyear, F. R. D. (1976). 'De inconstantia Cornelii Taciti' in *Acta omnium gentium ac nationum conventus Latinis litteris linguaeque fovendis* (Malta), 198–204

Goodyear, F. R. D. (1981). *The Annals of Tacitus*, vol. 2: *Annals* 1.55–81 and *Annals* 2. Cambridge

Goold, G. P. (1961). 'A Greek professorial circle at Rome', *TAPhA* 92.168–92

Gozzoli, S. (1976). 'Polibio e Dionigi d'Alicarnasso', *SCO* 25.149–76

Grant, M. (1971). *Roman Myths*. London

Gray, V. (1979). 'Two different approaches to the Battle of Sardis in 395 B.C.', *CSCA* 12.183–200

Groag, E. (1939). *Die römischen Reichsbeamten von Achaia bis auf Diokletian*. Vienna

Grube, G. M. A. (1965). *The Greek and Roman Critics*. London

Häussler, R. (1965). *Tacitus und das historische Bewusstsein*. Heidelberg

Halbfas, F. (1910). *Theorie und Praxis in der Geschichtsschreibung bei Dionys von Halikarnass*. Dissertation. Münster

Haller, B. (1967). *C. Asinius Pollio als Politiker und zeitkritischer Historiker*. Dissertation. Münster

Hanell, K. (1945). 'Bemerkungen zu der politischen Terminologie des Sallustius', *Eranos* 43. 263–76

Harris, W. V. (1979). *War and Imperialism in Republican Rome, 327–70 B.C.* Oxford

Hasluk, F. W. (1902). 'An inscribed basis from Cyzicus', *JHS* 22.126–34

Hasluk, F. W. (1910). *Cyzicus*. London

Hasluk, F. W.–Henderson, A. E. (1904). 'On the topography of Cyzicus', *JHS* 24.135–43

Hatzfeld, J. (1936). *Xénophon: Helléniques*, vol. 1. Paris

Hatzfeld, J. (1939). *Xénophon: Helléniques*, vol. 2. Paris

Hatzfeld, J. (1940). *Alcibiade*. Paris

Hellegouarc'h, J. (1963). *Le Vocabulaire latin des relations et des partis politiques sous la République*. Paris

Hennig, D. (1975). *L. Aelius Seianus. Untersuchungen zur Regierung des Tiberius*. Munich

Hercher, R. (1873). *Epistolographi Graeci*. Paris

Herkommer, E. (1968). *Die Topoi in den Proömien der römischen Geschichtswerke*. Dissertation. Tübingen

Heubner, H. (1963). *P. Cornelius Tacitus. Die Historien*, vol. 1: Book 1. Heidelberg

Heurgon, J. (1973). *The Rise of Rome to 264 B.C.* London

Hill, G. (1951). *Sources for Greek History between the Persian and Peloponnesian Wars*, new edition by R. Meiggs and A. Andrewes. Oxford

Hodkinson, S. and H. (1981). 'Mantinea and the Mantinike: settlement and society in a Greek polis', *ABSA* 76.239–96

Hölscher, T. (1967). *Victoria Romana*. Mainz

Hölscher, T. (1978). 'Die Anfänge römischer Repräsentationskunst', *MDAI(R)* 85.315–57

Hoffmann, W. (1942). *Livius und der zweite Punische Krieg*. Berlin

Hommel, H. (1981). 'Herodots Einleitungssatz: ein Schlüssel zur Analyse des Gesamtwerks?' in *Gnomosyne. Festschrift W. Marg* (Munich), ed. G. Kurz *et al.*, 271–87

How, W. W.–Wells, J. (1912). *A Commentary on Herodotus*, vol. 1. Oxford

Hude, C. (1930). *Xenophontis Historia Graeca*. Leipzig

Hunter, V. (1982). *Past and Process in Herodotus and Thucydides*. Princeton

Hurst, A. (1982). 'Un critique grec dans la Rome d'Auguste: Denys d'Halicarnasse' in *ANRW* II.30.1. 839–65

Ihm, M. (1901). 'Die sogenannte "villa Iovis" des Tiberius auf Capri und andere Suetoniana', *Hermes* 36.287–304

Immerwahr, H. R. (1960). '*Ergon*: history as a monument in Herodotus and Thucydides', *AJPh* 81.261–90

Jacoby, F. (1912). 'Hekataios' in *RE* 7.2, cols. 2667–2750. (Reprinted in his *Griechische Historiker* (Stuttgart, 1956), 186–227)

Jacoby, F. (1913a). 'Hellanikos' (7) in *RE* 8, cols. 104–53. (Reprinted in his *Griechische Historiker* (Stuttgart, 1956), 262–87)

Jacoby, F. (1913b). 'Herodotus' (7) in *RE* Supplementband 1.2, cols. 205–520

Janin, R. (1964). *Constantinople byzantine*, 2nd edition. Paris

Jones, C. P. (1966). 'Towards a chronology of Plutarch's works', *JRS* 56.61–74

Jones, C. P. (1971). *Plutarch and Rome*. Oxford

Kagan, D. (1969). *The Outbreak of the Peloponnesian War*. Ithaca, N.Y.

Kajanto, I. (1965). *The Latin Cognomina*. Helsinki

Kalligas, P. (1980). 'Τοπογραφικὰ τῆς πόλης τῆς ἀρχαίας Κερκύρας', *Κερκυραϊκὰ Χρονικά* 23.81–88

Kambanis, M. L. (1892). 'Le dessèchement du lac Copais par les anciens', *BCH* 16.121–37
Keil, H. *et al.* (1857–80). *Grammatici Latini*, 8 vols. Leipzig
Kennedy, G. (1972). *The Art of Rhetoric in the Roman World 300 B.C.–A.D. 300*. Princeton
Klotz, A. (1935). 'Über die Quelle Plutarchs in der Lebensbeschreibung des Q. Fabius Maximus', *RhM* 84.125–53
Klotz, A. (1940). *Livius und seine Vorgänger*. Berlin/Leipzig
Kniely, E. M. (1974). *Quellenkritische Studien zur Tätigkeit des M. Brutus im Osten*. Dissertation (Graz). Vienna
Knierim, E. (1939). *Die Bezeichnung 'dux' in der politischen Terminologie von Cicero bis Juvenal*. Dissertation. Giessen
Koenen, L. (1976). 'Fieldwork of the international photographic archive in Cairo: 2. A new fragment of the Oxyrhynchus historian', *StudPap* 15.55–76
Koldewey, R. (1890). *Die antiken Baureste der Insel Lesbos*. Leipzig
Kraft, K. (1952–53). 'Der goldene Kranz Caesars und der Kampf um die Entlarvung der Tyrannen', *JNG* 3–4.7–97
Kromayer, J.–Veith, G. (1928). *Heerwesen und Kriegführung der Griechen und Römer*. Munich
Laing, D. (1964). 'A new interpretation of the Athenian naval catalogue *IG* II² 1951'. Unpublished dissertation. University of Cincinnati
Laistner, M. L. W. (1947). *The Greater Roman Historians*. Berkeley
Lanzillotta, E. (1975). 'La battaglia di Nozio', *MGR* 4.135–61
Laslett, P. (1967). *John Locke: Two Treatises of Government. A critical edition with an introduction and apparatus criticus*, 2nd edition. Cambridge
Latacz, J. (1980). 'Die rätselhafte "Grosse Bewegung". Zum Eingang des Thukydideischen Geschichtswerks', *WJA* 6a. 77–99
Leavitt, M. L. (1966). 'Constitutional speculation in the antiquarians and annalists of the last century B.C., with special reference to the legends of Romulus and Servius Tullius in Livy, Cicero and Dionysius of Halicarnassus'. Unpublished B.Litt. thesis. University of Oxford
Lehmann-Hartleben, K. (1923). *Die antiken Hafenanlage des Mittelmeeres*. (= *Klio* Beiheft 14.) Leipzig
Lenardon, R. J. (1981). 'Thucydides and Hellanicus' in *Classical Contributions. Studies in honour of M. F. McGregor* (Locust Valley), ed. G. S. Shrimpton and D. J. McCargar, 59–70
Lendle, O. (1960). 'Zu Thukydides 5.20.2', *Hermes* 88.33–40
Lendle, O. (1964). 'Die Auseinandersetzung des Thukydides mit Hellanikos', *Hermes* 92.129–43. (Reprinted in *Thukydides. Wege der Forschung* 98 (Darmstadt, 1968), ed. H. Herter, 661–82)
Levick, B. M. (1976). *Tiberius the Politician*. London
Lewis, G. C. (1855). *An Inquiry into the Credibility of the Early Roman History*, 2 vols. London
Liers, H. (1886). *Die Theorie der Geschichtsschreibung des Dionys von Halikarnass*. Programm. Waldenburg

Lintott, A. W. (1968). *Violence in Republican Rome*. Oxford
Lintott, A. W. (1971). 'Lucan and the history of the Civil War', *CQ* 21.488–505
Lintott, A. W. (1972). 'Imperial expansion and moral decline in the Roman Republic', *Historia* 21.626–38
Lintott, A. W. (1976). 'A historian in Cicero *ad familiares* – *P. Licinius* [?] *Apollonius*', *RhM* 119.368
Lintott, A. W. (1982). *Violence, Civil Strife and Revolution in the Classical City 750–330 B.C.* London
Lloyd, A. B. (1975). *Herodotus Book II. Introduction*. Leyden.
Lloyd, A. B. (1976). *Herodotus Book II. Commentary 1–98*. Leyden
Lotze, D. (1967). 'Der Munichion 404 v.Chr. und das Problem der Schaltfolge im Athenischen Kalendar', *Philologus* 111.34–46
Luce, T. J. (1977). *Livy: the composition of his history*. Princeton
Luce, T. J. (1981). 'Tacitus' in *Ancient Writers: Greece and Rome* (New York), 2 vols., 2.1003–33
Luschnat, O. (1970). 'Thukydides der Historiker' in *RE* Supplementband 12, cols. 1085–1354
Macleod, C. W. (1977). 'Thucydides' Plataean debate', *GRBS* 18.227–46
Macleod, C. W. (1983). *Collected Essays*. Oxford
Magie, D. (1950). *Roman Rule in Asia Minor to the End of the Third Century after Christ*, 2 vols. Princeton
Malitz, J. (1982). 'Thukydides' Weg zur Geschichtsschreibung', *Historia* 31.257–89
Manuwald, B. (1979). *Cassius Dio und Augustus*. Wiesbaden
Marchant, E. C. (1920). *Xenophontis Opera Omnia: Opuscula*. Oxford
Marenghi, G. (n.d. [1970]). *Dionisio di Alicarnasso. Dinarco*. Milan
Marg, W. (1983). *Herodot, Geschichten und Geschichte, Bücher 5–9*. Translated by W. M.; revised by G. Strasburger; with an essay, 'Herodot als Geschichtsforcher', by H. Strasburger. Zürich/Munich
Martin, P. M. (1969). 'Le Dessein de Denys d'Halicarnasse dans les Antiquités Romaines et sa conception de l'histoire à travers sa préface du Livre 1', *Caesarodunum* 4.197–206
Martin, P. M. (1971). 'La Propagande augustéenne dans les Antiquités Romaines de Denys d'Halicarnasse (Livre 1)', *REL* 49.162–79
Martin, P. M. (1972). 'Héraklès en Italie d'après Denys d'Halicarnasse (*A.R.* 1.34–44)', *Athenaeum* 50.252–75
Martin, R. H. (1981). *Tacitus*. London/Berkeley
Maxfield, V. A. (1981). *The Military Decorations of the Roman Army*. London
Meek, R. (1976). *Social Science and the Ignoble Savage*. Cambridge
Meier, C. (1965). 'Populares' §§III and IV in *RE* Supplementband 10, cols. 580, 582, 590
Meier, C. (1978). 'Prozess und Ereignis in der griechischen Historiographie des 5. Jahrhunderts v. Chr. und vorher' in *Historische Prozesse. Theorie der Geschichte* vol. 2 (Munich), ed. K.-G. Faber, C. Meier, 69–97
Meiggs, R. (1972). *The Athenian Empire*. Oxford

Meinhardt, E. (1957). *Perikles bei Plutarch*. Dissertation. Frankfurt
Mercando, L.–Ioppolo, G.–Degrassi, A. (1966). 'Area sacra di S. Omobono. Esplorazione delle fase repubblicane I–III', *BCAR* 79 (for 1963–64). 35–93
Meritt, B. D. (1962). 'The seasons in Thucydides', *Historia* 11.436–46
Meritt, B. D. (1966). 'A Persian date in Thucydides', *CPh* 61.182–84
Meritt, B. D. (1979). 'Ten years and a few days – Thuc. 5.20', *AJPh* 100.107–10
Meritt, B. D.–McGregor, M. F. (1967). 'The Athenian quota-list of 421/0 B.C.', *Phoenix* 21.85–91
Meritt, B. D.–Wade-Gery, H. T.–McGregor, M. F. (1950). *The Athenian Tribute Lists*, vol. 3. Princeton
Mess, A. von (1909). 'Die Hellenika von Oxyrhynchos und die Berichte Xenophons und Diodors', *RhM* 64.235–43
Meucci, P. L. (1942). 'Le lettere greche di Bruto', *SIFC* 19.47–102
Meyer, E. (1965). 'Pras' (1–3) in *RE* Supplementband 10, cols. 651–52
Millar, F. (1964). *A Study of Cassius Dio*. Oxford
Miltner, F. (1958). *Ephesos*. Vienna
Moles, J. L. (1974). 'A commentary on Plutarch's Brutus'. Unpublished D.Phil. thesis. University of Oxford
Momigliano, A. (1957). 'Perizonius, Niebuhr and the character of early Roman tradition', *JRS* 47.104–14. (= Momigliano (1960a) 69–87)
Momigliano, A. (1958). 'Some observations on causes of war in ancient historiography' in *Acta Congressus Madrigiani. Proceedings of the Second International Congress of Classical Studies 1954* (Copenhagen), 1.199–211. (= Momigliano (1960a) 13–27)
Momigliano, A. (1960a). *Secondo contributo alla storia degli studi classici*. Rome
Momigliano, A. (1960b). 'Linee per una valutazione di Fabio Pittore', *RAL*[8] 15.310–20. (= Momigliano (1966) 55–68)
Momigliano, A. (1961). *Claudius: the emperor and his achievement*, 2nd edition. Cambridge
Momigliano, A. (1963). 'An interim report on the origins of Rome', *JRS* 53.95–121. (= Momigliano (1966) 545–98)
Momigliano, A. (1966). *Terzo contributo alla storia degli studi classici e del mondo antico*. Rome
Momigliano, A. (1967). 'L'ascesa della plebe nella storia arcaica di Roma', *RSI* 79.297–312. (= Momigliano (1969) 437–54)
Momigliano, A. (1969). *Quarto contributo alla storia degli studi classici e del mondo antico*. Rome
Momigliano, A. (1977). 'Prolegomena a ogni futura metafisica sulla plebe romana', *Labeo* 23.7–15. (= Momigliano (1980) 477–86)
Momigliano, A. (1978). 'The historians of the classical world and their audiences: some suggestions', *ASNP* 8.59–75. (= Momigliano (1980) 361–76)
Momigliano, A. (1980). *Sesto contributo alla storia degli studi classici e del mondo antico*. Rome

Morgan, M. G. (1973). 'Pliny, *NH* III 129, the Roman use of stades and the Elogium of C. Sempronius Tuditanus (*cos.* 129 BC)', *Philologus* 117.29–48

Müller, E. H. O. (1852). *De Tempore Quo Bellum Peloponnesiacum Initium Ceperit*. Marburg

Müller-Strübing, H. (1883). 'Das erste Jahr des peloponnesischen Krieges', *Jahrbücher für classische Philologie = Neue Jahrbücher für Philologie und Paedagogik* 127.577–612, 657–713

Münzer, F. (1891). *De Gente Valeria*. Dissertation. Opole

Münzer, F. (1920). *Römische Adelsparteien und Adelsfamilien*. Stuttgart

Musti, D. (1970). *Tendenze nella storiografia romana e greca su Roma arcaica. Studi su Livio e Dionigi d'Alicarnasso*. QUCC 10. Rome

Nagle, D. B. (1970). 'The failure of the Roman political process in 133 B.C.', *Athenaeum* 48.372–94

Nenci, G. (1955). 'Il motivo della autopsia nella storiografia greca', *SCO* 3.16–46

Nicolet, C. (1966). *L'Ordre équestre: l'époque républicaine (312–43 av. J.-C.)*, vol. 1. Paris

Niese, B. (1888). 'Die Chroniken des Hellanikos', *Hermes* 23.81–91

Noè, E. (1979). 'Ricerche su Dionigi d'Alicarnasso: la prima stasis a Roma e l'episodio di Coriolano' in *Ricerche di storiografia antica*, vol. 1: *Ricerche di storiografia greca di età romana* (Biblioteca di studi antici 22) (Pisa), with preface by E. Gabba, 21–116

Oberhummer, E. (1897). 'Byzantion' (1) in *RE* 3, cols. 1115–27

Ogilvie, R. M. (1965). *A Commentary on Livy I–V*. Oxford

Ogilvie, R. M. (1976). *Early Rome and the Etruscans*. London

Pabst, W. (1969). *Quellenkritische Studien zur inneren römischen Geschichte der älteren Zeit bei T. Livius und Dionys von Halikarnass*. Dissertation. Innsbruck

Parker, R. A.–Dubberstein, W. H. (1956). *Babylonian Chronology*. Providence

Parry, A. (1969). 'The language of Thucydides' description of the plague', *BICS* 16.106–18

Patterson, O. (1982). *Slavery and Social Death: a comparative study*. Cambridge, Mass./London

Pearson, L. (1942). *The Local Historians of Attica*. Philadelphia

Pelekidis, Ch. S. (1974). 'Συμβολή στην Ιστορία της Πεντηκονταετίας', *Dodone* 3.409–39

Pelling, C. B. R. (1979). 'Plutarch's method of work in the Roman Lives', *JHS* 99.74–96

Pelling, C. B. R. (1980). 'Plutarch's adaptation of his source-material', *JHS* 100.127–40

Peter, H. (1865). *Die Quellen Plutarchs*. Halle

Peter, H. (1906). *Historicorum Romanorum Reliquiae*, vol. 2. Leipzig

Peter, H. (1914). *Historicorum Romanorum Reliquiae*, vol. 1, 2nd edition. Leipzig

Platnauer, M. (1964). *Aristophanes' Peace*. Oxford

Plumb, J. H. (1969). *The Death of the Past*. London
Pohlenz, M. (1924). 'Eine politische Tendenzschrift aus Caesars Zeit', *Hermes* 59. 157–89
Pohlenz, M. (1927). 'Causae civilium armorum' in *Epitymbion H. Swoboda dargebracht* (Reichenberg), 201–10. (Reprinted in his *Kleine Schriften* (Hildesheim, 1965), 2.139–48)
Pouncey, P. R. (1980). *The Necessities of War. A study of Thucydides' pessimism*. New York
Pritchett, W. K. (1965). 'The Thucydidean summer of 411 B.C.', *CPh* 60.259–61
Pritchett, W. K. (1969). *Studies in Ancient Greek Topography*. Part II: *Battlefields*. University of California Publications: Classical Studies vol. 4. Berkeley/Los Angeles
Pritchett, W. K. (1975). *Dionysius of Halicarnassus: On Thucydides*. Berkeley
Pritchett, W. K.–Waerden, B. L. van der (1961). 'Thucydidean time-reckoning and Euctemon's seasonal calendar', *BCH* 85.17–52
Proctor, D. (1980). *The Experience of Thucydides*. Warminster
Raubitschek, A. E. (1957). 'Brutus in Athens', *Phoenix* 11.1–11
Raubitschek, A. E. (1959). 'The Brutus statue in Athens' in *Atti del terzo congresso internazionale di epigrafia greca e latina (Roma, 4–8 Settembre 1957)*, 15–21. Rome
Rawlings, H. R. (1981). *The Structure of Thucydides' History*. Princeton
Rawson, E. (1976). 'The first Latin annalists', *Latomus* 35.689–717
Rawson, E. (1980). Review of Wiseman (1979) in *THES* 378.18
Rawson, E. (1981). 'Chariot racing in the Roman Republic', *PBSR* 49.1–16
Rawson, E. (1982). 'Crassorum funera', *Latomus* 41.540–49
Regling, K. (1899). *De Belli Parthici Crassiani Fontibus*. Berlin
Reynolds, J. (1982). *Aphrodisias and Rome*. London
Rhodes, P. J. (1981). *A Commentary on the Aristotelian Athenaion Politeia*. Oxford
Rhys Roberts, W. (1897). 'Caecilius of Caleacte', *AJPh* 18.300–12
Rhys Roberts, W. (1900). 'The literary circle of Dionysius of Halicarnassus', *CR* 14.439–42
Rhys Roberts, W. (1901). *Dionysius of Halicarnassus. The three literary letters*. Cambridge
Rhys Roberts, W. (1910). *Dionysius of Halicarnassus. On literary composition*. London
Richards, G. C. (1938). 'The authorship of the περὶ ὕψους', *CQ* 32.133–34
Richardson, J. S. (1980). 'The ownership of Roman land: Tiberius Gracchus and the Italians', *JRS* 70.1–11
Rogers, B. B. (1913). *The Peace of Aristophanes*. London
Rosen, K. (1982). *Ammianus Marcellinus*. Erträge der Forschung 183. Darmstadt
Rühl, F. (1915). 'Die griechischen Briefe des Brutus', *RhM* 70.315–25
Russell, D. A. F. M. (1964). *'Longinus': On the Sublime*. Oxford

Russell, D. A. F. M. (1972). *Plutarch*. London

Sacks, K. S. (1983). 'Historiography in the rhetorical works of Dionysius of Halicarnassus', *Athenaeum* 61.65–87

Salles, C. (1981). 'Assem para et accipe auream fabulam: Quelques remarques sur la littérature populaire et le répertoire des conteurs publics dans le monde romain', *Latomus* 40.3–20

Scardigli, B. (1979). *Die Römerbiographien Plutarchs: Ein Forschungsbericht*. Munich

Scardigli, B. (1983). 'Asinius Pollio und Nikolaos von Damaskos', *Historia* 32.121–23

Scheller, P. (1911). *De Hellenistica Historiae Conscribendae Arte*. Dissertation. Leipzig

Schepens, G. (1970). 'Éphore sur la valeur de l'autopsie', *AncSoc* 1.163–82

Schürer, E. (1973). *The History of the Jewish People in the Age of Jesus Christ (175 B.C.–A.D.135)*. A new English version revised and edited by G. Vermes, F. Millar, P. Vermes, M. Black. Vol. 1. Edinburgh

Schwartz, E. (1903). 'Dionysios' (113 §1) in *RE* 5, cols. 934–61

Scobie, A. (1979). 'Storytellers, storytelling, and the novel in Greco-Roman antiquity', *RhM* 122.229–59

Seager, R. (1972). 'Cicero and the word *popularis*', *CQ* 22.328–38

Sherk, R. K. (1969). *Roman Documents from the Greek East*. Baltimore

Sherwin-White, A. N. (1973). *The Roman Citizenship*, 2nd edition. Oxford

Shochat, Y. (1970). 'The Lex Agraria of 133 B.C. and the Italian allies', *Athenaeum* 48.25–45

Shochat, Y. (1980). *Recruitment and the Programme of Tiberius Gracchus*. Collection Latomus 169. Brussels

Skutsch, O. (1968). *Studia Enniana*. London

Smart, J. D. (1972). 'Athens and Egesta', *JHS* 92.128–46

Smart, J. D. (1977a). 'Catalogues in Thucydides and Ephorus', *GRBS* 18.33–42

Smart, J. D. (1977b). 'The Athenian Empire', *Phoenix* 31.245–57

Smith, R. E. (1936). 'The Greek letters of M. Junius Brutus', *CQ* 30.194–203

Solodow, J. B. (1979). 'Livy and the story of Horatius, 1.24–26', *TAPhA* 109.251–68

Soltau, W. (1897). *Livius' Geschichtswerk*. Leipzig

Sommella, P. (1968). 'Area sacra di S. Omobono: contributo per una datazione della platea dei templi gemelli', *Quaderni, Istituto di Topografia antica, Università di Roma* 5.63ff.

Spelman, E. (1758). *The Roman Antiquities of Dionysius Halicarnassensis translated into English*, 4 vols. London

Spyropoulos, T. (1973). 'Εἰδήσεις ἐκ Βοιωτίας', *AAA* 6.376–92

Stadter, P. A. (1975). 'Plutarch's comparison of Pericles and Fabius Maximus', *GRBS* 16.77–85

Stählin, F. (1935). 'Narthakion' in *RE* 16.2, cols. 1760–64

Stahl, H.-P. (1966). *Thukydides. Die Stellung des Menschen im geschichtlichen Prozess.* Zetemata 40. Munich
Starkie, W. J. M. (1909). *The Acharnians of Aristophanes.* London
Stewart, A. F. (1977). 'To entertain an emperor: Sperlonga, Laokoon, and Tiberius at the dinner-table', *JRS* 67.76–90
Stewens, W. (1963). *M. Brutus als Politiker.* Dissertation. Zürich
Stibbe, C. *et al.* (1980). *Lapis Satricanus.* Nederlands Instituut te Rome: Scripta Minora 5. The Hague
Stockton, D. L. (1979). *The Gracchi.* Oxford
Strasburger, H. (1938). *Caesars Eintritt in die Geschichte.* Munich
Strasburger, H. (1966). 'Die Wesensbestimmung der Geschichte durch die antike Geschichtsschreibung', *Sitzungsberichte der wissenschaftlichen Gesellschaft an der Goethe-Universität, Frankfurt-am-Main* 5.47–96
Strasburger, H. (1972). *Homer und die Geschichtsschreibung.* SHAW 1. Heidelberg
Strauss, B. (1983). 'Aegospotami re-examined', *AJPh* 104.24–35
Strebel, H. G. (1935). *Wertung und Wirkung des Thukydideischen Geschichtswerkes in der griechisch-römischen Literatur.* Dissertation. Munich
Stroud, R. S. (1971). 'An ancient fort on Mount Oneion', *Hesperia* 41.127–45
Suerbaum, W. (1971). 'Der Historiker und die Freiheit des Wortes: Die Rede des Cremutius Cordus bei Tacitus, *Ann.* 4, 34/35' in *Politik und Literarische Kunst im Werk des Tacitus* (Stuttgart), ed. G. Radke, 61–99
Sumner, G. V. (1967). Review of Bowersock (1965) in *Phoenix* 21.130–35
Sydow, W. von (1973). 'Archäologische Funde und Forschungen im Bereich der Soprintendenz Rom 1957–73', *AA* 88.521–647
Syme, R. (1939). *The Roman Revolution.* Oxford
Syme, R. (1950). *A Roman Post-Mortem.* Tod Memorial Lecture. Sydney
Syme, R. (1958). *Tacitus,* 2 vols. Oxford
Syme, R. (1964). *Sallust.* Berkeley/Cambridge
Syme, R. (1970). *Ten Studies in Tacitus.* Oxford
Syme, R. (1978). *History in Ovid.* Oxford
Thompson, W. E. (1968). 'The chronology of 432/1', *Hermes* 96.216–32
Tibiletti, G. (1948). 'Il possesso dell' *ager publicus* e le norme *de modo agrorum* sino ai Gracchi', *Athenaeum* 26.173–236
Timpe, D. (1970–71). 'Le "Origini" di Catone e la storiografia latina', *AAPat* 83.5–33
Timpe, D. (1972). 'Fabius Pictor und die Anfänge der römischen Historiographie' in *ANRW* 1.2.928–69
Torelli, M. (1968). 'Il donario di M. Fulvio Flacco nell' area di S. Omobono', *Quaderni, Istituto di Topografia antica, Università di Roma* 5.71ff.
Torraca, L. (1959). *Marco Giunio Bruto, Epistole Greche.* Collana di studi greci 31. Naples
Toynbee, A. J. (1965). *Hannibal's Legacy,* 2 vols. London

Traenkle, H. (1965). 'Der Anfang des römischen Freistaats in der Darstellung des Livius', *Hermes* 93.311–37

Ullmann, B. L. (1942). 'History and tragedy', *TAPhA* 73.25–53

Underhill, G. E. (1900). *A Commentary with Introduction and Appendices on the Hellenica of Xenophon*. Oxford

Untersteiner, M. (1959). 'Dionisio di Alicarnasso, fondatore della critica pseudepigrafica', *AFC* 7.72–93

Usener, H.–Radermacher, L. (1899–1905). *Dionysii Halicarnasei Opuscula*, 2 vols. Leipzig

Usher, S. (1974). *Dionysius of Halicarnassus. The critical essays*, vol. 1. London/Cambridge, Mass.

Usher, S. (1982). 'The style of Dionysius of Halicarnassus in the "Antiquitates Romanae"' in *ANRW* II.30.1. 817–38

Verdin, H. (1974). 'La Fonction de l'histoire selon Denys d'Halicarnasse', *AncSoc* 5.289–307

Versnel, H. S. (1970). *Triumphus*. Leyden

Versnel, H. S. (1982). 'Die neue Inschrift von Satricum in historischer Sicht', *Gymnasium* 89.193–235

Wade-Gery, H. T. (1949). Review of A. W. Gomme, *A Historical Commentary on Thucydides Vol. 1* (Oxford, 1945) in *JHS* 69.83–85

Walbank, F. W. (1945). 'Polybius, Philinus and the First Punic War', *CQ* 39.1–18

Walbank, F. W. (1957). *A Historical Commentary on Polybius*, vol. 1. Oxford

Walbank, F. W. (1960). 'History and tragedy', *Historia* 9.216–34

Walbank, F. W. (n.d. [1965]). *Speeches in Greek Historians*. Third J. L. Myres Memorial Lecture. Oxford

Walbank, F. W. (1972). *Polybius*. Berkeley

Walsh, P. G. (1961). *Livy: his historical aims and methods*. Cambridge

Wardman, A. E. (1974). *Plutarch's Lives*. London

Warner, R. (1978). *Xenophon: A History of my Times* (*Hellenica*). Harmondsworth

Warren, L. B. (1970). 'Roman triumphs and Etruscan kings: the changing face of the triumph', *JRS* 60.49–66

Watson, A. (1975). *Rome of the XII Tables: persons and property*. Princeton

Weidauer, K. (1954). *Thukydides und die Hippokratischen Schriften. Der Einfluss der Medizin auf Zielsetzung und Darstellungsweise des Geschichtswerks*. Dissertation. Heidelberg

Weinstock, S. (1957). '*Victor* and *invictus*', *HThR* 50.211–47

Weinstock, S. (1971). *Divus Julius*. Oxford

Westlake, H. D. (1955). 'Thucydides and the Pentekontaetia', *CQ* 5.53–67. (Reprinted in *Essays on the Greek Historians and Greek History* (Manchester, 1969), 39–60)

Westlake, H. D. (1977). 'Thucydides on Pausanias and Themistocles – a written source', *CQ* 27.95–110

Wiedemann, T. (1979). 'Nunc ad inceptum redeo', *LCM* 4.13–16

Wilcken, U. (1907). 'Der Anonymus Argentinensis', *Hermes* 42.374–418

Williams, G. W. (1978). *Change and Decline. Roman literature in the early Empire*. Sather Classical Lectures 45. Berkeley

Winkler, J. (1980). 'Lollianos and the desperadoes', *JHS* 100.155–81

Wiseman, J. (1978). *The Land of the Ancient Corinthians*. Göteborg

Wiseman, T. P. (1964). 'Viae Anniae', *PBSR* 32.21–37

Wiseman, T. P. (1969). 'Viae Anniae again', *PBSR* 37.82–91

Wiseman, T. P. (1971). *New Men in the Roman Senate 139 B.C.–A.D. 14*. Oxford

Wiseman, T. P. (1979). *Clio's Cosmetics. Three studies in Greco-Roman literature*. Leicester

Wiseman, T. P. (1981). 'Practice and theory in Roman historiography', *History* 66.375–93

Wood, J. R. (1982). 'The *Haruspices* of the Roman Republic'. Unpublished Ph.D. thesis. University of London

Woodman, A. J. (1983a). *Velleius Paterculus: the Caesarian and Augustan narrative (2.41–93)*. Cambridge Classical Texts and Commentaries 25. Cambridge

Woodman, A. J. (1983b). 'Reading the ancient historians', *Omnibus* 5.24–27

Yavetz, Z. (1969). *Plebs et Princeps*. Oxford

Ziegler, K. (1929). 'Der Ursprung der Excurse im Thukydides', *RhM* 78.58–67

Indexes

General index

Index locorum

(Only passages central to the discussion in each article are included.)

Inscriptions

Coins